2 $\underline{50}$

D1359631

THE WORKS OF VIRGIL

TRANSLATED BY

JOHN DRYDEN

THE WORKS OF
VIRGIL

TRANSLATED BY
JOHN DRYDEN

WITH
AN INTRODUCTION BY
JAMES KINSLEY

OXFORD UNIVERSITY PRESS
1961

Oxford University Press, Amen House, London E.C.4

GLASGOW NEW YORK TORONTO MELBOURNE WELLINGTON
BOMBAY CALCUTTA MADRAS KARACHI KUALA LUMPUR
CAPE TOWN IBADAN NAIROBI ACCRA

PRINTED IN GREAT BRITAIN

CONTENTS

17304

CONTENTS

THE ÆNEIS

INTRODUCTION

NOWADAYS the main business of translation from the classics is to make remote literatures and cultures intelligible to a public which has little Latin and less Greek. For a society educated in the humanist tradition, however, literal versions of familiar authors have limited value; and in the time of Dryden the translator's first concern was to strengthen the ties which bound the ancients and their modern admirers and imitators. An old author was to be revived in a new medium, enriching both the language and the literature of his adoption. By such translation 'the slowness of invention is stimulated. The junior tongue, confronted with the problem or piqued by the challenge of keeping pace with its elders and betters, must develop missing organs, borrow for its deficiencies, strain itself to unsuspected capacities and attainments' (J. S. Phillimore). The Restoration poets who turned Virgil, Ovid, Horace, and Lucretius most successfully into English verse were literati rather than scholars, concerned with the general character and quality of their originals and valuing elegance above accuracy. The demand for scholarly translation grew stronger in the early eighteenth century, as the fashion in graceful poetic versions for the literary miscellanies declined.

In his Preface to *Ovid's Epistles Translated* (1680) Dryden distinguishes three kinds of version: literal 'metaphrase', 'paraphrase', or translation

with latitude', and free 'imitation'. His own prefer-
ence is for paraphrase, which he defends in the
Dedication of *Examen Poeticum* (1693):

> Sure I am, that if it be a fault, 'tis much more par-
> donable, than that of those, who run into the other
> extream, of a litteral, and close Translation, where the
> Poet is confin'd so streightly to his Author's Words,
> that he wants elbow-room, to express his Elegancies.
> He leaves him obscure ; he leaves him Prose, where he
> found him Verse. . . . I have . . . attempted to restore
> *Ovid* to his Native sweetness, easiness, and smoothness ;
> and to give my Poetry a kind of Cadence, and, as we
> call it, a run of Verse, as like the Original, as the
> *English* can come up to the *Latin*.

A translator, therefore, must have sympathy and
critical sensitivity as well as learning. 'He must
perfectly understand his Authors Tongue, and ab-
solutely command his own. So that to be a thorow
Translatour, he must be a thorow Poet.' In preserving the character of his original, Dryden felt free
to reduce expressions which 'wou'd not appear so
shining in the English' ; and where (in the miscel-
lany *Sylvae*, 1685)

> I have enlarg'd them, I desire the false Criticks wou'd
> not always think that those thoughts are wholly mine,
> but that either they are secretly in the Poet, or may
> be fairly deduc'd from him: or at least, if both these
> considerations should fail, that my own is of a piece
> with his, and that if he were living, and an *English-
> man*, they are such, as he wou'd probably have written.

From the time of the Tudors, translators had
been turning classical poets into Englishmen. But
Dryden's policy is notably systematic and critical.
It is part of the business of maintaining an author's
character—of making him 'appear as charming as
possibly he can', speaking (as Dryden's Juvenal
does) 'that kind of *English*, which he would have
spoken, had he lived in *England*, and had written
to this Age'. Dryden and his Augustan successors

understood that translation is, at its most refined,
an art of analogy: of 'reviving the old of past ages
to the present' by shaping it again in a modern
linguistic and cultural mould. So Pope took Trum-
bull's advice (given in a letter of 9 April 1708) to
make Homer 'speak good *English*, to dress his
admirable characters in . . . proper, significant, and
expressive conceptions, and to make his works as
useful and instructive to this degenerate age, as he
was to our friend *Horace*, when he read him at
Praeneste'. When such an ideal is realized, the gap
between original work and translation becomes
insignificant; the ancient author becomes culturally
effective, and the translator a 'noble collateral'
with him.

In the Preface to *Annus Mirabilis* (1667) Dryden
speaks of Virgil as his master. This devoted dis-
cipleship is illustrated throughout his critical
essays and his poetry. The qualities of Virgil's
style which he admired were a majesty maintained
'in the midst of plainness' and above the tricks of
hyperbole, epigram, and conceit; sensitiveness and
inimitable grace in the choice of words; harmony
and precise brevity; and the control of imagination
by decorum in metaphor—especially in epic poetry,
the language of which is 'almost wholly figurative'.

With the example of Virgil before him, and many
Renaissance precedents, Dryden had an early ambition to write a heroic poem 'intended chiefly for the
Honour of my Native Country'. But, he says in
the Dedication of his *Juvenal* (1693),

being encourag'd only with fair Words, by King Charles
II, my little Sallary ill paid, and no prospect of a future
Subsistence, I was then Discourag'd in the beginning
of my Attempt; and now Age has overtaken me; and
Want, a more insufferable Evil, through the Change of
the Times, has wholly disenabl'd me.

The translation of the *Aeneid* (1697) was as near

as he came to realizing his ambition. He had no mean idea of his task. The Postscript to the Reader has a noble and earnest simplicity, an awareness of inadequacy tempering his sense of achievement, recalling Milton's declaration of his poetic ideals and looking forward to Johnson's Preface to his *Dictionary*:

What *Virgil* wrote in the vigour of his Age, in Plenty and at Ease, I have undertaken to *Translate* in my Declining Years: struling with Wants, oppress'd with Sickness, curb'd in my Genius, lyable to be misconstrued in all I write. . . . Yet steady to my Principles, and not dispirited with my Afflictions, I have, by the Blessing of God on my Endeavours, overcome all difficulties. . . . For, what I have done, Imperfect as it is, for want of Health and leisure to Correct it, will be judg'd in after Ages, and possibly in the present, to be no dishonour to my Native Country; whose Language and Poetry wou'd be more esteem'd abroad, if they were better understood.

A translator 'must perfectly understand his Authors Tongue'. Recent scholarship has shown that Dryden's knowledge of the Latin poets and their language was, for his time, both extensive and exact; and his critical comments on Virgil, as on his other 'originals', are often admirable. Yet, when confronted with Virgil, he despaired. Literal translation, he says, is made impossible by the qualitative differences between Latin, 'a most severe and compendious language', and English; and Virgil's Latin in particular has a richness and concentration beyond the scope of any modern language. Of brevity and elegance, the two essential Virgilian qualities, the first defies translation into another tongue; and Dryden is forced to concentrate on preserving the second as best he can. Virgil's Latin is like ambergris, 'a Rich Perfume, but of so close and glutinous a Body, that it must be open'd with inferiour scents of Musk or Civet, or the sweetness will not be drawn out'. With his inexhaustible store of 'figurative, elegant, and sounding words', he called on Dryden 'in every line for some new word: And I paid so long, that I was almost Banckrupt'.

The gulf between the two poets was yet wider than Dryden suggests. Virgil's distinction is a close and subtle compression of meaning. Words in pattern induce new significances, or uncover latent significances, in each other; and Virgil so disposes his diction that he can evoke a rich complication of primary meaning and suggestion from a line or a phrase. This sets him apart from Dryden, not only in technique but in poetic quality. The traditional assessment of Dryden, from Wordsworth to T. S. Eliot, as a master of 'immense statement', misses much of the imaginative subtlety in his verse; but in organizing language for the sustained interplay of secondary meanings he is a much simpler artist than Virgil—or Shakespeare or Milton. Even on the level of syntax, the texture of his poetry is looser than that of Virgil's; and this is far more than the structural difference between the two languages, for in both Shakespeare and Milton English approaches the convolution of Latin verse. There is, too, a fundamental difference in the poetic personalities of Dryden and Virgil. In temper as in style Dryden stands closer to Homer, as he himself recognized. Virgil, he says in the Preface to the *Fables* (1700),

was of a quiet, sedate Temper; *Homer* was violent, impetuous, and full of Fire. The chief Talent of *Virgil* was Propriety of Thoughts, and Ornament of Words; *Homer* was rapid in his thoughts, and took all the Liberties both of Numbers, and of Expressions, which his Language, and the Age in which he liv'd allow'd him: *Homer*'s Invention was more copious, *Virgil*'s more confin'd . . . . One warms you by Degrees; the other sets you on fire all at once, and never intermits his

Heat. . . . This Vehemence of [*Homer*'s], I confess, is more suitable to my Temper: and therefore I have translated his First Book with greater Pleasure than any Part of *Virgil*.

A Homeric ardour and impetuosity of mind, sophisticated and controlled by Augustan rhetoric, is the essence of Dryden's style. He is a poet of muscle and sinew; he delights in action, in violent emotion, in strong and final utterance. His version of the *Aeneid* shows a persistent uneasiness, an impatience with the grave artistry of Virgil; and he makes spasmodic efforts to give the poem the pith and fire of his own natural manner. A translation which carries the quality of the Latin over into English, inevitably with some loss but without distortion, is not to be expected at his hands. There is much more to be said here for Gavin Douglas's *Eneados*, though even Scotsmen may feel that Professor C. S. Lewis has said it too emphatically. The virtues of Dryden's *Georgics* and *Æneis* are great; but they are the virtues of Dryden himself, in his singing robes; and too often they take the place of Virgilian qualities which he recognizes but cannot imitate.

Dryden was dissatisfied with the 'quiet, sedate Temper' of Virgil. There is some truth in Scott's notion that the Latin 'restrained [him] to a correct, steady, and even flight, . . . damped his energy by its regularity, and fettered his excursive imagination by the sobriety of its decorum'. But the paraphrastic method gave him due licence; and he is ever adding details to increase the vitality of the narrative, especially in scenes of slaughter, where he often comes nearer to Ovid than to Virgil. His natural energy is liberated—with a deal of help from 'our *Saxon* monosyllables' that he thought a limitation of the language—in such passages as the story of the Cyclops (*Aen*. iii) or of

Cacus and Alcides (viii), and in the time of blood
at the beginning and end of the poem:

> domus sanie dapibusque cruentis,
intus opaca, ingens.

*   *   *

> visceribus miserorum et sanguine vescitur atro.
vidi egomet duo de numero cum corpora nostro
prensa manu magna medio resupinus in antro
frangeret ad saxum, sanieque aspersa natarent
limina ; vidi atro cum membra fluentia tabo
manderet et tepidi tremerent sub dentibus artus.

The Cave, though large, was dark, the dismal Flore
Was pav'd with mangled Limbs and putrid Gore.

*   *   *

The Joints of slaughter'd Wretches are his Food:
And for his Wine he quaffs the streaming Blood.
Those Eyes beheld, when with his spacious Hand
He seiz'd two Captives of our *Grecian* Band ;
Stretch'd on his Back, he dash'd against the Stones
Their broken Bodies, and their crackling Bones:
With spouting Blood the Purple Pavement swims,
While the dire Glutton grinds the trembling Limbs.

Dryden makes explicit the hints of pompous
complacency that his age saw in *pius Aeneas*. He
turns the tensions of the debate between Turnus
and Drances ('a close Caballer, and Tongue-
valiant Lord'), and the domestic disputes of
Olympus, to satiric account. Fame (*Aen.* iv) has the
gratuitous aid of 'Court Informers . . . and Royal
Spyes'; the *indomiti agricolae* (*Aen.* vii) are pre-
sented as English militia, 'a boistrous, rude, un-
govern'd Crew' unpopular with Jacobites ; *vana
superstitio* is modernized for Puritan England as
'blind Devotion' and 'heady Zeal' (ibid.) ; *passimque
armenta videbant Romanoque foro* (Aen. viii) becomes

They view'd the ground of Rome's litigious Hall ;
Once Oxen low'd, where now the Lawyers bawl.

Indeed, says Scott, 'there are passages . . . which,
in the revolution of a few pages, transport our

ideas from the time of Troy's siege to that of the court of Augustus, and thence downwards to the reign of William the Third'.

Much of the vulgarity and colloquialism in the *Æneis* is deliberate, for Dryden has a fine sense of propriety in diction. I suspect that he found stretches of Virgil a bore, and the maintenance of 'majesty in the midst of plainness' a strain. He had admitted long before, in a discussion of tragi-comedy, that 'continued gravity keeps the spirit too much bent; we must refresh it sometimes, as we bait on a journey, that we may go on with greater ease'. The alloy of common speech and indecorous wit does not detract from the general strength of his heroic manner, and it is a carping purist who protests much.

Professor Lewis condemns the humanist mis-conception of Latin poetry which Dryden inherited: 'the spectral solemnity, the gradus epithets, the dictionary language'. But a diction removed from the colloquial, consecrated by poetic tradition, was one of Virgil's own aims; and in Dryden's *Virgil*, as in Pope's *Homer*, a measure of artifice in diction gives 'a certain ritual ceremony and a certain temporal distance to events and manners and modes of belief which could not be contemporary' (Bonamy Dobrée). Yet Dryden was not seriously infected with spectral solemnity and dictionary language. In his colloquialism, in occasional satiric intrusions, and in moments of sheer burlesque, he is running counter to the neo-classical tradition of the epic. Dr. Tillyard has suggested that the 'addition of the burlesque to the serious', as early as *Annus Mirabilis*, 'is potentially Dryden's original contribution to the course of the English epic', implying for him and for his age 'a high degree of self-consciousness, the refusal to be ultimately committed'. This ambivalent attitude to the heroic is reflected not only in the *Æneis*, but in the verse satires and in the translations of Boccaccio, Chaucer, and Homer. To set Dryden's version of the end of *Iliad* I after that of Pope is sufficient illustration:

Thus the blest Gods the genial day prolong,
In feasts ambrosial, and celestial song.
Apollo tun'd the lyre ; the Muses round
With voice alternate aid the silver sound.
Meantime the radiant sun, to mortal sight
Descending swift, roll'd down the rapid light.
Then to their starry domes the Gods depart,
The shining monuments of Vulcan's art :
Jove on his couch reclin'd his awful head,
And Juno slumber'd on the golden bed.

The Feast continu'd till declining Light :
They drank, they laugh'd, they lov'd, and then 'twas Night.
Nor wanted tuneful Harp, nor vocal Quire ;
The Muses sung ; *Apollo* touch'd the Lyre.
Drunken at last, and drowsy they depart,
Each to his House ; Adorn'd with labour'd Art
Of the lame Architect : The thund'ring God
His swimming Head to needful Sleep apply'd ;
And *Juno* lay unheeded by his side.

With Montaigne, Dryden thought the *Georgics* 'the best Poem of the best Poet'; and he 'labour'd and cultivated [it] with more care than any other part ... and as I think my self with more Success'. But he loses much of Virgil's delicacy in natural description, and he exaggerates the element of 'fancy', so nicely calculated in the Latin, to a degree of conceit which falsifies and cheapens. Virgil's deep sympathy with the miseries of the brutes in Book iii is turned into mock-elegy; the era of the *Ode on the Death of a Favourite Cat* and *Poor Mailie* has begun. Dryden is at his natural best when, 'enlarging' hints from Virgil in Books iii and iv, he humanizes the courtship of the animals and the life of the hive.

The *Virgil* is of great historical importance. Dryden, perhaps even more than Milton, set the tone in style and diction for the elevated 'kinds' of Augustan poetry; and he has left his mark on eighteenth-century heroic, mock-heroic, didactic, descriptive, and pastoral verse. The *Virgil* appealed as strongly to Burns, in Ayrshire, at the end of the century, as it had done to Pope in Twickenham at the beginning. It is, says Pope, 'the most noble and spirited translation that I know in any language'; and his *Homer* stands solidly on the foundation laid by Dryden. The *Æneis* held the eighteenth century in thrall not only as a model of the heroic style and a quarry for poetical language, but as a great epic poem in its own right. It 'became at once a substantive part of English literature, one of the greater English poems, and Virgil entered the eighteenth century an English citizen' (G. S. Gordon).

Dryden's best translations, judged by his own criterion of maintaining the author's character, are his versions of Juvenal, Ovid, and Lucretius. But the *Virgil* is his finest single achievement in twenty years of 'reviving the old of past ages' for English readers. There are more dependable cribs, even in verse; and Douglas's version may be, as Professor Lewis claims, 'the best possible preparation for a re-reading of the Latin'. But works of imagination, says Johnson,

excel by their allurement and delight; by their power of attracting and detaining the attention. That book is good in vain which the reader throws away. He only is the master who keeps the mind in pleasing captivity; whose pages are perused with eagerness, and in hope of new pleasure are perused again; and whose conclusion is perceived with an eye of sorrow. . . . By his proportion of this predomination I will consent that Dryden should be tried.

JAMES KINSLEY

Swansea, 1960

PASTORAL I

TITYRUS AND MELIBŒUS

THE ARGUMENT

The occasion of the first Pastoral was this. When Augustus had settled himself in the Roman empire, that he might reward his veteran troops for their past service, he distributed among them all the lands that lay about Cremona and Mantua, turning out the right owners for having sided with his enemies. Virgil was a sufferer among the rest; who afterward recovered his estate by Mæcenas' intercession, and, as an instance of his gratitude, composed the following Pastoral, where he sets out his own good fortune in the person of Tityrus, and the calamities of his Mantuan neighbours in the character of Melibœus.

M. BENEATH the shade which beechen boughs diffuse,
You, Tityrus, entertain your sylvan muse.
Round the wide world in banishment we roam,
Forced from our pleasing fields and native home;
While, stretched at ease, you sing your happy loves,
And Amaryllis fills the shady groves.
T. These blessings, friend, a deity bestowed:
For never can I deem him less than god.
The tender firstlings of my woolly breed
Shall on his holy altar often bleed.
He gave my kine to graze the flowery plain,
And to my pipe renewed the rural strain.
M. I envy not your fortune, but admire,
That, while the raging sword and wasteful fire
Destroy the wretched neighbourhood around,
No hostile arms approach your happy ground.
Far different is my fate: my feeble goats
With pains I drive from their forsaken cotes.
And this, you see, I scarcely drag along,

3

Who, yeaning, on the rocks has left her young ;
The hope and promise of my failing fold.
My loss, my dire portents, the gods foretold ;
For, had I not been blind, I might have seen :—
Yon riven oak, the fairest of the green,
And the hoarse raven, on the blasted bough,
By croaking from the left, presaged the coming blow.
But tell me, Tityrus, what heavenly power
Preserved your fortunes in that fatal hour?

   T. Fool that I was, I thought imperial Rome
Like Mantua, where on market-days we come,
And thither drive our tender lambs from home.
So kids and whelps their sires and dams express,
And so the great I measured by the less.
But country towns, compared with her, appear
Like shrubs, when lofty cypresses are near.

   M. What great occasion called you hence to Rome?
   T. Freedom, which came at length, though slow to
      come.
Nor did my search of liberty begin,
Till my black hairs were changed upon my chin ;
Nor Amaryllis would vouchsafe a look,
Till Galatea's meaner bonds I broke.
Till then a helpless, hopeless, homely swain,
I sought not freedom, nor aspired to gain :
Though many a victim from my folds was bought,
And many a cheese to country markets brought,
Yet all the little that I got, I spent,
And still returned as empty as I went.

   M. We stood amazed to see your mistress mourn,
Unknowing that she pined for your return :
We wondered why she kept her fruit so long,
For whom so late the ungathered apples hung.
But now the wonder ceases, since I see
She kept them only, Tityrus, for thee.
For thee the bubbling springs appeared to mourn,
And whispering pines made vows for thy return.

   T. What should I do?—While here I was enchained,
No glimpse of godlike liberty remained :
Nor could I hope, in any place but there

To find a god so present to my prayer.
There first the youth of heavenly birth I viewed,
For whom our monthly victims are renewed.
He heard my vows, and graciously decreed
My grounds to be restored, my former flocks to feed.

   M. O fortunate old man ! whose farm remains—
For you sufficient—and requites your pains ;
Though rushes overspread the neighbouring plains,
Though here the marshy grounds approach your fields,
And there the soil a stony harvest yields.
Your teeming ewes shall no strange meadows try,
Nor fear a rot from tainted company.
Behold ! yon bordering fence of sallow-trees
Is fraught with flowers ; the flowers are fraught with
      bees :
The busy bees, with a soft murmuring strain,
Invite to gentle sleep the labouring swain.
While from the neighbouring rock, with rural songs,
The pruner's voice the pleasing dream prolongs,
Stock-doves and turtles tell their amorous pain,
And, from the lofty elms, of love complain.

   T. The inhabitants of seas and skies shall change,
And fish on shore, and stags in air, shall range,
The banished Parthian dwell on Arar's brink,
And the blue German shall the Tigris drink,
Ere I, forsaking gratitude and truth,
Forget the figure of that godlike youth.

   M. But we must beg our bread in climes unknown,
Beneath the scorching or the freezing zone :
And some to far Oaxis shall be sold,
Or try the Libyan heat, or Scythian cold ;
The rest among the Britons be confined :
A race of men from all the world disjoined.
O ! must the wretched exiles ever mourn,
Nor, after length of rolling years, return ?
Are we condemned by fate's unjust decree,
No more our houses and our homes to see ?
Or shall we mount again the rural throne,
And rule the country kingdoms, once our own ?
Did we for these barbarians plant and sow ?

On these, on these, our happy fields bestow?
Good heaven! what dire effects from civil discord flow!
Now let me graff my pears, and prune the vine;
The fruit is theirs, the labour only, mine.
Farewell, my pastures, my paternal stock,
My fruitful fields, and my more fruitful flock!
No more, my goats, shall I behold you climb
The steepy cliffs, or crop the flowery thyme!
No more, extended in the grot below,
Shall see you browsing on the mountain's brow
The prickly shrubs, and after on the bare,
Lean down the deep abyss, and hang in air!
No more my sheep shall sip the morning dew;
No more my song shall please the rural crew:
Adieu, my tuneful pipe! and all the world, adieu!

   T. This night, at least, with me forget your care;
Chestnuts, and curds, and cream, shall be your fare;
The carpet-ground shall be with leaves o'erspread;
And boughs shall weave a covering for your head.
For, see, yon sunny hill the shade extends;
And curling smoke from cottages ascends.

PASTORAL II

ALEXIS

THE ARGUMENT

The commentators can by no means agree on the person of Alexis, but are all of opinion that some beautiful youth is meant by him, to whom Virgil here makes love, in Corydon's language and simplicity. His way of courtship is wholly pastoral: he complains of the boy's coyness; recommends himself for his beauty and skill in piping; invites the youth into the country, where he promises him the diversions of the place, with a suitable present of nuts and apples. But when he finds nothing will prevail, he resolves to quit his troublesome amour, and betake himself again to his former business.

YOUNG Corydon, the unhappy shepherd swain,
The fair Alexis loved, but loved in vain;
And underneath the beechen shade, alone,
Thus to the woods and mountains made his moan:
Is this, unkind Alexis, my reward?
And must I die unpitied, and unheard?
Now the green lizard in the grove is laid;
The sheep enjoy the coolness of the shade:
And Thestylis wild thyme and garlic beats,
For harvest hinds, o'erspent with toil and heats;
While in the scorching sun I trace in vain
Thy flying footsteps o'er the burning plain.
The creaking locusts with my voice conspire,
They fried with heat, and I with fierce desire.
How much more easy was it to sustain
Proud Amaryllis, and her haughty reign;
The scorns of young Menalcas, once my care,
Though he was black, and thou art heavenly fair!
Trust not too much to that enchanting face:

7

Beauty's a charm; but soon the charm will pass.
White lilies lie neglected on the plain,
While dusky hyacinths for use remain.
My passion is thy scorn; nor wilt thou know
What wealth I have, what gifts I can bestow;
What stores my dairies and my folds contain—
A thousand lambs that wander on the plain,
New milk that, all the winter, never fails,
And, all the summer, overflows the pails.
Amphion sung not sweeter to his herd,
When summoned stones the Theban turrets reared.
Nor am I so deformed; for late I stood
Upon the margin of the briny flood:
The winds were still; and, if the glass be true,
With Daphnis I may vie, though judged by you.
O leave the noisy town: O come and see
Our country cots, and live content with me!
To wound the flying deer, and from their cotes
With me to drive a-field the browsing goats;
To pipe and sing, and, in our country strain,
To copy, or perhaps contend with Pan.
Pan taught to join with wax unequal reeds;
Pan loves the shepherds, and their flocks he feeds.
Nor scorn the pipe: Amyntas, to be taught,
With all his kisses would my skill have bought.
Of seven smooth joints a mellow pipe I have,
Which with his dying breath Damœtas gave,
And said, 'This, Corydon, I leave to thee;
For only thou deserv'st it after me.'
His eyes Amyntas durst not upward lift;
For much he grudged the praise, but more the gift.
Besides, two kids, that in the valley strayed,
I found by chance, and to my fold conveyed;
They drain two bagging udders every day;
And these shall be companions of thy play;
Both flecked with white, the true Arcadian strain,
Which Thestylis had often begged in vain:
And she shall have them, if again she sues,
Since you the giver and the gift refuse.
Come to my longing arms, my lovely care!

And take the presents which the nymphs prepare.
White lilies in full canisters they bring,
With all the glories of the purple spring.
The daughters of the flood have searched the mead
For violets pale, and cropped the poppy's head,
The short narcissus and fair daffodil,
Pansies to please the sight, and cassia sweet to smell:
And set soft hyacinths with iron-blue,
To shade marsh marigolds of shining hue;
Some bound in order, others loosely strewed,
To dress thy bower, and trim thy new abode.
Myself will search our planted grounds at home,
For downy peaches and the glossy plum:
And thrash the chestnuts in the neighbouring grove,
Such as my Amaryllis used to love.
The laurel and the myrtle sweets agree;
And both in nosegays shall be bound for thee.
Ah, Corydon! ah, poor unhappy swain!
Alexis will thy homely gifts disdain;
Nor, shouldst thou offer all thy little store,
Will rich Iolas yield, but offer more.
What have I done, to name that wealthy swain!
So powerful are his presents, mine so mean!
The boar amidst my crystal streams I bring:
And southern winds to blast my flowery spring.
Ah, cruel creature! whom dost thou despise?
The gods, to live in woods, have left the skies:
And godlike Paris, in the Idæan grove,
To Priam's wealth preferred Œnone's love.
In cities, which she built, let Pallas reign;
Towers are for gods, but forests for the swain.
The greedy lioness the wolf pursues,
The wolf the kid, the wanton kid the browse;
Alexis, thou art chased by Corydon:
All follow several games, and each his own.
See, from afar the fields no longer smoke;
The sweating steers, unharnessed from the yoke,
Bring, as in triumph, back the crooked plough;
The shadows lengthen as the sun goes low;
Cool breezes now the raging heats remove;

Ah ! cruel heaven, that made no cure for love !
I wish for balmy sleep, but wish in vain :
Love has no bounds in pleasure, or in pain.
What frenzy, shepherd, has thy soul possessed ?
Thy vineyard lies half-pruned, and half-undressed
Quench, Corydon, thy long-unanswered fire,
Mind what the common wants of life require :
On willow twigs employ thy weaving care ;
And find an easier love, though not so fair.

PASTORAL III

PALÆMON

MENALCAS.   DAMŒTAS.   PALÆMON.

THE ARGUMENT

Damœtas and Menalcas, after some smart strokes of country raillery, resolve to try who has the most skill at song; and accordingly make their neighbour Palæmon judge of their performances; who, after a full hearing of both parties, declares himself unfit for the decision of so weighty a controversy, and leaves the victory undetermined.

   M. Ho, swain! what shepherd owns those ragged sheep?
   D. Ægon's they are: he gave them me to keep.
   M. Unhappy sheep of an unhappy swain!
While he Neæra courts, but courts in vain,
And fears that I the damsel shall obtain,
Thou, varlet, dost thy master's gains devour;
Thou milk'st his ewes, and often twice an hour;
Of grass and fodder thou defraud'st the dams,
And of their mother's dugs the starving lambs.
   D. Good words, young catamite, at least to men.
We know who did your business, how, and when;
And in what chapel too you played your prize,
And what the goats observed with leering eyes:
The nymphs were kind, and laughed; and there your
     safety lies.
   M. Yes, when I cropt the hedges of the leas,
Cut Micon's tender vines, and stole the stays!
   D. Or rather, when beneath yon ancient oak,
The bow of Daphnis, and the shafts, you broke,

11

When the fair boy received the gift of right;
And, but for mischief, you had died for spite.

M. What nonsense would the fool thy master prate,
When thou, his knave, canst talk at such a rate!
Did I not see you, rascal, did I not,
When you lay snug to snap young Damon's goat?
His mongrel barked: I ran to his relief,
And cried, 'There, there he goes! stop, stop the thief!'
Discovered, and defeated of your prey,
You skulked behind the fence, and sneaked away.

D. An honest man may freely take his own:
The goat was mine, by singing fairly won.
A solemn match was made: he lost the prize.
Ask Damon, ask, if he the debt denies.
I think he dares not: if he does, he lies.

M. Thou sing with him? thou booby! Never pipe
Was so profaned to touch that blubbered lip.
Dunce at the best! in streets but scarce allowed
To tickle, on thy straw, the stupid crowd.

D. To bring it to the trial, will you dare
Our pipes, our skill, our voices to compare?
My brinded heifer to the stake I lay:
Two thriving calves she suckles twice a day,
And twice besides her beestings never fail
To store the dairy with a brimming pail.
Now back your singing with an equal stake.

M. That should be seen, if I had one to make.
You know too well, I feed my father's flock:
What can I wager from the common stock?
A stepdame too I have, a cursed she,
Who rules my henpecked sire, and orders me.
Both number twice a day the milky dams;
And once she takes the tale of all the lambs.
But, since you will be mad, and since you may
Suspect my courage, if I should not lay;
The pawn I proffer shall be full as good:
Two bowls I have, well turned, of beechen wood;
Both by divine Alcimedon were made:
To neither of them yet the lip is laid.
The lids are ivy: grapes in clusters lurk

Beneath the carving of the curious work.
Two figures on the sides embossed appear—
Conon, and what's his name who made the spear,
And showed the seasons of the sliding year,
Instructed in his trade the labouring swain,
And when to reap, and when to sow the grain?

D. And I have two, to match your pair, at home;
The wood the same; from the same hand they come,
(The kimbo handles seem with bear's-foot carved),
And never yet to table have been served;
Where Orpheus on his lyre laments his love,
With beasts encompassed, and a dancing grove.
But these, nor all the proffers you can make,
Are worth the heifer which I set to stake.

M. No more delays, vain boaster, but begin!
I prophesy beforehand I shall win.
Palæmon shall be judge how ill you rhyme:
I'll teach you how to brag another time.

D. Rhymer, come on! and do the worst you can.
I fear not you, nor yet a better man.
With silence, neighbour, and attention, wait:
For 'tis a business of a high debate.

P. Sing, then: the shade affords a proper place;
The trees are clothed with leaves, the fields with
    grass;
The blossoms blow; the birds on bushes sing;
And Nature has accomplished all the spring.
The challenge to Damœtas shall belong;
Menalcas shall sustain his under-song:
Each in his turn, your tuneful numbers bring:
By turns the tuneful Muses love to sing.

D. From the great father of the gods above
My muse begins: for all is full of Jove;
To Jove the care of heaven and earth belongs;
My flocks he blesses, and he loves my songs.

M. Me Phœbus loves; for he my muse inspires;
And, in her songs, the warmth he gave, requires.
For him, the god of shepherds and their sheep,
My blushing hyacinths and my bays I keep.

D. My Phyllis me with pelted apples plies:

Then tripping to the woods the wanton hies,
And wishes to be seen before she flies.

M. But fair Amyntas comes unasked to me,
And offers love, and sits upon my knee :
Not Delia to my dogs is known so well as he.

D. To the dear mistress of my love-sick mind,
Her swain a pretty present has designed :
I saw two stock-doves billing, and ere long
Will take the nest ; and her's shall be the young.

M. Ten ruddy wildings in the wood I found,
And stood on tip-toes, reaching from the ground :
I sent Amyntas all my present store ;
And will, to-morrow, send as many more.

D. The lovely maid lay panting in my arms ;
And all she said and did was full of charms.
Winds ! on your wings to heaven her accents bear ;
Such words as heaven alone is fit to hear.

M. Ah ! what avails it me, my love's delight,
To call you mine, when absent from my sight ?
I hold the nets, while you pursue the prey ;
And must not share the dangers of the day.

D. I keep my birth-day : send my Phyllis home :
At shearing-time, Iolas, you may come.

M. With Phyllis I am more in grace than you :
Her sorrow did my parting steps pursue :
' Adieu, my dear ! (she said) a long adieu !'

D. The nightly wolf is baneful to the fold,
Storms to the wheat, to buds the bitter cold ;
But, from my frowning fair, more ills I find,
Than from the wolves, and storms, and winter wind.

M. The kids with pleasure browse the bushy plain ;
The showers are grateful to the swelling grain ;
To teeming ewes the sallow's tender tree ;
But, more than all the world, my love to me.

D. Pollio my rural verse vouchsafes to read :
A heifer, Muses, for your patron breed.

M. My Pollio writes himself : a bull he bred,
With spurning heels, and with a butting head.

D. Who Pollio loves, and who his muse admires,
Let Pollio's fortune crown his full desires,

Let myrrh instead of thorn his fences fill,
And showers of honey from his oaks distil.

M. Who hates not living Bavius, let him be
(Dead Mævius!) damned to love thy works and thee!
The same ill taste of sense would serve to join
Dog-foxes in the yoke, and shear the swine.

D. Ye boys, who pluck the flowers, and spoil the spring,
Beware the secret snake that shoots a sting.

M. Graze not too near the banks, my jolly sheep:
The ground is false; the running streams are deep:
See, they have caught the father of the flock,
Who dries his fleece upon the neighbouring rock.

D. From rivers drive the kids, and sling your hook:
Anon I'll wash them in the shallow brook.

M. To fold, my flock!—when milk is dried with heat,
In vain the milk-maid tugs an empty teat.

D. How lank my bulls from plenteous pasture come!
But love, that drains the herd, destroys the groom.

M. My flocks are free from love, yet look so thin,
Their bones are barely covered with their skin.
What magic has bewitched the woolly dams,
And what ill eyes beheld the tender lambs?

D. Say, where the round of heaven, which all contains,
To three short ells on earth our sight restrains:
Tell that, and rise a Phœbus for thy pains.

M. Nay, tell me first, in what new region springs
A flower, that bears inscribed the names of kings;
And thou shalt gain a present as divine
As Phœbus' self; for Phyllis shall be thine.

P. So nice a difference in your singing lies,
That both have won, or both deserved, the prize.
Rest equal happy both; and all who prove
The bitter sweets, and pleasing pains, of love.
Now dam the ditches, and the floods restrain:
Their moisture has already drenched the plain.

PASTORAL IV

POLLIO

THE ARGUMENT

The poet celebrates the birthday of Saloninus, the son of Pollio, born in the consulship of his father, after the taking of Salonæ, a city in Dalmatia. Many of the verses are translated from one of the Sibyls, who prophesied of our Savour's birth.

Sicilian muse, begin a loftier strain !
Though lowly shrubs, and trees that shade the plain,
Delight not all ; Sicilian muse, prepare
To make the vocal woods deserve a consul's care.
The last great age, foretold by sacred rhymes,
Renews its finished course : Saturnian times
Roll round again ; and mighty years, begun
From their first orb, in radiant circles run.
The base degenerate iron offspring ends :
A golden progeny from heaven descends.
O chaste Lucina ! speed the mother's pains ;
And haste the glorious birth ! thy own Apollo reigns !
The lovely boy, with his auspicious face,
Shall Pollio's consulship and triumph grace :
Majestic months set out with him to their appointed race.
The father banished virtue shall restore ;
And crimes shall threat the guilty world no more.
The son shall lead the life of gods, and be
By gods and heroes seen, and gods and heroes see.
The jarring nations he in peace shall bind,
And with paternal virtues rule mankind.
Unbidden earth shall wreathing ivy bring,

16

And fragrant herbs (the promises of spring),
As her first offerings to her infant king.
The goats with strutting dugs shall homeward speed,
And lowing herds secure from lions, feed.
His cradle shall with rising flowers be crowned :
The serpent's brood shall die ; the sacred ground
Shall weeds and poisonous plants refuse to bear ;
Each common bush shall Syrian roses wear.
But when heroic verse his youth shall raise,
And form it to hereditary praise,
Unlaboured harvests shall the fields adorn,
And clustered grapes shall blush on every thorn ;
The knotted oaks shall showers of honey weep,
And through the matted grass the liquid gold shall
    creep.
Yet, of old fraud some footsteps shall remain :
The merchant still shall plough the deep for gain ;
Great cities shall with walls be compassed round ;
And sharpened shares shall vex the fruitful ground ;
Another Tiphys shall new seas explore ;
Another Argo land the chiefs upon the Iberian shore ;
Another Helen other wars create,
And great Achilles urge the Trojan fate.
But when to ripened manhood he shall grow,
The greedy sailor shall the seas forego :
No keel shall cut the waves for foreign ware ;
For every soil shall every product bear.
The labouring hind his oxen shall disjoin ;
No plough shall hurt the glebe, nor pruning hook the
    vine ;
Nor wool shall in dissembled colours shine ;
But the luxurious father of the fold,
With native purple and unborrowed gold,
Beneath his pompous fleece shall proudly sweat ;
And under Tyrian robes the lamb shall bleat.
The Fates, when they this happy web have spun,
Shall bless the sacred clue, and bid it smoothly run.
Mature in years, to ready honours move,
O of celestial seed ! O foster-son of Jove !
See, labouring Nature calls thee to sustain

The nodding frame of heaven, and earth, and main !
See to their base restored, earth, seas, and air ;
And joyful ages, from behind, in crowding ranks appear.
To sing thy praise, would heaven my breath prolong,
Infusing spirits worthy such a song,
Not Thracian Orpheus should transcend my lays,
Nor Linus crowned with never-fading bays ;
Though each his heavenly parent should inspire ;
The muse instruct the voice, and Phœbus tune the lyre.
Should Pan contend in verse, and thou my theme,
Arcadian judges should their god condemn.
Begin, auspicious boy ! to cast about
Thy infant eyes, and, with a smile, thy mother single
    out.
Thy mother well deserves that short delight,
The nauseous qualms of ten long months and travail to
    requite.
Then smile ! the frowning infant's doom is read,
No god shall crown the board, nor goddess bless the bed.

PASTORAL V

DAPHNIS

Menalcas.   Mopsus.

THE ARGUMENT

Mopsus and Menalcas, two very expert shepherds at a song, begin
one, by consent, to the memory of Daphnis, who is supposed
by the best critics to represent Julius Cæsar. Mopsus laments
his death; Menalcas proclaims his divinity; the whole eclogue
consisting of an elegy and an apotheosis.

Men. Since on the downs our flocks together feed,
And since my voice can match your tuneful reed,
Why sit we not beneath the grateful shade,
Which hazels, intermixed with elms, have made?
Mop. Whether you please that sylvan scene to take,
Where whistling winds uncertain shadows make;
Or will you to the cooler cave succeed,
Whose mouth the curling vines have overspread?
Men. Your merit and your years command the choice:
Amyntas only rivals you in voice.
Mop. What will not that presuming shepherd dare,
Who thinks his voice with Phœbus may compare?
Men. Begin you first; if either Alcon's praise,
Or dying Phyllis, have inspired your lays:
If her you mourn, or Codrus you commend,
Begin; and Tityrus your flock shall tend.
Mop. Or shall I rather the sad verse repeat,
Which on the beech's bark I lately writ?
I writ, and sung betwixt. Now bring the swain
Whose voice you boast, and let him try the strain.

Men. Such as the shrub to the tall olive shows,
Or the pale sallow to the blushing rose :
Such is his voice, if I can judge aright,
Compared to thine, in sweetness and in height.

Mop. No more, but sit and hear the promised lay :
The gloomy grotto makes a doubtful day.
The nymphs about the breathless body wait
Of Daphnis, and lament his cruel fate.
The trees and floods were witness to their tears :
At length the rumour reached his mother's ears.
The wretched parent, with a pious haste,
Came running, and his lifeless limbs embraced.
She sighed, she sobbed ; and, furious with despair,
She rent her garments, and she tore her hair,
Accusing all the gods, and every star.
The swains forgot their sheep, nor near the brink
Of running waters brought their herds to drink.
The thirsty cattle, of themselves, abstained
From water, and their grassy fare disdained.
The death of Daphnis, woods and hills deplore ;
They cast the sound to Libya's desert shore ;
The Libyan lions hear, and hearing roar.
Fierce tigers Daphnis taught the yoke to bear,
And first with curling ivy dressed the spear.
Daphnis did rites to Bacchus first ordain,
And holy revels for his reeling train.
As vines the trees, as grapes the vines adorn,
As bulls the herds, and fields the yellow corn :
So bright a splendour, so divine a grace,
The glorious Daphnis cast on his illustrious race.
When envious Fate the godlike Daphnis took,
Our guardian gods the fields and plains forsook ;
Pales no longer swelled the teeming grain,
Nor Phœbus fed his oxen on the plain ;
No fruitful crop the sickly fields return ;
But oats and darnel choke the rising corn.
And where the vales with violets once were crowned,
Now knotty burrs and thorns disgrace the ground.
Come, shepherds, come, and strew with leaves the
          plain :

Such funeral rites your Daphnis did ordain.
With cypress boughs the crystal fountains hide
And softly let the running waters glide.
A lasting monument to Daphnis raise,
With this inscription to record his praise :
' Daphnis, the fields' delight, the shepherds' love.
Renowned on earth, and deified above ;
Whose flock excelled the fairest on the plains,
But less than he himself surpassed the swains.'
   Men. O heavenly poet ! such thy verse appears,
So sweet, so charming to my ravished ears,
As to the weary swain, with cares opprest,
Beneath the sylvan shade, refreshing rest ;
As to the feverish traveller, when first
He finds a crystal stream to quench his thirst.
In singing, as in piping, you excel ;
And scarce your master could perform so well.
O fortunate young man ! at least your lays
Are next to his, and claim the second praise.
Such as they are, my rural songs I join,
To raise our Daphnis to the powers divine ;
For Daphnis was so good, to love whate'er was mine.
   Mop. How is my soul with such a promise raised ;
For both the boy was worthy to be praised,
And Stimicon has often made me long
To hear, like him, so soft, so sweet a song.
   Men. Daphnis, the guest of heaven, with wondering
    eyes
Views, in the milky way, the starry skies,
And far beneath him, from the shining sphere,
Beholds the moving clouds, and rolling year.
For this, with cheerful cries the woods resound ;
The purple spring arrays the various ground ;
The nymphs and shepherds dance ; and Pan himself is
    crowned.
The wolf no longer prowls for nightly spoils,
Nor birds the springes fear, nor stags the toils ;
For Daphnis reigns above, and deals from thence
His mother's milder beams, and peaceful influence.
The mountain-tops unshorn, the rocks, rejoice ;

The lowly shrubs partake of human voice.
Assenting nature, with a gracious nod,
Proclaims him, and salutes the new-admitted god.
Be still propitious, ever good to thine !
Behold ! four hallowed altars we design ;
And two to thee, and two to Phœbus rise ;
On both is offered annual sacrifice.
The holy priests, at each returning year,
Two bowls of milk, and two of oil, shall bear ;
And I myself the guest with friendly bowls will cheer.
Two goblets will I crown with sparkling wine,
The generous vintage of the Chian vine ;
These will I pour to thee, and make the nectar thine.
In winter shall the genial feast be made
Before the fire ; by summer, in the shade.
Damœtas shall perform the rites divine ;
And Lyctian Ægon in the song shall join.
Alphesibœus tripping shall advance,
And mimic satyrs in his antic dance.
When to the nymphs our annual rites we pay,
And when our fields with victims we survey :
While savage boars delight in shady woods,
And finny fish inhabit in the floods :
While bees on thyme, and locusts feed on dew :
Thy grateful swains these honours shall renew.
Such honours as we pay to powers divine,
To Bacchus and to Ceres, shall be thine.
Such annual honours shall be given ; and thou
Shalt hear, and shalt condemn thy suppliants to their
    vow.
    Mop. What present, worth thy verse, can Mopsus find?
Not the soft whispers of the southern wind,
That play through trembling trees, delight me more ;
Nor murmuring billows on the sounding shore ;
Nor winding streams, that through the valley glide,
And the scarce-covered pebbles gently chide.
    Men. Receive you first this tuneful pipe, the same
That played my Corydon's unhappy flame ;
The same that sung Neæra's conquering eyes,
And, had the judge been just, had won the prize.

Mop. Accept from me this sheep-hook in exchange ;
The handle brass ; the knobs in equal range.
Antigenes, with kisses often tried
To beg this present in his beauty's pride,
When youth and love are hard to be denied.
But what I could refuse to his request,
Is yours unasked ; for you deserve it best.

PASTORAL VI

SILENUS

THE ARGUMENT

Two young shepherds, Chromis and Mnasylus, having been often
promised a song by Silenus, chance to catch him asleep in this
Pastoral; where they bind him hand and foot, and then claim
his promise. Silenus, finding they would be put off no longer,
begins his song, in which he describes the formation of the
universe, and the original of animals, according to the Epicurean
philosophy; and then runs through the most surprising trans-
formations which have happened in Nature since her birth. This
Pastoral was designed as a compliment to Syron the Epicurean,
who instructed Virgil and Varus in the principles of that philosophy. Silenus acts as tutor, Chromis and Mnasylus as the two
pupils.

I FIRST transferred to Rome Sicilian strains :
Nor blushed the Doric Muse to dwell on Mantuan
    plains.
But when I tried her tender voice, too young,
And fighting kings and bloody battles sung,
Apollo checked my pride, and bade me feed
My fattening flocks, nor dare beyond the reed.
Admonished thus, while every pen prepares
To write thy praises, Varus, and thy wars,
My pastoral muse her humble tribute brings ;
And yet not wholly uninspired she sings ;
For all who read, and, reading, not disdain
These rural poems, and their lowly strain,
The name of Varus oft inscribed shall see
In every grove, and every vocal tree ;
And all the sylvan reign shall sing of thee :
Thy name, to Phœbus and the muses known,

24

Shall in the front of every page be shown;
For he who sings thy praise secures his own.
Proceed, my muse!—Two satyrs, on the ground,
Stretched at his ease, their sire Silenus found,
Dosed with his fumes, and heavy with his load,
They found him snoring in his dark abode,
And seized with youthful arms the drunken god.
His rosy wreath was dropt not long before,
Borne by the tide of wine, and floating on the floor.
His empty can, with ears half worn away,
Was hung on high, to boast the triumph of the day.
Invaded thus, for want of better bands,
His garland they unstring, and bind his hands:
For, by the fraudful god deluded long,
They now resolve to have their promised song.
Ægle came in, to make their party good,
The fairest Naïs of the neighbouring flood;
And, while he stares around with stupid eyes,
His brows with berries, and his temples, dyes.
He finds the fraud, and, with a smile, demands
On what design the boys had bound his hands.
' Loose me (he cried :) 'twas impudence to find
A sleeping god; 'tis sacrilege to bind.
To you the promised poem I will pay;
The nymph shall be rewarded in her way.'
He raised his voice; and soon a numerous throng
Of tripping satyrs crowded to the song;
And sylvan fauns, and savage beasts, advanced;
And nodding forests to the numbers danced.
Not by Hæmonian hills the Thracian bard,
Nor awful Phœbus, was on Pindus heard
With deeper silence or with more regard.
He sung the secret seeds of nature's frame;
How seas, and earth, and air, and active flame,
Fell through the mighty void, and, in their fall,
Were blindly gathered in this goodly ball.
The tender soil then, stiffening by degrees,
Shut from the bounded earth the bounding seas.
Then earth and ocean various forms disclose;
And a new sun to the new world arose;

And mists, condensed to clouds, obscure the sky;
And clouds, dissolved, the thirsty ground supply.
The rising trees the lofty mountains grace :
The lofty mountains feed the savage race,
Yet few, and strangers, in the unpeopled place.
From thence the birth of man the song pursued,
And how the world was lost, and how renewed :
The reign of Saturn, and the golden age ;
Prometheus' theft, and Jove's avenging rage :
The cries of Argonauts for Hylas drowned,
With whose repeated name the shores resound ;
Then mourns the madness of the Cretan queen :
Happy for her, if herds had never been.
What fury, wretched woman, seized thy breast ?
The maids of Argos (though with rage possessed,
Their imitated lowings filled the grove)
Yet shunned the guilt of thy preposterous love,
Nor sought the youthful husband of the herd,
Though labouring yokes on their own necks they
          feed,
And felt for budding horns on their smooth foreheads
          reared.
Ah, wretched queen ! you range the pathless wood,
While on a flowery bank he chews the cud,
Or sleeps in shades, or through the forest roves,
And roars with anguish for his absent loves.
' Ye nymphs, with toils his forest-walk surround,
And trace his wandering footsteps on the ground.
But ah ! perhaps my passion he disdains,
And courts the milky mothers of the plains.
We search the ungrateful fugitive abroad,
While they at home sustain their happy load.'
He sung the lover's fraud ; the longing maid,
With golden fruit, like all the sex, betrayed ;
The sisters mourning for their brother's loss ;
Their bodies hid in bark, and furred with moss :
How each a rising alder now appears,
And o'er the Po distils her gummy tears :
Then sung, how Gallus, by a muse's hand,
Was led and welcomed to the sacred strand ;

The senate rising to salute their guest;
And Linus thus their gratitude expressed:
' Receive this present, by the muses made,
The pipe on which the Ascræan pastor played;
With which of old he charmed the savage train,
And called the mountain ashes to the plain.
Sing thou, on this, thy Phœbus; and the wood
Where once his fane of Parian marble stood:
On this his ancient oracles rehearse;
And with new numbers grace the god of verse.'
Why should I sing the double Scylla's fate?
The first by love transformed, the last by hate—
A beauteous maid above; but magic arts
With barking dogs deformed her nether parts:
What vengeance on the passing fleet she poured,
The master frighted and the mates devoured.
Then ravished Philomel the song exprest;
The crime revealed; the sisters' cruel feast;
And how in fields the lapwing Tereus reigns,
The warbling nightingale in woods complains;
While Procne makes on chimney-tops her moan;
And hovers o'er the palace once her own.
Whatever songs besides the Delphian god
Had taught the laurels, and the Spartan flood,
Silenus sung: the vales his voice rebound,
And carry to the skies the sacred sound.
And now the setting sun had warned the swain
To call his counted cattle from the plain;
Yet still the unwearied sire pursues the tuneful strain,
Till, unperceived, the heavens with stars were hung,
And sudden night surprised the yet unfinished song.

PASTORAL VII

MELIBŒUS

MELIBŒUS.   CORYDON.   THYRSIS.

THE ARGUMENT

Melibœus here gives us the relation of a sharp poetical contest
between Thyrsis and Corydon, at which he himself and Daphnis
were present; who both declared for Corydon.

M. BENEATH a holm, repaired two jolly swains
(Their sheep and goats together grazed the plains),
Both young Arcadians, both alike inspired
To sing, and answer as the song required.
Daphnis, as umpire, took the middle seat;
And fortune thither led my weary feet.
For, while I fenced my myrtles from the cold,
The father of my flock had wandered from the fold.
Of Daphnis I inquired: he smiling said,
'Dismiss your fear,' and pointed where he fed:
'And, if no greater cares disturb your mind,
Sit here with us, in covert of the wind.
Your lowing heifers, of their own accord,
At watering time will seek the neighbouring ford.
Here wanton Mincius winds along the meads,
And shades his happy banks with bending reeds.
And see, from yon old oak that mates the skies,
How black the clouds of swarming bees arise.'
What should I do? nor was Alcippe nigh,
Nor absent Phyllis could my care supply,
To house, and feed by hand, my weaning lambs,
And drain the strutting udders of their dams.

28

Great was the strife betwixt the singing swains :
And I preferred my pleasure to my gains.
Alternate rhyme the ready champions chose :
These Corydon rehearsed and Thyrsis those.

   C. Ye muses, ever fair, and ever young,
Assist my numbers, and inspire my song.
With all my Codrus, O ! inspire my breast :
For Codrus, after Phœbus, sings the best.
Or, if my wishes have presumed too high,
And stretched their bounds beyond mortality,
The praise of artful numbers I resign,
And hang my pipe upon the sacred pine.

   T. Arcadian swains, your youthful poet crown
With ivy-wreaths ; though surly Codrus frown.
Or, if he blast my muse with envious praise,
Then fence my brows with amulets of bays,
Lest his ill arts or his malicious tongue
Should poison or bewitch my growing song.

   C. These branches of a stag, this tusky boar
(The first essay of arms untried before),
Young Micon offers, Delia, to thy shrine.
But speed his hunting with thy power divine ;
Thy statue then of Parian stone shall stand ;
Thy legs in buskins with a purple band.

   T. This bowl of milk, these cakes (our country fare),
For thee, Priapus, yearly we prepare,
Because a little garden is thy care.
But, if the falling lambs increase my fold,
Thy marble statue shall be turned to gold.

   C. Fair Galatea, with thy silver feet,
O, whiter than the swan, and more than Hybla sweet !
Tall as a poplar, taper as the bole !
Come, charm thy shepherd, and restore my soul
Come, when my lated sheep at night return ;
And crown the silent hours, and stop the rosy morn.

   T. May I become as abject in thy sight,
As sea-weed on the shore, and black as night ;
Rough as a burr, deformed like him who chaws
Sardinian herbage to contract his jaws ;
Such and so monstrous let thy swain appear,

If one day's absence looks not like a year.
Hence from the field, for shame ! the flock deserves
No better feeding, while the shepherd starves.

   C. Ye mossy springs, inviting easy sleep,
Ye trees whose leafy shades those mossy fountains keep,
Defend my flock ! The summer heats are near,
And blossoms on the swelling vines appear.

   T. With heapy fires our cheerful hearth is crowned ;
And firs for torches in the woods abound :
We fear not more the winds, and wintry cold,
Than streams the banks, or wolves the bleating fold.

   C. Our woods with juniper and chestnuts crowned,
With falling fruits and berries paint the ground ;
And lavish nature laughs, and strews her stores around.
But, if Alexis from our mountains fly,
E'en running rivers leave their channels dry.

   T. Parched are the plains, and frying is the field,
Nor withering vines their juicy vintage yield.
But, if returning Phyllis bless the plain,
The grass revives ; the woods are green again ;
And Jove descends in showers of kindly rain.

   C. The poplar is by great Alcides worn ;
The brows of Phœbus his own bays adorn ;
The branching vine the jolly Bacchus loves ;
The Cyprian queen delights in myrtle groves ;
With hazel Phyllis crowns her flowing hair ;
And, while she loves that common wreath to wear,
Nor bays, nor myrtle boughs, with hazel shall compare.

   T. The towering ash is fairest in the woods ;
In gardens pines, and poplars by the floods ;
But, if my Lycidas will ease my pains,
And often visit our forsaken plains,
To him the towering ash shall yield in woods,
In gardens pines, and poplars by the floods.

   M. These rhymes I did to memory commend,
When vanquished Thyrsis did in vain contend ;
Since when, 'tis Corydon among the swains ;
Young Corydon without a rival reigns.

PASTORAL VIII

PHARMACEUTRIA

THE ARGUMENT

This Pastoral contains the songs of Damon and Alphesibœus. The first of them bewails the loss of his mistress, and repines at the success of his rival Mopsus. The other repeats the charms of some enchantress, who endeavoured by her spells and magic to make Daphnis in love with her.

THE mournful muse of two despairing swains,
The love rejected, and the lover's pains ;
To which the savage lynxes listening stood ;
The rivers stood on heaps, and stopped the running
    flood ;
The hungry herd their needful food refuse—
Of two despairing swains, I sing the mournful muse.
    Great Pollio ! thou, for whom thy Rome prepares
The ready triumph of thy finished wars,
Whether Timavus or the Illyrian coast,
Whatever land or sea thy presence boast :
Is there an hour in fate reserved for me,
To sing thy deeds in numbers worthy thee ?
In numbers like to thine, could I rehearse
Thy lofty tragic scenes, thy laboured verse ;
The world another Sophocles in thee,
Another Homer should behold in me.
Amidst thy laurels let this ivy twine :
Thine was my earliest muse ; my latest shall be thine.
    Scarce from the world the shades of night withdrew,
Scarce were the flocks refreshed with morning dew,
When Damon, stretched beneath an olive shade,

And wildly staring upwards, thus inveighed
Against the conscious gods, and cursed the cruel maid :
' Star of the morning, why dost thou delay ?
Come, Lucifer, drive on the lagging day,
While I my Nisa's perjured faith deplore—
Witness, ye powers, by whom she falsely swore !
The gods, alas ! are witnesses in vain :
Yet shall my dying breath to heaven complain.
Begin with me, my flute, the sweet Mænalian strain.

   The pines of Mænalus, the vocal grove,
Are ever full of verse, and full of love ;
They hear the hinds, they hear their god complain,
Who suffered not the reeds to rise in vain.
Begin with me, my flute, the sweet Mænalian strain.

   Mopsus triumphs : he weds the willing fair !
When such is Nisa's choice, what lover can despair ?
Now griffons join with mares ; another age
Shall-see the hound and hind their thirst assuage,
Promiscuous at the spring.   Prepare the lights,
O Mopsus ! and perform the bridal rites.
Scatter thy nuts among the scrambling boys :
Thine is the night, and thine the nuptial joys.
For thee the sun declines : O happy swain !
Begin with me, my flute, the sweet Mænalian strain.

   O Nisa ! justly to thy choice condemned !
Whom hast thou taken, whom hast thou contemned ?
For him thou hast refused my browsing herd,
Scorned my thick eyebrows and my shaggy beard.
Unhappy Damon sighs and sings in vain,
While Nisa thinks no god regards a lover's pain.
Begin with me, my flute, the sweet Mænalian strain.

   I viewed thee first (how fatal was the view !)
And led thee where the ruddy wildings grew,
High on the planted hedge, and wet with morning
    dew.
Then scarce the bending branches I could win ;
The callow down began to clothe my chin.
I saw ; I perished ; yet indulged my pain.
Begin with me, my flute, the sweet Mænalian strain.

   I know thee, Love ! in deserts thou wert bred,

And at the dugs of savage tigers fed ;
Alien of birth, usurper of the plains !
Begin with me, my flute, the sweet Mænalian strains.
  Relentless Love the cruel mother led
The blood of her unhappy babes to shed :
Love lent the sword ; the mother struck the blow ;
Inhuman she ; but more inhuman thou :
Alien of birth, usurper of the plains !
Begin with me, my flute, the sweet Mænalian strains.
  Old doting nature, change thy course anew ;
And let the trembling lamb the wolf pursue :
Let oaks now glitter with Hesperian fruit,
And purple daffodils from alder shoot ;
Fat amber let the tamarisk distil,
And hooting owls contend with swans in skill ;
Hoarse Tityrus strive with Orpheus in the woods,
And challenge famed Arion on the floods.
Or, oh ! let nature cease, and chaos reign !
Begin with me, my flute, the sweet Mænalian strain.
  Let earth be sea ; and let the whelming tide
The lifeless limbs of luckless Damon hide :
Farewell, ye secret woods, and shady groves,
Haunts of my youth, and conscious of my loves !
From yon high cliff I plunge into the main :
Take the last present of thy dying swain :
And cease, my silent flute, the sweet Mænalian strain.'
  Now take your turns, ye muses, to rehearse
His friend's complaints, and mighty magic verse.
  ' Bring running water : bind those altars round
With fillets, and with vervain strew the ground :
Make fat with frankincense the sacred fires,
To reinflame my Daphnis with desires.
'Tis done ; we want but verse. Restore, my charms,
My lingering Daphnis to my longing arms.
  Pale Phœbe, drawn by verse, from heaven descends ;
And Circe changed with charms Ulysses' friends.
Verse breaks the ground, and penetrates the brake,
And in the winding cavern splits the snake.
Verse fires the frozen veins. Restore, my charms,
My lingering Daphnis to my longing arms.

Around his waxen image first I wind
Three woollen fillets, of three colours joined ;
Thrice bind about his thrice-devoted head,
Which round the sacred altar thrice is led.
Unequal numbers please the gods.   My charms,
Restore my Daphnis to my longing arms.

Knit with three knots the fillets : knit them strait :
Then say, "These knots to Love I consecrate !"
Haste, Amaryllis, haste !   Restore, my charms,
My lovely Daphnis to my longing arms.

As fire this figure hardens, made of clay,
And this of wax with fire consumes away ;
Such let the soul of cruel Daphnis be—
Hard to the rest of women, soft to me.
Crumble the sacred mole of salt and corn :
Next in the fire the bays with brimstone burn
And, while it crackles in the sulphur, say,
"This I for Daphnis burn ; thus Daphnis burn away !
This laurel is his fate."   Restore, my charms,
My lovely Daphnis to my longing arms.

As when the raging heifer, through the grove,
Stung with desire, pursues her wandering love ;
Faint at the last, she seeks the weedy pools,
To quench her thirst, and on the rushes rolls,
Careless of night, unmindful to return ;
Such fruitless fires perfidious Daphnis burn,
While I so scorn his love !   Restore, my charms,
My lingering Daphnis to my longing arms.

These garments once were his, and left to me,
The pledges of his promised loyalty,
Which underneath my threshold I bestow.
These pawns, O sacred earth ! to me my Daphnis owe.
As these were his, so mine is he.   My charms,
Restore their lingering lord to my deluded arms.

These poisonous plants, for magic use designed
(The noblest and the best of all the baneful kind),
Old Mœris brought me from the Pontic strand,
And culled the mischief of a bounteous land.
Smeared with these powerful juices, on the plain
He howls a wolf among the hungry train ;

And oft the mighty necromancer boasts,
With these to call from tombs the stalking ghosts,
And from the roots to tear the standing corn,
Which, whirled aloft, to distant fields is borne:
Such is the strength of spells.   Restore, my charms,
My lingering Daphnis to my longing arms.

    Bear out these ashes ; cast them in the brook ;
Cast backwards o'er your head ; nor turn your look :
Since neither gods nor godlike verse can move,
Break out, ye smothered fires, and kindle smothered
      love.
Exert your utmost power, my lingering charms ;
And force my Daphnis to my longing arms.

    See, while my last endeavours I delay,
The waking ashes rise, and round our altars play !
Run to the threshold, Amaryllis—hark !
Our Hylax opens, and begins to bark.
Good heaven ! may lovers what they wish believe ?
Or dream their wishes, and those dreams deceive ?
No more ! my Daphnis comes ! no more, my charms !
He comes, he runs, he leaps to my desiring arms.'

PASTORAL IX

LYCIDAS AND MŒRIS

THE ARGUMENT

When Virgil, by the favour of Augustus, had recovered his patrimony near Mantua, and went in hope to take possession, he was
in danger to be slain by Arius the centurion, to whom those
lands were assigned by the emperor, in reward of his service
against Brutus and Cassius. This Pastoral therefore is filled
with complaints of his hard usage; and the persons introduced
are the bailiff of Virgil, Mœris, and his friend Lycidas.

L. Ho, Mœris! whither on thy way so fast?
This leads to town.

                M. O Lycidas! at last
The time is come I never thought to see,
(Strange revolution for my farm and me!)
When the grim captain in a surly tone
Cries out, 'Pack up, ye rascals, and be gone.'
Kicked out, we set the best face on't we could;
And these two kids, to appease his angry mood,
I bear,—of which the Furies give him good!
   L. Your country friends were told another tale—
That, from the sloping mountain to the vale
And doddered oak, and all the banks along,
Menalcas saved his fortune with a song.
   M. Such was the news, indeed; but songs and
      rhymes
Prevail as much in these hard iron times,
As would a plump of trembling fowl, that rise
Against an eagle sousing from the skies.
And, had not Phœbus warned me, by the croak

Of an old raven from a hollow oak,
To shun debate, Menalcas had been slain,
And Mœris not survived him, to complain.

    L. Now heaven defend ! could barbarous rage induce
The brutal son of Mars to insult the sacred muse?
Who then should sing the nymphs? or who rehearse
The waters gliding in a smoother verse !
Or Amaryllis praise that heavenly lay,
That shortened, as we went, our tedious way—
' O Tityrus ! tend my herd, and see them fed ;
To morning pastures, evening waters led ;
And 'ware the Libyan ridgil's butting head.'

    M. Or what unfinished he to Varus read—
' Thy name, O Varus ! (if the kinder powers
Preserve our plains, and shield the Mantuan towers,
Obnoxious by Cremona's neighbouring crime),
The wings of swans, and stronger-pinioned rhyme,
Shall raise aloft, and soaring bear above—
The immortal gift of gratitude to Jove.'

    L. Sing on, sing on : for I can ne'er be cloyed.
So may thy swarms the baleful yew avoid :
So may thy cows their burdened bags distend,
And trees to goats their willing branches bend.
Mean as I am, yet have the muses made
Me free, a member of the tuneful trade :
At least the shepherds seem to like my lays,
But I discern their flattery from their praise :
I nor to Cinna's ears, nor Varus', dare aspire,
But gabble, like a goose, amidst the swan-like choir.

    M. 'Tis what I have been conning in my mind ;
Nor are they verses of a vulgar kind.
' Come, Galatea ! come ! the seas forsake !
What pleasures can the tides with their hoarse
      murmurs make?
See, on the shore inhabits purple spring ;
Where nightingales their love-sick ditty sing :
See, meads with purling streams, with flowers the
      ground
The grottoes cool, with shady poplars crowned,
And creeping vines on arbours weaved around.

Come then, and leave the waves' tumultuous roar ;
Let the wild surges vainly beat the shore.'
    L. Or that sweet song I heard with such delight ;
The same you sung alone one starry night.
The tune I still retain, but not the words.
    M. 'Why, Daphnis, dost thou search in old records,
To know the seasons when the stars arise ?
See, Cæsar's lamp is lighted in the skies—
The star, whose rays the blushing grapes adorn,
And swell the kindly ripening ears of corn.
Under this influence, graft the tender shoot ;
Thy children's children shall enjoy the fruit.'
The rest I have forgot ; for cares and time
Change all things, and untune my soul to rhyme.
I could have once sung down a summer's sun :
But now the chime of poetry is done :
My voice grows hoarse ; I feel the notes decay,
As if the wolves had seen me first to-day.
But these, and more than I to mind can bring,
Menalcas has not yet forgot to sing.
    L. Thy faint excuses but inflame me more :
And now the waves roll silent to the shore ;
Hushed winds the topmost branches scarcely bend,
As if thy tuneful song they did attend :
Already we have half our way o'ercome ;
Far off I can discern Bianor's tomb.
Here, where the labourers' hands have formed a bower
Of wreathing trees, in singing waste an hour.
Rest here thy weary limbs ; thy kids lay down ;
We've day before us yet, to reach the town ;
Or if, ere night, the gathering clouds we fear,
A song will help, the beating storm to bear.
And, that thou may'st not be too late abroad,
Sing, and I'll ease thy shoulders of thy load.
    M. Cease to request me ; let us mind our way :
Another song requires another day.
When good Menalcas comes, if he rejoice,
And find a friend at court, I'll find a voice.

PASTORAL X

GALLUS

THE ARGUMENT

Gallus, a great patron of Virgil, and an excellent poet, was very deeply in love with one Cytheris, whom he calls Lycoris, and who had forsaken him for the company of a soldier. The poet therefore supposes his friend Gallus retired, in his height of melancholy, into the solitudes of Arcadia (the celebrated scene of pastorals), where he represents him in a very languishing condition, with all the rural deities about him, pitying his hard usage, and condoling his misfortune.

THY sacred succour, Arethusa, bring,
To crown my labour ('tis the last I sing),
Which proud Lycoris may with pity view :
The muse is mournful, though the numbers few.
Refuse me not a verse, to grief and Gallus due.
So may thy silver streams beneath the tide,
Unmixed with briny seas, securely glide.
Sing then my Gallus, and his hopeless vows ;
Sing while my cattle crop the tender browse.
The vocal grove shall answer to the sound,
And echo, from the vales, the tuneful voice rebound.

What lawns or woods withheld you from his aid,
Ye nymphs, when Gallus was to love betrayed,
To love, unpitied by the cruel maid ?
Not steepy Pindus could retard your course,
Nor cleft Parnassus, nor the Aonian source :
Nothing that owns the muses, could suspend
Your aid to Gallus :—Gallus is their friend.
For him the lofty laurel stands in tears,
And hung with humid pearls the lowly shrub appears.

Mænalian pines the god-like swain bemoan,
When, spread beneath a rock, he sighed alone ;
And cold Lycæus wept from every dropping stone.
The sheep surround their shepherd as he lies :
Blush not, sweet poet, nor the name despise :
Along the streams, his flock Adonis fed ;
And yet the queen of beauty blest his bed.
The swains and tardy neat-herds came, and last
Menalcas, wet with beating winter mast.
Wondering, they asked from whence arose thy flame.
Yet more amazed, thy own Apollo came.
Flushed were his cheeks, and glowing were his eyes :
' Is she thy care?   Is she thy care? (he cries)
Thy false Lycoris flies thy love and thee,
And for thy rival, tempts the raging sea,
The forms of horrid war, and heaven's inclemency.'
Silvanus came : his brows a country crown
Of fennel, and of nodding lilies, drown.
Great Pan arrived ; and we beheld him too,
His cheeks and temples of vermilion hue.
' Why, Gallus, this immoderate grief? (he cried)
Think'st thou that love with tears is satisfied ?
The meads are sooner drunk with morning dews,
The bees with flowery shrubs, the goats with browse.'
Unmoved, and with dejected eyes, he mourned :
He paused, and then these broken words returned :
' 'Tis past ; and pity gives me no relief :
But you, Arcadian swains, shall sing my grief,
And on your hills my last complaints renew :
So sad a song is only worthy you.
How light would lie the turf upon my breast,
If you my sufferings in your songs exprest !
Ah ! that your birth and business had been mine—
To pen the sheep, and press the swelling vine !
Had Phyllis or Amyntas caused my pain,
Or any nymph or shepherd on the plain,
(Though Phyllis brown, though black, Amyntas were,
Are violets not sweet, because not fair ?)
Beneath the sallows and the shady vine,
My loves had mixed their pliant limbs with mine :

Phyllis with myrtle wreaths had crowned my hair,
And soft Amyntas sung away my care.
Come, see what pleasures in our plains abound ;
The woods, the fountains and the flowery ground.
As you are beauteous, were you half so true,
Here could I live, and love, and die, with only you.
Now I to fighting fields am sent afar,
And strive in winter camps with toils of war ;
While you (alas, that I should find it so !)
To shun my sight, your native soil forego,
And climb the frozen Alps, and tread the eternal
    snow.
Ye frosts and snows, her tender body spare !
Those are not limbs for icicles to tear.
For me, the wilds and deserts are my choice ;
The muses, once my care ; my once harmonious voice.
There will I sing, forsaken and alone :
The rocks and hollow caves shall echo to my moan.
The rind of every plant her name shall know ;
And as the rind extends, the love shall grow.
Then on Arcadian mountains will I chase
(Mixed with the woodland nymphs) the savage race ;
Nor cold shall hinder me, with horns and hounds
To thrid the thickets, or to leap the mounds.
And now methinks o'er steepy rocks I go,
And rush through sounding woods, and bend the Par-
    thian bow ;
As if with sports my sufferings I could ease,
Or by my pains the god of love appease.
My frenzy changes : I delight no more
On mountain-tops to chase the tusky boar :
No game but hopeless love my thoughts pursue :
Once more, ye nymphs, and songs, and sounding
    woods, adieu !
Love alters not for us his hard decrees,
Not though beneath the Thracian clime we freeze,
Or Italy's indulgent heaven forego,
And in mid-winter tread Sithonian snow ;
Or, when the barks of elms are scorched, we keep
On Meroë's burning plains the Libyan sheep.

In hell, and earth, and seas, and heaven above,
Love conquers all ; and we must yield to Love.'
　My muses, here your sacred raptures end :
The verse was what I owed my suffering friend.
Thus while I sung, my sorrows I deceived,
And bending osiers into baskets weaved.
The song, because inspired by you, shall shine ;
And Gallus will approve, because 'tis mine—
Gallus, for whom my holy flames renew,
Each hour, and every moment rise in view ;
As alders, in the spring, their boles extend,
And heave so fiercely, that the bark they rend.
Now let us rise ; for hoarseness oft invades
The singer's voice, who sings beneath the shades.
From juniper unwholesome dews distil,
That blast the sooty corn, the withering herbage kill :
Away, my goats, away ! for you have browsed your fill.

GEORGICS

BOOK I

THE ARGUMENT

The poet, in the beginning of this book, propounds the general design of each Georgic: and, after a solemn invocation of all the gods who are any way related to his subject, he addresses himself, in particular, to Augustus, whom he compliments with divinity; and after strikes into his business. He shews the different kinds of tillage proper to different soils; traces out the original of agriculture; gives a catalogue of the husbandman's tools; specifies the employments peculiar to each season; describes the changes of the weather, with the signs in heaven and earth that forbode them; instances many of the prodigies that happened near the time of Julius Cæsar's death; and shuts up all with a supplication to the gods for the safety of Augustus, and the preservation of Rome.

WHAT makes a plenteous harvest, when to turn
The fruitful soil, and when to sow the corn;
The care of sheep, of oxen, and of kine;
And how to raise on elms the teeming vine;
The birth and genius of the frugal bee,
I sing, Mæcenas, and I sing to thee.
 Ye deities! who fields and plains protect,
Who rule the seasons, and the year direct,
Bacchus and fostering Ceres, powers divine,
Who gave us corn for mast, for water, wine:
Ye Fauns, propitious to the rural swains,
Ye Nymphs that haunt the mountains and the plains,
Join in my work, and to my numbers bring
Your needful succour; for your gifts I sing.
And thou, whose trident struck the teeming earth,
And made a passage for the courser's birth;
And thou, for whom the Cean shore sustains
The milky herds that graze the flowery plains;
And thou, the shepherds' tutelary god,
Leave, for awhile, O Pan! thy loved abode;

And, if Arcadian fleeces be thy care,
From fields and mountains to my song repair.
Inventor, Pallas, of the fattening oil,
Thou founder of the plough, and ploughman's toil;
And thou, whose hands the shroud-like cypress rear:
Come, all ye gods and goddesses, that wear
The rural honours, and increase the year;
You, who supply the ground with seeds of grain;
And you, who swell those seeds with kindly rain;
And chiefly thou, whose undetermined state
Is yet the business of the gods' debate,
Whether in after-times to be declared
The patron of the world, and Rome's peculiar guard,
Or o'er the fruits and seasons to preside,
And the round circuit of the year to guide—
Powerful of blessings, which thou strew'st around,
And with thy goddess-mother's myrtle crowned.
Or wilt thou, Cæsar, choose the watery reign,
To smooth the surges, and correct the main?
Then mariners, in storms, to thee shall pray;
E'en utmost Thulè shall thy power obey;
And Neptune shall resign the fasces of the sea.
The watery virgins for thy bed shall strive,
And Tethys all her waves in dowry give.
Or wilt thou bless our summers with thy rays,
And, seated near the Balance, poise the days,
Where, in the void of heaven, a space is free,
Betwixt the Scorpion and the Maid, for thee?
The Scorpion, ready to receive thy laws,
Yields half his region, and contracts his claws.
Whatever part of heaven thou shalt obtain,
(For let not hell presume of such a reign;
Nor let so dire a thirst of empire move
Thy mind, to leave thy kindred gods above;
Though Greece admires Elysium's blest retreat,
Though Proserpine affects her silent seat,
And, importuned by Ceres to remove,
Prefers the fields below to those above),
Be thou propitious, Cæsar! guide my course,
And to my bold endeavours add thy force:

Pity the poet's and the ploughman's cares ;
Interest thy greatness in our mean affairs,
And use thyself betimes to hear and grant our prayers.
　While yet the spring is young, while earth unbinds
Her frozen bosom to the western winds ;
While mountain snows dissolve against the sun,
And streams yet new, from precipices run ;
E'en in this early dawning of the year,
Produce the plough, and yoke the sturdy steer,
And goad him till he groans beneath his toil,
Till the bright share is buried in the soil.
That crop rewards the greedy peasant's pains,
Which twice the sun, and twice the cold sustains,
And bursts the crowded barns with more than promised
　　gains.
But, ere we stir the yet unbroken ground,
The various course of seasons must be found ;
The weather, and the setting of the winds,
The culture suiting to the several kinds
Of seeds and plants, and what will thrive and rise,
And what the genius of the soil denies.
This ground with Bacchus, that with Ceres, suits :
That other loads the trees with happy fruits :
A fourth, with grass unbidden, decks the ground.
Thus Tmolus is with yellow saffron crowned :
India black ebon and white ivory bears ;
And soft Idumè weeps her od'rous tears.
Thus Pontus sends her beaver-stones from far ;
And naked Spaniards temper steel for war :
Epirus, for the Elean chariot, breeds
(In hopes of palms) a race of running steeds.
　This is the original contract ; these the laws
Imposed by Nature, and by Nature's cause,
On sundry places, when Deucalion hurled
His mother's entrails on the desert world ;
Whence men, a hard laborious kind, were born.
Then borrow part of winter for thy corn,
And early, with thy team, the glebe in furrows turn ;
That, while the turf lies open and unbound,
Succeeding suns may bake the mellow ground.

But, if the soil be barren, only scar
The surface, and but lightly print the share,
When cold Arcturus rises with the sun ;
Lest wicked weeds the corn should overrun
In watery soils ; or lest the barren sand
Should suck the moisture from the thirsty land.
Both these unhappy soils the swain forbears,
And keeps a sabbath of alternate years,
That the spent earth may gather heart again,
And, bettered by cessation, bear the grain.
At least where vetches, pulse, and tares, have stood,
And stalks of lupines grew (a stubborn wood),
The ensuing season, in return, may bear
The bearded product of the golden year :
For flax and oats will burn the tender field,
And sleepy poppies harmful harvests yield.
But sweet vicissitudes of rest and toil
Make easy labour, and renew the soil.
Yet sprinkle sordid ashes all around,
And load with fattening dung thy fallow ground.
Thus change of seeds for meagre soils is best ;
And earth manured, not idle, though at rest.
  Long practice has a sure improvement found,
With kindled fires to burn the barren ground,
When the light stubble, to the flames resigned,
Is driven along, and crackles in the wind.
Whether from hence the hollow womb of earth
Is warmed with secret strength for better birth ;
Or, when the latent vice is cured by fire,
Redundant humours through the pores expire ;
Or that the warmth distends the chinks, and makes
New breathings, whence new nourishment she takes ;
Or that the heat the gaping ground constrains,
New knits the surface, and new strings the veins ;
Lest soaking showers should pierce her secret seat,
Or freezing Boreas chill her genial heat,
Or scorching suns too violently beat.
  Nor is the profit small the peasant makes,
Who smooths with harrows, or who pounds with rakes,
The crumbling clods ; nor Ceres from on high

Regards his labours with a grudging eye ;
Nor his, who ploughs across the furrowed grounds,
And on the back of earth inflicts new wounds ;
For he, with frequent exercise, commands
The unwilling soil, and tames the stubborn lands.
   Ye swains, invoke the powers who rule the sky,
For a moist summer, and a winter dry ;
For winter drought rewards the peasant's pain,
And broods indulgent on the buried grain.
Hence Mysia boasts her harvests, and the tops
Of Gargarus admire their happy crops.
When first the soil receives the fruitful seed
Make no delay, but cover it with speed :
So fenced from cold, the pliant furrows break,
Before the surly clod resists the rake ;
And calls the floods from high, to rush amain
With pregnant streams, to swell the teeming grain.
Then, when the fiery suns too fiercely play,
And shrivelled herbs on withering stems decay,
The wary ploughman, on the mountain's brow,
Undams his watery stores—huge torrents flow,
And, rattling down the rocks, large moisture yield,
Tempering the thirsty fever of the field ;
And, lest the stem, too feeble for the freight,
Should scarce sustain the head's unwieldy weight,
Sends in his feeding flocks betimes, to invade
The rising bulk of the luxuriant blade,
Ere yet the aspiring offspring of the grain
O'ertops the ridges of the furrowed plain ;
And drains the standing waters, when they yield
Too large a beverage to the drunken field :
But most in autumn, and the showery spring,
When dubious months uncertain weather bring ;
When fountains open, when impetuous rain
Swells hasty brooks, and pours upon the plain ;
When earth with slime and mud is covered o'er,
Or hollow places spew their watery store.
   Nor yet the ploughman, nor the labouring steer,
Sustain alone the hazards of the year :
But glutton geese, and the Strymonian crane,

With foreign troops invade the tender grain ;
And towering weeds malignant shadows yield ;
And spreading succory chokes the rising field.
The sire of gods and men, with hard decrees,
Forbids our plenty to be bought with ease,
And wills that mortal men, inured to toil,
Should exercise with pains, the grudging soil ;
Himself invented first the shining share,
And whetted human industry by care ;
Himself did handicrafts and arts ordain,
Nor suffered sloth to rust his active reign.
Ere this, no peasant vexed the peaceful ground,
Which only turfs and greens for altars, found :
No fences parted fields, nor marks nor bounds
Distinguished acres of litigious grounds ;
But all was common, and the fruitful earth
Was free to give her unexacted birth.
Jove added venom to the viper's brood,
And swelled, with raging storms, the peaceful flood ;
Commissioned hungry wolves to infest the fold,
And shook from oaken leaves the liquid gold ;
Removed from human reach the cheerful fire,
And from the rivers bade the wine retire ;
That studious need might useful arts explore ;
From furrowed fields to reap the foodful store,
And force the veins of clashing flints to expire
The lurking seeds of their celestial fire.
Then first on seas the hollowed alder swam ;
Then sailors quartered heaven, and found a name
For every fixed and every wandering star—
The Pleiads, Hyads, and the Northern Car.
Then toils for beasts, and lime for birds, were found,
And deep-mouthed dogs did forest walks surround ;
And casting-nets were spread in shallow brooks,
Drags in the deep, and baits were hung on hooks.
Then saws were toothed, and sounding axes made ;
(For wedges first did yielding wood invade) ;
And various arts in order did succeed,
(What cannot endless labour, urged by need ?)
     First Ceres taught, the ground with grain to sow,

And armed with iron shares the crooked plough ;
When now Dodonian oaks no more supplied
Their mast, and trees their forest-fruit denied.
Soon was his labour doubled to the swain,
And blasting mildews blackened all his grain ;
Tough thistles choked the fields, and killed the corn,
And an unthrifty crop of weeds was born :
Then burs and brambles, an unbidden crew
Of graceless guests, the unhappy field subdue ;
And oats unblest, and darnel domineers
And shoots its head above the shining ears ;
So that, unless the land with daily care
Is exercised, and, with an iron war
Of rakes and harrows, the proud foes expelled,
And birds with clamours frighted from the field—
Unless the boughs are lopped that shade the plain,
And heaven invoked with vows for fruitful rain—
On others' crops you may with envy look,
And shake for food the long-abandoned oak.
    Nor must we pass untold what arms they wield,
Who labour tillage and the furrowed field ;
Without whose aid the ground her corn denies,
And nothing can be sown, and nothing rise—
The crooked plough, the share, the towering height
Of waggons, and the cart's unwieldy weight,
The sled, the tumbril, hurdles, and the flail,
The fan of Bacchus, with the flying sail—
These all must be prepared, if ploughmen hope
The promised blessing of a bounteous crop.
Young elms, with early force, in copses bow,
Fit for the figure of the crooked plough.
Of eight feet long a fastened beam prepare
On either side the head, produce an ear ;
And sink a socket for the shining share.
Of beech the plough-tail, and the bending yoke,
Or softer linden hardened in the smoke.
I could be long in precepts, but I fear
So mean a subject might offend your ear.
    Delve of convenient depth your thrashing-floor :
With tempered clay then fill and face it o'er ;

And let the weighty roller run the round,
To smooth the surface of the unequal ground ;
Lest, cracked with summer heats, the flooring flies,
Or sinks, and through the crannies weeds arise :
For sundry foes the rural realm surround :
The field-mouse builds her garner under ground
For gathered grain : the blind laborious mole
In winding mazes works her hidden hole :
In hollow caverns vermin make abode—
The hissing serpent, and the swelling toad :
The corn-devouring weasel here abides,
And the wise ant her wintry store provides.
    Mark well the flowering almonds in the wood ;
If odorous blooms the bearing branches load,
The glebe will answer to the sylvan reign ;
Great heats will follow, and large crops of grain.
But, if a wood of leaves o'ershade the tree,
Such and so barren will thy harvest be :
In vain the hind shall vex the thrashing-floor ;
For empty chaff and straw will be thy store.
Some steep their seed, and some in cauldrons boil,
With vigorous nitre and with lees of oil,
O'er gentle fires, the exuberant juice to drain,
And swell the flattering husks with fruitful grain.
Yet is not the success for years assured,
Though chosen is the seed, and fully cured,
Unless the peasant, with his annual pain,
Renews his choice, and culls the largest grain.
Thus all below, whether by Nature's curse,
Or Fate's decree, degenerate still to worse.
So the boat's brawny crew the current stem,
And, slow advancing, struggle with the stream :
But if they slack their hands, or cease to strive,
Then down the flood with headlong haste they drive.
    Nor must the ploughman less observe the skies,
When the Kids, Dragon, and Arcturus, rise,
Than sailors homeward bent, who cut their way
Through Helle's stormy straits, and oyster-breeding
        sea.
But, when Astæa's Balance hung on high,

Betwixt the nights and days divides the sky,
Then yoke your oxen, sow your winter-grain,
Till cold December comes with driving rain.
Linseed and fruitful poppy bury warm,
In a dry season, and prevent the storm.
Sow beans and clover in a rotten soil,
And millet rising from your annual toil,
When with his golden horns, in full career,
The Bull beats down the barriers of the year,
And Argo and the Dog forsake the northern sphere.
 But, if your care to wheat alone extend,
Let Maia with her sisters first descend,
And the bright Gnossian diadem downward bend,
Before you trust in earth your future hope ;
Or else expect a listless lazy crop.
Some swains have sown before ; but most have found
A husky harvest from the grudging ground,
Vile vetches would you sow, or lentils lean ?
The growth of Egypt, or the kidney-bean,
Begin when the slow Waggoner descends ;
Nor cease your sowing till mid-winter ends.
For this, through twelve bright signs Apollo guides
The year, and earth in several climes divides.
Five girdles bind the skies : the torrid zone
Glows with the passing and repassing sun :
Far on the right and left, the extremes of heaven
To frosts and snows and bitter blasts are given ;
Betwixt the midst and these, the gods assigned
Two habitable seats for human kind,
And, 'cross their limits, cut a sloping way,
Which the twelve signs in beauteous order sway.
Two poles turn round the globe ; one seen to rise
O'er Scythian hills, and one in Libyan skies ;
The first sublime in heaven, the last is whirled
Below the regions of the nether world.
 Around our pole the spiry Dragon glides,
And, like a winding stream, the Bears divides—
The less and greater, who by Fate's decree,
Abhor to dive beneath the northern sea.
There, as they say, perpetual night is found

In silence brooding on the unhappy ground :
Or, when Aurora leaves our northern sphere,
She lights the downward heaven, and rises there ;
And, when on us she breathes the living light,
Red Vesper kindles there the tapers of the night.
From hence uncertain seasons we may know,
And when to reap the grain, and when to sow ;
Or when to fell the furzes ; when 'tis meet
To spread the flying canvas for the fleet.
Observe what stars arise or disappear ;
And the four quarters of the rolling year.
But, when cold weather and continued rain
The labouring husband in his house restrain,
Let him forecast his work with timely care,
Which else is huddled, when the skies are fair :
Then let him mark the sheep, or whet the shining
　　　share,
Or hollow trees for boats, or number o'er
His sacks, or measure his increasing store,
Or sharpen stakes, or head the forks, or twine
The sallow twigs to tie the straggling vine ;
Or wicker baskets weave, or air the corn,
Or grinded grain betwixt two marbles turn.
No laws, divine or human, can restrain
From necessary works the labouring swain.
E'en holidays and feasts permission yield
To float the meadows, or to fence the field,
To fire the brambles, snare the birds, and steep
In wholesome water-falls the woolly sheep.
And oft the drudging ass is driven with toil,
To neighbouring towns with apples and with oil ;
Returning, late and laden, home with gain
Of bartered pitch, and hand-mills for the grain.
　The lucky days, in each revolving moon,
For labour choose ; the fifth be sure to shun ;
That gave the Furies and pale Pluto birth,
And armed, against the skies, the sons of earth.
With mountains piled on mountains, thrice they
　　　strove
To scale the steepy battlements of Jove ;

And thrice his lightning and red thunder played,
And their demolished works in ruin laid.
The seventh is, next the tenth, the best to join
Young oxen to the yoke, and plant the vine.
Then, weavers, stretch your stays upon the weft :
The ninth is good for travel, bad for theft.
Some works in dead of night are better done,
Or when the morning dew prevents the sun.
Parched meads and stubble, mow by Phœbe's light,
Which both require the coolness of the night ;
For moisture then abounds, and pearly rains
Descend in silence to refresh the plains.
The wife and husband equally conspire
To work by night, and rake the winter fire :
He sharpens torches in the glimmering room ;
She shoots the flying shuttle through the loom ;
Or boils in kettles must of wine, and skims,
With leaves, the dregs that overflow the brims :
And till the watchful cock awakes the day,
She sings, to drive the tedious hours away.
But, in warm weather, when the skies are clear,
By daylight reap the product of the year ;
And in the sun your golden grain display,
And thrash it out, and winnow it by day.
Plough naked, swain, and naked sow the land ;
For lazy winter numbs the labouring hand.
In genial winter, swains enjoy their store,
Forget their hardships and recruit for more.
The farmer to full bowls invites his friends,
And, what he got with pains, with pleasure spends.
So sailors, when escaped from stormy seas,
First crown their vessels, then indulge their ease.
Yet that's the proper time to thrash the wood
For mast of oak, your fathers' homely food ;
To gather laurel-berries, and the spoil
Of bloody myrtles, and to press your oil ;
For stalking cranes to set the guileful snare ;
To inclose the stags in toils, and hunt the hare ;
With Balearic slings, or Gnossian bow,
To persecute from far the flying doe,

Then, when the fleecy skies new-clothe the wood,
And cakes of rustling ice come rolling down the flood.
  Now sing we stormy stars, when autumn weighs
The year, and adds to nights, and shortens days,
And suns declining shine with feeble rays;
What cares must then attend the toiling swain;
Or when the lowering spring, with lavish rain,
Beats down the slender stem and bearded grain,
While yet the head is green, or, lightly swelled
With milky moisture, overlooks the field.
E'en when the farmer, now secure of fear,
Sends in the swains to spoil the finished year,
E'en while the reaper fills his greedy hands,
And binds the golden sheaves in brittle bands,
Oft have I seen a sudden storm arise,
From all the warring winds that sweep the skies:
The heavy harvest from the root is torn,
And whirled aloft, the lighter stubble borne:
With such a force the flying rack is driven,
And such a winter wears the face of heaven:
And oft whole sheets descend of sluicy rain,
Sucked by the spongy clouds from off the main:
The lofty skies at once come pouring down,
The promised crop and golden labours drown.
The dikes are filled; and, with a roaring sound,
The rising rivers float the nether ground;
And rocks the bellowing voice of boiling seas rebound.
The father of the gods his glory shrouds,
Involved in tempests, and a night of clouds;
And from the middle darkness flashing out,
By fits he deals his fiery bolts about.
Earth feels the motions of her angry god:
Her entrails tremble, and her mountains nod,
And flying beasts in forests seek abode:
Deep horror seizes every human breast;
Their pride is humbled and their fear confessed,
While he from high his rolling thunder throws,
And fires the mountains with repeated blows:
The rocks are from their old foundation rent;
The winds redouble, and the rains augment:

The waves on heaps are dashed against the shore ;
And now the woods, and now the billows, roar.
   In fear of this, observe the starry signs,
Where Saturn houses, and where Hermes joins.
But first to heaven thy due devotions pay,
And annual gifts on Ceres' altars lay.
When winter's rage abates, when cheerful hours
Awake the spring, the spring awakes the flowers,
On the green turf thy careless limbs display,
And celebrate the mighty Mother's day ;
For then the hills with pleasing shades are crowned,
And sleeps are sweeter on the silken ground :
With milder beams the sun securely shines ;
Fat are the lambs, and luscious are the wines.
Let every swain adore her power divine,
And milk and honey mix with sparkling wine ;
Let all the choir of clowns attend the show,
In long procession, shouting as they go ;
Invoking her to bless their yearly stores,
Inviting plenty to their crowded floors.
Thus in the spring, and thus in summer's heat,
Before the sickles touch the ripening wheat,
On Ceres call ; and let the labouring hind
With oaken wreaths his hollow temples bind :
On Ceres let him call, and Ceres praise,
With uncouth dances, and with country lays.
   And that by certain signs we may presage
Of heats and rains, and winds' impetuous rage,
The sovereign of the heavens has set on high
The moon to mark the changes of the sky ;
When southern blasts should cease, and when the swain
Should near their folds his feeding flocks restrain.
For, e'er the rising winds begin to roar,
The working seas advance to wash the shore ;
Soft whispers run along the leafy woods,
And mountains whistle to the murmuring floods.
E'en then the doubtful billows scarce abstain
From the tossed vessel on the troubled main ;
When crying cormorants forsake the sea,
And, stretching to the covert, wing their way ;

When sportful coots run skimming o'er the strand,
When watchful herons leave their watery stand,
And, mounting upward with erected flight,
Gain on the skies, and soar above the sight.
And oft, before tempestuous winds arise,
The seeming stars fall headlong from the skies,
And, shooting through the darkness, gild the night
With sweeping glories, and long trails of light;
And chaff with eddy winds is whirled around,
And dancing leaves are lifted from the ground;
And floating feathers on the waters play.
    But when the wingèd thunder takes his way
From the cold north, and east and west engage,
And at their frontiers meet with equal rage,
The clouds are crushed; a glut of gathered rain
The hollow ditches fills, and floats the plain;
And sailors furl their dropping sheets amain.
Wet weather seldom hurts the most unwise;
So plain the signs, such prophets are the skies.
The wary crane foresees it first, and sails
Above the storm, and leaves the lowly vales;
The cow looks up, and from afar can find
The change of heaven, and snuffs it in the wind;
The swallow skims the river's watery face;
The frogs renew the croaks of their loquacious race;
The careful ant her secret cell forsakes,
And drags her eggs along the narrow tracks:
At either horn the rainbow drinks the flood;
Huge flocks of rising rooks forsake their food,
And, crying, seek the shelter of the wood.
Besides, the several sorts of watery fowls,
That swim the seas, or haunt the standing pools,
The swans that sail along the silver flood,
And dive with stretching necks to search their food,
Then lave their backs with sprinkling dews in vain,
And stem the stream to meet the promised rain.
The crow with clamorous cries the shower demands,
And single stalks along the desert sands.
The nightly virgin, while her wheel she plies,
Foresees the storm impending in the skies,

When sparkling lamps their sputtering light advance,
And in the sockets oily bubbles dance.
   Then, after showers, 'tis easy to descry
Returning suns, and a serener sky :
The stars shine smarter ; and the moon adorns,
As with unborrowed beams, her sharpened horns.
The filmy gossamer now flits no more,
Nor halcyons bask on the short sunny shore ;
Their litter is not tossed by sows unclean ;
But a blue droughty mist descends upon the plain ;
And owls, that mark the setting sun, declare
A star-light evening, and a morning fair.
Towering aloft, avenging Nisus flies,
While, dared, below the guilty Scylla lies.
Wherever frighted Scylla flies away,
Swift Nisus follows and pursues his prey :
Where injured Nisus takes his airy course,
Thence trembling Scylla flies, and shuns his force :
This punishment pursues the unhappy maid,
And thus the purple hair is dearly paid.
   Then, thrice the ravens rend the liquid air,
And croaking notes proclaim the settled fair.
Then round their airy palaces they fly,
To greet the sun ; and seized with secret joy,
When storms are overblown, with food repair
To their forsaken nests and callow care.
Not that I think their breasts with heavenly souls
Inspired, as man, who destiny controls :
But, with the changeful temper of the skies,
As rains condense, and sunshine rarefies,
So turn the species in their altered minds,
Composed by calms, and discomposed by winds.
From hence proceeds the birds' harmonious voice ;
From hence the cows exult, and frisking lambs rejoice.
   Observe the daily circle of the sun,
And the short year of each revolving moon :
By them thou shalt foresee the following day,
Nor shall a starry night thy hopes betray.
When first the moon appears, if then she shrouds
Her silver crescent tipped with sable clouds,

Conclude she bodes a tempest on the main,
And brews for fields impetuous floods of rain.
Or, if her face with fiery flushing glow,
Expect the rattling winds aloft to blow.
But, four nights old (for that's the surest sign),
With sharpened horns if glorious then she shine,
Next day, not only that, but all the moon,
Till her revolving race be wholly run,
Are void of tempests, both by land and sea ;
And sailors in the port their promised vow shall pay.
   Above the rest, the sun, who never lies,
Foretells the change of weather in the skies :
For, if he rise unwilling to his race,
Clouds on his brow, and spots upon his face :
Or if through mists he shoots his sullen beams,
Frugal of light, in loose and straggling streams ;
Suspect a drizzling day, with southern rain,
Fatal to fruits, and flocks, and promised grain.
Or if Aurora, with half-opened eyes,
And a pale sickly cheek, salute the skies ;
How shall the vine, with tender leaves, defend
Her teeming clusters, when the storms descend,
When ridgy roofs and tiles can scarce avail
To bar the ruin of the rattling hail ?
   But, more than all, the setting sun survey,
When down the steep of heaven he drives the day :
For oft we find him finishing his race,
With various colours erring on his face.
If fiery red his glowing globe descends,
High winds and furious tempests he portends :
But, if his cheeks are swoln with livid blue,
He bodes wet weather by his watery hue :
If dusky spots are varied on his brow,
And, streaked with red, a troubled colour show ;
That sullen mixture shall at once declare
Winds, rain, and storms, and elemental war.
What desperate madman then would venture o'er
The frith, or haul his cables from the shore ?
But, if with purple rays he brings the light,
And a pure heaven resigns to quiet night,

No rising winds, or falling storms are nigh;
But northern breezes through the forests fly,
And drive the rack, and purge the ruffled sky.
The unerring sun by certain signs declares,
What the late e'en or early morn prepares,
And when the south projects a stormy day,
And when the clearing north will puff the clouds away.

The sun reveals the secrets of the sky;
And who dares give the source of light the lie?
The change of empires often he declares,
Fierce tumults, hidden treasons, open wars.
He first the fate of Cæsar did foretell,
And pitied Rome, when Rome in Cæsar fell;
In iron clouds concealed the public light;
And impious mortals feared eternal night.

Nor was the fact foretold by him alone:
Nature herself stood forth, and seconded the sun.
Earth, air, and seas, with prodigies were signed;
And birds obscene, and howling dogs, divined.
What rocks did Ætna's bellowing mouth expire
From her torn entrails! and what floods of fire!
What clanks were heard, in German skies afar,
Of arms, and armies, rushing to the war!
Dire earthquakes rent the solid Alps below,
And from their summits shook the eternal snow;
Pale spectres in the close of night were seen,
And voices heard, of more than mortal men,
In silent groves: dumb sheep and oxen spoke;
And streams ran backward, and their beds forsook;
The yawning earth disclosed the abyss of hell:
The weeping statues did the wars foretell;
And holy sweat from brazen idols fell.
Then, rising in his might, the king of floods
Rushed through the forests, tore the lofty woods,
And, rolling onward, with a sweepy sway,
Bore houses, herds, and labouring hinds away.
Blood sprang from wells; wolves howled in towns by
      night.
And boding victims did the priests affright.
Such peals of thunder never poured from high,

Nor forky lightnings flashed from such a sullen sky.
Red meteors ran across the ethereal space ;
Stars disappeared, and comets took their place.
For this, the Emathian plains once more were strewed
With Roman bodies, and just heaven thought good
To fatten twice those fields with Roman blood.
Then, after length of time, the labouring swains
Who turn the turfs of those unhappy plains,
Shall rusty piles from the ploughed furrows take,
And over empty helmets pass the rake—
Amazed at antique titles on the stones,
And mighty relics of gigantic bones.

　　Ye home-born deities, of mortal birth !
Thou father Romulus, and mother Earth,
Goddess unmoved ! whose guardian arms extend
O'er Tuscan Tiber's course, and Roman towers defend ;
With youthful Cæsar your joint powers engage,
Nor hinder him to save the sinking age.
O ! let the blood, already spilt, atone
For the past crimes of cursed Laomedon !
Heaven wants thee there ; and long the gods, we know,
Have grudged thee, Cæsar, to the world below,
Where fraud and rapine right and wrong confound,
Where impious arms from every part resound,
And monstrous crimes in every shape are crowned.
The peaceful peasant to the wars is pressed ;
The fields lie fallow in inglorious rest ;
The plain no pasture to the flock affords ;
The crooked scythes are straightened into swords :
And there Euphrates her soft offspring arms,
And here the Rhine rebellows with alarms ;
The neighbouring cities range on several sides ;
Perfidious Mars long-plighted leagues divides,
And o'er the wasted world in triumph rides.
So four fierce coursers, starting to the race,
Scour through the plain, and lengthen every pace ;
Nor reins, nor curbs, nor threatening cries, they fear,
But force along the trembling charioteer.

BOOK II

THE ARGUMENT

The subject of the following book is planting: in handling of which
argument, the poet shews all the different methods of raising
trees, describes their variety, and gives rules for the management
of each in particular. He then points out the soils in which the
several plants thrive best, and thence takes occasion to run out
into the praises of Italy; after which, he gives some directions for
discovering the nature of every soil, prescribes rules for dressing
of vines, olives, etc., and concludes the Georgic with a panegyric
on a country life.

Thus far of tillage, and of heavenly signs:
Now sing, my muse, the growth of generous vines.
The shady groves, the woodland progeny,
And the slow product of Minerva's tree.

   Great father Bacchus! to my song repair;
For clustering grapes are thy peculiar care:
For thee, large bunches load the bending vine;
And the last blessings of the year are thine.
To thee his joys the jolly Autumn owes,
When the fermenting juice the vat o'erflows.
Come, strip with me, my god! come drench all o'er
Thy limbs in must of wine, and drink at every pore.

   Some trees their birth to bounteous Nature owe;
For some, without the pains of planting, grow.
With osiers thus the banks of brooks abound,
Sprung from the watery genius of the ground.
From the same principles gray willows come,
Herculean poplar, and the tender broom.
But some, from seeds inclosed in earth, arise;
For thus the mastful chestnut mates the skies.
Hence rise the branching beech and vocal oak,

Where Jove of old oraculously spoke.
Some from the root a rising wood disclose:
Thus elms, and thus the savage cherry grows:
Thus the green bay, that binds the poet's brows,
Shoots, and is sheltered by the mother's boughs.
　These ways of planting, Nature did ordain
For trees and shrubs, and all the sylvan reign.
Others there are, by late experience found:
Some cut the shoots, and plant in furrowed ground;
Some cover rooted stalks in deeper mould;
Some, cloven stakes; and (wondrous to behold!)
Their sharpened ends in earth their footing place;
And the dry poles produce a living race.
Some bow their vines, which buried in the plain,
Their tops in distant arches rise again.
Others no root require; the labourer cuts
Young slips, and in the soil securely puts.
E'en stumps of olives, bared of leaves, and dead,
Revive, and oft redeem their withered head.
'Tis usual now an inmate graff to see
With insolence invade a foreign tree:
Thus pears and quinces from the crab-tree come,
And thus the ruddy cornel bears the plum.
　Then let the learnèd gardener mark with care
The kinds of stocks, and what those kinds will bear:
Explore the nature of each several tree,
And, known, improve with artful industry:
And let no spot of idle earth be found,
But cultivate the genius of the ground:
For open Ismarus will Bacchus please;
Taburnus loves the shade of olive-trees.
　The virtues of the several soils I sing.—
Mæcenas, now thy needful succour bring!
O thou! the better part of my renown,
Inspire thy poet, and thy poem crown:
Embark with me, while I new tracts explore,
With flying sails and breezes from the shore:
Not that my song, in such a scanty space,
So large a subject fully can embrace—
Not though I were supplied with iron lungs,

A hundred mouths, filled with as many tongues :
But steer my vessel with a steady hand,
And coast along the shore in sight of land.
Nor will I tire thy patience with a train
Of preface, or what ancient poets feign.
   The trees, which of themselves advance in air,
Are barren kinds, but strongly built and fair,
Because the vigour of the native earth
Maintains the plant, and makes a manly birth.
Yet these, receiving graffs of other kind,
Or thence transplanted, change their savage mind,
Their wildness lose, and, quitting nature's part,
Obey the rules and discipline of art.
The same do trees, that, sprung from barren roots,
In open fields transplanted bear their fruits.
For, where they grow, the native energy
Turns all into the substance of the tree,
Starves and destroys the fruit, is only made
For brawny bulk, and for a barren shade.
The plant that shoots from seed, a sullen tree,
At leisure grows, for late posterity ;
The generous flavour lost, the fruits decay,
And savage grapes are made the birds' ignoble prey.
   Much labour is required in trees, to tame
Their wild disorder, and in ranks reclaim.
Well must the ground be digged, and better dressed,
New soil to make, and meliorate the rest.
Old stakes of olive trees in plants revive ;
By the same method Paphian myrtles live ;
But nobler vines by propagation thrive.
From roots hard hazels, and, from scions, rise
Tall ash, and taller oak that mates the skies ;
Palm, poplar, fir, descending from the steep
Of hills, to try the dangers of the deep.
The thin-leaved arbute, hazel-graffs receives ;
And planes huge apples bear, that bore but leaves
Thus mastful beech the bristly chestnut bears,
And the wild ash is white with blooming pears,
And greedy swine, from grafted elms are fed
With falling acorns, that on oaks are bred.

3   D

But various are the ways to change the state
Of plants, to bud, to graff, to inoculate.
For, where the tender rinds of trees disclose
Their shooting gems, a swelling knot there grows:
Just in that space a narrow slit we make,
Then other buds from bearing trees we take ;
Inserted thus, the wounded rind we close,
In whose moist womb the admitted infant grows.
But, when the smoother bole from knots is free,
We make a deep incision in the tree,
And in the solid wood the slip inclose ;
The battening bastard shoots again and grows ;
And in short space the laden boughs arise,
With happy fruit advancing to the skies.
The mother plant admires the leaves unknown
Of alien trees, and apples not her own.

Of vegetable woods are various kinds,
And the same species are of several minds.
Lotes, willows, elms, have different forms allowed ;
So funeral cypress, rising like a shroud.
Fat olive-trees of sundry sorts appear,
Of sundry shapes their unctuous berries bear.
Radii long olives, Orchites round produce,
And bitter Pausia, pounded for the juice.
Alcinous' orchard various apples bears :
Unlike are bergamots and pounder pears.
Nor our Italian vines produce the shape,
Or taste, or flavour, of the Lesbian grape.
The Thasian vines in richer soils abound ;
The Mareotic grow in barren ground.
The Psythian grape we dry : Lagean juice
Will stammering tongues and staggering feet produce
Rath ripe are some, and some of later kind ;
Of golden some, and some of purple rind.
How shall I praise the Rhætian grape divine,
Which yet contends not with Falernian wine ?
The Aminean many a consulship survives,
And longer than the Lydian vintage lives,
Or high Phanæus, king of Chian growth :
But, for large quantities and lasting, both,

The less Argitis bears the prize away.
The Rhodian, sacred to the solemn day,
In second services is poured to Jove,
And best accepted by the gods above.
Nor must Bumastus his old honours lose,
In length and largeness like the dugs of cows.
I pass the rest, whose every race, and name,
And kinds, are less material to my theme ;
Which who would learn, as soon may tell the sands,
Driven by the western wind on Libyan lands,
Or number, when the blustering Eurus roars,
The billows beating on Ionian shores.

Nor every plant on every soil will grow :
The sallow loves the watery ground, and low ;
The marshes, alders : Nature seems to ordain
The rocky cliff for the wild ash's reign ;
The baleful yew to northern blasts assigns,
To shores the myrtles, and to mounts the vines.

Regard the extremest cultivated coast,
From hot Arabia to the Scythian frost :
All sorts of trees their several countries know ;
Black ebon only will in India grow,
And odorous frankincense on the Sabæan bough.
Balm slowly trickles through the bleeding veins
Of happy shrubs in Idumæan plains.
The green Egyptian thorn, for med'cine good,
With Æthiops' hoary trees and woolly wood,
Let others tell ; and how the Seres spin
Their fleecy forests in a slender twine ;
With mighty trunks of trees on Indian shores,
Whose height above the feathered arrow soars,
Shot from the toughest bow, and, by the brawn
Of expert archers, with vast vigour drawn.
Sharp-tasted citrons, Median climes produce,
(Bitter the rind, but generous is the juice),
A cordial fruit, a present antidote
Against the direful stepdame's deadly draught,
Who, mixing wicked weeds with words impure,
The fate of envied orphans would procure.
Large is the plant, and like a laurel grows,

And, did it not a different scent disclose,
A laurel were : the fragrant flowers contemn
The stormy winds, tenacious of their stem.
With this, the Medes to labouring age bequeath
New lungs, and cure the sourness of the breath.
    But neither Median woods (a plenteous land),
Fair Ganges, Hermus rolling golden sand,
Nor Bactria, nor the richer Indian fields,
Nor all the gummy stores Arabia yields,
Nor any foreign earth of greater name,
Can with sweet Italy contend in fame.
No bulls, whose nostrils breathe a living flame,
Have turned our turf ; no teeth of serpents here
Were sown, an armèd host and iron crop to bear.
But fruitful vines, and the fat olive's freight,
And harvests heavy with their fruitful weight,
Adorn our fields ; and on the cheerful green
The grazing flocks and lowing herds are seen.
The warrior horse, here bred, is taught to train :
There flows Clitumnus through the flowery plain,
Whose waves, for triumphs after prosperous war,
The victim ox and snowy sheep prepare.
Perpetual spring our happy climate sees :
Twice breed the cattle, and twice bear the trees ;
And summer suns recede by slow degrees.
    Our land is from the rage of tigers freed,
Nor nourishes the lion's angry seed ;
Nor poisonous aconite is here produced,
Or grows unknown, or is, when known, refused ;
Nor in so vast a length our serpents glide,
Or raised on such a spiry volume ride.
    Next add our cities of illustrious name,
Their costly labour, and stupendous frame ;
Our forts on steepy hills, that far below
See wanton streams in winding valleys flow ;
Our twofold seas, that, washing either side,
A rich recruit of foreign stores provide ;
Our spacious lakes ; thee, Larius, first ; and next
Benacus, with tempestuous billows vexed.
Or shall I praise thy ports, or mention make

Of the vast mound that binds the Lucrine lake?
Or the disdainful sea, that, shut from thence,
Roars round the structure, and invades the fence,
There, where secure the Julian waters glide,
Or where Avernus' jaws admit the Tyrrhene tide?
Our quarries, deep in earth, were famed of old
For veins of silver, and for ore of gold.
The inhabitants themselves their country grace;
Hence rose the Marsian and Sabellian race,
Strong-limbed and stout, and to the wars inclined,
And hard Ligurians a laborious kind,
And Volscians armed with iron-headed darts.
Besides—an offspring of undaunted hearts—
The Decii, Marii, great Camillus, came
From hence, and greater Scipio's double name,
And mighty Cæsar, whose victorious arms
To farthest Asia carry fierce alarms,
Avert unwarlike Indians from his Rome,
Triumph abroad, secure our peace at home.
　Hail, sweet Saturnian soil! of fruitful grain
Great parent, greater of illustrious men!
For thee my tuneful accents will I raise,
And treat of arts disclosed in ancient days,
Once more unlocked for thee the sacred spring,
And old Ascræan verse in Roman cities sing.
　The nature of the several soils now see,
Their strength, their colour, their fertility:
And first for heath, and barren hilly ground,
Where meagre clay and flinty stones abound,
Where the poor soil all succour seems to want—
Yet this suffices the Palladian plant.
Undoubted signs of such a soil are found;
For here wild olive-shoots o'erspread the ground,
And heaps of berries strew the fields around.
But, where the soil, with fattening moisture filled,
Is clothed with grass, and fruitful to be tilled,
Such as in cheerful vales we view from high,
Which dripping rocks with rolling streams supply,
And feed with ooze; where rising hillocks run
In length, and open to the southern sun;

Where fern succeeds, ungrateful to the plough—
That gentle ground to generous grapes allow.
Strong stocks of vines it will in time produce,
And overflow the vats with friendly juice,
Such as our priests in golden goblets pour
To gods, the givers of the cheerful hour,
Then when the bloated Tuscan blows his horn,
And reeking entrails are in chargers borne.
　　If herds or fleecy flocks be more thy care,
Or goats that graze the field, and burn it bare,
Then seek Tarentum's lawns, and farthest coast,
Or such a field as hapless Mantua lost,
Where silver swans sail down the watery road,
And graze the floating herbage of the flood.
There crystal streams perpetual tenor keep,
Nor food nor springs are wanting to thy sheep;
For, what the day devours, the nightly dew
Shall to the morn in pearly drops renew.
Fat crumbling earth is fitter for the plough,
Putrid and loose above, and black below;
For ploughing is an imitative toil,
Resembling nature in an easy soil.
No land for seed like this; no fields afford
So large an income to the village lord:
No toiling teams from harvest-labour come
So late at night, so heavy-laden home.
The like of forest land is understood,
From whence the surly ploughman grubs the wood,
Which had for length of ages idle stood.
Then birds forsake the ruins of their seat,
And, flying from their nests, their callow young forget.
The coarse lean gravel, on the mountain-sides,
Scarce dewy beverage for the bees provides;
Nor chalk, nor crumbling stones, the food of snakes,
That work in hollow earth their winding tracks.
The soil exhaling clouds of subtle dews,
Imbibing moisture which with ease she spews,
Which rusts not iron, and whose mould is clean,
Well clothed with cheerful grass, and ever green,
Is good for olives, and aspiring vines,

Embracing husband elms in amorous twines ;
Is fit for feeding cattle, fit to sow,
And equal to the pasture and the plough.
Such is the soil of fat Campanian fields ;
Such large increase the land that joins Vesuvius yields ;
And such a country could Acerræ boast,
Till Clanius overflowed the unhappy coast.
    I teach thee next the differing soils to know,
The light for vines, the heavier for the plough.
Choose first a place for such a purpose fit :
There dig the solid earth, and sink a pit ;
Next fill the hole with its own earth again,
And trample with thy feet, and tread it in :
Then, if it rise not to the former height
Of superfice, conclude that soil is light,
A proper ground for pasturage and vines.
But, if the sullen earth, so pressed, repines
Within its native mansion to retire,
And stays without, a heap of heavy mire,
'Tis good for arable, a glebe that asks
Tough teams of oxen, and laborious tasks.
    Salt earth and bitter are not fit to sow.
Nor will be tamed and mended by the plough.
Sweet grapes degenerate there ; and fruits declined
From their first flavorous taste, renounce their kind.
This truth by sure experiment is tried ;
For first an osier colander provide
Of twigs thick wrought (such, toiling peasants twine,
When through strait passages they strain their wine :)
In this close vessel place that earth accursed,
But filled brimful with wholesome water first ;
Then run it through ; the drops will rope around,
And, by the bitter taste, disclose the ground.
The fatter earth by handling we may find,
With ease distinguished from the meagre kind :
Poor soil will crumble into dust ; the rich
Will to the fingers cleave like clammy pitch :
Moist earth produces corn and grass, but both
Too rank and too luxuriant in their growth.
Let not my land so large a promise boast,

Lest the lank ears in length of stem be lost.
The heavier earth is by her weight betrayed ;
The lighter in the poising hand is weighed.
'Tis easy to distinguish by the sight,
The colour of the soil, and black from white.
But the cold ground is difficult to know ;
Yet this, the plants that prosper there, will show—
Black ivy, pitch-trees, and the baleful yew.

These rules considered well, with early care
The vineyard destined for thy vines prepare :
But long before the planting, dig the ground,
With furrows deep that cast a rising mound.
The clods, exposed to winter winds, will bake ;
For putrid earth will best in vineyards take ;
And hoary frosts, after the painful toil
Of delving hinds, will rot the mellow soil.

Some peasants, not to omit the nicest care,
Of the same soil their nursery prepare,
With that of their plantation ; lest the tree,
Translated, should not with the soil agree.
Beside, to plant it as it was, they mark
The heaven's four quarters on the tender bark,
And to the north or south, restore the side,
Which at their birth did heat or cold abide :
So strong is custom ; such effects can use
In tender souls of pliant plants produce.

Choose next a province for thy vineyard's reign
On hills above, or in the lowly plain.
If fertile fields or valleys be thy choice,
Plant thick ; for bounteous Bacchus will rejoice
In close plantations there ; but, if the vine
On rising ground be placed, or hills supine,
Extend thy loose battalions largely wide,
Opening thy ranks and files on either side,
But marshalled all in order as they stand ;
And let no soldier straggle from his band.
As legions in the field their front display,
To try the fortune of some doubtful day,
And move to meet their foes with sober pace,
Strict to their figure, though in wider space,

Before the battle joins, while from afar
The field yet glitters with the pomp of war,
And equal Mars, like an impartial lord,
Leaves all to fortune, and the dint of sword:
So let thy vines in intervals be set,
But not their rural discipline forget;
Indulge their width, and add a roomy space,
That their extremest lines may scarce embrace:
Nor this alone to indulge a vain delight,
And make a pleasing prospect for the sight,
But for the ground itself; this only way
Can equal vigour to the plants convey,
Which, crowded, want the room, their branches to
    display.

  How deep they must be planted, wouldst thou know?
In shallow furrows vines securely grow.
Not so the rest of plants; for Jove's own tree,
That holds the woods in awful sovereignty,
Requires a depth of lodging in the ground,
And, next the lower skies, a bed profound:
High as his topmost boughs to heaven ascend,
So low his roots to hell's dominion tend.
Therefore, nor winds, nor winter's rage, o'erthrows
His bulky body, but unmoved he grows;
For length of ages lasts his happy reign,
And lives of mortal man contend in vain.
Full in the midst of his own strength he stands,
Stretching his brawny arms, and leafy hands:
His shade protects the plains, his head the hills
    commands.

  The hurtful hazel in thy vineyard shun;
Nor plant it to receive the setting sun;
Nor break the topmost branches from the tree;
Nor prune, with blunted knife, the progeny.
Root up wild olives from thy laboured lands;
For sparkling fire, from hinds' unwary hands,
Is often scattered o'er their unctuous rinds,
And after spread abroad by raging winds:
For first the smouldering flame the trunk receives;
Ascending thence, it crackles in the leaves;

At length victorious to the top aspires,
Involving all the wood in smoky fires;
But most, when driven by winds, the flaming storm
Of the long files destroys the beauteous form.
In ashes then the unhappy vineyard lies;
Nor will the blasted plants from ruin rise;
Nor will the withered stock be green again;
But the wild olive shoots, and shades the ungrateful
     plain.
Be not seduced with wisdom's empty shows,
To stir the peaceful ground when Boreas blows.
When winter frosts constrain the field with cold,
The fainty root can take no steady hold.
But when the golden spring reveals the year,
And the white bird returns, whom serpents fear,
That season deem the best to plant thy vines:
Next that, is when autumnal warmth declines,
Ere heat is quite decayed, or cold begun,
Or Capricorn admits the winter sun.
     The spring adorns the woods, renews the leaves;
The womb of earth the genial seed receives:
For then almighty Jove descends, and pours
Into his buxom bride his fruitful showers;
And, mixing his large limbs with hers, he feeds
Her births with kindly juice, and fosters teeming seeds.
Then joyous birds frequent the lonely grove,
And beasts, by nature stung, renew their love.
Then fields the blades of buried corn disclose;
And, while the balmy western spirit blows,
Earth to the breath her bosom dares expose.
With kindly moisture then the plants abound;
The grass securely springs above the ground;
The tender twig shoots upward to the skies,
And on the faith of the new sun relies.
The swerving vines on the tall elms prevail;
Unhurt by southern showers, or northern hail,
They spread their gems, the genial warmth to share,
And boldly trust their buds in open air.
     In this soft season (let me dare to sing),
The world was hatched by heaven's imperial king—

In prime of all the year, and holidays of spring.
Then did the new creation first appear ;
Nor other was the tenor of the year,
When laughing heaven did the great birth attend ;
And eastern winds their wintry breath suspend :
Then sheep first saw the sun in open fields ;
And savage beasts were sent to stock the wilds ;
And golden stars flew up to light the skies ;
And man's relentless race from stony quarries rise.
Nor could the tender new creation bear
The excessive heats or coldness of the year,
But, chilled by winter, or by summer fired,
The middle temper of the spring required,
When warmth and moisture did at once abound,
And heaven's indulgence brooded on the ground.
   For what remains, in depth of earth secure
Thy covered plants, and dung with hot manure ;
And shells and gravel in the ground inclose ;
For through their hollow chinks the water flows,
Which, thus imbibed, returns in misty dews,
And, steaming up, the rising plant renews.
Some husbandmen, of late, have found the way,
A hilly heap of stones above to lay,
And press the plants with shards of potters' clay.
This fence against immoderate rain they found,
Or when the dog-star cleaves the thirsty ground.
   Be mindful, when thou hast entombed the shoot ;
With store of earth around to feed the root ;
With iron teeth of rakes and prongs, to move
The crusted earth, and loosen it above.
Then exercise thy sturdy steers to plough
Betwixt thy vines, and teach the feeble row
To mount on reeds, and wands, and, upward led,
On ashen poles to raise their forky head.
On these new crutches let them learn to walk,
Till, swerving upwards with a stronger stalk,
They brave the winds, and, clinging to their guide,
On tops of elms at length triumphant ride.
But, in their tender nonage, while they spread
Their springing leaves, and lift their infant head,

And upward while they shoot in open air,
Indulge their childhood, and the nurselings spare;
Nor exercise thy rage on new-born life;
But let thy hand supply the pruning-knife,
And crop luxuriant stragglers, nor be loth
To strip the branches of their leafy growth.
But, when the rooted vines, with steady hold,
Can clasp their elms, then, husbandman, be bold
To lop the disobedient boughs, that strayed
Beyond their ranks; let crooked steel invade
The lawless troops, which discipline disclaim,
And their superfluous growth with rigour tame.
   Next, fenced with hedges and deep ditches round,
Exclude the encroaching cattle from thy ground,
While yet the tender germs but just appear,
Unable to sustain the uncertain year,
Whose leaves are not alone foul winter's prey,
But oft by summer suns are scorched away;
And, worse than both, become the unworthy browse
Of buffaloes, salt goats, and hungry cows.
For not December's frost, that burns the boughs,
Nor dog-days' parching heat, that splits the rocks,
Are half so harmful as the greedy flocks,
Their venomed bite, and scars indented on the stocks.
For this, the malefactor goat was laid
On Bacchus' altar, and his forfeit paid.
   At Athens thus old comedy began,
When round the streets the reeling actors ran,
In country villages, and crossing ways,
Contending for the prizes of their plays;
And, glad with Bacchus, on the grassy soil,
Leaped o'er the skins of goats besmeared with oil.
Thus Roman youth, derived from ruined Troy,
In rude Saturnian rhymes express their joy;
With taunts, and laughter loud, their audience please,
Deformed with vizards, cut from barks of trees:
In jolly hymns they praise the god of wine,
Whose earthen images adorn the pine,
And there are hung on high, in honour of the vine.
A madness so devout the vineyard fills;

In hollow valleys and on rising hills,
On whate'er side he turns his honest face,
And dances in the wind, those fields are in his grace.
To Bacchus therefore let us tune our lays,
And in our mother-tongue resound his praise.
Thin cakes in chargers, and a guilty goat,
Dragged by the horns, be to his altars brought ;
Whose offered entrails shall his crime reproach,
And drip their fatness from the hazel broach.

To dress thy vines, new labour is required ;
Nor must the painful husbandman be tired :
For thrice, at least, in compass of the year,
Thy vineyard must employ the sturdy steer
To turn the glebe ; besides thy daily pain
To break the clods, and make the surface plain,
To unload the branches, or the leaves to thin,
That suck the vital moisture of the vine.
Thus in a circle runs the peasant's pain,
And the year rolls within itself again.
E'en in the lowest months, when storms have shed
From vines the hairy honours of their head,
Not then the drudging hind his labour ends,
But to the coming year his care extends.
E'en then the naked vine he persecutes ;
His pruning-knife at once reforms and cuts.
Be first to dig the ground ; be first to burn
The branches lopt ; and first the props return
Into thy house, that bore the burdened vines ;
But last to reap the vintage of thy wines.

Twice in the year luxuriant leaves o'ershade
The encumbered vine ; rough brambles twice invade.
Hard labour both ! Commend the large excess
Of spacious vineyards ; cultivate the less.
Besides, in woods the shrubs of prickly thorn,
Sallows and reeds on banks of rivers born,
Remain to cut ; for vineyards, useful found
To stay thy vines, and fence thy fruitful ground.
Nor when thy tender trees at length are bound ;
When peaceful vines from pruning-hooks are free,
When husbands have surveyed the last degree,

And utmost files of plants, and ordered every tree ;
E'en when they sing at ease in full content,
Insulting o'er the toils they underwent ;
Yet still they find a future task remain,
To turn the soil, and break the clods again ;
And, after all, their joys are insincere,
While falling rains on ripening grapes they fear.
Quite opposite to these are olives found :
No dressing they require, and dread no wound,
Nor rakes nor harrows need ; but, fixed below,
Rejoice in open air, and unconcern'dly grow.
The soil itself due nourishment supplies :
Plough but the furrows, and the fruits arise,
Content with small endeavours, till they spring.
Soft peace they figure, and sweet plenty bring :
Then olives plant, and hymns to Pallas sing.

   Thus apple-trees, whose trunks are strong to bear
Their spreading boughs, exert themselves in air,
Want no supply, but stand secure alone,
Not trusting foreign forces, but their own,
Till with the ruddy freight the bending branches groan.

   Thus trees of nature, and each common bush,
Uncultivated thrive, and with red berries blush.
Vile shrubs are shorn for browse ; the towering height
Of unctuous trees are torches for the night.
And shall we doubt (indulging easy sloth),
To sow, to set, and to reform their growth ?
To leave the lofty plants—the lowly kind
Are for the shepherd or the sheep designed.
E'en humble broom and osiers have their use,
And shade for sheep, and food for flocks, produce ;
Hedges for corn, and honey for the bees,
Besides the pleasing prospect of the trees.
How goodly looks Cytorus, ever green
With boxen groves ! with what delight are seen
Narycian woods of pitch, whose gloomy shade
Seems for retreat of heavenly muses made ;
But much more pleasing are those fields to see,
That need not ploughs, nor human industry.
E'en cold Caucasean rocks with trees are spread,

And wear green forests on their hilly head.
Though bending from the blast of eastern storms,
Though shent their leaves, and shattered are their arms,
Yet heaven their various plants for use designs—
For houses, cedars—and, for shipping, pines—
Cypress provides for spokes and wheels of wains,
And all for keels of ships, that scour the watery
       plains.
Willows in twigs are fruitful, elms in leaves;
The war, from stubborn myrtle, shafts receives—
From cornels, javelins; and the tougher yew
Receives the bending figure of a bow.
Nor box, nor limes, without their use are made,
Smooth-grained, and proper for the turner's trade
Which curious hands may carve, and steel with ease
       invade.
Light alder stems the Po's impetuous tide,
And bees in hollow oaks their honey hide.
Now balance, with these gifts, the fumy joys
Of wine, attended with eternal noise,
Wine urged to lawless lust the Centaurs' train;
Through wine they quarrelled, and through wine were
       slain.
  O happy, if he knew his happy state,
The swain, who, free from business and debate,
Receives his easy food from nature's hand,
And just returns of cultivated land!
No palace, with a lofty gate, he wants,
To admit the tides of early visitants,
With eager eyes devouring, as they pass,
The breathing figures of Corinthian brass.
No statues threaten, from high pedestals;
No Persian arras hides his homely walls,
With antic vests, which, through their shady fold,
Betray the streaks of ill-dissembled gold:
He boasts no wool, whose native white is dyed
With purple poison of Assyrian pride;
No costly drugs of Araby defile,
With foreign scents, the sweetness of his oil:
But easy quiet, a secure retreat,

A harmless life that knows not how to cheat,
With home-bred plenty, the rich owner bless,
And rural pleasures crown his happiness.
Unvexed with quarrels, undisturbed with noise,
The country king his peaceful realm enjoys—
Cool grots, and living lakes, the flowery pride
Of meads, and streams that through the valley glide,
And shady groves that easy sleep invite,
And after toilsome days, a soft repose at night.
Wild beasts of nature in his woods abound ;
And youth, of labour patient, plough the ground,
Inured to hardship, and to homely fare.
Nor venerable age is wanting there,
In great examples to the youthful train ;
Nor are the gods adored with rites profane.
From hence Astræa took her flight ; and here
The prints of her departing steps appear.

Ye sacred muses ! with whose beauty fired,
My soul is ravished, and my brain inspired—
Whose priest I am, whose holy fillets wear—
Would you your poet's first petition hear ;
Give me the ways of wandering stars to know,
The depths of heaven above, and earth below :
Teach me the various labours of the moon,
And whence proceed the eclipses of the sun ;
Why flowing tides prevail upon the main,
And in what dark recess they shrink again ;
What shakes the solid earth ; what cause delays
The summer nights, and shortens winter days.
But, if my heavy blood restrain the flight
Of my free soul, aspiring to the height
Of nature, and unclouded fields of light—
My next desire is, void of care and strife,
To lead a soft, secure, inglorious life—
A country cottage near a crystal flood,
A winding valley, and a lofty wood.
Some god conduct me to the sacred shades,
Where Bacchanals are sung by Spartan maids,
Or lift me high to Hæmus' hilly crown,
Or in the plains of Tempè lay me down,

Or lead me to some solitary place,
And cover my retreat from human race.
  Happy the man, who, studying nature's laws,
Through known effects can trace the secret cause—
His mind possessing in a quiet state,
Fearless of Fortune, and resigned to Fate !
And happy too is he, who decks the bowers
Of sylvans, and adores the rural powers—
Whose mind, unmoved, the bribes of courts can see,
Their glittering baits, and purple slavery—
Nor hopes the people's praise, nor fears their frown,
Nor, when contending kindred tear the crown,
Will set up one, or pull another down.
  Without concern he hears, but hears from far,
Of tumults, and descents, and distant war ;
Nor with a superstitious fear is awed,
For what befalls at home, or what abroad.
Nor his own peace disturbs with pity for the poor.
Nor envies he the rich their happy store,
He feeds on fruits, which, of their own accord,
The willing ground and laden trees afford.
From his loved home no lucre him can draw ;
The senate's mad decrees he never saw ;
Nor heard, at bawling bars, corrupted law.
Some to the seas, and some to camps, resort,
And some with impudence invade the court :
In foreign countries, others seek renown ;
With wars and taxes, others waste their own,
And houses burn, and household gods deface,
To drink in bowls which glittering gems enchase,
To loll on couches, rich with citron steds,
And lay their guilty limbs in Tyrian beds.
This wretch in earth entombs his golden ore,
Hovering and brooding on his buried store.
Some patriot fools to popular praise aspire
Of public speeches, which worse fools admire,
While, from both benches, with redoubled sounds,
The applause of lords and commoners abounds.
Some, through ambition, or through thirst of gold,
Have slain their brothers, or their country sold,

And, leaving their sweet homes, in exile run
To lands that lie beneath another sun.
   The peasant, innocent of all these ills,
With crooked ploughs the fertile fallows tills,
And the round year with daily labour fills.
And hence the country markets are supplied :
Enough remains for household charge beside,
His wife and tender children to sustain,
And gratefully to feed his dumb deserving train.
Nor cease his labours till the yellow field
A full return of bearded harvest yield—
A crop so plenteous, as the land to load,
O'ercome the crowded barns, and lodge on ricks abroad.
   Thus every several season is employed,
Some spent in toil, and some in ease enjoyed.
The yeaning ewes prevent the springing year ;
The laden boughs their fruits in autumn bear :
'Tis then the vine her liquid harvest yields,
Baked in the sunshine of ascending fields.
The winter comes ; and then the falling mast
For greedy swine provides a full repast :
Then olives, ground in mills, their fatness boast,
And winter fruits are mellowed by the frost.
His cares are eased with intervals of bliss ;
His little children, climbing for a kiss,
Welcome their father's late return at night ;
His faithful bed is crowned with chaste delight.
His kine with swelling udders ready stand,
And, lowing for the pail, invite the milker's hand.
His wanton kids, with budding horns prepared,
Fight harmless battles in his homely yard :
Himself, in rustic pomp, on holidays,
To rural powers a just oblation pays,
And on the green his careless limbs displays.
The hearth is in the midst ; the herdsmen, round
The cheerful fire, provoke his health in goblets
    crowned.
He calls on Bacchus, and propounds the prize ;
The groom his fellow-groom at butts defies,
And bends his bow, and levels with his eyes ;

Or, stript for wrestling, smears his limbs with oil,
And watches, with a trip his foe to foil.
 Such was the life the frugal Sabines led ;
So Remus and his brother-god were bred,
From whom the austere Etrurian virtue rose ;
And this rude life our homely fathers chose.
Old Rome from such a race derived her birth,
(The seat of empire and the conquered earth),
Which now on seven high hills triumphant reigns,
And in that compass all the world contains.
Ere Saturn's rebel son usurped the skies,
When beasts were only slain for sacrifice,
While peaceful Crete enjoyed her ancient lord,
Ere sounding hammers forged the inhuman sword,
Ere hollow drums were beat, before the breath
Of brazen trumpets rung the peals of death,
The good old god his hunger did assuage
With roots and herbs, and gave the golden age.
 But, over-laboured with so long a course,
Tis time to set at ease the smoking horse.

BOOK III

THE ARGUMENT

This book begins with the invocation of some rural deities, and a compliment to Augustus; after which Virgil directs himself to Mæcenas, and enters on his subject. He lays down rules for the breeding and management of horses, oxen, sheep, goats, and dogs; and interweaves several pleasant descriptions of a chariot-race, of the battle of the bulls, of the force of love, and of the Scythian winter. In the latter part of the book, he relates the diseases incident to cattle; and ends with the description of a fatal murrain that formerly raged among the Alps.

THY fields, propitious Pales, I rehearse;
And sing thy pastures in no vulgar verse,
Amphrysian shepherd! the Lycæan woods,
Arcadia's flowery plains, and pleasing floods.
  All other themes, that careless minds invite,
Are worn with use, unworthy me to write.
Busiris' altars, and the dire decrees
Of hard Eurystheus, every reader sees:
Hylas the boy, Latona's erring isle,
And Pelops' ivory shoulder, and his toil
For fair Hippodamè, with all the rest
Of Grecian tales, by poets are expressed.
New ways I must attempt, my grovelling name
To raise aloft, and wing my flight to fame.
  I, first of Romans, shall in triumph come
From conquered Greece, and bring her trophies home,
With foreign spoils adorn my native place,
And with Idume's palms my Mantua grace.
Of Parian stone a temple will I raise,
Where the slow Mincius through the valley strays,
Where cooling streams invite the flocks to drink,

And reeds defend the winding water's brink.
Full in the midst shall mighty Cæsar stand,
Hold the chief honours, and the dome command.
Then I, conspicuous in my Tyrian gown
(Submitting to his godhead my renown),
A hundred coursers from the goal will drive:
The rival chariots in the race shall strive.
All Greece shall flock from far, my games to see;
The whorlbat, and the rapid race, shall be
Reserved for Cæsar, and ordained by me.
Myself, with olive crowned, the gifts will bear.
E'en now methinks the public shouts I hear;
The passing pageants, and the pomps appear.
I to the temple will conduct the crew,
The sacrifice and sacrificers view,
From thence return, attended with my train,
Where the proud theatres disclose the scene,
Which interwoven Britons seem to raise,
And show the triumph which their shame displays.
High o'er the gate, in elephant and gold,
The crowd shall Cæsar's Indian war behold:
The Nile shall flow beneath; and on the side
His shattered ships on brazen pillars ride.
Next him Niphates, with inverted urn,
And drooping sedge, shall his Armenian mourn;
And Asian cities in our triumph borne.
With backward bows the Parthians shall be there,
And, spurring from the fight, confess their fear.
A double wreath shall crown our Cæsar's brows—
Two differing trophies, from two different foes.
Europe with Afric in his fame shall join;
But neither shore his conquest shall confine.
The Parian marble there shall seem to move
In breathing statues, not unworthy Jove,
Resembling heroes, whose ethereal root
Is Jove himself, and Cæsar is the fruit.
Tros and his race the sculptor shall employ;
And he—the god who built the walls of Troy.
Envy herself at last, grown pale and dumb
(By Cæsar combated and overcome),

Shall give her hands, and fear the curling snakes
Of lashing Furies, and the burning lakes ;
The pains of famished Tantalus shall feel,
And Sisyphus, that labours up the hill
The rolling rock in vain ; and curst Ixion's wheel.

    Meantime we must pursue the sylvan lands
(The abode of nymphs), untouched by former hands :
For such, Mæcenas, are thy hard commands.
Without thee, nothing lofty can I sing :
Come then, and, with thyself, thy genius bring,
With which inspired, I brook no dull delay :
Cithæron loudly calls me to my way ;
Thy hounds, Taygetus, open, and pursue their prey.
High Epidaurus urges on my speed,
Famed for his hills, and for his horses' breed :
From hills and dales the cheerful cries rebound ;
For Echo hunts along, and propagates the sound.

    A time will come, when my maturer muse,
In Cæsar's wars, a nobler theme shall choose,
And through more ages bear my sovereign's praise,
Than have from Tithon past to Cæsar's days.

    The generous youth, who, studious of the prize,
The race of running coursers multiplies,
Or to the plough the sturdy bullock breeds,
May know, that from the dam the worth of each
      proceeds.
The mother-cow must wear a lowering look,
Sour-headed, strongly necked, to bear the yoke.
Her double dewlap from her chin descends,
And at her thighs the ponderous burden ends.
Long are her sides and large ; her limbs are great ;
Rough are her ears, and broad her horny feet.
Her colour shining black, but flecked with white ;
She tosses from the yoke ; provokes the fight :
She rises in her gait, is free from fears,
And in her face a bull's resemblance bears :
Her ample forehead with a star is crowned,
And with her length of tail she sweeps the ground.
The bull's insult at four she may sustain ;
But, after ten, from nuptial rites refrain.

Six seasons use; but then release the cow,
Unfit for love, and for the labouring plough.
  Now, while their youth is filled with kindly fire,
Submit thy females to the lusty sire:
Watch the quick motions of the frisking tail;
Then serve their fury with the rushing male,
Indulging pleasure, lest the breed should fail.
  In youth alone unhappy mortals live;
But ah! the mighty bliss is fugitive:
Discoloured sickness, anxious labours, come,
And age, and death's inexorable doom.
  Yearly thy herds in vigour will impair.
Recruit and mend them with thy yearly care:
Still propagate; for still they fall away:
'Tis prudence to prevent the entire decay.
  Like diligence requires the courser's race,
In early choice, and for a longer space,
The colt, that for a stallion is designed,
By sure presages shows his generous kind:
Of able body, sound of limb and wind,
Upright he walks, on pasterns firm and straight;
His motions easy; prancing in his gait;
The first to lead the way, to tempt the flood,
To pass the bridge unknown, nor fear the trembling
    wood;
Dauntless at empty noises; lofty necked;
Sharp-headed, barrel-bellied, broadly backed:
Brawny his chest, and deep; his colour gray;
For beauty, dappled, or the brightest bay:
Faint white and dun will scarce the rearing pay.
  The fiery courser, when he hears from far
The sprightly trumpets, and the shouts of war,
Pricks up his ears; and, trembling with delight,
Shifts place, and paws, and hopes the promised
    fight.
On his right shoulder his thick mane reclined,
Ruffles at speed, and dances in the wind.
His horny hoofs are jetted black and round;
His chine is double; starting with a bound
He turns the turf, and shakes the solid ground.

Fire from his eyes, clouds from his nostrils, flow:
He bears his rider headlong on the foe.

Such was the steed in Grecian poets famed,
Proud Cyllarus, by Spartan Pollux tamed:
Such coursers bore to fight the god of Thrace;
And such, Achilles, was thy warlike race.
In such a shape, grim Saturn did restrain
His heavenly limbs, and flowed with such a mane,
When, half-surprised, and fearing to be seen,
The lecher galloped from his jealous queen;
Ran up the ridges of the rocks amain,
And with shrill neighings filled the neighbouring plain.

But, worn with years, when dire diseases come,
Then hide his not ignoble age at home,
In peace to enjoy his former palms and pains;
And gratefully be kind to his remains.
For, when his blood no youthful spirits move,
He languishes and labours in his love;
And, when the sprightly seed should swiftly come,
Dribbling he drudges, and defrauds the womb.
In vain he burns, like hasty stubble fires,
And in himself his former self requires.

His age and courage weigh; nor those alone,
But note his father's virtues and his own:
Observe if he disdains to yield the prize,
Of loss impatient, proud of victories.
Hast thou beheld, when from the goal they start,
The youthful charioteers with heaving heart
Rush to the race; and, panting, scarcely bear
The extremes of feverish hope and chilling fear;
Stoop to the reins, and lash with all their force?
The flying chariot kindles in the course:
And now alow, and now aloft, they fly,
As borne through air, and seem to touch the sky.
No stop, no stay: but clouds of sand arise,
Spurned and cast backward on the followers' eyes.
The hindmost blows the foam upon the firs:
Such is the love of praise, an honourable thirst.

Bold Erichthonius was the first who joined
Four horses for the rapid race designed,

And o'er the dusty wheels presiding sat :
The Lapithæ, to chariots, add the state
Of bits and bridles ; taught the steed to bound,
To run the ring, and trace the mazy round ;
To stop, to fly, the rules of war to know ;
To obey the rider, and to dare the foe.
  To choose a youthful steed with courage fired,
To breed him, break him, back him, are required
Experienced masters ; and, in sundry ways,
Their labours equal, and alike their praise.
But, once again, the battered horse beware :
The weak old stallion will deceive thy care,
Though famous in his youth for force and speed,
Or was of Argos or Epirian breed,
Or did from Neptune's race, or from himself, proceed.
  These things premised, when now the nuptial time
Approaches for the stately steed to climb,
With food enable him to make his court ;
Distend his chine, and pamper him for sport :
Feed him with herbs, whatever thou canst find,
Of generous warmth, and of salacious kind :
Then water him, and (drinking what he can)
Encourage him to thirst again, with bran.
Instructed thus, produce him to the fair,
And join in wedlock to the longing mare.
For, if the sire be faint, or out of case,
He will be copied in his famished race,
And sink beneath the pleasing task assigned :
(For all's too little for the craving kind.)
  As for the females, with industrious care
Take down their mettle ; keep them lean and bare :
When conscious of their past delight, and keen
To take the leap, and prove the sport again,
With scanty measure then supply their food ;
And, when athirst, restrain them from the flood ;
Their bodies harass ; sink them when they run ;
And fry their melting marrow in the sun.
Starve them, when barns beneath their burden groan,
And winnowed chaff by western winds is blown ;
For fear the rankness of the swelling womb

Should scant the passage, and confine the room ;
Lest the fat furrows should the sense destroy
Of genial lust, and dull the seat of joy.
But let them suck the seed with greedy force,
And close involve the vigour of the horse.

    The male has done : thy care must now proceed
To teeming females, and the promised breed.
First let them run at large, and never know
The taming yoke, or draw the crooked plough.
Let them not leap the ditch, or swim the flood,
Or lumber o'er the meads, or cross the wood ;
But range the forest, by the silver side
Of some cool stream, where nature shall provide
Green grass and fattening clover for their fare,
And mossy caverns for their noontide lair,
With rocks above, to shield the sharp nocturnal air.

    About the Alburnian groves, with holly green,
Of wingèd insects mighty swarms are seen :
This flying plague (to mark its quality)
Œstros the Grecians call—Asylus, we—
A fierce loud-buzzing breeze—their stings draw blood,
And drive the cattle gadding through the wood.
Seized with unusual pains, they loudly cry :
Tanagrus hastens thence, and leaves his channel dry.
This curse the jealous Juno did invent,
And first employed for Iö's punishment.
To shun this ill, the cunning leech ordains,
In summer's sultry heats (for then it reigns)
To feed the females ere the sun arise,
Or late at night, when stars adorn the skies.
When she has calved, then set the dam aside,
And for the tender progeny provide.
Distinguish all betimes with branding fire,
To note the tribe, the lineage and the sire ;
Whom to reserve for husband of the herd ;
Or who shall be to sacrifice preferred ;
Or whom thou shalt to turn thy glebe allow,
To smooth the furrows, and sustain the plough :
The rest, for whom no lot is yet decreed,
May run in pastures, and at pleasure feed.

The calf, by nature and by genius made
To turn the glebe, breed to the rural trade.
Set him betimes to school ; and let him be
Instructed there in rules of husbandry.
While yet his youth is flexible and green,
Nor bad examples of the world has seen.
Early begin the stubborn child to break ;
For his soft neck, a supple collar make
Of bending osiers ; and (with time and care
Inured that easy servitude to bear)
Thy flattering method on the youth pursue :
Joined with his schoolfellows by two and two,
Persuade them first to lead an empty wheel,
That scarce the dust can raise, or they can feel :
In length of time produce the labouring yoke,
And shining shares, that make the furrow smoke.
Ere the licentious youth be thus restrained,
Or moral precepts on their minds have gained,
Their wanton appetites not only feed
With delicates of leaves, and marshy weed,
But with thy sickle reap the rankest land,
And minister the blade with bounteous hand :
Nor be with harmful parsimony won
To follow what our homely sires have done,
Who filled the pail with beestings of the cow,
But all her udder to the calf allow.
    If to the warlike steed thy studies bend,
Or for the prize in chariots to contend,
Near Pisa's flood the rapid wheels to guide,
Or in Olympian groves aloft to ride,
The generous labours of the courser, first,
Must be with sight of arms and sounds of trumpets
        nursed ;
Inured tne groaning axle-tree to bear,
And let him clashing whips in stables hear.
Soothe him with praise, and make him understand
The loud applauses of his master's hand :
This, from his weaning, let him well be taught ;
And then betimes in a soft snaffle wrought,
Before his tender joints with nerves are knit,

Untried in arms, and trembling at the bit.
But, when to four full springs his years advance,
Teach him to run the ground, with pride to prance,
And (rightly managed) equal time to beat,
To turn, to bound in measure, and curvet.
Let him to this, with easy pains, be brought,
And seem to labour, when he labours not.
Thus formed for speed, he challenges the wind,
And leaves the Scythian arrow far behind:
He scours along the field, with loosened reins,
And treads so light, he scarcely prints the plains;
Like Boreas in his race, when, rushing forth,
He sweeps the skies, and clears the cloudy north:
The waving harvest bends beneath his blast,
The forest shakes, the groves their honours cast;
He flies aloft, and with impetuous roar
Pursues the foaming surges to the shore.
Thus, o'er the Elean plains, thy well-breathed horse
Impels the flying car, and wins the course,
Or, bred to Belgian waggons, leads the way,
Untired at night, and cheerful all the day,
　When once he's broken, feed him full and high;
Indulge his growth, and his gaunt sides supply.
Before his training, keep him poor and low;
For his stout stomach with his food will grow:
The pampered colt will discipline disdain,
Impatient of the lash, and restive to the rein.
　Wouldst thou their courage and their strength improve?
Too soon they must not feel the stings of love.
Whether the bull or courser be thy care,
Let him not leap the cow, or mount the mare.
The youthful bull must wander in the wood,
Behind the mountain, or beyond the flood,
Or in the stall at home his fodder find,
Far from the charms of that alluring kind.
With two fair eyes his mistress burns his breast:
He looks, and languishes, and leaves his rest,
Forsakes his food, and, pining for the lass,
Is joyless of the grove, and spurns the growing grass.

The soft seducer, with enticing looks,
The bellowing rivals to the fight provokes.
   A beauteous heifer in the wood is bred :
The stooping warriors, aiming head to head,
Engage their clashing horns : with dreadful sound
The forest rattles, and the rocks rebound.
They fence, they push, and, pushing, loudly roar :
Their dewlaps and their sides are bathed in gore.
Nor, when the war is over, is it peace ;
Nor will the vanquished bull his claim release ;
But, feeding in his breast his ancient fires,
And cursing fate, from his proud foe retires.
Driven from his native land to foreign grounds,
He with a generous rage resents his wounds,
His ignominious flight, the victor's boast,
And, more than both, the loves which unrevenged he
    lost.
Often he turns his eyes, and, with a groan,
Surveys the pleasing kingdoms, once his own :
And therefore to repair his strength he tries,
Hardening his limbs with painful exercise,
And rough upon the flinty rock he lies.
On prickly leaves and on sharp herbs he feeds,
Then to the prelude of a war proceeds.
His horns, yet sore, he tries against a tree,
And meditates his absent enemy.
He snuffs the wind ; his heels the sand excite ;
But, when he stands collected in his might,
He roars, and promises a more successful fight.
Then, to redeem his honour at a blow,
He moves his camp, to meet his careless foe.
Not with more madness, rolling from afar,
The spumy waves proclaim the watery war,
And mounting upwards, with a mighty roar,
March onwards, and insult the rocky shore.
They mate the middle region with their height,
And fall no less than with a mountain's weight ;
The waters boil, and, belching, from below
Black sands, as from a forceful engine, throw.
   Thus every creature, and of every kind,

The secret joys of sweet coition find.
Not only man's imperial race, but they
That wing the liquid air, or swim the sea,
Or haunt the desert, rush into the flame :
For Love is lord of all, and is in all the same.
    'Tis with this rage, the mother-lion stung,
Scours o'er the plain, regardless of her young :
Demanding rites of love, she sternly stalks,
And hunts her lover in his lonely walks.
'Tis then the shapeless bear his den forsakes ;
In woods and fields, a wild destruction makes :
Boars with their tusks ; to battle tigers move,
Enraged with hunger, more enraged with love.
Then woe to him, that, in the desert land
Of Libya, travels o'er the burning sand !
The stallion snuffs the well-known scent afar,
And snorts and trembles for the distant mare ;
Nor bits nor bridles can his rage restrain,
And rugged rocks are interposed in vain :
He makes his way o'er mountains, and contemns
Unruly torrents, and unforded streams.
The bristled boar, who feels the pleasing wound,
New grinds his arming tusks, and digs the ground.
The sleepy lecher shuts his little eyes ;
About his churning chaps the frothy bubbles rise :
He rubs his sides against a tree ; prepares
And hardens both his shoulders for the wars.
    What did the youth, when Love's unerring dart
Transfixed his liver, and inflamed his heart ?
Alone, by night, his watery way he took ;
About him, and above, the billows broke ;
The sluices of the sky were open spread,
And rolling thunder rattled o'er his head ;
The raging tempests called him back in vain,
And every boding omen of the main :
Nor could his kindred, nor the kindly force
Of weeping parents, change his fatal course ;
No, not the dying maid, who must deplore
His floating carcase on the Sestian shore.
    I pass the wars that spotted lynxes make

With their fierce rivals for the female's sake,
The howling wolves', the mastiffs' amorous rage ;
When e'en the fearful stag dares for his hind engage.
But, far above the rest, the furious mare,
Barred from the male, is frantic with despair :
For, when her pouting vent declares her pain,
She tears the harness, and she rends the rein.
For this (when Venus gave them rage and power)
Their master's mangled members they devour,
Of love defrauded in their longing hour.
For love, they force through thickets of the wood,
They climb the steepy hills, and stem the flood.

  When, at the spring's approach, their marrow burns,
(For with the spring their genial warmth returns),
The mares to cliffs of rugged rocks repair,
And with wide nostrils snuff the western air :
When (wondrous to relate !) the parent wind,
Without the stallion, propagates the kind,
Then, fired with amorous rage, they take their flight
Through plains, and mount the hills' unequal height ;
Nor to the north, nor to the rising sun,
Nor southward to the rainy regions, run,
But boring to the west, and hovering there,
With gaping mouths, they draw prolific air ;
With which impregnate, from their groins they shed,
A slimy juice, by false conception bred.
The shepherd knows it well, and calls by name
Hippomanes, to note the mother's flame.
This, gathered in the planetary hour,
With noxious weeds, and spelled with words of power,
Dire stepdames in the magic bowl infuse,
And mix, for deadly draughts, the poisonous juice.

  But time is lost, which never will renew,
While we too far the pleasing path pursue,
Surveying nature with too nice a view.
Let this suffice for herds ; our following care
Shall woolly flocks and shaggy goats declare.
Nor can I doubt what toil I must bestow,
To raise my subject from a ground so low ;
And the mean matter, which my theme affords,

To embellish with magnificence of words.
But the commanding muse my chariot guides,
Which o'er the dubious cliff securely rides ;
And pleased I am, no beaten road to take,
But first the way to new discoveries make.
    Now, sacred Pales ! in a lofty strain
I sing the rural honours of thy reign.
First, with assiduous care from winter keep,
Well foddered in the stalls, thy tender sheep :
Then spread with straw the bedding of thy fold,
With fern beneath, to 'fend the bitter cold ;
That free from gouts thou mayest preserve thy care,
And clear from scabs, produced by freezing air.
Next let thy goats officiously be nursed,
And led to living streams, to quench their thirst.
Feed them with winter-browse ; and, for their lair,
A cote, that opens to the south, prepare ;
Where basking in the sunshine they may lie,
And the short remnants of his heat enjoy.
This during winter's drizzly reign be done,
Till the new Ram receives the exalted sun.
For hairy goats of equal profit are
With woolly sheep, and ask an equal care.
'Tis true, the fleece, when drunk with Tyrian juice,
Is dearly sold ; but not for needful use :
For the salacious goat increases more,
And twice as largely yields her milky store.
The still-distended udders never fail,
But, when they seem exhausted, swell the pail.
Meantime the pastor shears their hoary beards,
And eases of their hair the laden herds.
Their camelots, warm in tents, the soldier hold,
And shield the shivering mariner from cold.
    On shrubs they browse, and, on the bleaky top
Of rugged hills, the thorny bramble crop.
Attended with their bleating kids, they come
At night, unasked, and mindful of their home ;
And scarce their swelling bags the threshold overcome.
So much the more thy diligence bestow
In depth of winter, to defend the snow,

By how much less the tender helpless kind,
For their own ills, can fit provision find.
Then minister the browse with bounteous hand,
And open let thy sacks all winter stand.
But, when the western winds with vital power
Call forth the tender grass and budding flower,
Then, at the last, produce in open air
Both flocks, and send them to their summer fare.
Before the sun while Hesperus appears,
First let them sip from herbs the pearly tears
Of morning dews, and after break their fast
On greensward ground—a cool and grateful taste.
But, when the day's fourth hour has drawn the dews,
And the sun's sultry heat their thirst renews;
When creaking grasshoppers on shrubs complain,
Then lead them to their watering-troughs again.
In summer's heat, some bending valley find,
Closed from the sun, but open to the wind;
Or seek some ancient oak, whose arms extend
In ample breadth, thy cattle to defend,
Or solitary grove, or gloomy glade,
To shield them with its venerable shade.
Once more to watering lead; and feed again
When the low sun is sinking to the main,
When rising Cynthia sheds her silver dews,
And the cool evening-breeze the meads renews,
When linnets fill the woods with tuneful sound,
And hollow shores the halcyon's voice rebound.
  Why should my muse enlarge on Libyan swains,
Their scattered cottages, and ample plains,
Where oft the flocks without a leader stray,
Or through continued deserts take their way,
And, feeding, add the length of night to day?
Whole months they wander, grazing as they go;
Nor folds nor hospitable harbour know:
Such an extent of plains, so vast a space
Of wilds unknown, and of untasted grass,
Allures their eyes: the shepherd last appears,
And with him all his patrimony bears,
His house, and household gods, his trade of war,

E

His bow and quiver, and his trusty cur.
Thus, under heavy arms, the youth of Rome
Their long laborious marches overcome,
Cheerly their tedious travels undergo,
And pitch their sudden camp before the foe.

Not so the Scythian shepherd tends his fold,
Nor he who bears in Thrace the bitter cold,
Nor he who treads the bleak Mæotian strand,
Or where proud Ister rolls his yellow sand.
Early they stall their flocks and herds ; for there
No grass the fields, no leaves the forests, wear :
The frozen earth lies buried there, below
A hilly heap, seven cubits deep in snow ;
And all the west allies of stormy Boreas blow.

The sun from far peeps with a sickly face,
Too weak, the clouds and mighty fogs to chase,
When up the skies he shoots his rosy head,
Or in the ruddy ocean seeks his bed.
Swift rivers are with sudden ice constrained :
And studded wheels are on its back sustained ;
A hostry now for waggons, which before
Tall ships of burden on its bosom bore.
The brazen cauldrons with the frost are flawed ;
The garment, stiff with ice, at hearths is thawed ;
With axes first they cleave the wine ; and thence,
By weight, the solid portions they dispense.
From locks uncombed, and from the frozen beard,
Long icicles depend, and crackling sounds are heard.
Meantime perpetual sleet, and driving snow,
Obscure the skies, and hang on herds below.
The starving cattle perish in their stalls ;
Huge oxen stand inclosed in wintry walls
Of snow congealed ; whole herds are buried there
Of mighty stags, and scarce their horns appear.
The dexterous huntsman wounds not these afar
With shafts or darts, or makes a distant war
With dogs, or pitches toils to stop their flight,
But close engages in unequal fight ;
And, while they strive in vain to make their way
Through hills of snow, and pitifully bray,

Assaults with dint of sword, or pointed spears,
And homeward, on his back, the joyful burden bears.
The men to subterranean caves retire,
Secure from cold, and crowd the cheerful fire ;
With trunks of elms and oaks the hearth they load,
Nor tempt the inclemency of heaven abroad.
Their jovial nights in frolics and in play
They pass, to drive the tedious hours away,
And their cold stomachs with crowned goblets cheer
Of windy cider, and of barmy beer.
Such are the cold Rhipæan race, and such
The savage Scythian, and unwarlike Dutch,
Where skins of beasts the rude barbarians wear,
The spoils of foxes, and the furry bear.

   Is wool thy care ? let not thy cattle go
Where bushes are, where burs and thistles grow ;
Nor in too rank a pasture let them feed ;
Then of the purest white select thy breed.
E'en though a snowy ram thou shalt behold,
Prefer him not in haste for husband to thy fold :
But search his mouth ; and if a swarthy tongue
Is underneath his humid palate hung,
Reject him, lest he darken all the flock,
And substitute another from thy stock.
'Twas thus, with fleeces milky-white (if we
May trust report), Pan, god of Arcady,
Did bribe thee, Cynthia ; nor didst thou disdain,
When called in woody shades, to cure a lover's pain.

   If milk be thy design, with plenteous hand
Bring clover-grass ; and from the marshy land
Salt herbage for the foddering rack provide,
To fill their bags, and swell the milky tide.
These raise their thirst, and to the taste restore
The savour of the salt, on which they fed before.

   Some, when the kids their dams too deeply drain,
With gags and muzzles their soft mouths restrain.
Their morning milk the peasants press at night ;
Their evening meal, before the rising light,
To market bear ; or sparingly they steep
With seasoning salt, and stored for winter keep.

Nor, last, forget thy faithful dogs ; but feed
With fattening whey the mastiff's generous breed,
And Spartan race, who, for the fold's relief,
Will persecute with cries the nightly thief,
Repulse the prowling wolf, and hold at bay
The mountain robbers rushing to the prey.
With cries of hounds, thou mayst pursue the fear
Of flying hares, and chase the fallow deer,
Rouse from their desert dens the bristled rage
Of boars, and beamy stags in toils engage.
With smoke of burning cedar scent thy walls,
And fume with stinking galbanum thy stalls,
With that rank odour, from thy dwelling-place
To drive the viper's brood, and all the venomed race :
For often, under stalls unmoved, they lie,
Obscure in shades, and shunning heaven's broad eye :
And snakes, familiar, to the hearth succeed,
Disclose their eggs, and near the chimney breed—
Whether to roofy houses they repair,
Or sun themselves abroad in open air,
In all abodes, of pestilential kind
To sheep and oxen, and the painful hind.
Take, shepherd, take a plant of stubborn oak,
And labour him with many a sturdy stroke,
Or with hard stones demolish from afar
His haughty crest, the seat of all the war ;
Invade his hissing throat, and winding spires ;
Till, stretched in length, the unfolded foe retires.
He drags his tail, and for his head provides,
And in some secret cranny slowly glides ;
But leaves exposed to blows his back and battered sides.
In fair Calabria's woods a snake is bred,
With curling crest, and with advancing head :
Waving he rolls, and makes a winding track ;
His belly spotted, burnished is his back.
While springs are broken, while the southern air
And dropping heavens the moistened earth repair,
He lives on standing lakes and trembling bogs,
And fills his maw with fish, or with loquacious frogs :
But when, in muddy pools, the water sinks,

And the chapped earth is furrowed o'er with chinks,
He leaves the fens, and leaps upon the ground,
And, hissing, rolls his glaring eyes around.
With thirst inflamed, impatient of the heats,
He rages in the fields, and wide destruction threats.
O ! let not sleep my closing eyes invade
In open plains, or in the secret shade,
When he, renewed in all the speckled pride
Of pompous youth, has cast his slough aside,
And in his summer livery rolls along,
Erect, and brandishing his forky tongue,
Leaving his nest, and his imperfect young,
And, thoughtless of his eggs, forgets to rear
The hopes of poison for the following year.
  The causes and the signs shall next be told,
Of every sickness that infects the fold.
A scabby tetter on their pelts will stick,
When the raw rain has pierced them to the quick,
Or searching frosts have eaten through the skin,
Or burning icicles are lodged within ;
Or, when the fleece is shorn, if sweat remains
Unwashed, and soaks into their empty veins ;
When their defenceless limbs the brambles tear,
Short of their wool, and naked from the shear.
  Good shepherds, after shearing, drench their sheep :
And their flock's father (forced from high to leap)
Swims down the stream, and plunges in the deep.
They oint their naked limbs with mothered oil ;
Or, from the founts where living sulphurs boil,
They mix a med'cine to foment their limbs,
With scum that on the molten silver swims ;
Fat pitch, and black bitumen, add to these,
Besides the waxen labour of the bees,
And hellebore, and squills deep-rooted in the seas.
Receipts abound ; but, searching all thy store,
The best is still at hand, to lance the sore,
And cut the head ; for, till the core be found,
The secret vice is fed, and gathers ground,
While, making fruitless moan, the shepherd stands,
And, when the lancing-knife requires his hands,

Vain help, with idle prayers, from heaven demands.
Deep in their bones when fevers fix their seat,
And rack their limbs, and lick the vital heat,
The ready cure to cool the raging pain
Is underneath the foot to breathe a vein.
This remedy the Scythian shepherds found :
The inhabitants of Thracia's hilly ground,
And Gelons, use it, when for drink and food
They mix their curdled milk with horses' blood.

  But, where thou seest a single sheep remain
In shades aloof, or couched upon the plain,
Or listlessly to crop the tender grass,
Or late to lag behind with truant pace ;
Revenge the crime, and take the traitor's head,
Ere in the faultless flock the dire contagion spread.

  On winter seas we fewer storms behold,
Than foul diseases that infect the fold.
Nor do those ills on single bodies prey,
But oftener bring the nation to decay,
And sweep the present stock and future hope away.

  A dire example of this truth appears,
When, after such a length of rolling years,
We see the naked Alps, and thin remains
Of scattered cots, and yet unpeopled plains,
Once filled with grazing flocks, the shepherds' happy
          reigns.
Here, from the vicious air, and sickly skies,
A plague did on the dumb creation rise :
During the autumnal heats the infection grew
Tame cattle and the beasts of nature slew,
Poisoning the standing lakes, and pools impure ;
Nor was the foodful grass in fields secure.
Strange death ! for, when the thirsty fire had drunk
Their vital blood, and the dry nerves were shrunk,
When the contracted limbs were cramped, e'en then
A waterish humour swelled and oozed again,
Converting into bane the kindly juice,
Ordained by nature for a better use.

  The victim ox, that was for altars prest,
Trimmed with white ribbons, and with garlands drest,

Sunk of himself, without the gods' command,
Preventing the slow sacrificer's hand.
Or, by the holy butcher if he fell,
The inspected entrails could no fates foretell;
Nor, laid on altars, did pure flames arise;
But clouds of smouldering smoke forbade the sacrifice.
Scarcely the knife was reddened with his gore,
Or the black poison stained the sandy floor.
The thriven calves in meads their food forsake,
And render their sweet souls before the plenteous rack.

The fawning dog runs mad; the wheezing swine
With coughs is choked, and labours from the chine:
The victor horse, forgetful of his food,
The palm renounces, and abhors the flood.
He paws the ground; and on his hanging ears
A doubtful sweat in clammy drops appears:
Parched is his hide, and rugged are his hairs.
Such are the symptoms of the young disease;
But, in time's process, when his pains increase,
He rolls his mournful eyes; he deeply groans
With patient sobbing, and with manly moans.
He heaves for breath; which, from his lungs supplied,
And fetched from far, distends his labouring side.
To his rough palate his dry tongue succeeds;
And ropy gore he from his nostrils bleeds.
A drench of wine has with success been used,
And through a horn the generous juice infused,
Which, timely taken, oped his closing jaws,
But, if too late, the patient's death did cause:
For the too vigorous dose too fiercely wrought,
And added fury to the strength it brought.
Recruited into rage, he grinds his teeth
In his own flesh, and feeds approaching death.
Ye gods, to better fate good men dispose,
And turn that impious error on our foes!

The steer, who to the yoke was bred to bow
(Studious of tillage, and the crooked plough),
Falls down and dies; and, dying, spews a flood
Of foamy madness, mixed with clotted blood.
The clown, who, cursing Providence, repines,

His mournful fellow from the team disjoins ;
With many a groan forsakes his fruitless care,
And in the unfinished furrow leaves the share.
The pining steer nor shades of lofty woods,
Nor flowery meads can ease, nor crystal floods
Rolled from the rock : his flabby flanks decrease ;
His eyes are settled in a stupid peace ;
His bulk too weighty for his thighs is grown.
And his unwieldy neck hangs drooping down.
Now what avails his well-deserving toil
To turn the glebe, or smooth the rugged soil ?
And yet he never supped in solemn state,
(Nor undigested feasts did urge his fate),
Nor day to night luxuriously did join,
Nor surfeited on rich Campanian wine.
Simple his beverage, homely was his food,
The wholesome herbage, and the running flood :
No dreadful dreams awaked him with affright ;
His pains by day, secured his rest by night.
   'Twas then that buffaloes, ill paired, were seen
To draw the car of Jove's imperial queen,
For want of oxen ; and the labouring swain
Scratched, with a rake, a furrow for his grain,
And covered with his hand the shallow seed again.
He yokes himself, and up the hilly height,
With his own shoulders, draws the waggon's weight.
   The nightly wolf, that round the inclosure prowled,
To leap the fence, now plots not on the fold,
Tamed with a sharper pain.   The fearful doe,
And flying stag, amidst the greyhounds go,
And round the dwellings roam of man, their fiercer
      foe.
The scaly nations of the sea profound,
Like shipwrecked carcases, are driven aground,
And mighty phocæ, never seen before
In shallow streams, are stranded on the shore.
The viper dead within her hole is found :
Defenceless was the shelter of the ground.
The water-snake, whom fish and paddocks fed,
With staring scales lies poisoned in his bed :

To birds their native heavens contagious prove ;
From clouds they fall, and leave their souls above.
   Besides, to change their pasture 'tis in vain,
Or trust to physic ; physic is their bane.
The learnèd leeches in despair depart,
And shake their heads, desponding of their art.
   Tisiphone, let loose from under ground,
Majestically pale, now treads the round,
Before her drives diseases and affright,
And every moment rises to the sight,
Aspiring to the skies, encroaching on the light.
The rivers, and their banks, and hills around,
With lowings and with dying bleats resound.
At length, she strikes a universal blow ;
To death at once whole herds of cattle go ;
Sheep, oxen, horses, fall ; and heaped on high,
The differing species in confusion lie,
Till, warned by frequent ills, the way they found
To lodge their loathsome carrion under ground :
For useless to the currier were their hides ;
Nor could their tainted flesh with ocean tides
Be freed from filth ; nor could Vulcanian flame
The stench abolish, or the savour tame.
Nor safely could they shear their fleecy store
(Made drunk with poisonous juice, and stiff with gore),
Or touch the web : but, if the vest they wear,
Red blisters rising on their paps appear,
And flaming carbuncles, and noisome sweat,
And clammy dews, that loathsome lice beget :
Till the slow-creeping evil eats his way,
Consumes the parching limbs, and makes the life his
    prey.

BOOK IV

THE ARGUMENT

Virgil has taken care to raise the subject of each Georgic. In the first, he deals only with dead matter. In the second, he just steps on the world of life, and describes that of vegetables. In the third, he advances to animals: and in the last, he singles out the bee, the most sagacious of them, for his subject.

In this Georgic, he shews us what station is most proper for the bees, and when they begin to gather honey; how to call them home when they swarm, and how to part them when they are engaged in battle. From hence he takes occasion to discover their different kinds; and, after an excursion, relates their prudent and politic administration of affairs, and the diseases that often rage in their hives, with the proper symptoms and remedies of each. In the last place he lays down a method of repairing their kind, supposing their whole breed lost; and gives the history of its invention.

THE gifts of Heaven my following song pursues,
Aërial honey, and ambrosial dews.
Mæcenas, read this other part, that sings
Embattled squadrons and adventurous kings—
A mighty pomp, though made of little things.
Their arms, their arts, their manners, I disclose,
And how they war, and whence the people rose.
Slight is the subject, but the praise not small,
If Heaven assist, and Phœbus hear my call.

First, for thy bees a quiet station find,
And lodge them under covert of the wind
(For winds, when homeward they return, will drive
The loaded carriers from their evening hive),
Far from the cows' and goats' insulting crew,
That trample down the flowers, and brush the dew.
The painted lizard, and the birds of prey,
Foes of the frugal kind, be far away—

106

The titmouse, and the pecker's hungry brood,
And Procne, with her bosom stained in blood :
These rob the trading citizens, and bear
The trembling captives through the liquid air,
And for their callow young a cruel feast prepare.
But near a living stream their mansion place,
Edged round with moss, and tufts of matted grass :
And plant (the winds' impetuous rage to stop)
Wild olive trees, or palms, before the busy shop ;
That, when the youthful prince, with proud alarm,
Calls out the venturous colony to swarm—
When first their way through yielding air they wing,
New to the pleasures of their native spring—
The banks of brooks may make a cool retreat
For the raw soldiers from the scalding heat,
And neighbouring trees with friendly shade invite
The troops, unused to long laborious flight.
Then o'er the running stream, or standing lake,
A passage for thy weary people make ;
With osier floats the standing waters strew ;
Of massy stones make bridges, if it flow ;
That basking in the sun thy bees may lie,
And resting there, their flaggy pinions dry,
When late returning home, the laden host
By raging winds is wrecked upon the coast.
Wild thyme and savory set around their cell,
Sweet to the taste, and fragrant to the smell :
Set rows of rosemary with flowering stem,
And let the purple violets drink the stream.

    Whether thou build the palace of thy bees
With twisted osiers, or with barks of trees,
Make but a narrow mouth : for, as the cold
Congeals into a lump the liquid gold,
So 'tis again dissolved by summer's heat ;
And the sweet labours both extremes defeat.
And therefore, not in vain, the industrious kind
With dauby wax and flowers the chinks have lined,
And, with their stores of gathered glue, contrive
To stop the vents and crannies of their hive.
Not bird lime, or Idæan pitch, produce

A more tenacious mass of clammy juice.

Nor bees are lodged in hives alone, but found
In chambers of their own beneath the ground:
Their vaulted roofs are hung in pumices,
And in the rotten trunks of hollow trees.

But plaster thou the chinky hives with clay,
And leafy branches o'er their lodgings lay:
Nor place them where too deep a water flows,
Or where the yew, their poisonous neighbour, grows;
Nor roast red crabs, to offend the niceness of their
    nose;
Nor near the steaming stench of muddy ground;
Nor hollow rocks, that render back the sound,
And double images of voice rebound.

For what remains, when golden suns appear,
And under earth have driven the winter year,
The wingèd nation wanders through the skies,
And o'er the plains and shady forest flies:
Then, stooping on the meads and leafy bowers,
They skim the floods, and sip the purple flowers.
Exalted hence, and drunk with secret joy,
Their young succession all their cares employ;
They breed, they brood, instruct, and educate,
And make provision for the future state:
They work their waxen lodgings in their hives,
And labour honey to sustain their lives.

But when thou seest a swarming cloud arise,
That sweeps aloft, and darkens all the skies,
The motions of their hasty flight attend;
And know, to floods or woods, their airy march they
    bend.
Then melfoil beat, and honey-suckles pound;
With these alluring savours strew the ground;
And mix with tinkling brass the cymbal's droning
    sound.
Straight to their ancient cells, recalled from air,
The reconciled deserters will repair.
But, if intestine broils alarm the hive
(For two pretenders oft for empire strive),
The vulgar in divided factions jar;

And murmuring sounds proclaim the civil war.
Inflamed with ire, and trembling with disdain,
Scarce can their limbs their mighty souls contain.
With shouts, the coward's courage they excite,
And martial clangours call them out to fight:
With hoarse alarms the hollow camp rebounds,
That imitate the trumpet's angry sounds:
Then to their common standard they repair;
The nimble horsemen scour the fields of air;
In form of battle drawn, they issue forth,
And every knight is proud to prove his worth.
Prest for their country's honour and their king's,
On their sharp beaks they whet their pointed stings,
And exercise their arms, and tremble with their wings.
Full in the midst the haughty monarchs ride;
The trusty guards come up, and close the side;
With shouts the daring foe to battle is defied.

    Thus in the season of unclouded spring,
To war they follow their undaunted king;
Crowd through their gates; and, in the fields of light,
The shocking squadrons meet in mortal fight.
Headlong they fall from high, and wounded wound;
And heaps of slaughtered soldiers bite the ground.
Hard hail-stones lie not thicker on the plain,
Nor shaken oaks such showers of acorns rain.
With gorgeous wings, the marks of sovereign sway,
The two contending princes make their way;
Intrepid through the midst of danger go,
Their friends encourage, and amaze the foe.
With mighty souls in narrow bodies prest,
They challenge, and encounter breast to breast;
So fixed on fame, unknowing how to fly,
And obstinately bent to win or die,
That long the doubtful combat they maintain,
Till one prevails—for only one can reign.
Yet all these dreadful deeds, this deadly fray,
A cast of scattered dust will soon allay,
And undecided leave the fortune of the day.

    When both the chiefs are sundered from the fight,
Then to the lawful king restore his right;

And let the wasteful prodigal be slain,
That he, who best deserves, alone may reign.
With ease distinguished is the regal race :
One monarch wears an honest open face :
Shaped to his size, and godlike to behold,
His royal body shines with specks of gold,
And ruddy scales ; for empire he designed,
Is better born, and of a nobler kind.
That other looks like nature in disgrace :
Gaunt are his sides, and sullen is his face ;
And like their grisly prince appear his gloomy race,
Grim, ghastly, rugged, like a thirsty train
That long have travelled through a desert plain,
And spit from their dry chaps the gathered dust again.
The better brood, unlike the bastard crew,
Are marked with royal streaks of shining hue ;
Glittering and ardent, though in body less :
From these, at 'pointed seasons, hope to press
Huge heavy honeycombs, of golden juice,
Not only sweet, but pure, and fit for use,
To allay the strength and hardness of the wine,
And with old Bacchus new metheglin join.

But, when the swarms are eager of their play,
And loathe their empty hives, and idly stray,
Restrain the wanton fugitives, and take
A timely care to bring the truants back.
The task is easy—but to clip the wings
Of their high-flying arbitrary kings.
At their command, the people swarm away :
Confine the tyrant, and the slaves will stay.

Sweet gardens, full of saffron flowers, invite
The wandering gluttons, and retard their flight—
Besides the god obscene, who frights away,
With his lath sword, the thieves and birds of prey,
With his own hand, the guardian of the bees,
For slips of pines may search the mountain trees,
And with wild thyme and savory plant the plain,
Till his hard horny fingers ache with pain ;
And deck with fruitful trees the fields around,
And with refreshing waters drench the ground.

Now, did I not so near my labours end,
Strike sail, and hastening to the harbour tend,
My song to flowery gardens might extend—
To teach the vegetable arts, to sing
The Pæstan roses, and their double spring;
How succory drinks the running streams, and how
Green beds of parsley near the river grow;
How cucumbers along the surface creep,
With crooked bodies, and with bellies deep—
The late narcissus, and the winding trail
Of bear's-foot, myrtles green, and ivy pale:
For, where with stately towers Tarentum stands,
And deep Galæsus soaks the yellow sands,
I chanced an old Corycian swain to know,
Lord of few acres, and those barren too,
Unfit for sheep or vines, and more unfit to sow;
Yet, labouring well his little spot of ground,
Some scattering pot-herbs here and there he found,
Which cultivated with his daily care,
And bruised with vervain, were his frugal fare.
Sometimes white lilies did their leaves afford,
With wholesome poppy-flowers, to mend his homely
    board;
For, late returning home, he supped at ease,
And wisely deemed the wealth of monarchs less:
The little of his own, because his own, did please.
    To quit his care, he gathered, first of all,
In spring the roses, apples in the fall;
And, when cold winter split the rocks in twain,
And ice the running rivers did restrain,
He stripped the bear's-foot of its leafy growth,
And, calling western winds, accused the spring of sloth.
He therefore first among the swains was found
To reap the product of his laboured ground,
And squeeze the combs with golden liquor crowned.
His limes were first in flowers; his lofty pines,
With friendly shade, secured his tender vines.
For every bloom his trees in spring afford,
An autumn apple was by tale restored.
He knew to rank his elms in even rows,

For fruit the grafted pear-tree to dispose,
And tame to plums the sourness of the sloes.
With spreading planes he made a cool retreat,
To shade good fellows from the summer's heat.
But, straitened in my space, I must forsake
This task, for others afterwards to take.

　　Describe we next the nature of the bees,
Bestowed by Jove for secret services,
When, by the tinkling sound of timbrels led,
The king of heaven in Cretan caves they fed.
Of all the race of animals, alone
The bees have common cities of their own,
And common sons ; beneath one law they live,
And with one common stock their traffic drive.
Each has a certain home, a several stall :
All is the state's ; the state provides for all.
Mindful of coming cold, they share the pain,
And hoard, for winter's use, the summer's gain.
Some o'er the public magazines preside ;
And some are sent new forage to provide :
These drudge in fields abroad ; and those at home
Lay deep foundations for the laboured comb,
With dew, narcissus leaves, and clammy gum.
To pitch the waxen flooring some contrive ;
Some nurse the future nation of the hive :
Sweet honey some condense ; some purge the grout ;
The rest, in cells apart, the liquid nectar shut :
All, with united force, combine to drive
The lazy drones from the laborious hive :
With envy stung, they view each other's deeds :
With diligence the fragrant work proceeds.

　　As when the Cyclops, at the almighty nod,
New thunder hasten for their angry god,
Subdued in fire the stubborn metal lies ;
One brawny smith the puffing bellows plies,
And draws and blows reciprocating air :
Others to quench the hissing mass prepare :
With lifted arms they order every blow,
And chime their sounding hammers in a row :
With laboured anvils Ætna groans below.

Strongly they strike ; huge flakes of flames expire ;
With tongs they turn the steel, and vex it in the fire.
If little things with great we may compare,
Such are the bees, and such their busy care :
Studious of honey each in his degree,
The youthful swain, the grave experienced bee—
That in the field ; this, in affairs of state
Employed at home, abides within the gate,
To fortify the combs, to build the wall,
To prop the ruins, lest the fabric fall :
But, late at night, with weary pinions come
The labouring youth, and heavy laden, home.
Plains, meads, and orchards, all the day he plies ;
The gleans of yellow thyme distend his thighs ·
He spoils the saffron flowers ; he sips the blues
Of violets, wilding blooms, and willow dews.
   Their toil is common, common is their sleep ;
They shake their wings when morn begins to peep ;
Rush through the city gates without delay ;
Nor ends their work, but with declining day.
Then, having spent the last remains of light,
They give their bodies due repose at night,
When hollow murmurs of their evening bells
Dismiss the sleepy swains, and toll them to their cells.
When once in beds their weary limbs they steep,
No buzzing sounds disturb their golden sleep.
'Tis sacred silence all.   Nor dare they stray,
When rain is promised, or a stormy day ;
But near the city walls their watering take,
Nor forage far, but short excursions make.
   And as, when empty barks on billows float,
With sandy ballast sailors trim the boat ;
So bees bear gravel-stones, whose poising weight
Steers through the whistling winds their steady flight.
   But (what's more strange) their modest appetites,
Averse from Venus, fly the nuptial rites.
No lust enervates their heroic mind,
Nor wastes their strength on wanton womankind ;
But in their mouths reside their genial powers :
They gather children from the leaves and flowers.

Thus make they kings to fill the regal seat
And thus their little citizens create,
And waxen cities build, the palaces of state.
And oft on rocks their tender wings they tear,
And sink beneath the burdens which they bear:
Such rage of honey in their bosom beats;
And such a zeal they have for flowery sweets.

Thus though the race of life they quickly run,
Which in the space of seven short years is done,
The immortal line in sure succession reigns:
The fortune of the family remains;
And grandsires' grandsires the long list contains.

Besides, not Egypt, India, Media, more
With servile awe their idol king adore:
While he survives, in concord and content
The commons live, by no divisions rent;
But the great monarch's death dissolves the government.
All goes to ruin; they themselves contrive
To rob the honey, and subvert the hive.
The king presides, his subjects' toil surveys;
The servile rout their careful Cæsar praise:
Him they extol; they worship him alone;
They crowd his levees, and support his throne:
They raise him on their shoulders with a shout:
And, when their sovereign's quarrel calls them out,
His foes to mortal combat they defy,
And think it honour at his feet to die.

Induced by such examples, some have taught
That bees have portions of ethereal thought—
Endued with particles of heavenly fires;
For God the whole created mass inspires.
Through heaven, and earth, and ocean's depth, he
    throws
His influence round, and kindles as he goes.
Hence flocks, and herds, and men, and beasts, and fowls,
With breath are quickened, and attract their souls;
Hence take the forms his prescience did ordain,
And into him at length resolve again.
No room is left for death: they mount the sky,
And to their own congenial planets fly.

Now, when thou hast decreed to seize their stores,
And by prerogative to break their doors,
With sprinkled water first the city choke,
And then pursue the citizens with smoke.
Two honey harvests fall in every year:
First, when the pleasing Pleiades appear,
And, springing upward, spurn the briny seas:
Again, when their affrighted choir surveys
The watery Scorpion mend his pace behind,
With a black train of storms and winter wind,
They plunge into the deep, and safe protection find.
Prone to revenge, the bees, a wrathful race,
When once provoked, assault the aggressor's face,
And through the purple veins a passage find;
There fix their stings, and leave their souls behind.
    But, if a pinching winter thou foresee,
And wouldst preserve thy famished family;
With fragrant thyme the city fumigate,
And break the waxen walls to save the state.
For lurking lizards often lodge, by stealth,
Within the suburbs, and purloin their wealth;
And worms, that shun the light, a dark retreat
Have found in combs, and undermined the seat;
Or lazy drones, without their share of pain,
In winter-quarters, free, devour the gain;
Or wasps infest the camps with loud alarms,
And mix in battle with unequal arms;
Or secret moths are there in silence fed;
Or spiders in the vault their snary webs have spread.
    The more oppressed by foes, or famine-pined,
The more increase thy care to save the sinking kind:
With greens and flowers recruit their empty hives,
And seek fresh forage to sustain their lives.
    But, since they share with man one common fate,
In health and sickness, and in turns of state,—
Observe the symptoms. When they fall away,
And languish with insensible decay,
They change their hue; with haggard eyes they stare:
Lean are their looks, and shagged is their hair:
And crowds of dead, that never must return

To their loved hives, in decent pomp are borne :
Their friends attend the hearse ; the next relations
    mourn.
The sick, for air, before the portal gasp,
Their feeble legs within each other clasp,
Or idle in their empty hives remain,
Benumbed with cold, and listless of their gain.
Soft whispers then, and broken sounds, are heard,
As when the woods by gentle winds are stirred ;
Such stifled noise as the close furnace hides,
Or dying murmurs of departing tides.
This when thou seest, galbanean odours use,
And honey in the sickly hive infuse.
Through reeden pipes convey the golden flood,
To invite the people to their wonted food,
Mix it with thickened juice of sodden wines,
And raisins from the grapes of Psythian vines :
To these add pounded galls, and roses dry,
And, with Cecropian thyme, strong-scented centaury.
   A flower there is, that grows in meadow ground,
Amellus called, and easy to be found ;
For, from one root, the rising stem bestows
A wood of leaves, and violet purple boughs :
The flower itself is glorious to behold,
And shines on altars like refulgent gold—
Sharp to the taste—by shepherds near the stream
Of Mella found ; and thence they gave the name.
Boil this restoring root in generous wine,
And set beside the door, the sickly stock to dine.
But, if the labouring kind be wholly lost,
And not to be retrieved with care or cost ;
'Tis time to touch the precepts of an art,
The Arcadian master did of old impart ;
And how he stocked his empty hives again,
Renewed with putrid gore of oxen slain.
An ancient legend I prepare to sing,
And upward follow Fame's immortal spring :
   For, where with seven-fold horns mysterious Nile
Surrounds the skirts of Egypt's fruitful isle,
And where in pomp the sun-burnt people ride,

On painted barges, o'er the teeming tide,
Which, pouring down from Ethiopian lands,
Makes green the soil with slime, and black prolific
    sands:
That length of region, and large tract of ground,
In this one art a sure relief have found.
  First, in a place by nature close, they build
A narrow flooring, guttered, walled, and tiled.
In this, four windows are contrived, that strike,
To the four winds opposed, their beams oblique.
A steer of two years old they take, whose head
Now first with burnished horns begins to spread:
They stop his nostrils, while he strives in vain
To breathe free air, and struggles with his pain.
Knocked down, he dies: his bowels, bruised within,
Betray no wound on his unbroken skin.
Extended thus, in this obscene abode
They leave the beast; but first sweet flowers are strewed
Beneath his body, broken boughs and thyme,
And pleasing cassia, just renewed in prime.
This must be done ere spring makes equal day,
When western winds on curling waters play;
Ere painted meads produce their flowery crops,
Or swallows twitter on the chimney tops.
The tainted blood, in this close prison pent,
Begins to boil, and through the bones ferment.
Then (wondrous to behold) new creatures rise,
A moving mass at first, and short of thighs;
Till, shooting out with legs, and imped with wings,
The grubs proceed to bees with pointed stings,
And, more and more affecting air, they try
Their tender pinions, and begin to fly:
At length, like summer storms from spreading clouds,
That burst at once, and pour impetuous floods—
Or flights of arrows from the Parthian bows,
When from afar they gall embattled foes—
With such a tempest through the skies they steer;
And such a form the wingèd squadrons bear.
  What god, O Muse! this useful science taught?
Or by what man's experience was it brought?

Sad Aristæus from fair Tempè fled—
His bees with famine or diseases dead.
On Penëus' banks he stood, and near his holy head;
And, while his falling tears the stream supplied,
Thus, mourning, to his mother goddess cried:
'Mother Cyrene! mother, whose abode
Is in the depth of this immortal flood!
What boots it, that from Phœbus' loins I spring,
The third, by him and thee, from heaven's high
          king?
O! where is all thy boasted pity gone,
And promise of the skies to thy deluded son?
Why didst thou me, unhappy me, create,
Odious to gods, and born to bitter fate?
Whom scarce my sheep, and scarce my painful plough
The needful aids of human life allow:
So wretched is thy son, so hard a mother thou!
Proceed, inhuman parent, in thy scorn;
Root up my trees; with blights destroy my corn;
My vineyards ruin, and my sheepfolds burn.
Let loose thy rage; let all thy spite be shown,
Since thus thy hate pursues the praises of thy son.'
But, from her mossy bower below the ground,
His careful mother heard the plaintive sound—
Encompassed with her sea-green sisters round.
One common work they plied; their distaffs full
With carded locks of blue Milesian wool.
Spio, with Drymo brown, and Xantho fair,
And sweet Phyllodocè with long dishevelled hair;
Cydippè with Lycorias, once a maid,
And one that once had called Lucina's aid;
Clio and Beroë, from one father both;
Both girt with gold, and clad in particoloured cloth;
Opis the meek, and Deïopeia proud:
Nisæa lofty, with Ligea loud;
Thalia joyous, Ephyrè the sad,
And Arethusa, once Diana's maid,
But now (her quiver left) to love betrayed.
To these Clymenè the sweet theft declares
Of Mars; and Vulcan's unavailing cares;

And all the rapes of gods, and every love.
From ancient Chaos down to youthful Jove.
   Thus while she sings, the sisters turn the wheel,
Empty the woolly rock, and fill the reel.
A mournful sound again the mother hears ;
Again the mournful sound invades the sisters' ears.
Starting at once from their green seats, they rise—
Fear in their heart, amazement in their eyes.
But Arethusa, leaping from her bed,
First lifts above the waves her beauteous head,
And, crying from afar, thus to Cyrene said :
'O sister, not with causeless fear possest !
No stranger voice disturbs thy tender breast.
'Tis Aristæus, 'tis thy darling son,
Who to his careless mother makes his moan.
Near his paternal stream he sadly stands,
With downcast eyes, wet cheeks, and folded hands,
Upbraiding heaven, from whence his lineage came,
And cruel calls the gods, and cruel thee, by name.'
   Cyrene, moved with love, and seized with fear,
Cries out, ' Conduct my son, conduct him here :
'Tis lawful for the youth, derived from gods,
To view the secrets of our deep abodes.'
At once she waved her hand on either side ;
At once the ranks of swelling streams divide.
Two rising heaps of liquid crystal stand,
And leave a space betwixt of empty sand.
Thus safe received, the downward track he treads,
Which to his mother's watery palace leads.
With wondering eyes he views the secret store
Of lakes, that, pent in hollow caverns, roar :
He hears the crackling sounds of coral woods,
And sees the secret source of subterranean floods ;
And where, distinguished in their several cells,
The fount of Phasis, and of Lycus, dwells ;
Where swift Enipeus in his bed appears,
And Tiber his majestic forehead rears ;
Whence Anio flows, and Hypanis profound
Breaks through the opposing rocks with raging sound :
Where Po first issues from his dark abodes,

And, awful in his cradle, rules the floods:
Two golden horns on his large front he wears,
And his grim face a bull's resemblance bears:
With rapid course he seeks the sacred main,
And fattens, as he runs, the fruitful plain.
    Now, to the court arrived, the admiring son
Beholds the vaulted roofs of pory stone,
Now to his mother goddess tells his grief,
Which she with pity hears, and promises relief.
The officious nymphs attending in a ring,
With waters drawn from their perpetual spring,
From earthly dregs his body purify,
And rub his temples, with fine towels, dry;
Then load the tables with a liberal feast,
And honour with full bowls their friendly guest.
The sacred altars are involved in smoke;
And the bright choir their kindred gods invoke.
Two bowls the mother fills with Lydian wine;
Then thus: ' Let these be poured with rites divine,
To the great authors of our watery line—
To father Ocean, this; and this (she said)
Be to the nymphs his sacred sisters paid,
Who rule the watery plains, and hold the woodland
        shade.'
She sprinkled thrice, with wine, the Vestal fire,
Thrice to the vaulted roofs the flames aspire.
Raised with so blest an omen, she begun,
With words like these, to cheer her drooping son;
' In the Carpathian bottom, makes abode
The shepherd of the seas, a prophet, and a god.
High o'er the main in watery pomp he rides,
His azure car and finny coursers guides—
Proteus his name.—To his Pallenian port
I see from far the weary god resort.
Him, not alone, we river gods adore,
But aged Nereus hearkens to his lore.
With sure foresight, and with unerring doom,
He sees what is, and was, and is to come.
This Neptune gave him, when he gave to keep
His scaly flocks, that graze the watery deep.

Implore his aid ; for Proteus only knows
The secret cause, and cure, of all thy woes.
But first the wily wizard must be caught :
For, unconstrained, he nothing tells for nought ;
Nor is with prayers or bribes, or flattery bought.
Surprise him first, and with hard fetters bind ;
Then all his frauds will vanish into wind.
I will myself conduct thee on thy way ;
When next the southing sun inflames the day,
When the dry herbage thirsts for dews in vain,
And sheep, in shades, avoid the parching plain ;
Then will I lead thee to his secret seat,
When, weary with his toil, and scorched with heat,
The wayward sire frequents his cool retreat.
His eyes with heavy slumber overcast—
With force invade his limbs, and bind him fast.
Thus surely bound, yet be not over bold :
The slippery god will try to loose his hold,
And various forms assume, to cheat thy sight,
And with vain images of beasts affright ;
With foamy tusks will seem a bristly boar,
Or imitate the lion's angry roar :
Break out in crackling flames to shun thy snare,
Or hiss a dragon, or a tiger stare ;
Or, with a wile thy caution to betray,
In fleeting streams attempt to slide away.
But thou, the more he varies forms, beware
To strain his fetters with a stricter care,
Till, tiring all his arts, he turns again
To his true shape, in which he first was seen.'
    This said, with nectar she her son anoints,
Infusing vigour through his mortal joints ;
Down from his head the liquid odours ran :
He breathed of heaven, and looked above a man.
    Within a mountain's hollow womb there lies
A large recess, concealed from human eyes,
Where heaps of billows, driven by wind and tide,
In form of war, their watery ranks divide,
And there, like sentries set, without the mouth abide ;
A station safe for ships, when tempests roar,

A silent harbour, and a covered shore.
Secure within resides the various god,
And draws a rock upon his dark abode.
Hither with silent steps, secure from sight,
The goddess guides her son, and turns him from the
        light:
Herself, involved in clouds, precipitates her flight.

    'Twas noon; the sultry Dog-star from the sky
Scorched Indian swains; the rivelled grass was dry;
The sun with flaming arrows pierced the flood,
And, darting to the bottom, baked the mud;
When weary Proteus, from the briny waves,
Retired for shelter to his wonted caves.
His finny flocks about their shepherd play,
And, rolling round him, spirt the bitter sea.
Unwieldily they wallow first in ooze,
Then in the shady covert seek repose.
Himself, their herdsman, on the middle mount,
Takes of his mustered flocks a just account.
So, seated on a rock, a shepherd's groom
Surveys his evening flocks returning home,
When lowing calves and bleating lambs from far,
Provoke the prowling wolf to nightly war.

    The occasion offers, and the youth complies:
For scarce the weary god had closed his eyes,
When, rushing on with shouts, he binds in chains
The drowsy prophet, and his limbs constrains.
He, not unmindful of his usual art,
First in dissembled fire attempts to part:
Then roaring beasts, and running streams, he tries,
And wearies all his miracles of lies:
But, having shifted every form to 'scape,
Convinced of conquest, he resumed his shape,
And, thus, at length, in human accent spoke:
'Audacious youth! what madness could provoke
A mortal man to invade a sleeping god?
What business brought thee to my dark abode?'

    To this the audacious youth: 'Thou knowest full well
My name and business, god; nor need I tell.
No man can Proteus cheat: but, Proteus, leave

Thy fraudful arts, and do not thou deceive.
Following the gods' command, I come to implore
Thy help, my perished people to restore.'
The seer, who could not yet his wrath assuage,
Rolled his green eyes, that sparkled with his rage,
And gnashed his teeth, and cried, 'No vulgar god
Pursues thy crimes, nor with a common rod.
Thy great misdeeds have met a due reward;
And Orpheus' dying prayers at length are heard.
For crimes not his, the lover lost his life,
And at thy hands requires his murdered wife:
Nor (if the Fates assist not) canst thou 'scape
The just revenge of that intended rape.
To shun thy lawless lust, the dying bride,
Unwary, took along the river's side,
Nor at her heels perceived the deadly snake,
That kept the bank, in covert of the brake.
But all her fellow-nymphs the mountains tear
With loud laments, and break the yielding air:
The realms of Mars remurmur all around,
And echoes to the Athenian shores rebound.
The unhappy husband, husband now no more,
Did on his tuneful harp his loss deplore,
And sought his mournful mind with music to restore.
On thee, dear wife, in deserts all alone,
He called, sighed, sung: his griefs with day begun,
Nor were they finished with the setting sun.
E'en to the dark dominions of the night
He took his way, through forests void of light,
And dared amidst the trembling ghosts to sing,
And stood before the inexorable king.
The infernal troops like passing shadows glide,
And, listening, crowd the sweet musician's side—
(Not flocks of birds, when driven by storms or night,
Stretch to the forest with so thick a flight)—
Men, matrons, children, and the unmarried maid,
The mighty hero's more majestic shade,
And youths, on funeral piles before their parents laid.
All these Cocytus bounds with squalid reeds,
With muddy ditches, and with deadly weeds;

And baleful Styx encompasses around,
With nine slow circling streams, the unhappy ground.
E'en from the depths of hell the damned advance ;
The infernal mansions, nodding, seem to dance ;
The gaping three-mouthed dog forgets to snarl ;
The Furies hearken, and their snakes uncurl ;
Ixion seems no more his pain to feel,
But leans attentive on his standing wheel.
All dangers past, at length the lovely bride
In safety goes, with her melodious guide,
Longing the common light again to share,
And draw the vital breath of upper air—
He first ; and close behind him followed she ;
For such was Proserpine's severe decree—
When strong desires the impatient youth invade,
By little caution and much love betrayed :
A fault, which easy pardon might receive,
Were lovers judges, or could hell forgive :
For near the confines of ethereal light,
And longing for the glimmering of a sight,
The unwary lover cast his eyes behind,
Forgetful of the law, nor master of his mind.
Straight all his hopes exhaled in empty smoke ;
And his long toils were forfeit for a look.
Three flashes of blue lightning gave the sign
Of covenants broke ; three peals of thunder join.
Then thus the bride : ' What fury seized on thee,
Unhappy man ! to lose thyself and me ?
Dragged back again by cruel Destinies,
An iron slumber shuts my swimming eyes.
And now farewell ! Involved in shades of night,
For ever I am ravished from thy sight.
In vain I reach my feeble hands to join
In sweet embraces—ah ! no longer thine !'
She said : and from his eyes the fleeting fair
Retired like subtle smoke dissolved in air,
And left her hopeless lover in despair.
In vain, with folding arms, the youth essayed
To stop her flight, and strain the flying shade :
He prays ; he raves ; all means in vain he tries,

With rage inflamed, astonished with surprise;
But she returned no more, to bless his longing eyes.
Nor would the infernal ferryman once more
Be bribed to waft him to the farther shore.
What should he do, who twice had lost his love?
What notes invent? what new petitions move?
Her soul already was consigned to fate,
And shivering in the leaky sculler sat.
For seven continued months, if fame say true,
The wretched swain his sorrows did renew:
By Strymon's freezing streams he sat alone:
The rocks were moved to pity with his moan:
Trees bent their heads to hear him sing his wrongs:
Fierce tigers couched around, and lolled their fawning
          tongues.
So, close in poplar shades, her children gone,
The mother nightingale laments alone,
Whose nest some prying churl had found, and thence
By stealth, conveyed the unfeathered innocence.
But she supplies the night with mournful strains;
And melancholy music fills the plains.
Sad Orpheus thus his tedious hours employs,
Averse from Venus, and from nuptial joys.
Alone he tempts the frozen floods, alone
The unhappy climes, where spring was never known:
He mourned his wretched wife, in vain restored,
And Pluto's unavailing boon deplored.
The Thracian matrons—who the youth accused
Of love disdained, and marriage-rites refused—
With furies and nocturnal orgies fired,
At length against his sacred life conspired.
Whom e'en the savage beasts had spared, they killed,
And strewed the mangled limbs about the field.
Then, when his head, from his fair shoulders torn,
Washed by the waters, was on Hebrus borne,
E'en then his trembling tongue invoked his bride;
With his last voice, "Eurydice," he cried,
"Eurydice," the rocks and river-banks replied.'
    This answer Proteus gave; nor more he said,
But in the billows plunged his hoary head;

And, where he leaped, the waves in circles widely
    spread.
  The nymph returned, her drooping son to cheer,
And bade him banish his superfluous fear :
' For now (said she) the cause is known, from whence
Thy woe succeeded, and for what offence.
The nymphs, companions of the unhappy maid,
This punishment upon thy crimes have laid ;
And sent a plague among thy thriving bees.—
With vows and suppliant prayers their powers ap-
    pease :
The soft Napæan race will soon relent
Their anger, and remit the punishment.
The secret in an easy method lies ;
Select four brawny bulls for sacrifice,
Which on Lycæus graze without a guide ;
Add four fair heifers yet in yoke untried ;
For these, four altars in their temple rear,
And then adore the woodland powers with prayer.
From the slain victims pour the streaming blood,
And leave their bodies in the shady wood :
Nine mornings thence, Lethæan poppy bring,
To appease the manes of the poet's king,
And, to propitiate his offended bride,
A fatted calf and a black ewe provide :
This finished, to the former woods repair.'
His mother's precepts he performs with care ;
The temple visits, and adores with prayer ;
Four altars raises ; from his herd he culls,
For slaughter, four the fairest of his bulls :
Four heifers from his female store he took,
All fair, and all unknowing of the yoke.
Nine mornings thence, with sacrifice and prayers,
The powers atoned, he to the grove repairs.
Behold a prodigy ! for, from within
The broken bowels and the bloated skin,
A buzzing noise of bees his ears alarms ;
Straight issue through the sides assembling swarms.
Dark as a cloud, they make a wheeling flight,
Then on a neighbouring tree, descending, light :

Like a large cluster of black grapes they shew,
And make a large dependance from the bough.
　　Thus have I sung of fields, of flocks, and trees,
And of the waxen work of labouring bees:
While mighty Cæsar, thundering from afar,
Seeks on Euphrates' banks the spoils of war;
With conquering arts asserts his country's cause,
With arts of peace the willing people draws;
On the glad earth the golden age renews,
And his great father's path to heaven pursues;
While I at Naples pass my peaceful days,
Affecting studies of less noisy praise;
And, bold through youth, beneath the beechen shade,
The lays of shepherds, and their loves, have played.

THE ÆNEIS

BOOK I

THE ARGUMENT

The Trojans, after a seven years' voyage, set sail for Italy, but are overtaken by a dreadful storm, which Æolus raises at Juno's request. The tempest sinks one ship, and scatters the rest. Neptune drives off the winds, and calms the sea. Æneas, with his own ship and six more, arrives safe at an African port. Venus complains to Jupiter of her son's misfortunes. Jupiter comforts her, and sends Mercury to procure him a kind reception among the Carthaginians. Æneas, going out to discover the country, meets his mother in the shape of a huntress, who conveys him in a cloud to Carthage, where he sees his friends whom he thought lost, and receives a kind entertainment from the queen. Dido, by a device of Venus, begins to have a passion for him, and after some discourse with him, desires the history of his adventures since the siege of Troy, which is the subject of the two following books.

ARMS, and the man I sing, who, forced by Fate,
And haughty Juno's unrelenting hate,
Expelled and exiled, left the Trojan shore.
Long labours, both by sea and land, he bore,
And in the doubtful war, before he won
The Latian realm, and built the destined town;
His banished gods restored to rites divine;
And settled sure succession in his line,
From whence the race of Alban fathers come,
And the long glories of majestic Rome.

O muse! the causes and the crimes relate;
What goddess was provoked, and whence her hate;
For what offence the queen of heaven began
To persecute so brave, so just a man;
Involved his anxious life in endless cares,
Exposed to wants, and hurried into wars!
Can heavenly minds such high resentment show,
Or exercise their spite in human woe?

Against the Tiber's mouth, but far away,
An ancient town was seated on the sea—
A Tyrian colony—the people made
Stout for the war, and studious for their trade:
Carthage the name—beloved by Juno more
Than her own Argos, or the Samian shore.
Here stood her chariot; here, if heaven were kind,
The seat of awful empire she designed.
Yet she had heard an ancient rumour fly
(Long cited by the people of the sky),
That times to come should see the Trojan race
Her Carthage ruin, and her towers deface;
Nor thus confined, the yoke of sovereign sway
Should on the necks of all the nations lay.
She pondered this, and feared it was in fate;
Nor could forget the war she waged of late,
For conquering Greece, against the Trojan state,
Besides, long causes working in her mind,
And secret seeds of envy, lay behind:
Deep graven in her heart, the doom remained
Of partial Paris, and her form disdained;
The grace bestowed on ravished Ganymed,
Electra's glories, and her injured bed.
Each was a cause alone; and all combined
To kindle vengeance in her haughty mind.
For this, far distant from the Latian coast,
She drove the remnants of the Trojan host;
And seven long years the unhappy wandering train
Were tossed by storms, and scattered through the
        main.
Such time, such toil, required the Roman name,
Such length of labour for so vast a frame!
Now scarce the Trojan fleet, with sails and oars,
Had left behind the fair Sicilian shores,
Entering with cheerful shouts the watery reign,
And ploughing frothy furrows in the main;
When, lab'ring still with endless discontent,
The queen of heaven did thus her fury vent:
  'Then am I vanquished? must I yield? (said she)
And must the Trojans reign in Italy?

So Fate will have it; and Jove adds his force;
Nor can my power divert their happy course.
Could angry Pallas, with revengeful spleen,
The Grecian navy burn, and drown the men?
She, for the fault of one offending foe,
The bolts of Jove himself presumed to throw:
With whirlwinds from beneath she tossed the ship,
And bare exposed the bosom of the deep:
Then—as an eagle gripes the trembling game—
The wretch, yet hissing with her father's flame,
She strongly seized, and, with a burning wound
Transfixed, and naked on a rock she bound.
But I, who walk in awful state above,
The majesty of heaven, the sister-wife of Jove,
For length of years my fruitless force employ
Against the thin remains of ruined Troy!
What nations now to Juno's power will pray,
Or offerings on my slighted altars lay?'

    Thus raged the goddess; and with fury fraught,
The restless regions of the storms she sought,
Where, in a spacious cave of living stone,
The tyrant Æolus, from his airy throne,
With power imperial curbs the struggling winds,
And sounding tempests in dark prisons binds:
This way, and that, the impatient captives tend,
And, pressing for release, the mountains rend.
High in his hall the undaunted monarch stands,
And shakes his sceptre, and their rage commands;
Which did he not, their unresisted sway
Would sweep the world before them in their way;
Earth, air, and seas, through empty space would roll,
And heaven would fly before the driving soul.
In fear of this, the father of the gods
Confined their fury to those dark abodes,
And locked them safe within, oppressed with mountain
    loads:
Imposed a king with arbitrary sway,
To loose their fetters, or their force allay;
To whom the suppliant queen her prayers addressed,
And thus the tenor of her suit expressed:

'O Æolus!—for to thee the king of heaven
The power of tempests and of winds has given;
Thy force alone their fury can restrain,
And smooth the waves, or swell the troubled main—
A race of wandering slaves, abhorred by me,
With prosperous passage cut the Tuscan sea:
To fruitful Italy their course they steer,
And, for their vanquished gods design new temples there.
Raise all thy winds; with night involve the skies;
Sink or disperse my fatal enemies!
Twice seven—the charming daughters of the main,
Around my person wait, and bear my train:
Succeed my wish, and second my design;
The fairest, Deiopeia, shall be thine,
And make thee father of a happy line.'

To this the god: ''Tis yours, O queen! to will
The work, which duty binds me to fulfil.
These airy kingdoms, and this wide command,
Are all the presents of your bounteous hand:
Yours is my sovereign's grace; and as your guest,
I sit with gods at their celestial feast.
Raise tempests at your pleasure, or subdue;
Dispose of empire, which I hold from you.'

He said, and hurled against the mountain side
His quivering spear, and all the god applied.
The raging winds rush through the hollow wound,
And dance aloft in air, and skim along the ground;
Then, settling on the sea, the surges sweep,
Raise liquid mountains, and disclose the deep.
South, East, and West, with mixed confusion roar,
And roll the foaming billows to the shore.
The cables crack; the sailors' fearful cries
Ascend; and sable night involves the skies;
And heaven itself is ravished from their eyes.
Loud peals of thunder from the poles ensue;
Then flashing fires the transient light renew;
The face of things a frightful image bears;
And present death in various forms appears.
Struck with unusual fright, the Trojan chief,
With lifted hands and eyes, invokes relief;

And, 'Thrice and four times happy those (he cried),
That under Ilian walls, before their parents, died !
Tydides, bravest of the Grecian train !
Why could not I by that strong arm be slain,
And lie by noble Hector on the plain,
Or great Sarpedon ; in those bloody fields,
Where Simoïs rolls the bodies and the shields
Of heroes, whose dismembered hands yet bear
The dart aloft, and clench the pointed spear ?'
   Thus while the pious prince his fate bewails,
Fierce Boreas drove against his flying sails,
And rent the sheets : the raging billows rise,
And mount the tossing vessel to the skies ;
Nor can the shivering oars sustain the blow :
The galley gives her side, and turns her prow ;
While those astern, descending down the steep,
Through gaping waves behold the boiling deep.
Three ships were hurried by the southern blast,
And on the secret shelves with fury cast.
Those hidden rocks the Ausonian sailors knew :
They called them Altars, when they rose in view,
And shewed their spacious backs above the flood.
Three more, fierce Eurus in his angry mood,
Dashed on the shallows of the moving sand,
And in mid ocean left them moored a-land.
Orontes' bark, that bore the Lycian crew,
(A horrid sight !) e'en in the hero's view,
From stem to stern by waves was overborne ·
The trembling pilot, from his rudder torn,
Was headlong hurled : thrice round, the ship was
    tossed,
Then bulged at once, and in the deep was lost ;
And here and there above the waves were seen
Arms, pictures, precious goods, and floating men.
The stoutest vessel to the storm gave way,
And sucked through loosened planks the rushing sea.
Ilioneus was her chief : Aletes old,
Achates faithful, Abas young and bold,
Endured not less : their ships, with gaping seams,
Admit the deluge of the briny streams.

Meantime imperial Neptune heard the sound
Of raging billows breaking on the ground.
Displeased, and fearing for his watery reign,
He reared his awful head above the main,
Serene in majesty,—then rolled his eyes
Around the space of earth, and seas, and skies.
He saw the Trojan fleet dispersed, distressed,
By stormy winds and wintry heaven oppressed.
Full well the god his sister's envy knew,
And what her aims and what her arts pursue.
He summoned Eurus and the western blast,
And first an angry glance on both he cast,
Then thus rebuked : ' Audacious winds ! from whence
This bold attempt, this rebel insolence?
Is it for you to ravage seas and land,
Unauthorized by my supreme command?
To raise such mountains on the troubled main?
Whom I—but first 'tis fit the billows to restrain ;
And then you shall be taught obedience to my reign.
Hence ! to your lord my royal mandate bear—
The realms of ocean and the fields of air
Are mine, not his.   By fatal lot to me
The liquid empire fell, and trident of the sea.
His power to hollow caverns is confined :
There let him reign the jailor of the wind,
With hoarse commands his breathing subjects call,
And boast and bluster in his empty h ll.'
He spoke ; and while he spoke, he smoothed the sea,
Dispelled the darkness, and restored the day.
Cymothoë, Triton, and the sea-green train
Of beauteous nymphs, the daughters of the main,
Clear from the rocks the vessels with their hands :
The god himself with ready trident stands,
And opes the deep, and spreads the moving sands ;
Then heaves them off the shoals. — Where'er he
      guides
His finny coursers, and in triumph rides,
The waves unruffle, and the sea subsides.
As, when in tumults rise the ignoble crowd,
Mad are their motions, and their tongues are loud ;

And stones and brands in rattling volleys fly,
And all the rustic arms that fury can supply :
If then some grave and pious man appear,
They hush their noise, and lend a listening ear :
He soothes with sober words their angry mood,
And quenches their innate desire of blood :
So, when the father of the flood appears,
And o'er the seas his sovereign trident rears,
Their fury falls : he skims the liquid plains,
High on his chariot, and, with loosened reins,
Majestic moves along, and awful peace maintains.
The weary Trojans ply their shattered oars
To nearest land, and make the Libyan shores.
    Within a long recess there lies a bay :
An island shades it from the rolling sea,
And forms a port secure for ships to ride :
Broke by the jutting land, on either side,
In double streams the briny waters glide,
Betwixt two rows of rocks : a sylvan scene
Appears above, and groves for ever green :
A grot is formed beneath, with mossy seats,
To rest the Nereïds, and exclude the heats.
Down through the crannies of the living walls,
The crystal streams descend in murmuring falls.
No halsers need to bind the vessels here,
Nor bearded anchors ; for no storms they fear.
Seven ships within this happy harbour meet,
The thin remainders of the scattered fleet.
The Trojans, worn with toils, and spent with woes,
Leap on the welcome land, and seek their wished repose.
    First, good Achates, with repeated strokes
Of clashing flints, their hidden fire provokes :
Short flame succeeds : a bed of withered leaves
The dying sparkles in their fall receives :
Caught into life, in fiery fumes they rise,
And, fed with stronger food, invade the skies.
The Trojans, dropping wet, or stand around
The cheerful blaze, or lie along the ground.
Some dry their corn infected with the brine,
Then grind with marbles, and prepare to dine.

Æneas climbs the mountain's airy brow,
And takes a prospect of the seas below,
If Capys thence, or Antheus, he could spy,
Or see the streamers of Caïcus fly.
No vessels were in view ; but, on the plain,
Three beamy stags command a lordly train
Of branching heads : the more ignoble throng
Attend their stately steps, and slowly graze along.
He stood ; and, while secure they fed below,
He took the quiver and the trusty bow
Achates used to bear : the leaders first
He laid along, and then the vulgar pierced ;
Nor ceased his arrows, till the shady plain
Seven mighty bodies with their blood distain.
For the seven ships he made an equal share,
And to the port returned triumphant from the war.
The jars of generous wine (Acestes' gift,
When his Trinacrian shores the navy left)
He set abroach, and for the feast prepared,
In equal portions with the ven'son shared.
Thus while he dealt it round, the pious chief
With cheerful words allayed the common grief :—
' Endure, and conquer ! Jove will soon dispose
To future good, our past and present woes.
With me, the rocks of Scylla you have tried ;
The inhuman Cyclops, and his den, defied.
What greater ills hereafter can you bear ?
Resume your courage, and dismiss your care :
An hour will come, with pleasure to relate
Your sorrows past, as benefits of fate.
Through various hazards and events, we move
To Latium, and the realms foredoomed by Jove.
Called to the seat (the promise of the skies)
Where Trojan kingdoms once again may rise,
Endure the hardships of your present state ;
Live, and reserve yourselves for better fate.'
　　These words he spoke, but spoke not from his heart ;
His outward smiles concealed his inward smart.
The jolly crew, unmindful of the past,
The quarry share, their plenteous dinner haste.

Some strip the skin ; some portion out the spoil ;
The limbs, yet trembling, in the caldrons boil ;
Some on the fire the reeking entrails broil.
Stretched on the grassy turf, at ease they dine,
Restore their strength with meat, and cheer their souls
    with wine.
Their hunger thus appeased, their care attends
The doubtful fortune of their absent friends :
Alternate hopes and fears their minds possess,
Whether to deem them dead, or in distress.
Above the rest, Æneas mourns the fate
Of brave Orontes, and the uncertain state
Of Gyas, Lycus, and of Amycus.
The day, but not their sorrows, ended thus.

    When from aloft, almighty Jove surveys
Earth, air, and shores, and navigable seas :
At length, on Libyan realms he fixed his eyes :
Whom, pondering thus on human miseries,
When Venus saw, she with a lowly look,
Not free from tears, her heavenly sire bespoke :
' O king of gods and men ! whose awful hand
Disperses thunder on the seas and land ;
Disposes all with absolute command ;
How could my pious son thy power incense ?
Or what, alas ! is vanished Troy's offence ?
Our hope of Italy not only lost ;
On various seas by various tempests tossed,
But shut from every shore, and barred from every
    coast.
You promised once, a progeny divine,
Of Romans, rising from the Trojan line,
In after-times should hold the world in awe,
And to the land and ocean give the law.
How is your doom reversed, which eased my care
When Troy was ruined in that cruel war !
Then fates to fates I could oppose ; but now,
When fortune still pursues her former blow,
What can I hope ? What worse can still succeed ?
What end of labours has your will decreed ?
Antenor, from the midst of Grecian hosts

Could pass secure, and pierce the Illyrian coasts:
Where, rolling down the steep, Timavus raves,
And through nine channels disembogues his waves.
At length he founded Padua's happy seat,
And gave his Trojans a secure retreat:
There fixed their arms, and there renewed their name;
And there in quiet rules, and crowned with fame.
But we, descended from your sacred line,
Entitled to your heaven and rites divine,
Are banished earth, and, for the wrath of one,
Removed from Latium, and the promised throne.
Are these our sceptres? these our due rewards?
And is it thus that Jove his plighted faith regards?'
   To whom the father of the immortal race,
Smiling, with that serene indulgent face
With which he drives the clouds and clears the skies—
First gave a holy kiss; then thus replies:
'Daughter, dismiss thy fears: to thy desire,
The fates of thine are fixed, and stand entire.
Thou shalt behold thy wished Lavinian walls;
And, ripe for heaven, when fate Æneas calls,
Then shalt thou bear him up, sublime, to me:
No counsels have reversed my firm decree.
And, lest new fears disturb thy happy state,
Know, I have searched the mystic rolls of fate:
Thy son (nor is the appointed season far)
In Italy shall wage successful war:
Shall tame fierce nations in the bloody field;
And sovereign laws impose, and cities build;
Till, after every foe subdued, the sun
Thrice through the signs his annual race shall run
This is his time prefixed.   Ascanius then,
Now called Iülus, shall begin his reign.
He, thirty rolling years the crown shall wear;
Then from Lavinium shall the seat transfer,
And with hard labour, Alba-longa build:
The throne with his succession shall be filled,
Three hundred circuits more: then shall be seen
Ilia the fair, a priestess and a queen,
Who, full of Mars, in time, with kindly throes,

Shall at a birth two goodly boys disclose.
The royal babes a tawny wolf shall drain:
Then Romulus his grandsire's throne shall gain,
Of martial towers the founder shall become,
The people Romans call, the city Rome.
To them no bounds of empire I assign,
Nor term of years to their immortal line.
E'en haughty Juno, who, with endless broils,
Earth, seas, and heaven, and Jove himself, turmoils,
At length atoned, her friendly power shall join,
To cherish and advance the Trojan line.
The subject world shall Rome's dominion own,
And, prostrate, shall adore the nation of the gown.

An age is ripening in revolving fate,
When Troy shall overturn the Grecian state,
And sweet revenge her conquering sons shall call,
To crush the people that conspired her fall.
Then Cæsar from the Julian stock shall rise,
Whose empire ocean, and whose fame the skies
Alone shall bound; whom, fraught with eastern spoils,
Our heaven, the just reward of human toils,
Securely shall repay with rights divine;
And incense shall ascend before his sacred shrine.
Then dire debate, and impious war, shall cease,
And the stern age be softened into peace:
Then banished Faith shall once again return,
And Vestal fires in hallowed temples burn;
And Remus, with Quirinus shall sustain
The righteous laws, and fraud and force restrain.
Janus himself before his fane shall wait,
And keep the dreadful issues of his gate
With bolts and iron bars: within remains
Imprisoned Fury, bound in brazen chains:
High on a trophy raised, of useless arms,
He sits, and threats the world with vain alarms.'

He said, and sent Cyllenius with command
To free the ports, and ope the Punic land
To Trojan guests; lest, ignorant of fate,
The queen might force them from her town and state.
Down from the steep of heaven Cyllenius flies,

And cleaves with all his wings the yielding skies.
Soon on the Libyan shore descends the god,
Performs his message, and displays his rod.
The surly murmurs of the people cease;
And, as the fates required, they give the peace.
The queen herself suspends the rigid laws,
The Trojans pities, and protects their cause.

Meantime, in shades of night Æneas lies:
Care seized his soul, and sleep forsook his eyes.
But when the sun restored the cheerful day,
He rose, the coast and country to survey;
Anxious and eager to discover more.
It looked a wild uncultivated shore:
But, whether human kind, or beasts alone
Possessed the new-found region, was unknown.
Beneath a ledge of rocks his fleet he hides:
Tall trees surround the mountain's shady sides:
The bending brow above, a safe retreat provides.
Armed with two pointed darts, he leaves his friends;
And true Achates on his steps attends.
Lo! in the deep recesses of the wood,
Before his eyes his goddess mother stood:
A huntress in her habit and her mien;
Her dress, a maid, her air, confessed a queen.
Bare were her knees, and knots her garments bind;
Loose was her hair, and wantoned in the wind;
Her hand sustained a bow; her quiver hung behind.
She seemed a virgin of the Spartan blood:
With such array Harpalyce bestrode
Her Thracian courser, and outstripped the rapid flood.
'Ho! strangers! have you lately seen (she said),
One of my sisters, like myself arrayed,
Who crossed the lawn, or in the forest strayed?
A painted quiver at her back she bore;
Varied with spots, a lynx's hide she wore;
And at full cry pursued the tusky boar.'

Thus Venus: thus her son replied again:
'None of your sisters have we heard or seen,
O virgin! or what other name you bear
Above that style—O more than mortal fair!

Your voice and mien celestial birth betray.
If, as you seem, the sister of the day,
Or one at least of chaste Diana's train,
Let not an humble suppliant sue in vain ;
But tell a stranger, long in tempests tossed,
What earth we tread, and who commands the coast ?
Then on your name shall wretched mortals call,
And offered victims at your altars fall.'
 ' I dare not (she replied) assume the name
Of goddess, or celestial honours claim ;
For Tyrian virgins bows and quivers bear,
And purple buskins o'er their ankles wear.
Know, gentle youth, in Libyan lands you are
A people rude in peace, and rough in war.
The rising city, which from far you see,
Is Carthage, and a Tyrian colony.
Phœnician Dido rules the growing state ;
Who fled from Tyre, to shun her brother's hate.
Great were her wrongs, her story full of fate ;
Which I will sum in short. Sichæus, known
For wealth, and brother to the Punic throne,
Possessed fair Dido's bed ; and either heart
At once was wounded with an equal dart.
Her father gave her, yet a spotless maid :
Pygmalion then the Tyrian sceptre swayed—
One who contemned divine and human laws :
Then strife ensued, and cursèd gold the cause.
The monarch, blinded with desire of wealth,
With steel invades his brother's life by stealth ;
Before the sacred altar made him bleed,
And long from her concealed the cruel deed.
Some tale, some new pretence, he daily coined
To soothe his sister, and delude her mind.
 At length, in dead of night, the ghost appears
Of her unhappy lord : the spectre stares,
And, with erected eyes, his bloody bosom bares.
The cruel altars, and his fate, he tells,
And the dire secret of his house reveals ;
Then warns the widow, with her household gods,
To seek a refuge in remote abodes.

Last, to support her in so long a way,
He shows her where his hidden treasure lay.
Admonished thus, and seized with mortal fright,
The queen provides companions of her flight :
They meet, and all combine to leave the state,
Who hate the tyrant, or who fear his hate.
They seize a fleet, which ready rigged they find ;
Nor is Pygmalion's treasure left behind.
The vessels, heavy laden, put to sea
With prosperous winds : a woman leads the way.
I know not, if by stress of weather driven,
Or was their fatal course disposed by Heaven :
At last they landed, where from far, your eyes
May view the turrets of new Carthage rise :
There, bought a space of ground, which (Byrsa call
From the bull's hide) they first enclosed, and wall
But whence are you ? what country claims **your**
    birth ?
What seek you, strangers, on our Libyan earth ?'
  To whom, with sorrow streaming from his eyes,
And deeply sighing, thus her son replies :
' Could you with patience hear, or I relate,
O nymph ! the tedious annals of our fate,
Through such a train of woes if I should run,
The day would sooner than the tale be done.
From ancient Troy, by force expelled, we came—
If you by chance have heard the Trojan name.
On various seas by various tempests tossed,
At length we landed on your Libyan coast.
The good Æneas am I called—a name,
While Fortune favoured, not unknown to fame.
My household gods, companions of my woes,
With pious care I rescued from our foes.
To fruitful Italy my course was bent ;
And from the king of heaven is my descent.
With twice ten sail I crossed the Phrygian sea ;
Fate and my mother-goddess led my way.
Scarce seven, the thin remainders of my fleet,
From storms preserved, within your harbour meet.
Myself distressed, an exile, and unknown,

Debarred from Europe, and from Asia thrown,
In Libyan deserts wander thus alone.'
   His tender parent could no longer bear,
But, interposing, sought to soothe his care.
'Whoe'er you are—not unbeloved by Heaven,
Since on our friendly shore your ships are driven—
Have courage : to the gods permit the rest,
And to the queen expose your just request.
Now take this earnest of success for more :
Your scattered fleet is joined upon the shore ;
The winds are changed, your friends from danger free ;
Or I renounce my skill in augury.
Twelve swans behold in beauteous order move,
And stoop with closing pinions from above ;
Whom late the bird of Jove had driven along,
And through the clouds pursued the scattering throng :
Now, all united in a goodly team,
They skim the ground, and seek the quiet stream.
As they, with joy returning, clap their wings,
And ride the circuit of the skies in rings :
Not otherwise your ships, and every friend,
Already hold the port, or with swift sails descend.
No more advice is needful ; but pursue
The path before you, and the town in view.'
   Thus having said, she turned, and made appear
Her neck refulgent, and dishevelled hair,
Which, flowing from her shoulders, reached the ground,
And widely spread ambrosial scents around.
In length of train descends her sweeping gown ;
And by her graceful walk, the queen of love is known.
The prince pursued the parting deity
With words like these : 'Ah ! whither do you fly ?
Unkind and cruel ! to deceive your son
In borrowed shapes, and his embrace to shun :
Never to bless my sight but thus, unknown ;
And still to speak in accents not your own.'
Against the goddess these complaints he made,
But took the path, and her commands obeyed.
They march obscure ; for Venus kindly shrouds
With mists their persons, and involves in clouds,

That, thus unseen, their passage none might stay,
Or force to tell the causes of their way.
This part performed, the goddess flies sublime,
To visit Paphos, and her native clime;
Where garlands, ever green and ever fair,
With vows are offered, and with solemn prayer:
A hundred altars in her temples smoke:
A thousand bleeding hearts her power invoke.

They climb the next ascent, and, looking down,
Now at a nearer distance view the town.
The prince with wonder sees the stately towers
(Which late were huts, and shepherds' homely bowers),
The gates and streets; and hears from every part
The noise and busy concourse of the mart.
The toiling Tyrians on each other call,
To ply their labour: some extend the wall;
Some build the citadel; the brawny throng
Or dig, or push unwieldy stones along.
Some for their dwellings choose a spot of ground,
Which, first designed, with ditches they surround.
Some laws ordain; and some attend the choice
Of holy senates, and elect by voice.
Here some design a mole, while others there
Lay deep foundations for a theatre,
From marble quarries mighty columns hew,
For ornaments of scenes, and future view.
Such is their toil, and such their busy pains,
As exercise the bees in flowery plains,
When winter past, and summer scarce begun,
Invites them forth to labour in the sun;
Some lead their youth abroad, while some condense
Their liquid store, and some in cells dispense:
Some at the gate stand ready to receive
The golden burden, and their friends relieve:
All, with united force, combine to drive
The lazy drones from the laborious hive.
With envy stung, they view each other's deeds:
The fragrant work with diligence proceeds.
'Thrice happy you, whose walls already rise!'
Æneas said, and viewed, with lifted eyes,

Their lofty towers : then entering at the gate,
Concealed in clouds (prodigious to relate),
He mixed, unmarked, among the busy throng,
Borne by the tide, and passed unseen along.

Full in the centre of the town there stood,
Thick set with trees, a venerable wood :
The Tyrians, landing near this holy ground,
And digging here, a prosperous omen found :
From under earth a courser's head they drew,
Their growth and future fortune to foreshow :
This fated sign their foundress Juno gave,
Of a soil fruitful, and a people brave.
Sidonian Dido here with solemn state
Did Juno's temple build, and consecrate ;
Enriched with gifts, and with a golden shrine ;
But more the goddess made the place divine.
On brazen steps the marble threshold rose,
And brazen plates the cedar beams inclose :
The rafters are with brazen coverings crowned ;
The lofty doors on brazen hinges sound.
What first Æneas in this place beheld,
Revived his courage, and his fears expelled.
For, while expecting there the queen, he raised
His wondering eyes, and round the temple gazed,
Admired the fortune of the rising town,
The striving artists, and their art's renown—
He saw, in order painted on the wall,
Whatever did unhappy Troy befall :
The wars that fame around the world had blown,
All to the life, and every leader known.
There Agamemnon, Priam here, he spies,
And fierce Achilles, who both kings defies.
He stopped, and weeping said : ' O friend, e'en here
The monuments of Trojan woes appear !
Our known disasters fill e'en foreign lands :
See there, where old unhappy Priam stands !
E'en the mute walls relate the warrior's fame,
And Trojan griefs the Tyrians' pity claim.'

He said—(his tears a ready passage find)
Devouring what he saw so well designed ;

And with an empty picture fed his mind :
For there he saw the fainting Grecians yield,
And here the trembling Trojans quit the field,
Pursued by fierce Achilles through the plain,
On his high chariot driving o'er the slain.
The tents of Rhesus next his grief renew,
By their white sails betrayed to nightly view ;
And wakeful Diomede, whose cruel sword
The sentries slew, nor spared their slumbering lord ;
Then took the fiery steeds, ere yet the food
Of Troy they taste, or drink the Xanthian flood.
Elsewhere, he saw where Troïlus defied
Achilles, and unequal combat tried ;
Then, where the boy disarmed, with loosened reins,
Was by his horses hurried o'er the plains,
Hung by the neck and hair, and dragged around :
The hostile spear, yet sticking in his wound,
With tracks of blood inscribed the dusty ground.
   Meantime the Trojan dames, oppressed with woe,
To Pallas' fane in long procession go,
In hopes to reconcile their heavenly foe :
They weep ; they beat their breasts ; they rend their hair,
And rich embroidered vests for presents bear ;
But the stern goddess stands unmoved with prayer.
   Thrice round the Trojan walls Achilles drew
The corpse of Hector, whom in fight he slew.
Here Priam sues ; and there, for sums of gold,
The lifeless body of his son is sold.
So sad an object, and so well expressed,
Drew sighs and groans from the grieved hero's breast,
To see the figure of his lifeless friend,
And his old sire his helpless hands extend.
Himself he saw amidst the Grecian train,
Mixed in the bloody battle on the plain.
And swarthy Memnon in his arms he knew,
His pompous ensigns, and his Indian crew.
Penthesilea there, with haughty grace,
Leads to the wars an Amazonian race :
In their right hands a pointed dart they wield ;
The left, for ward, sustains the lunar shield.

Athwart her breast a golden belt she throws,
Amidst the press alone provokes a thousand foes,
And dares her maiden arms to manly force oppose.

Thus while the Trojan prince employs his eyes,
Fixed on the walls with wonder and surprise,
The beauteous Dido, with a numerous train,
And pomp of guards, ascends the sacred fane.
Such on Eurotas' banks, or Cynthus' height,
Diana seems ; and so she charms the sight,
When in the dance the graceful goddess leads
The choir of nymphs, and overtops their heads.
Known by her quiver, and her lofty mien,
She walks majestic, and she looks their queen :
Latona sees her shine above the rest,
And feeds with secret joy her silent breast.
Such Dido was ; with such becoming state,
Amidst the crowd, she walks serenely great.
Their labour to her future sway she speeds,
And passing with a gracious glance proceeds ;
Then mounts the throne, high placed before the shrine :
In crowds around the swarming people join.
She takes petitions, and dispenses laws,
Hears and determines every private cause ;
Their tasks in equal portions she divides,
And, where unequal, there by lot decides.

Another way by chance Æneas bends
His eyes, and unexpected sees his friends,
Antheus, Sergestus brave, Cloanthus strong,
And at their backs a mighty Trojan throng,
Whom late the tempest on the billows tossed,
And widely scattered on another coast.
The prince, unseen, surprised with wonder stands,
And longs, with joyful haste, to join their hands ;
But, doubtful of the wished event, he stays,
And from the hollow cloud his friends surveys,
Impatient, till they told their present state,
And where they left their ships, and what their fate,
And why they came, and what was their request :
For these were sent commissioned by the rest,
To sue for leave to land their sickly men,

And gain admission to the gracious queen.
Entering, with cries they filled the holy fane;
Then thus, with lowly voice, Ilioneus began:
' O queen ! indulged by favour of the gods
To found an empire in these new abodes ;
To build a town ; with statutes to restrain
The wild inhabitants beneath thy reign :
We wretched Trojans, tossed on every shore,
From sea to sea, thy clemency implore !
Forbid the fires our shipping to deface :
Receive the unhappy fugitives to grace,
And spare the remnant of a pious race !
We come not with design of wasteful prey,
To drive the country, force the swains away :
Nor such our strength, nor such is our desire:
The vanquished dare not to such thoughts aspire.
A land there is, Hesperia named of old—
The soil is fruitful, and the men are bold
(The Œnotrians held it once)—by common fame
Now called Italia, from the leader's name.
To that sweet region was our voyage bent,
When winds and every warring element
Disturbed our course, and, far from sight of land
Cast our torn vessels on the moving sand.
The sea came on ; the South, with mighty roar,
Dispersed and dashed the rest upon the rocky shore.
Those few you see, escaped the storm, and fear
(Unless you interpose) a shipwreck here.
What men, what monsters, what inhuman race,
What laws, what barbarous customs of the place,
Shut up a desert shore to drowning men,
And drive us to the cruel seas again !
If our hard fortune no compassion draws,
Nor hospitable rights, nor human laws,
The gods are just, and will revenge our cause.
   Æneas was our prince : a juster lord,
Or nobler warrior, never drew a sword :
Observant of the right, religious of his word.
If yet he lives, and draws this vital air,
Nor we, his friends, of safety shall despair,

Nor you, great queen, these offices repent,
Which he will equal, and perhaps augment.
We want not cities, nor Sicilian coasts,
Where king Acestes Trojan lineage boasts.
Permit our ships a shelter on your shores,
Refitted from your woods with planks and oars,
That, if our prince be safe, we may renew
Our destined course, and Italy pursue.
But if, O best of men ! the Fates ordain
That thou art swallowed in the Libyan main,
And if our young Iülus be no more,
Dismiss our navy from your friendly shore,
That we to good Acestes may return,
And with our friends our common losses mourn.'

   Thus spoke Ilioneus : the Trojan crew
With cries and clamours his request renew.
The modest queen awhile, with downcast eyes,
Pondered the speech, then briefly thus replies :
'Trojans ! dismiss your fears : my cruel fate,
And doubts attending an unsettled state,
Force me to guard my coast from foreign foes.
Who has not heard the story of your woes,
The name and fortune of your native place,
The fame and valour of the Phrygian race ?
We Tyrians are not so devoid of sense,
Nor so remote from Phœbus' influence.
Whether to Latian shores your course is bent,
Or, driven by tempests from your first intent,
You seek the good Acestes' government,
Your men shall be received, your fleet repaired,
And sail, with ships of convoy for your guard :
Or, would you stay, and join your friendly powers
To raise and to defend the Tyrian towers,
My wealth, my city, and myself, are yours.
And would to heaven, the storm you felt would bring
On Carthaginian coasts your wandering king.
My people shall, by my command, explore
The ports and creeks of every winding shore,
And towns, and wilds, and shady woods, in quest
Of so renowned, and so desired a guest.'

Raised in his mind the Trojan hero stood,
And longed to break from out his ambient cloud :
Achates found it, and thus urged his way :
' From whence, O goddess-born, this long delay?
What more can you desire, your welcome sure,
Your fleet in safety, and your friends secure?
One only wants ; and him we saw in vain
Oppose the storm, and swallowed in the main.
Orontes in his fate our forfeit paid :
The rest agrees with what your mother said.'
  Scarce had he spoken, when the cloud gave way ;
The mists flew upward, and dissolved in day.
The Trojan chief appeared in open sight,
August in visage, and serenely bright.
His mother-goddess, with her hands divine,
Had formed his curling locks, and made his temples shine,
And given his rolling eyes a sparkling grace,
And breathed a youthful vigour on his face ;
Like polished ivory, beauteous to behold,
Or Parian marble, when enchased in gold :
Thus radiant from the circling cloud he broke ;
And thus with manly modesty he spoke :
' He whom you seek am I ; by tempests tossed,
And saved from shipwreck on your Libyan coast
Presenting, gracious queen, before your throne,
A prince that owes his life to you alone :
Fair majesty ! the refuge and redress
Of those whom fate pursues, and wants oppress !
You, who your pious offices employ
To save the relics of abandoned Troy ;
Receive the shipwrecked on your friendly shore ;
With hospitable rites relieve the poor ;
Associate in your town a wandering train,
And strangers in your palace entertain.
What thanks can wretched fugitives return,
Who, scattered through the world in exile mourn?
The gods (if gods to goodness are inclined :
If acts of mercy touch their heavenly mind),
And, more than all the gods, your generous heart,
Conscious of worth, requite its own desert !

In you this age is happy, and this earth ;
And parents more than mortal gave you birth.
While rolling rivers into seas shall run,
And round the space of heaven the radiant sun ;
While trees the mountain-tops with shades supply,
Your honour, name, and praise, shall never die.
Whate'er abode my fortune has assigned,
Your image shall be present in my mind.'
Thus having said, he turned with pious haste,
And joyful his expecting friends embraced :
With his right hand Ilioneus he graced,
Sergestus with his left ; then to his breast
Cloanthus and the noble Gyas pressed ;
And so by turns descended to the rest.

The Tyrian queen stood fixed upon his face,
Pleased with his motions, ravished with his grace ;
Admired his fortunes, more admired the man ;
Then re-collected stood, and thus began :
'What fate, O goddess-born ! what angry powers
Have cast you shipwrecked on our barren shores ?
Are you the great Æneas, known to fame,
Who from celestial seed your lineage claim ?
The same Æneas, whom fair Venus bore
To famed Anchises on the Idæan shore ?
It calls into my mind, though then a child,
When Teucer came, from Salamis exiled,
And sought my father's aid, to be restored :
My father, Belus, then with fire and sword
Invaded Cyprus, made the region bare,
And, conquering, finished the successful war.
From him the Trojan siege I understood,
The Grecian chiefs, and your illustrious blood.
Your foe himself the Dardan valour praised,
And his own ancestry from Trojans raised.
Enter, my noble guest ! and you shall find,
If not a costly welcome, yet a kind :
For I myself, like you, have been distressed,
Till Heaven afforded me this place of rest :
Like you, an alien in a land unknown,
I learn to pity woes so like my own.'

She said, and to the palace led her guest;
Then offered incense, and proclaimed a feast.
Nor yet less careful for her absent friends,
Twice ten fat oxen to the ships she sends:
Besides a hundred boars, a hundred lambs,
With bleating cries, attend their milky dams;
And jars of generous wine, and spacious bowls
She gives, to cheer the sailors' drooping souls.
Now purple hangings clothe the palace-walls,
And sumptuous feasts are made in splendid halls:
On Tyrian carpets, richly wrought, they dine;
With loads of massy plate the sideboards shine,
And antique vases all of gold, embossed
(The gold itself inferior to the cost
Of curious work), where on the sides were seen
The fights and figures of illustrious men,
From their first founder to the present queen.
  The good Æneas, whose paternal care
Iülus' absence could no longer bear,
Dispatched Achates to the ships in haste,
To give a glad relation of the past,
And, fraught with precious gifts, to bring the boy,
Snatched from the ruins of unhappy Troy.
A robe of tissue, stiff with golden wire;
An upper vest, once Helen's rich attire,
From Argos by the famed adult'ress brought,
With golden flowers and winding foliage wrought:
Her mother Leda's present, when she came
To ruin Troy, and set the world on flame;
The sceptre Priam's eldest daughter bore,
Her orient necklace, and the crown she wore
Of double texture, glorious to behold:
One order set with gems, and one with gold.
Instructed thus, the wise Achates goes,
And, in his diligence, his duty shews.
  But Venus, anxious for her son's affairs,
New counsels tries, and new designs prepares:
That Cupid should assume the shape and face
Of sweet Ascanius, and the sprightly grace;
Should bring the presents, in her nephew's stead,

And in Eliza's veins the gentle poison shed :
For much she feared the Tyrians, double-tongued :
And knew the town to Juno's care belonged.
These thoughts by night her golden slumbers broke ;
And thus, alarmed, to wingèd Love she spoke :
' My son, my strength, whose mighty power alone
Controls the Thunderer on his awful throne !
To thee thy much-afflicted mother flies,
And on thy succour and thy faith relies.
Thou knowest, my son, how Jove's revengeful wife
By force and fraud, attempts thy brother's life ;
And often hast thou mourned with me his pains.
Him Dido now with blandishment detains ;
But I suspect the town where Juno reigns.
For this, 'tis needful to prevent her art,
And fire with love the proud Phœnician's heart—
A love so violent, so strong, so sure,
That neither age can change, nor art can cure.
How this may be performed, now take my mind :
Ascanius, by his father is designed
To come with presents laden, from the port,
To gratify the queen, and gain the court.
I mean to plunge the boy in pleasing sleep,
And, ravished, in Idalian bowers to keep,
Or high Cythera, that the sweet deceit
May pass unseen, and none prevent the cheat.
Take thou his form and shape.   I beg the grace
But only for a night's revolving space :
Thyself a boy, assume a boy's dissembled face ;
That when, amidst the fervour of the feast,
The Tyrian hugs and fonds thee on her breast,
And with sweet kisses in her arms constrains,
Thou mayest infuse thy venom in her veins.'
The god of love obeys, and sets aside
His bow and quiver, and his plumy pride :
He walks Iülus in his mother's sight,
And in the sweet resemblance takes delight.

The goddess then to young Ascanius flies,
And in a pleasing slumber seals his eyes :
Lulled in her lap, amidst a train of Loves,

She gently bears him to her blissful groves;
Then with a wreath of myrtle crowns his head,
And softly lays him on a flowery bed.
    Cupid meantime assumed his form and face,
Following Achates with a shorter pace,
And brought the gifts. The queen already sat
Amidst the Trojan lords, in shining state,
High on a golden bed: her princely guest
Was next her side; in order sat the rest.
Then canisters with bread are heaped on high:
The attendants water for their hands supply,
And, having washed, with silken towels dry.
Next fifty handmaids in long order bore
The censers, and with fumes the gods adore;
Then youths and virgins, twice as many, join
To place the dishes, and to serve the wine.
The Tyrian train, admitted to the feast,
Approach, and on the painted couches rest.
All on the Trojan gifts with wonder gaze,
But view the beauteous boy with more amaze:
His rosy-coloured cheeks, his radiant eyes,
His motions, voice, and shape, and all the god's disguise;
Nor pass unpraised the vest and veil divine,
Which wandering foliage and rich flowers entwine.
But far above the rest, the royal dame
(Already doomed to love's disastrous flame),
With eyes insatiate, and tumultuous joy,
Beholds the presents, and admires the boy.
The guileful god about the hero, long,
With children's play, and false embraces, hung;
Then sought the queen: she took him to her arms
With greedy pleasure, and devoured his charms.
Unhappy Dido little thought, what guest,
How dire a god she drew so near her breast.
But he, not mindless of his mother's prayer,
Works in the pliant bosom of the fair,
And moulds her heart anew, and blots her former care.
The dead is to the living love resigned;
And all Æneas enters in her mind.
    Now, when the rage of hunger was appeased,

The meat removed, and every guest was pleased,
The golden bowls with sparkling wine are crowned,
And through the palace cheerful cries resound.
From gilded roofs depending lamps display
Nocturnal beams, that emulate the day.
A golden bowl, that shone with gems divine,
The queen commanded to be crowned with wine—
The bowl that Belus used, and all the Tyrian line.
Then, silence through the hall proclaimed, she spoke:
'O hospitable Jove! we thus invoke
With solemn rites, thy sacred name and power:
Bless to both nations this auspicious hour!
So may the Trojan and the Tyrian line
In lasting concord from this day combine.
Thou, Bacchus, god of joys and friendly cheer,
And gracious Juno, both, be present here!
And you, my lords of Tyre, your vows address
To heaven with mine, to ratify the peace.'
The goblet then she took, with nectar crowned
(Sprinkling the first libations on the ground),
And raised it to her mouth with sober grace,
Then, sipping, offered to the next in place.
'Twas Bitias whom she called—a thirsty soul:
He took the challenge, and embraced the bowl,
With pleasure swilled the gold, nor ceased to draw
Till he the bottom of the brimmer saw.
The goblet goes around: Iöpas brought
His golden lyre, and sung what ancient Atlas taught—
The various labours of the wandering moon,
And whence proceed the eclipses of the sun;
The original of men and beasts; and whence
The rains arise, and fires their warmth dispense,
And fixed and erring stars dispose their influence;
What shakes the solid earth; what cause delays
The summer nights, and shortens winter days.
With peals of shouts the Tyrians praise the song;
Those peals are echoed by the Trojan throng.
The unhappy queen with talk prolonged the night,
And drank large draughts of love with vast delight:
Of Priam much inquired, of Hector more;

Then asked what arms the swarthy Memnon wore,
What troops he landed on the Trojan shore :
The steeds of Diomede varied the discourse,
And fierce Achilles, with his matchless force :
At length, as Fate and her ill stars required,
To hear the series of the war desired.
' Relate at large, my godlike guest (she said),
The Grecian stratagems, the town betrayed :
The fatal issue of so long a war,
Your flight, your wanderings, and your woes declare :
For, since on every sea, on every coast,
Your men have been distressed, your navy tossed,
Seven times the sun has either tropic viewed,
The winter banished, and the spring renewed.'

BOOK II

THE ARGUMENT

Æneas relates how the city of Troy was taken, after a ten years' siege, by the treachery of Sinon, and the stratagem of a wooden horse. He declares the fixed resolution he had taken not to survive the ruin of his country, and the various adventures he met with in the defence of it. At last, having been before advised by Hector's ghost, and now by the appearance of his mother Venus, he is prevailed upon to leave the town, and settle his household gods in another country. In order to this, he carries off his father on his shoulders, and leads his little son by the hand, his wife following him behind. When he comes to the place appointed for the general rendezvous, he finds a great confluence of people, but misses his wife, whose ghost afterwards appears to him, and tells him the land which was designed for him.

ALL were attentive to the godlike man,
When from his lofty couch he thus began :
' Great queen, what you command me to relate,
Renews the sad remembrance of our fate :
An empire from its old foundations rent,
And every woe the Trojans underwent ;
A peopled city made a desert place ;
All that I saw, and part of which I was ;
Not e'en the hardest of our foes could hear,
Nor stern Ulysses tell, without a tear.
And now the latter watch of wasting night,
And setting stars, to kindly rest invite.
But since you take such interest in our woe,
And Troy's disastrous end desire to know,
I will restrain my tears, and briefly tell
What in our last and fatal night befell.
   By destiny compelled, and in despair,

The Greeks grew weary of the tedious war,
And by Minerva's aid, a fabric reared,
Which like a steed of monstrous height appeared :
The sides were planked with pine : they feigned it made
For their return, and this the vow they paid.
Thus they pretend ; but in the hollow side,
Selected numbers of their soldiers hide :
With inward arms the dire machine they load ;
And iron bowels stuff the dark abode.
In sight of Troy lies Tenedos, an isle
(While Fortune did on Priam's empire smile)
Renowned for wealth ; but since, a faithless bay,
Where ships exposed to wind and weather lay.
There was their fleet concealed. We thought, for Greece,
Their sails were hoisted, and our fears release.
The Trojans, cooped within their walls so long,
Unbar their gates, and issue in a throng
Like swarming bees, and with delight survey
The camp deserted, where the Grecians lay :
The quarters of the several chiefs they showed :
Here Phœnix, here Achilles, made abode ;
Here joined the battles ; there the navy rode.
Part on the pile their wondering eyes employ—
The pile by Pallas raised to ruin Troy.
Thymœtes first ('tis doubtful whether hired,
Or so the Trojan destiny required)
Moved that the ramparts might be broken down,
To lodge the monster fabric in the town.
But Capys, and the rest of sounder mind,
The fatal present to the flames designed,
Or to the watery deep : at least to bore
The hollow sides, and hidden frauds explore.
The giddy vulgar, as their fancies guide,
With noise say nothing, and in parts divide.
Laocoön, followed by a numerous crowd,
Ran from the fort, and cried from far, aloud :
"O wretched countrymen ! what fury reigns ?
What more than madness has possessed your brains ?
Think you the Grecians from your coasts are gone ?
And are Ulysses' arts no better known ?

This hollow fabric either must inclose
Within its blind recess, our secret foes ;
Or 'tis an engine raised above the town
To overlook the walls, and then to batter down.
Somewhat is sure designed by fraud or force :
Trust not their presents, nor admit the horse."
Thus having said, against the steed he threw
His forceful spear, which, hissing as it flew,
Pierced through the yielding planks of jointed wood.
And trembling in the hollow belly stood.
The sides, transpierced, return a rattling sound ;
And groans of Greeks inclosed come issuing through
    the wound.
And had not Heaven the fall of Troy designed,
Or had not men been fated to be blind,
Enough was said and done t' inspire a better mind.
Then had our lances pierced the treacherous wood,
And Ilian towers and Priam's empire stood.

    Meantime, with shouts, the Trojan shepherds bring
A captive Greek in bands, before the king—
Taken, to take—who made himself their prey
To impose on their belief, and Troy betray :
Fixed on his aim, and obstinately bent
To die undaunted, or to circumvent.
About the captive, tides of Trojans flow ;
All press to see, and some insult the foe.
Now hear how well the Greeks their wiles disguised :
Behold a nation in a man comprised !
Trembling the miscreant stood : unarmed and bound,
He stared, and rolled his haggard eyes around,
Then said, "Alas ! what earth remains, what sea,
Is open to receive unhappy me ?
What fate a wretched fugitive attends,
Scorned by my foes, abandoned by my friends ?"
He said, and sighed, and cast a rueful eye :
Our pity kindles, and our passions die.
We cheer the youth to make his own defence,
And freely tell us what he was, and whence :
What news he could impart we long to know,
And what to credit from a captive foe.

His fear at length dismissed, he said, "Whate'er
My fate ordains, my words shall be sincere;
I neither can nor dare my birth disclaim;
Greece is my country, Sinon is my name:
Though plunged by Fortune's power in misery,
'Tis not in Fortune's power to make me lie.
If any chance has hither brought the name
Of Palamedes, not unknown to fame,
Who suffered from the malice of the times,
Accused and sentenced for pretended crimes,
Because these fatal wars he would prevent:
Whose death the wretched Greeks too late lament.
Me, then a boy, my father, poor and bare
Of other means, committed to his care,
His kinsman and companion in the war.
While fortune favoured, while his arms support
The cause, and ruled the counsels of the court,
I made some figure there; nor was my name
Obscure, nor I without my share of fame.
But when Ulysses, with fallacious arts,
Had made impression in the people's hearts,
And forged a treason in my patron's name
(I speak of things too far divulged by fame),
My kinsman fell. Then I, without support,
In private mourned his loss, and left the court.
Mad as I was, I could not bear his fate
With silent grief, but loudly blamed the state,
And cursed the direful author of my woes.—
'Twas told again; and hence my ruin rose.
I threatened, if indulgent Heaven once more
Would land me safely on my native shore,
His death with double vengeance to restore.
This moved the murderer's hate; and soon ensued
The effects of malice from a man so proud.
Ambiguous rumours through the camp he spread,
And sought, by treason, my devoted head;
New crimes invented; left unturned no stone,
To make my guilt appear, and hide his own;
Till Calchas was by force and threatening wrought—
But why—why dwell I on that anxious thought?

If on my nation just revenge you seek.
(And 'tis to appear a foe, to appear a Greek);
Already you my name and country know:
Assuage your thirst of blood, and strike the blow:
My death will both the kingly brothers please,
And set insatiate Ithacus at ease."
This fair unfinished tale, these broken starts,
Raised expectations in our longing hearts;
Unknowing as we were in Grecian arts.
His former trembling once again renewed,
With acted fear, the villain thus pursued:
" Long had the Grecians (tired with fruitless care
And wearied with an unsuccessful war)
Resolved to raise the siege, and leave the town;
And had the gods permitted, they had gone.
But oft the wintry seas, and southern winds,
Withstood their passage home, and changed their minds,
Portents and prodigies their souls amazed;
But most, when this stupendous pile was raised;
Then flaming meteors, hung in air, were seen,
And thunders rattled through a sky serene.
Dismayed, and fearful of some dire event,
Eurypylus, to inquire their fate, was sent.
He from the gods this dreadful answer brought:
' O Grecians, when the Trojan shores you sought,
Your passage with a virgin's blood was bought:
So must your safe return be bought again,
And Grecian blood once more atone the main.'
The spreading rumour round the people ran;
All feared, and each believed himself the man.
Ulysses took the advantage of their fright;
Called Calchas, and produced in open sight;
Then bade him name the wretch, ordained by fate
The public victim, to redeem the state.
Already some presaged the dire event,
And saw what sacrifice Ulysses meant.
For twice five days, the good old seer withstood
The intended treason, and was dumb to blood,
Till, tired with endless clamours and pursuit
Of Ithacus, he stood no longer mute,

But, as it was agreed, pronounced that I
Was destined by the wrathful gods to die.
All praised the sentence, pleased the storm should fall
On one alone, whose fury threatened all.
The dismal day was come ; the priests prepare
Their leavened cakes, and fillets for my hair.
I followed nature's laws, and must avow,
I broke my bonds, and fled the fatal blow.
Hid in a weedy lake all night I lay,
Secure of safety when they sailed away.
But now, what further hopes for me remain
To see my friends, or native soil again ;
My tender infants, or my careful sire,
Whom they, returning, will to death require ;
Will perpetrate on them their first design,
And take the forfeit of their heads for mine ?
Which, O ! if pity mortal minds can move,
If there be faith below, or gods above,
If innocence and truth can claim desert,
Ye Trojans, from an injured wretch avert !"
   False tears true pity move : the king commands
To loose his fetters, and unbind his hands ;
Then adds these friendly words : " Dismiss thy fears ;
Forget the Greeks ; be mine as thou wert theirs ;
But truly tell, was it for force or guile,
Or some religious end, you raised the pile ?"
Thus said the king. He, full of fraudful arts,
This well-invented tale for truth imparts :
" Ye lamps of heaven ! (he said, and lifted high
His hands, now free) Thou venerable sky !
Inviolable powers, adored with dread !
Ye fatal fillets, that once bound this head !
Ye sacred altars, from whose flames I fled !
Be all of you adjured ; and grant I may
Without a crime, the ungrateful Greeks betray,
Reveal the secrets of the guilty state,
And justly punish whom I justly hate !
But you, O king ! preserve the faith you gave,
If I to save myself, your empire save.
The Grecian hopes, and all the attempts they made.

Were only founded on Minerva's aid.
But from the time when impious Diomede,
And false Ulysses, that inventive head,
Her fatal image from the temple drew,
The sleeping guardians of the castle slew,
Her virgin statue with their bloody hands
Polluted, and profaned her holy bands;
From thence the tide of fortune left their shore,
And ebbed much faster than it flowed before:
Their courage languished, as their hopes decayed;
And Pallas, now averse, refused her aid.
Nor did the goddess doubtfully declare
Her altered mind, and alienated care.
When first her fatal image touched the ground,
She sternly cast her glaring eyes around,
That sparkled as they rolled, and seemed to threat:
Her heavenly limbs distilled a briny sweat.
Thrice from the ground she leaped, was seen to wield
Her brandished lance, and shake her horrid shield.
Then Calchas bade our host for flight prepare,
And hope no conquest from the tedious war,
Till first they sailed for Greece; with prayers besought
Her injured power, and better omens brought.
And now their navy ploughs the watery main,
Yet soon expect it on your shores again,
With Pallas pleased; as Calchas did ordain.
But first, to reconcile the blue-eyed maid
For her stolen statue and her tower betrayed,
Warned by the seer, to her offended name
We raised and dedicate this wondrous frame,
So lofty, lest through your forbidden gates
It pass, and intercept our better fates:
For, once admitted there, our hopes are lost;
And Troy may then a new Palladium boast:
For so religion and the gods ordain,
That, if you violate with hands profane
Minerva's gift, your town in flames shall burn;
(Which omen, O ye gods, on Græcia turn!)
But if it climb, with your assisting hands,
The Trojan walls, and in the city stands;

Then Troy shall Argos and Mycenæ burn,
And the reverse of fate on us return."
  With such deceits he gained their easy hearts,
Too prone to credit his perfidious arts.
What Diomede, nor Thetis' greater son,
A thousand ships, nor ten years' siege, had done—
False tears and fawning words the city won.
  A greater omen, and of worse portent,
Did our unwary minds with fear torment,
Concurring to produce the dire event.
Laocoön, Neptune's priest by lot that year,
With solemn pomp then sacrificed a steer ;
When (dreadful to behold !) from sea we spied
Two serpents, ranked abreast, the seas divide,
And smoothly sweep along the swelling tide.
Their flaming crests above the waves they shew ;
Their bellies seem to burn the seas below ;
Their speckled tails advance to steer their course,
And on the sounding shore the flying billows force.
And now the strand, and now the plain, they held :
Their ardent eyes with bloody streaks were filled ;
Their nimble tongues they brandished as they came,
And licked their hissing jaws, that sputtered flame.
We fled amazed ; their destined way they take,
And to Laocoön and his children make :
And first around the tender boys they wind,
Then with their sharpened fangs their limbs and bodies
    grind.
The wretched father, running to their aid
With pious haste, but vain, they next invade :
Twice round his waist their winding volumes rolled ;
And twice about his gasping throat they fold.
The priest thus doubly choked—their crests divide,
And towering o'er his head in triumph ride.
With both his hands he labours at the knots ;
His holy fillets the blue venom blots ;
His roaring fills the flitting air around.
Thus, when an ox receives a glancing wound,
He breaks his bands, the fatal altar flies,
And with loud bellowings breaks the yielding skies.

Their tasks performed, the serpents quit their prey,
And to the tower of Pallas make their way :
Couched at her feet they lie, protected there
By her large buckler, and protended spear.
   Amazement seizes all : the general cry
Proclaims Laocoön justly doomed to die,
Whose hand the will of Pallas had withstood,
And dared to violate the sacred wood.
All vote to admit the steed ; that vows be paid,
And incense offered, to the offended maid.
A spacious breach is made : the town lies bare :
Some hoisting-levers, some the wheels prepare,
And fasten to the horse's feet : the rest
With cables haul along the unwieldy beast.
Each on his fellow for assistance calls :
At length, the fatal fabric mounts the walls,
Big with destruction. Boys with chaplets crowned,
And choirs of virgins, sing and dance around.
Thus raised aloft, and then descending down,
It enters o'er our heads, and threats the town.
O sacred city, built by hands divine !
O valiant heroes of the Trojan line !
Four times he struck : as oft the clashing sound
Of arms was heard, and inward groans rebound.
Yet mad with zeal, and blinded with our fate,
We haul along the horse in solemn state ;
Then place the dire portent within the tower.
Cassandra cried, and cursed the unhappy hour ;
Foretold our fate ; but, by the god's decree,
All heard, and none believed the prophecy.
With branches we the fanes adorn, and waste
In jollity the day ordained to be the last.
   Meantime the rapid heavens rolled down the light,
And on the shaded ocean rushed the night :
Our men, secure, nor guards nor sentries held ;
But easy sleep their weary limbs compelled.
The Grecians had embarked their naval powers
From Tenedos, and sought our well-known shores,
Safe under covert of the silent night,
And guided by the imperial galley's light ;

When Sinon, favoured by the partial gods,
Unlocked the horse, and oped his dark abodes;
Restored to vital air our hidden foes,
Who joyful from their long confinement rose.
Thessander bold, and Sthenelus their guide,
And dire Ulysses, down the cable slide:
Then Thoas, Athamas, and Pyrrhus, haste;
Nor was the Podalirian hero last,
Nor injured Menelaüs, nor the famed
Epeus, who the fatal engine framed.
A nameless crowd succeed; their forces join
To invade the town, oppressed with sleep and wine.
Those few they find awake, first meet their fate;
Then to their fellows they unbar the gate.

'Twas in the dead of night, when sleep repairs
Our bodies, worn with toils, our minds, with cares,
When Hector's ghost before my sight appears:
A bloody shroud he seemed, and bathed in tears;
Such as he was, when, by Pelides slain,
Thessalian coursers dragged him o'er the plain.
Swoln were his feet, as when the thongs were thrust
Through the bored holes: his body black with
          dust:
Unlike that Hector who returned from toils
Of war, triumphant in Æacian spoils;
Or him, who made the fainting Greeks retire,
And launched against their navy Phrygian fire.
His hair and beard stood stiffened with his gore;
And all the wounds he for his country bore
Now streamed afresh, and with new purple ran.
I wept to see the visionary man,
And, while my trance continued, thus began:
"O light of Trojans, and support of Troy,
Thy father's champion, and thy country's joy!
O, long expected by thy friends! from whence
Art thou so late returned for our defence?
Do we behold thee, wearied as we are
With length of labours, and with toils of war?
After so many funerals of thy own,
Art thou restored to thy declining town?

But say, what wounds are these? what new disgrace
Deforms the manly features of thy face?"
  To this, the spectre no reply did frame,
But answered to the cause for which he came;
And, groaning from the bottom of his breast,
This warning, in these mournful words, expressed:
"O goddess-born! escape, by timely flight,
The flames and horrors of this fatal night.
The foes already have possessed the wall:
Troy nods from high, and totters to her fall.
Enough is paid to Priam's royal name,
More than enough to duty and to fame.
If by a mortal hand my father's throne
Could be defended, 'twas by mine alone.
Now Troy to thee commends her future state,
And gives her gods companions of thy fate;
From their assistance, happier walls expect,
Which wand'ring long, at last thou shalt erect."
He said, and brought me, from their blest abodes,
The venerable statues of the gods;
With ancient Vesta from the sacred choir,
The wreaths and relics of the immortal fire.
  Now peals of shouts came thundering from afar,
Cries, threats, and loud laments, and mingled war:
The noise approaches, though our palace stood
Aloof from streets, encompassed with a wood.
Louder, and yet more loud, I hear the alarms
Of human cries, distinct, and clashing arms.
Fear broke my slumbers; I no longer stay,
But mount the terrace, thence the town survey,
And hearken, what the frightful sounds convey.
Thus, when a flood of fire by wind is borne,
Crackling it rolls, and mows the standing corn;
Or deluges, descending on the plains,
Sweep o'er the yellow year, destroy the pains
Of lab'ring oxen, and the peasant's gains;
Unroot the forest oaks, and bear away
Flocks, folds, and trees, an undistinguished prey:
The shepherd climbs the cliff, and sees from far
The wasteful ravage of the watery war.

Then Hector's faith was manifestly cleared ;
And Grecian frauds in open light appeared.
The palace of Deïphobus ascends
In smoky flames, and catches on his friends'.
Ucalegon's burns next : the seas are bright
With splendour not their own, and shine with Trojan light.
New clamours and new clangours now arise,
The sound of trumpets mixed with fighting-cries.
With frenzy seized, I run to meet the alarms,
Resolved on death, resolved to die in arms,
But first to gather friends, with them to oppose
(If fortune favoured) and repel the foes :
Spurred by my courage, by my country fired
With sense of honour, and revenge inspired.

Panthus, Apollo's priest, a sacred name,
Had 'scaped the Grecian swords and passed the flame.
With relics laden, to my doors he fled,
And by the hand his tender grandson led.
"What hope, O Panthus ! whither can we run ?
Where make a stand ? and what may yet be done ?"
Scarce had I said, when Panthus, with a groan :
"Troy is no more, and Ilium was a town !
The fatal day, the appointed hour is come,
When wrathful Jove's irrevocable doom
Transfers the Trojan state to Grecian hands.
The fire consumes the town, the foe commands ;
And armed hosts, an unexpected force,
Break from the bowels of the fatal horse.
Within the gates, proud Sinon throws about
The flames ; and foes, for entrance press without,
With thousand others, whom I fear to name,
More than from Argos or Mycenæ came.
To several posts their parties they divide :
Some block the narrow streets, some scour the wide,
The bold they kill, the unwary they surprise ;
Who fights finds death, and death finds him who flies.
The warders of the gate but scarce maintain
The unequal combat, and resist in vain."

I heard ; and heaven, that well-born souls inspires,
Prompts me, through lifted swords and rising fires,

To run, where clashing arms and clamour calls,
And rush undaunted to defend the walls.
Ripheus and Iphitus by my side engage ;
For valour one renowned, and one for age.
Dymas and Hypanis by moonlight knew
My motions and my mien, and to my party drew ;
With young Chorœbus, who by love was led
To win renown, and fair Cassandra's bed ;
And lately brought his troops to Priam's aid,
Forewarned in vain by the prophetic maid ;
Whom when I saw resolved in arms to fall,
And that one spirit animated all,
" Brave souls ! (said I) but brave, alas ! in vain ;
Come, finish what our cruel fates ordain :
You see the desperate state of our affairs ;
And Heaven's protecting powers are deaf to prayers.
The passive gods behold the Greeks defile
Their temples, and abandon to the spoil
Their own abodes : we, feeble few, conspire
To save a sinking town, involved in fire.
Then let us fall, but fall amidst our foes :
Despair of life the means of living shows."
So bold a speech encouraged their desire
Of death, and added fuel to their fire.

As hungry wolves, with raging appetite,
Scour through the fields, nor fear the stormy night ·
Their whelps at home expect the promised food,
And long to temper their dry chaps in blood :
So rushed we forth at once : resolved to die,
Resolved, in death, the last extremes to try,
We leave the narrow lanes behind, and dare
The unequal combat in the public square :
Night was our friend ; our leader was despair.
What tongue can tell the slaughter of that night?
What eyes can weep the sorrows and affright?
An ancient and imperial city falls ;
The streets are filled with frequent funerals ;
Houses and holy temples float in blood ;
And hostile nations make a common flood.
Not only Trojans fall ; but, in their turn,

The vanquished triumph, and the victors mourn.
Ours take new courage from despair and night .
Confused the fortune is, confused the fight.
All parts resound with tumults, plaints, and fears ;
And grisly death in sundry shapes appears.
    Androgeos fell among us, with his band,
Who thought us Grecians newly come to land.
" From whence (said he), my friends, this long delay?
You loiter, while the spoils are borne away :
Our ships are laden with the Trojan store ;
And you, like truants, come too late ashore."
He said, but soon corrected his mistake,
Found by the doubtful answers which we make.
Amazed, he would have shunned the unequal fight ;
But we, more numerous, intercept his flight.
As when some peasant in a bushy brake
Has with unwary footing pressed a snake,
He starts aside, astonished, when he spies
His rising crest, blue neck, and rolling eyes.
So, from our arms, surprised Androgeos flies
In vain ; for him and his we compass round,
Possessed with fear, unknowing of the ground,
And of their lives an easy conquest found.
Thus fortune on our first endeavour smiled.
    Chorœbus then, with youthful hopes beguiled,
Swoln with success, and of a daring mind,
This new invention fatally designed
" My friends (said he), since fortune shews the way,
'Tis fit we should the auspicious guide obey ;
For what has she those Grecian arms bestowed,
But their destruction, and the Trojans' good ?
Then change we shields, and their devices bear :
Let fraud supply the want of force in war.
They find us arms."   This said, himself he dressed
In dead Androgeos' spoils, his upper vest,
His painted buckler, and his plumy crest.
Thus Ripheus, Dymas, all the Trojan train,
Lay down their own attire, and strip the slain.
Mixed with the Greeks, we go with ill presage,
Flattered with hopes to glut our greedy rage ;

Unknown, assaulting whom we blindly meet,
And strew with Grecian carcases, the street.
Thus while their straggling parties we defeat,
Some to the shore and safer ships retreat ;
And some, oppressed with more ignoble fear,
Remount the hollow horse, and pant in secret there.
   But ah ! what use of valour can be made,
When heaven's propitious powers refuse their aid ?
Behold the royal prophetess, the fair
Cassandra, dragged by her dishevelled hair ;
Whom not Minerva's shrine, nor sacred bands,
In safety could protect from sacrilegious hands.
On heaven she cast her eyes, she sighed, she cried—
'Twas all she could—her tender arms were tied.
So sad a sight Choroebus could not bear ;
But, fired with rage, distracted with despair,
Amid the barbarous ravishers he flew :
Our leader's rash example we pursue.
But storms of stones, from the proud temple's height
Pour down, and on our battered helms alight :
We from our friends received this fatal blow,
Who thought us Grecians, as we seemed in show.
They aim at the mistaken crests, from high ;
And ours beneath the ponderous ruin lie.
Then, moved with anger and disdain, to see
Their troops dispersed, the royal virgin free,
The Grecians rally, and their powers unite,
With fury charge us, and renew the fight.
The brother-kings with Ajax join their force,
And the whole squadron of Thessalian horse.
   Thus, when the rival winds their quarrel try,
Contending for the empire of the sky,
South, East, and West, on airy coursers borne :
The whirlwind gathers, and the woods are torn :
Then Nereus strikes the deep : the billows rise,
And, mixed with ooze and sand, pollute the skies.
The troops we squandered first, again appear
From several quarters, and inclose the rear.
They first observe, and to the rest betray
Our different speech : our borrowed arms survey.

Oppressed with odds, we fall ; Chorœbus first,
At Pallas' altar, by Peneleus pierced.
Then Ripheus followed, in the unequal fight ;
Just of his word, observant of the right :
Heaven thought not so.   Dymas their fate attends,
With Hypanis, mistaken by their friends.
Nor, Panthus, thee, thy mitre nor the bands
Of awful Phœbus, saved from impious hands.
Ye Trojan flames ! your testimony bear,
What I performed and what I suffered there ;
No sword avoiding in the fatal strife,
Exposed to death, and prodigal of life.
Witness ye heavens ! I live not by my fault :
I strove to have deserved the death I sought.
But when I could not fight, and would have died ;
Borne off to distance by the growing tide,
Old Iphitus and I were hurried thence,
With Pelias, wounded, and without defence.
New clamours from the invested palace ring :
We run to die, or disengage the king.
So hot the assault, so high the tumult rose,
While ours defend, and while the Greeks oppose,
As all the Dardan and Argolic race
Has been contracted in that narrow space ;
Or, as all Ilium else were void of fear,
And tumult, war, and slaughter, only there.
Their targets in a tortoise cast, the foes,
Secure advancing, to the turrets rose :
Some mount the scaling ladders ; some, more bold,
Swerve upwards, and by posts and pillars hold :
Their left hand gripes their bucklers in the ascent,
While with the right they seize the battlement.
From the demolished towers, the Trojans throw
Huge heaps of stones, that, falling, crush the foe :
And heavy beams and rafters from the sides
(Such arms their last necessity provides !)
And gilded roofs, come tumbling from on high,
The marks of state and ancient royalty.
The guards below, fixed in the pass, attend
The charge, undaunted, and the gate defend.

Renewed in courage with recovered breath,
A second time we ran to tempt our death,
To clear the palace from the foe, succeed
The weary living, and revenge the dead.

A postern-door, yet unobserved and free,
Joined by the length of a blind gallery,
To the king's closet led (a way well-known
To Hector's wife, while Priam held the throne—
Through which she brought Astyanax, unseen,
To cheer his grandsire, and his grandsire's queen).
Through this we pass, and mount the tower, from whence
With unavailing arms the Trojans make defence.
From this the trembling king had oft descried
The Grecian camp, and saw their navy ride.
Beams from its lofty height with swords we hew,
Then, wrenching with our hands, the assault renew,
And where the rafters on the columns meet,
We push them headlong with our arms and feet.
The lightning flies not swifter than the fall;
Nor thunder louder than the ruined wall:
Down goes the top at once: the Greeks beneath
Are piecemeal torn, or pounded into death.
Yet more succeed, and more to death are sent:
We cease not from above, nor they below relent.

Before the gate stood Pyrrhus, threatening loud,
With glittering arms conspicuous in the crowd.
So shines, renewed in youth, the crested snake
Who slept the winter in a thorny brake,
And casting off his slough when spring returns,
Now looks aloft, and with new glory burns,
Restored with poisonous herbs; his ardent sides
Reflect the sun; and, raised on spires, he rides
High o'er the grass: hissing he rolls along,
And brandishes by fits his forky tongue.
Proud Periphas, and fierce Automedon,
His father's charioteer, together run
To force the gate: the Scyrian infantry
Rush on in crowds, and the barred passage free.
Entering the court, with shouts the skies they rend,
And flaming firebrands to the roofs ascend.

Himself, among the foremost, deals his blows,
And with his axe repeated strokes bestows
On the strong doors : then all their shoulders ply,
Till from the posts the brazen hinges fly.
He hews apace : the double bars at length
Yield to his axe, and unresisted strength.
A mighty breach is made ; the rooms concealed,
Appear, and all the palace is revealed :
The halls of audience, and of public state,
And where the lonely queen in secret sat.
  Armed soldiers now by trembling maids are seen,
With not a door, and scarce a space between.
The house is filled with loud laments and cries ;
And shrieks of women rend the vaulted skies.
The fearful matrons run from place to place,
And kiss the thresholds, and the posts embrace.
The fatal work inhuman Pyrrhus plies ;
And all his father sparkles in his eyes.
No bars nor fighting guards his force sustain :
The bars are broken, and the guards are slain.
In rush the Greeks, and all the apartments fill ;
Those few defendants whom they find, they kill.
Not with so fierce a rage, the foaming flood
Roars when he finds his rapid course withstood,
Bears down the dams with unresisted sway,
And sweeps the cattle and the cots away.
These eyes beheld him when he marched between
The brother-kings : I saw the unhappy queen,
The hundred wives, and where old Priam stood,
To stain his hallowed altar with his blood.
The fifty nuptial beds (such hopes had he,
So large a promise of a progeny),
The posts of plated gold, and hung with spoils.
Fell the reward of the proud victor's toils.
Where'er the raging fire had left a space,
The Grecians enter, and possess the place.
  Perhaps you may of Priam's fate inquire.
He, when he saw his regal town on fire,
His ruined palace, and his entering foes,
On every side, inevitable woes :

In arms disused invests his limbs, decayed
Like them with age : a late and useless aid.
His feeble shoulders scarce the weight sustain :
Loaded, not armed, he creeps along with pain,
Despairing of success, ambitious to be slain !
Uncovered but by heaven, there stood in view
An altar : near the hearth a laurel grew,
Doddered with age, whose boughs encompass round
The household gods, and shade the holy ground.
Here Hecuba, with all her helpless train
Of dames, for shelter sought, but sought in vain.
Driven like a flock of doves along the sky,
Their images they hug, and to their altars fly.
The queen, when she beheld her trembling lord,
And hanging by his side a heavy sword :
" What rage (she cried) has seized my husband's mind ?
What arms are these, and to what use designed ?
These times want other aids ! Were Hector here,
E'en Hector now in vain, like Priam, would appear.
With us, one common shelter thou shalt find,
Or in one common fate with us be joined."
She said, and with a last salute embraced
The poor old man, and by the laurel placed.
Behold ! Polites, one of Priam's sons,
Pursued by Pyrrhus, there for safety runs.
Through swords and foes, amazed and hurt, he flies
Through empty courts, and open galleries.
Him Pyrrhus, urging with his lance, pursues,
And often reaches, and his thrusts renews.
The youth, transfixed, with lamentable cries
Expires before his wretched parents' eyes :
Whom gasping at his feet when Priam saw,
The fear of death gave place to Nature's law ;
And, shaking more with anger than with age :
" The gods (said he) requite thy brutal rage !
(As sure they will, barbarian, sure they must,
If there be gods in heaven, and gods be just)
Who takest in wrongs an insolent delight ;
With a son's death to infect a father's sight.
Not he, whom thou and lying fame conspire

To call thee his—not he, thy vaunted sire
Thus used my wretched age : the gods he feared,
The laws of nature and of nations heard.
He cheered my sorrows, and, for sums of gold,
The bloodless carcase of my Hector sold ;
Pitied the woes a parent underwent,
And sent me back in safety from his tent."

    This said, his feeble hand a javelin threw,
Which, fluttering, seemed to loiter as it flew :
Just, and but barely, to the mark it held,
And faintly tinkled on the brazen shield.

    Then Pyrrhus thus : " Go thou from me to fate,
And to my father my foul deeds relate.
Now die !"   With that he dragged the trembling sire,
Sliddering through clottered blood and holy mire
(The mingled paste his murdered son had made),
Hauled from beneath the violated shade,
And on the sacred pile the royal victim laid.
His right hand held his bloody falchion bare ;
His left he twisted in his hoary hair ;
Then, with a speeding thrust his heart he found :
The lukewarm blood came rushing through the wound,
And sanguine streams distained the sacred ground.
Thus Priam fell, and shared one common fate
With Troy in ashes, and his ruined state :
He, who the sceptre of all Asia swayed,
Whom monarchs like domestic slaves obeyed !
On the bleak shore now lies the abandoned king,
A headless carcase, and a nameless thing !

    Then, not before, I felt my curdled blood
Congealed with fear ; my hair with horror stood :
My father's image filled my pious mind,
Lest equal years might equal fortune find.
Again I thought on my forsaken wife,
And trembled for my son's abandoned life.
I looked about, but found myself alone,
Deserted at my need !   My friends were gone !
Some spent with toil, some with despair oppressed
Leaped headlong from the heights ; the flames consumed
    the rest

Thus, wandering in my way without a guide,
The graceless Helen in the porch I spied
Of Vesta's temple ; there she lurked alone ;
Muffled she sat, and what she could, unknown ;
But by the flames that cast their blaze around,
That common bane of Greece and Troy I found :
For Ilium burnt, she dreads the Trojan sword ;
More dreads the vengeance of her injured lord :
E'en by those gods who refuged her, abhorred.
Trembling with rage, the strumpet I regard,
Resolved to give her guilt the due reward.
"Shall she triumphant sail before the wind,
And leave in flames unhappy Troy behind ?
Shall she her kingdom and her friends review,
In state attended with a captive crew,
While unrevenged the good old Priam falls,
And Grecian fires consume the Trojan walls ?
For this the Phrygian fields and Xanthian flood
Were swelled with bodies, and were drunk with blood !
'Tis true, a soldier can small honour gain,
And boast no conquest from a woman slain ;
Yet shall the fact not pass without applause,
Of vengeance taken in so just a cause.
The punished crime shall set my soul at ease,
And murmuring manes of my friends appease."

    Thus while I rave, a gleam of pleasing light
Spread o'er the place ; and, shining heavenly bright,
My mother stood revealed before my sight
(Never so radiant did her eyes appear ;
Not her own star confessed a light so clear) :
Great in her charms, as when on gods above
She looks, and breathes herself into their love.
She held my hand, the destined blow to break ;
Then from her rosy lips began to speak :
"My son ! from whence this madness, this neglect
Of my commands, and those whom I protect ?
Why this unmanly rage ?   Recall to mind
Whom you forsake, what pledges leave behind.
Look if your helpless father yet survive,
Or if Ascanius or Creüsa live.

Around your house the greedy Grecians err;
And these had perished in the nightly war
But for my presence, and protecting care.
Not Helen's face, nor Paris, was in fault;
But by the gods was this destruction brought.
Now cast your eyes around, while I dissolve
The mists and films that mortal eyes involve,
Purge from your sight the dross, and make you see
The shape of each avenging deity.
Enlightened thus, my just commands fulfil,
Nor fear obedience to your mother's will.
Where yon disordered heap of ruin lies,
Stones rent from stones—where clouds of dust arise,—
Amid that smother, Neptune holds his place,
Below the wall's foundation drives his mace,
And heaves the building from the solid base.
Look! where in arms, imperial Juno stands,
Full in the Scæan gate, with loud commands
Urging on shore the tardy Grecian bands.
See! Pallas, of her snaky buckler proud,
Bestrides the tower, refulgent through the cloud:
See! Jove new courage to the foe supplies,
And arms against the town the partial deities.
Haste hence, my son! this fruitless labour end:
Haste! where your trembling spouse and sire attend:
Haste! and a mother's care your passage shall befriend."
She said, and swiftly vanished from my sight,
Obscure in clouds, and gloomy shades of night.

I looked, I listened! dreadful sounds I hear;
And the dire forms of hostile gods appear,
Troy sunk in flames I saw (nor could prevent),
And Ilium from its old foundations rent—
Rent like a mountain-ash, which dared the winds,
And stood the sturdy strokes of labouring hinds.
About the roots the cruel axe resounds;
The stumps are pierced with oft-repeated wounds:
The war is felt on high; the nodding crown
Now threats a fall, and throws the leafy honours down.
To their united force it yields, though late,
And mourns with mortal groans the approaching fate:

The roots no more their upper load sustain ;
But down she falls, and spreads a ruin through the plain.
  Descending thence, I 'scape through foes and fire :
Before the goddess, foes and flames retire.
Arrived at home, he, for whose only sake,
Or most for his, such toils I undertake—
The good Anchises—whom, by timely flight,
I purposed to secure on Ida's height—
Refused the journey, resolute to die,
And add his funerals to the fate of Troy,
Rather than exile and old age sustain.
" Go you, whose blood runs warm in every vein.
Had heaven decreed that I should life enjoy,
Heaven had decreed to save unhappy Troy.
'Tis, sure, enough, if not too much, for one,
Twice to have seen our Ilium overthrown.
Make haste to save the poor remaining crew ;
And give this useless corpse a long adieu.
These weak old hands suffice to stop my breath :
At least the pitying foes will aid my death,
To take my spoils, and leave my body bare :
As for my sepulchre, let Heaven take care.
'Tis long since I, for my celestial wife
Loathed by the gods, have dragged a lingering life ;
Since every hour and moment I expire,
Blasted from heaven by Jove's avenging fire."
This oft repeated, he stood fixed to die :
Myself, my wife, my son, my family,
Intreat, pray, beg, and raise a doleful cry—
" What ! will he still persist, on death resolve,
And in his ruin all his house involve ?"
He still persists his reasons to maintain ;
Our prayers, our tears, our loud laments are vain.
  Urged by despair, again I go to try
The fate of arms, resolved in fight to die.
What hope remains, but what my death must give ?
" Can I without so dear a father, live ?
You term it prudence, what I baseness call :
Could such a word from such a parent fall ?
If fortune please, and so the gods ordain,

That nothing should of ruined Troy remain,
And you conspire with fortune to be slain ;
The way to death is wide, the approaches near ;
For soon relentless Pyrrhus will appear,
Reeking with Priam's blood—the wretch who slew
The son (inhuman) in the father's view ;
And then the sire himself to the dire altar drew.
O goddess mother ! give me back to fate ;
Your gift was undesired, and came too late.
Did you, for this, unhappy me convey
Through foes and fires, to see my house a prey !
Shall I my father, wife, and son, behold
Weltering in blood, each other's arms infold ?
Haste ! gird my sword, though spent and overcome;
'Tis the last summons to receive our doom.
I hear thee, fate ! and I obey thy call !
Not unrevenged the foe shall see my fall.
Restore me to the yet unfinished fight :
My death is wanting to conclude the night."
Armed once again, my glittering sword I wield,
While the other hand sustains my weighty shield ;
And forth I rush to seek the abandoned field.
I went ; but sad Creüsa stopped my way,
And 'cross the threshold in my passage lay,
Embraced my knees, and, when I would have gone,
Shewed me my feeble sire, and tender son.
" If death be your design—at least (said she)
Take us along, to share your destiny.
If any farther hopes in arms remain,
This place, these pledges of your love, maintain.
To whom do you expose your father's life,
Your son's, and mine, your now forgotten wife ?"
    While thus she fills the house with clamorous cries,
Our hearing is diverted by our eyes :
For, while I held my son, in the short space
Betwixt our kisses and our last embrace,
(Strange to relate !) from young Iülus' head
A lambent flame arose, which gently spread
Around his brows, and on his temples fed.
Amazed, with running water we prepare

To quench the sacred fire, and slake his hair ;
But old Anchises, versed in omens, reared
His hands to heaven, and this request preferred :
" If any vows, almighty Jove, can bend
Thy will, if piety can prayers commend ;
Confirm the glad presage which thou art pleased to send."
Scarce had he said, when on our left we hear
A peal of rattling thunder roll in air :
There shot a streaming lamp along the sky,
Which on the wingèd lightning seemed to fly ;
From o'er the roof the blaze began to move,
And, trailing, vanished in the Idean grove.
It swept a path in heaven, and shone a guide,
Then in a steaming stench of sulphur died.

The good old man with suppliant hands implored
The gods' protection, and their star adored.
" Now, now (said he), my son, no more delay !
I yield, I follow where heaven shows the way.
Keep (O my country gods !) our dwelling-place,
And guard the relic of this Trojan race,
This tender child !—These omens are your own ;
And you can yet restore the ruined town.
At least accomplish what your signs foreshow :
I stand resigned, and am prepared to go."

He said ; the crackling flames appear on high,
And driving sparkles dance along the sky ;
With Vulcan's rage the rising winds conspire,
And near our palace roll the flood of fire.
" Haste, my dear father ! ('tis no time to wait)
And load my shoulders with a willing freight.
Whate'er befalls, your life shall be my care ;
One death, or one deliverance we will share.
My hand shall lead our little son ; and you,
My faithful consort, shall our steps pursue.
Next, you my servants, heed my strict commands :
Without the walls a ruined temple stands,
To Ceres hallowed once : a cypress nigh
Shoots up her venerable head on high,
By long religion kept : there bend your feet ;
And in divided parties let us meet.

Our country gods, the relics, and the bands,
Hold you, my father, in your guiltless hands:
In me 'tis impious, holy things to bear,
Red as I am with slaughter, new from war,
Till in some living stream I cleanse the guilt
Of dire debate, and blood in battle spilt."
Thus, ordering all that prudence could provide,
I clothe my shoulders with a lion's hide
And yellow spoils; then, on my bending back,
The welcome load of my dear father take;
While on my better hand Ascanius hung,
And with unequal paces tript along.
Creüsa kept behind: by choice we stray
Through every dark and every devious way.
I, who so bold and dauntless, just before,
The Grecian darts and shock of lances bore,
At every shadow now, am seized with fear,
Not for myself, but for the charge I bear;
Till, near the ruined gate arrived at last,
Secure, and deeming all the danger past,
A frightful noise of trampling feet we hear.
My father, looking through the shades with fear,
Cried out, "Haste, haste, my son! the foes are nigh;
Their swords and shining armour I descry."
Some hostile god, for some unknown offence,
Had sure bereft my mind of better sense;
For, while through winding ways I took my flight,
And sought the shelter of the gloomy night,
Alas! I lost Creüsa: hard to tell
If by her fatal destiny she fell,
Or weary sat, or wandered with affright;
But she was lost for ever to my sight.
I knew not, or reflected, till I meet
My friends at Ceres' now-deserted seat.
We met: not one was wanting; only she
Deceived her friends, her son, and wretched me.
What mad expressions did my tongue refuse?
Whom did I not of gods or men accuse?
This was the fatal blow, that pained me more
Than all I felt from ruined Troy before.

Stung with my loss, and raving with despair,
Abandoning my now-forgotten care,
Of counsel, comfort, and of hope bereft,
My sire, my son, my country gods, I left.
In shining armour once again I sheath
My limbs, not feeling wounds, nor fearing death ;
Then headlong to the burning walls I run,
And seek the danger I was forced to shun.
I tread my former tracks, through night explore
Each passage, every street I crossed before.
All things were full of horror and affright,
And dreadful e'en the silence of the night.
Then to my father's house I make repair,
With some small glimpse of hope to find her there.
Instead of her, the cruel Greeks I met :
The house was filled with foes, with flames beset.
Driven on the wings of winds, whole sheets of fire
Through air transported, to the roofs aspire.
From thence to Priam's palace I resort,
And search the citadel, and desert court.
Then, unobserved, I pass by Juno's church :
A guard of Grecians had possessed the porch ;
There Phœnix and Ulysses watch the prey ;
And thither all the wealth of Troy convey :
The spoils which they from ransacked houses brought ;
And golden bowls from burning altars caught ;
The tables of the gods, the purple vests,
The people's treasure, and the pomp of priests.
A rank of wretched youths, with pinioned hands,
And captive matrons, in long order stands.
Then, with ungoverned madness, I proclaim
Through all the silent streets Creüsa's name :
Creüsa still I call : at length she hears,
And sudden, through the shades of night, appears—
Appears, no more Creüsa, nor my wife,
But a pale spectre, larger than the life.
Aghast, astonished, and struck dumb with fear
I stood : like bristles rose my stiffened hair.
Then thus the ghost began to soothe my grief :
" Nor tears, nor cries, can give the dead relief.

Desist, my much-loved lord, to indulge your pain ;
You bear no more than what the gods ordain.
My fates permit me not from hence to fly ;
Nor he, the great controller of the sky.
Long wand'ring ways for you the powers decree :
On land, hard labours, and a length of sea.
Then, after many painful years are past,
On Latium's happy shore you shall be cast ;
Where gentle Tiber from his bed beholds
The flowery meadows, and the feeding folds.
There, end your toils, and there your fates provide
A quiet kingdom, and a royal bride :
There Fortune shall the Trojan line restore ;
And you for lost Creüsa weep no more.
Fear not that I shall watch, with servile shame,
The imperious looks of some proud Grecian dame ;
Or, stooping to the victor's lust, disgrace
My goddess-mother, or my royal race.
And now, farewell ! the parent of the gods
Restrains my fleeting soul in her abodes.
I trust our common issue to your care."
She said, and gliding passed unseen in air.
I strove to speak ; but horror tied my tongue ;
And thrice about her neck my arms I flung,
And thrice deceived, on vain embraces hung :
Light as an empty dream at break of day,
Or as a blast of wind, she rushed away.

Thus having passed the night in fruitless pain,
I to my longing friends return again
(Amazed the augmented number to behold,
Of men and matrons mixed, of young and old) :
A wretched exiled crew together brought,
With arms appointed, and with treasure fraught,
Resolved, and willing, under my command
To run all hazards both of sea and land.
The Morn begun, from Ida, to display
Her rosy cheeks ; and Phosphor led the day :
Before the gates the Grecians took their post,
And all pretence of late relief was lost.
I yield to Fate, unwillingly retire,
And, loaded, up the hill convey my sire.

BOOK III

THE ARGUMENT

Æneas proceeds in his relation: he gives an account of the fleet with which he sailed, and the success of his first voyage to Thrace. From thence he directs his course to Delos, and asks the oracle what place the gods had appointed for his habitation. By a mistake of the oracle's answer, he settles in Crete. His household gods give him the true sense of the oracle in a dream. He follows their advice, and makes the best of his way for Italy. He is cast on several shores, and meets with very surprising adventures, till at length he lands on Sicily, where his father Anchises dies. This is the place which he was sailing from, when the tempest rose, and threw him upon the Carthaginian coast.

' When Heaven had overturned the Trojan state
And Priam's throne, by too severe a fate;
When ruined Troy became the Grecian's prey,
And Ilium's lofty towers in ashes lay;
Warned by celestial omens, we retreat,
To seek in foreign lands a happier seat.
Near old Antandros, and at Ida's foot,
The timber of the sacred groves we cut,
And build our fleet—uncertain yet to find
What place the gods for our repose assigned.
Friends daily flock; and scarce the kindly spring
Began to clothe the ground, and birds to sing,
When old Anchises summoned all to sea:
The crew, my father and the Fates obey.
With sighs and tears I leave my native shore,
And empty fields, where Ilium stood before.
My sire, my son, our less and greater gods,
All sail at once, and cleave the briny floods.

Against our coast appears a spacious land,
Which once the fierce Lycurgus did command

187

(Thracia the name—the people bold in war—
Vast are their fields, and tillage is their care),
A hospitable realm while Fate was kind,
With Troy in friendship and religion joined.
I land with luckless omens ; then adore
Their gods, and draw a line along the shore :
I lay the deep foundations of a wall,
And Ænos, named from me, the city call.
To Dionæan Venus vows are paid,
And all the powers that rising labours aid ;
A bull on Jove's imperial altar laid.
Not far, a rising hillock stood in view .
Sharp myrtles on the sides, and cornels grew.
There, while I went to crop the sylvan scenes,
And shade our altar with their leafy greens,
I pulled a plant (with horror I relate
A prodigy so strange, and full of fate),
The rooted fibres rose, and from the wound,
Black bloody drops distilled upon the ground.
Mute and amazed, my hair with terror stood ;
Fear shrunk my sinews, and congealed my blood.
Manned once again, another plant I try ;
That other gushed with the same sanguine dye.
Then fearing guilt for some offence unknown,
With prayers and vows the Dryads I atone,
With all the sisters of the woods, and most
The god of arms, who rules the Thracian coast—
That they, or he, these omens would avert,
Release our fears, and better signs impart.
Cleared, as I thought, and fully fixed at length
To learn the cause, I tugged with all my strength :
I bent my knees against the ground : once more
The violated myrtle ran with gore.
Scarce dare I tell the sequel : from the womb
Of wounded earth, and caverns of the tomb,
A groan, as of a troubled ghost, renewed
My fright, and then these dreadful words ensued :
" Why dost thou thus my buried body rend ?
O ! spare the corpse of thy unhappy friend !
Spare to pollute thy pious hands with blood :

The tears distil not from the wounded wood ;
But every drop this living tree contains,
Is kindred blood, and ran in Trojan veins.
O ! fly from this unhospitable shore,
Warned by my fate ; for I am Polydore !
Here loads of lances, in my blood embrued,
Again shoot upward, by my blood renewed."
   My faltering tongue and shivering limbs declare
My horror, and in bristles rose my hair.
When Troy with Grecian arms was closely pent,
Old Priam, fearful of the war's event,
This hapless Polydore to Thracia sent :
Loaded with gold, he sent his darling far
From noise and tumults, and destructive war :
Committed to the faithless tyrant's care ;
Who, when he saw the power of Troy decline,
Forsook the weaker, with the strong to join :
Broke every bond of nature and of truth,
And murdered, for his wealth, the royal youth.
O sacred hunger of pernicious gold !
What bands of faith can impious lucre hold ?
Now, when my soul had shaken off her fears,
I call my father, and the Trojan peers—
Relate the prodigies of heaven—require
What he commands, and their advice desire.
All vote to leave that execrable shore,
Polluted with the blood of Polydore ;
But, ere we sail, his funeral rites prepare ;
Then to his ghost, a tomb and altars rear.
In mournful pomp the matrons walk the round,
With baleful cypress and blue fillets crowned,
With eyes dejected, and with hair unbound.
Then bowls of tepid milk and blood we pour,
And thrice invoke the soul of Polydore.
   Now, when the raging storms no longer reign,
But southern gales invite us to the main,
We launch our vessels, with a prosperous wind,
And leave the cities and the shores behind.
   An island in the Ægæan main appears :
Neptune and watery Doris claim it theirs.

It floated once, till Phœbus fixed the sides
To rooted earth ; and now it braves the tides.
Here, borne by friendly winds, we come ashore,
With needful ease our weary limbs restore,
And the Sun's temple and his town adore.
   Anius, the priest and king, with laurel crowned,
His hoary locks with purple fillets bound,
Who saw my sire the Delian shore ascend,
Came forth with eager haste to meet his friend :
Invites him to his palace ; and in sign
Of ancient love, their plighted hands they join.
Then to the temple of the god I went,
And thus, before the shrine, my vows present :
" Give, O Thymbræus ! give a resting-place
To the sad relics of the Trojan race :
A seat secure, a region of their own,
A lasting empire, and a happier town.
Where shall we fix ? where shall our labours end ?
Whom shall we follow, and what fate attend ?
Let not my prayers a doubtful answer find ;
But in clear auguries unveil thy mind."
Scarce had I said : he shook the holy ground,
The laurels, and the lofty hills around ;
And from the tripos rushed a bellowing sound.
Prostrate we fell ; confessed the present god,
Who gave this answer from his dark abode :
" Undaunted youths ! go, seek that mother earth
From which your ancestors derive their birth.
The soil that sent you forth, her ancient race,
In her old bosom shall again embrace.
Through the wide world the Æneian house shall reign,
And children's children shall the crown sustain."
Thus Phœbus did our future fates disclose ;
A mighty tumult, mixed with joy, arose.
All are concerned to know what place the god
Assigned, and where determined our abode.
My father, long revolving in his mind
The race and lineage of the Trojan kind,
Thus answered their demands : " Ye princes ! hear
Your pleasing fortune, and dispel your fear.

The fruitful isle of Crete, well-known to fame,
Sacred of old to Jove's imperial name,
In the mid ocean lies, with large command ;
And on its plains a hundred cities stand.
Another Ida rises there ; and we
From thence derive our Trojan ancestry.
From thence, as 'tis divulged by certain fame,
To the Rhœtean shores old Teucer came ;
There fixed, and there the seat of empire chose,
Ere Ilium and the Trojan towers arose.
In humble vales they built their soft abodes ;
Till Cybele, the mother of the gods,
With tinkling cymbals charmed the Idean woods.
She secret rites and ceremonies taught,
And to the yoke the savage lions brought.
Let us the land which Heaven appoints, explore ;
Appease the winds, and seek the Gnossian shore.
If Jove assists the passage of our fleet,
The third propitious dawn discovers Crete."
Thus having said, the sacrifices, laid
On smoking altars, to the gods he paid :
A bull to Neptune, an oblation due,
Another bull to bright Apollo, slew :
A milk-white ewe, the western winds to please,
And one coal-black, to calm the stormy seas.
Ere this, a flying rumour had been spread,
That fierce Idomeneus from Crete was fled,
Expelled and exiled ; that the coast was free
From foreign or domestic enemy.
We leave the Delian ports, and put to sea ;
By Naxos, famed for vintage, make our way ;
Then green Donysa pass ; and sail in sight
Of Paros' isle, with marble quarries white.
We pass the scattered isles of Cyclades,
That, scarce distinguished, seem to stud the seas.
The shouts of sailors double near the shores ;
They stretch their canvas, and they ply their oars.
"All hands aloft ! for Crete ! for Crete !" they cry,
And swiftly through the foamy billows fly.
Full on the promised land at length we bore,

With joy descending on the Cretan shore.
With eager haste a rising town I frame,
Which from the Trojan Pergamus I name:
The name itself was grateful:—I exhort
To found their houses, and erect a fort.
Our ships are hauled upon the yellow strand:
The youth begin to till the laboured land ;
And I myself new marriages promote,
Give laws ; and dwellings I divide by lot :
When rising vapours choke the wholesome air,
And blasts of noisome winds corrupt the year :
The trees, devouring caterpillars burn :
Parched was the grass, and blighted was the corn :
Nor 'scape the beasts ; for Sirius, from on high
With pestilential heat infects the sky :
My men—some fall, the rest in fevers fry.
Again my father bids me seek the shore
Of sacred Delos, and the god implore,
To learn what end of woes we might expect,
And to what clime our weary course direct.
    'Twas night, when every creature void of cares,
The common gift of balmy slumber shares :
The statues of my gods (for such they seemed—
Those gods whom I from flaming Troy redeemed),
Before me stood, majestically bright,
Full in the beams of Phœbe's entering light.
Then thus they spoke, and eased my troubled mind :
" What from the Delian god thou goest to find,
He tells thee here, and sends us to relate.
Those powers are we, companions of thy fate,
Who from the burning town by thee were brought,
Thy fortune followed, and thy safety wrought.
Through seas and lands as we thy steps attend,
So shall our care thy glorious race befriend.
An ample realm for thee thy fates ordain,
A town, that o'er the conquered world shall reign.
Thou, mighty walls for mighty nations build ;
Nor let thy weary mind to labours yield :
But change thy seat ; for not the Delian god
Nor we, have given thee Crete for our abode.

A land there is, Hesperia called of old,
(The soil is fruitful, and the natives bold—
The Œnotrians held it once), by later fame
Now called Italia, from the leader's name.
Iäsius there, and Dardanus, were born:
From thence we came, and thither must return.
Rise, and thy sire with these glad tidings greet:
Search Italy; for Jove denies thee Crete."

    Astonished at their voices and their sight,
(Nor were they dreams but visions of the night;
I saw, I knew their faces, and descried
In perfect view, their hair with fillets tied)
I started from my couch: a clammy sweat
On all my limbs, and shivering body, sat.
To heaven I lift my hands with pious haste,
And sacred incense in the flames I cast.
Thus to the gods their perfect honours done,
More cheerful to my good old sire I run,
And tell the pleasing news.   In little space
He found his error of the double race,
Not, as before he deemed, derived from Crete;
No more deluded by the doubtful seat;
Then said: "O son, turmoiled in Trojan fate!
Such things as these Cassandra did relate.
This day revives within my mind, what she
Foretold of Troy renewed in Italy,
And Latian lands: but who could then have thought
That Phrygian gods to Latium should be brought;
Or who believed what mad Cassandra taught?
Now let us go where Phœbus leads the way."

    He said; and we with glad consent obey;
Forsake the seat; and, leaving few behind,
We spread our sails before the willing wind.
Now from the sight of land our galleys move,
With only seas around, and skies above;
When o'er our heads descends a burst of rain,
And night with sable clouds involves the main;
The ruffling winds the foamy billows raise;
The scattered fleet is forced to several ways;
The face of heaven is ravished from our eyes;

37   H

And in redoubled peals the roaring thunder flies.
Cast from our course, we wander in the dark ;
No stars to guide, no point of land to mark.
E'en Palinurus no distinction found
Betwixt the night and day ; such darkness reigned
    around.
Three starless nights the doubtful navy strays
Without distinction, and three sunless days :
The fourth renews the light ; and from our shrouds
We view a rising land, like distant clouds ;
The mountain-tops confirm the pleasing sight,
And curling smoke ascending from their height.
The canvas falls ; their oars the sailors ply ;
From the rude strokes the whirling waters fly.

    At length I land upon the Strophades,
Safe from the danger of the stormy seas.
Those isles are compassed by the Ionian main ;
The dire abode where the foul Harpies reign,
Forced by the wingèd warriors to repair
To their old homes, and leave their costly fare.
Monsters more fierce, offended Heaven ne'er sent
From hell's abyss, for human punishment :
With virgin-faces, but with wombs obscene,
Foul paunches, and with ordure still unclean ;
With claws for hands, and looks for ever lean.

    We landed at the port, and soon beheld
Fat herds of oxen graze the flowery field ;
And wanton goats without a keeper strayed.
With weapons we the welcome prey invade ;
Then call the gods for partners of our feast,
And Jove himself, the chief invited guest.
We spread the tables on the greensward ground ;
We feed with hunger, and the bowls go round ;
When from the mountain-tops, with hideous cry,
And clattering wings, the hungry Harpies fly :
They snatch the meat, defiling all they find,
And parting, leave a loathsome stench behind.
Close by a hollow rock, again we sit,
New-dress the dinner, and the beds refit,
Secure from sight, beneath a pleasing shade,

Where tufted trees a native arbour made.
Again the holy fires on altars burn;
And once again the ravenous birds return,
Or from the dark recesses where they lie,
Or from another quarter of the sky:
With filthy claws their odious meal repeat,
And mix their loathsome ordures with their meat.

    I bid my friends for vengeance then prepare,
And with the hellish nation wage the war.
They, as commanded, for the fight provide,
And in the grass their glittering weapons hide;
Then, when along the crooked shore we hear
Their clattering wings, and saw the foes appear,
Misenus sounds a charge: we take the alarm,
And our strong hands with swords and bucklers arm.
In this new kind of combat, all employ
Their utmost force, the monsters to destroy—
In vain:—the fated skin is proof to wounds;
And from their plumes the shining sword rebounds.
At length rebuffed, they leave their mangled prey,
And their stretched pinions to the skies display.
Yet one remained—the messenger of fate:
High on a craggy cliff Celæno sat,
And thus her dismal errand did relate:
" What ! not contented with our oxen slain,
Dare you with heaven an impious war maintain,
And drive the Harpies from their native reign?
Heed therefore what I say; and keep in mind
What Jove decrees, what Phœbus has designed,
And I, the Furies' queen, from both relate—
You seek the Italian shores: foredoomed by fate,
The Italian shores are granted you to find,
And a safe passage to the port assigned.
But know, that, ere your promised walls you build,
My curses shall severely be fulfilled.
Fierce famine is your lot : for this misdeed,
Reduced to grind the plates on which you feed."
She said, and to the neighbouring forest flew.
Our courage fails us, and our fears renew.
Hopeless to win by war, to prayers we fall,

And on the offended Harpies humbly call,
And (whether gods or birds obscene they were)
Our vows, for pardon and for peace, prefer.
But old Anchises, offering sacrifice,
And lifting up to heaven his hands and eyes,
Adored the greater gods—" Avert (said he)
These omens ! render vain this prophecy,
And from the impending curse a pious people free."
    Thus having said, he bids us put to sea.
We loose from shore our halsers, and obey,
And soon with swelling sails pursue our watery way.
Amidst our course, Zacynthian woods appear ;
And next by rocky Neritos we steer :
We fly from Ithaca's detested shore,
And curse the land which dire Ulysses bore.
At length Leucate's cloudy top appears,
And the Sun's temple, which the sailor fears.
Resolved to breathe awhile from labour past,
Our crooked anchors from the prow we cast,
And joyful to the little city haste.
Here, safe beyond our hopes, our vows we pay
To Jove, the guide and patron of our way.
The customs of our country we pursue,
And Trojan games on Actian shores renew.
Our youth their naked limbs besmear with oil,
And exercise the wrestlers' noble toil :
Pleased to have sailed so long before the wind,
And left so many Grecian towns behind.
    The sun had now fulfilled his annual course,
And Boreas on the seas displayed his force :
I fixed upon the temple's lofty door
The brazen shield which vanquished Abas bore :
The verse beneath, my name and action speaks :
"These arms Æneas took from conquering Greeks."
Then I command to weigh : the seamen ply
Their sweeping oars : the smoking billows fly.
The sight of high Phæacia soon we lost,
And skimmed along Epirus' rocky coast.
Then to Chaonia's port our course we bend,
And, landed, to Buthrotus' heights ascend.

Here wondrous things were loudly blazed by Fame:
How Helenus revived the Trojan name,
And reigned in Greece; that Priam's captive son
Succeeded Pyrrhus in his bed and throne;
And fair Andromache, restored by fate,
Once more was happy in a Trojan mate.
I leave my galleys riding in the port,
And long to see the new Dardanian court.
   By chance, the mournful queen, before the gate,
Then solemnized her former husband's fate.
Green altars, raised of turf, with gifts she crowned;
And sacred priests in order stand around,
And thrice the name of hapless Hector sound.
The grove itself resembles Ida's wood;
And Simoïs seemed the well-dissembled flood.
But when, at nearer distance, she beheld
My shining armour and my Trojan shield,
Astonished at the sight, the vital heat
Forsakes her limbs, her veins no longer beat:
She faints, she falls, and scarce recovering strength,
Thus, with a faltering tongue, she speaks at length:
" Are you alive, O goddess-born! (she said)
Or, if a ghost, then where is Hector's shade?"
At this she cast a loud and frightful cry.
With broken words I made this brief reply:
" All of me that remains, appears in sight;
I live; if living be to loathe the light—
No phantom; but I drag a wretched life;
My fate resembling that of Hector's wife.
What have you suffered since you lost your lord?
By what strange blessing are you now restored?
Still are you Hector's? or is Hector fled,
And his remembrance lost in Pyrrhus' bed?"
With eyes dejected, in a lowly tone,
After a modest pause, she thus begun:
" O only happy maid of Priam's race,
Whom death delivered from the foe's embrace!
Commanded on Achilles' tomb to die,
Not forced, like us, to hard captivity,
Or in a haughty master's arms to lie.

In Grecian ships, unhappy we were borne,
Endured the victor's lust, sustained the scorn:
Thus I submitted to the lawless pride
Of Pyrrhus, more a handmaid than a bride.
Cloyed with possession, he forsook my bed,
And Helen's lovely daughter sought to wed;
Then, me to Trojan Helenus resigned,
And his two slaves in equal marriage joined;
Till young Orestes, pierced with deep despair,
And longing to redeem the promised fair,
Before Apollo's altar slew the ravisher.
By Pyrrhus' death the kingdom we regained:
At least one half with Helenus remained.
Our part, from Chaon, he Chaonia calls;
And names, from Pergamus, his rising walls.
But you, what fates have landed on our coast?
What gods have sent you, or what storms have tossed?
Does young Ascanius life and health enjoy,
Saved from the ruins of unhappy Troy?
O! tell me how his mother's loss he bears,
What hopes are promised from his blooming years,
How much of Hector in his face appears?"
She spoke; and mixed her speech with mournful cries;
And fruitless tears came trickling from her eyes.
At length her lord descends upon the plain,
In pomp, attended with a numerous train;
Receives his friends, and to the city leads,
And tears of joy amidst his welcome sheds.
Proceeding on, another Troy I see,
Or in less compass, Troy's epitome.
A rivulet by the name of Xanthus ran;
And I embrace the Scæan gate again.
My friends in porticoes were entertained;
And feasts and pleasures through the city reigned.
The tables filled the spacious hall around;
And golden bowls with sparkling wine were crowned.
Two days we passed in mirth, till friendly gales,
Blown from the south, supplied our swelling sails;
Then to the royal seer I thus began:
"O thou who knowest beyond the reach of man,

The laws of heaven, and what the stars decree;
Whom Phœbus taught unerring prophecy,
From his own tripod, and his holy tree—
Skilled in the winged inhabitants of air,
What auspices their notes and flights declare—
O! say—(for all religious rights portend
A happy voyage, and a prosperous end;
And every power and omen of the sky
Direct my course for destined Italy;
But only dire Celæno, from the gods,
A dismal famine fatally forebodes)—
O! say, what dangers I am first to shun,
What toils to vanquish, and what course to run."
　　The prophet first with sacrifice adores
The greater gods; their pardon then implores;
Unbinds the fillet from his holy head;
To Phœbus, next, my trembling steps he led,
Full of religious doubts and awful dread.
Then, with his god possessed, before the shrine
These words proceeded from his mouth divine:
" O goddess-born! (for heaven's appointed will,
With greater auspices of good than ill,
Foreshows thy voyage, and thy course directs;
Thy fates conspire, and Jove himself protects),
Of many things, some few I shall explain,
Teach thee to shun the dangers of the main,
And how at length the promised shore to gain.
The rest, the fates from Helenus conceal,
And Juno's angry power forbids to tell.
First then, that happy shore that seems so nigh,
Will far from your deluded wishes fly:
Long tracts of seas divide your hopes from Italy.
For you must cruise along Sicilian shores,
And stem the currents with your struggling oars;
Then round the Italian coast your navy steer;
And, after this, to Circe's island veer;
And last, before your new foundations rise,
Must pass the Stygian lake, and view the nether skies.
Now mark the signs of future ease and rest;
And bear them safely treasured in thy breast.

When, in the shady shelter of a wood,
And near the margin of a gentle flood,
Thou shalt behold a sow upon the ground,
With thirty sucking young encompassed round
(The dam and offspring white as falling snow);
These, on thy city shall their name bestow;
And there, shall end thy labours and thy woe.
Nor let the threatened famine fright thy mind;
For Phœbus will assist; and Fate the way will find.
Let not thy course to that ill coast be bent,
Which fronts from far the Epirian continent:
Those parts are all by Grecian foes possessed.
The savage Locrians here the shores infest:
There fierce Idomeneus his city builds,
And guards with arms the Salentinian fields;
And on the mountain's brow Petilia stands,
Which Philoctetes with his troops commands.
E'en when thy fleet is landed on the shore,
And priests with holy vows the gods adore,
Then with a purple veil involve your eyes,
Lest hostile faces blast the sacrifice.
These rites and customs to the rest commend,
That to your pious race they may descend.
    When, parted hence, the wind that ready waits
For Sicily, shall bear you to the straits:
Where proud Pelorus opes a wider way,
Tack to the larboard, and stand off to sea:
Veer starboard sea and land. The Italian shore
And fair Sicilia's coast were one, before
An earthquake caused the flaw: the roaring tides
The passage broke, that land from land divides;
And, where the lands retired, the rushing ocean rides
Distinguished by the straits, on either hand,
Now rising cities in long order stand,
And fruitful fields :—so much can time invade
The mouldering work, that beauteous Nature made.
Far on the right, her dogs foul Scylla hides :
Charybdis roaring on the left presides,
And in her greedy whirlpool sucks the tides,
Then spouts them from below : with fury driven,

The waves mount up, and wash the face of heaven.
But Scylla from her den, with open jaws,
The sinking vessel in her eddy draws,
Then dashes on the rocks.—A human face,
And virgin bosom, hide her tail's disgrace:
Her parts obscene below the waves descend,
With dogs inclosed, and in a dolphin end.
'Tis safer, then, to bear aloof to sea,
And coast Pachynus, though with more delay,
Than once to view mis-shapen Scylla near,
And the loud yell of watery wolves to hear.

Besides, if faith to Helenus be due,
And if prophetic Phœbus tell me true,
Do not this precept of your friend forget,
Which therefore more than once I must repeat
Above the rest, great Juno's name adore;
Pay vows to Juno; Juno's aid implore.
Let gifts be to the mighty queen designed;
And mollify with prayers her haughty mind.
Thus, at the length, your passage shall be free,
And you shall safe descend on Italy.

Arrived at Cumæ, when you view the flood
Of black Avernus, and the sounding wood,
The mad prophetic Sibyl you shall find,
Dark in a cave, and on a rock reclined.
She sings the fates, and in her frantic fits,
The notes and names, inscribed, to leaves commits.
What she commits to leaves, in order laid,
Before the cavern's entrance are displayed:
Unmoved they lie; but, if a blast of wind
Without, or vapours issue from behind,
The leaves are borne aloft in liquid air,
And she resumes no more her museful care;
Nor gathers from the rocks her scattered verse,
Nor sets in order what the winds disperse.
Thus, many not succeeding, most upbraid
The madness of the visionary maid,
And with loud curses leave the mystic shade.

Think it not loss of time awhile to stay,
Though thy companions chide thy long delay;

Though summoned to the seas ; though pleasing gales
Invite thy course, and stretch thy swelling sails ;
But beg the sacred priestess to relate
With willing words, and not to write, thy fate.
The fierce Italian people she will show,
And all thy wars, and all thy future woe ;
And what thou may'st avoid, and what must undergo.
She shall direct thy course, instruct thy mind,
And teach thee how the happy shores to find.
This is what heaven allows me to relate :
Now part in peace ; pursue thy better fate,
And raise, by strength of arms, the Trojan state."

    This when the priest with friendly voice declared,
He gave me license, and rich gifts prepared :
Bounteous of treasure, he supplied my want
With heavy gold, and polished elephant ;
Then Dodonæan caldrons put on board ;
And every ship with sums of silver stored.
A trusty coat of mail to me he sent,
Thrice chained with gold, for use and ornament ;
The helm of Pyrrhus added to the rest,
That flourished with a plume and waving crest.
Nor was my sire forgotten, nor my friends ;
And large recruits he to my navy sends :
Men, horses, captains, arms, and warlike stores ;
Supplies new pilots, and new sweeping oars.
Meantime, my sire commands to hoist our sails,
Lest we should lose the first auspicious gales.
The prophet blessed the parting crew, and last,
With words like these, his ancient friend embraced :
" Old happy man, the care of gods above !
Whom heavenly Venus honoured with her love,
And twice preserved thy life when Troy was lost ;
Behold from far the wished Ausonian coast !
There land ; but take a larger compass round ;
For that, before, is all forbidden ground.
The shore that Phœbus has designed for you,
At farther distance lies, concealed from view.
Go happy hence, and seek your new abodes,
Blessed in a son, and favoured by the gods ;

For I with useless words prolong your stay,
When southern gales have summoned you away."
  Nor less the queen our parting thence deplored,
Nor was less bounteous than her Trojan lord.
A noble present to my son she brought,
A robe with flowers on golden tissue wrought:
A Phrygian vest; and loads with gifts beside
Of precious texture, and of Asian pride.
"Accept (she said) these monuments of love,
Which in my youth with happier hands I wove:
Regard these trifles for the giver's sake:
'Tis the last present Hector's wife can make.
Thou call'st my lost Astyanax to mind:
In thee, his features and his form I find;
His eyes so sparkled with a lively flame;
Such were his motions; such was all his frame;
And ah! had heaven so pleased, his years had been the
  With tears I took my last adieu, and said: [same."
"Your fortune, happy pair, already made,
Leaves you no farther wish. My different state,
Avoiding one, incurs another fate.
To you a quiet seat the gods allow:
You have no shores to search, no seas to plough;
Nor fields of flying Italy to chase—
Deluding visions and a vain embrace!
You see another Simoïs, and enjoy
The labours of your hands, another Troy,
With better auspice than her ancient towers;
And less obnoxious to the Grecian powers.
If e'er the gods whom I with vows adore,
Conduct my steps to Tiber's happy shore:
If ever I ascend the Latian throne,
And build a city I may call my own:
As both of us our birth from Troy derive;
So let our kindred lines in concord live;
And both in acts of equal friendship strive.
Our fortunes, good or bad, shall be the same:
The double Troy shall differ but in name:
That what we now begin, may never end,
But long to late posterity descend."

Near the Ceraunian rocks our course we bore—
The shortest passage to the Italian shore.
Now had the sun withdrawn his radiant light,
And hills were hid in dusky shades of night :
We land, and, on the bosom of the ground,
A safe retreat and a bare lodging found.
Close by the shore we lay ; the sailors keep
Their watches, and the rest securely sleep.
The night, proceeding on with silent pace,
Stood in her noon, and viewed with equal face
Her steepy rise, and her declining race.
Then wakeful Palinurus rose, to spy
The face of heaven, and the nocturnal sky ;
And listened every breath of air to try ;
Observes the stars, and notes their sliding course,
The Pleiads, Hyads, and their watery force ;
And both the Bears is careful to behold,
And bright Orion, armed with burnished gold.
Then, when he saw no threatening tempest nigh,
But a sure promise of a settled sky,
He gave the sign to weigh : we break our sleep,
Forsake the pleasing shore, and plough the deep.

And now the rising morn with rosy light
Adorns the skies, and puts the stars to flight ;
When we from far, like bluish mists, descry
The hills, and then the plains, of Italy.
Achates first pronounced the joyful sound ;
Then ' Italy !' the cheerful crew rebound.
My sire Anchises crowned a cup with wine,
And, offering, thus implored the powers divine :
" Ye gods, presiding over lands and seas,
And you, who raging winds and waves appease,
Breathe on our swelling sails a prosperous wind,
And smooth our passage to the port assigned."
The gentle gales their flagging force renew ;
And now the happy harbour is in view.
Minerva's temple then salutes our sight,
Placed, as a landmark, on the mountain's height.
We furl our sails, and turn the prows to shore :
The curling waters round the galleys roar.

The land lies open to the raging east,
Then, bending like a bow, with rocks compressed,
Shuts out the storms; the wind and waves complain,
And vent their malice on the cliffs in vain.
The port lies hid within; on either side,
The towering rocks the narrow mouth divide.
The temple, which aloft we viewed before,
To distance flies, and seems to shun the shore.
  Scarce landed, the first omens I beheld
Were four white steeds, that cropped the flowery
    field.
" War, war is threatened from this foreign ground
(My father cried), where warlike steeds are found.
Yet since reclaimed, to chariots they submit,
And bend to stubborn yokes, and champ the bit,
Peace may succeed to war."—Our way we bend
To Pallas, and the sacred hill ascend;
There, prostrate, to the fierce virago pray,
Whose temple was the landmark of our way.
Each with a Phrygian mantle veiled his head,
And all commands of Helenus obeyed;
And pious rites to Grecian Juno paid.
  These dues performed, we stretch our sails and stand
To sea, forsaking that suspected land.
From hence Tarentum's bay appears in view,
For Hercules renowned, if fame be true.
Just opposite, Lacinian Juno stands;
Caulonian towers, and Scylacæan strands
For shipwrecks feared.   Mount Ætna thence we spy,
Known by the smoky flames which cloud the sky.
Far off we hear the waves with surly sound
Invade the rocks, the rocks their groans rebound.
The billows break upon the sounding strand,
And roll the rising tide, impure with sand.
Then thus, Anchises, in experience old:
" 'Tis that Charybdis which the seer foretold,
And those the promised rocks!   Bear off to sea!"
With haste the frighted mariners obey.
First Palinurus to the larboard veered;
Then all the fleet by his example steered.

To heaven aloft on ridgy waves we ride,
Then down to hell descend, when they divide;
And thrice our galleys knocked the stony ground,
And thrice the hollow rocks return the sound,
And thrice we saw the stars that stood with dews around.
The flagging winds forsook us, with the sun;
And, wearied, on Cyclopean shores we run.

   The port, capacious and secure from wind,
Is to the foot of thundering Ætna joined.
By turns a pitchy cloud she rolls on high;
By turns hot embers from her entrails fly,
And flakes of mountain flames, that lick the sky.
Oft from her bowels massy rocks are thrown,
And shivered by the force, come piece-meal down:
Oft liquid lakes of burning sulphur flow,
Fed from the fiery springs that boil below.
Enceladus, they say, transfixed by Jove,
With blasted limbs came tumbling from above;
And where he fell, the avenging father drew
This flaming hill, and on his body threw.
As often as he turns his weary sides,
He shakes the solid isle, and smoke, the heavens hides.
In shady woods we pass the tedious night,
Where bellowing sounds and groans our souls affright,
Of which no cause is offered to the sight;
For not one star was kindled in the sky;
Nor could the moon her borrowed light supply;
For misty clouds involved the firmament:
The stars were muffled, and the moon was pent.

   Scarce had the rising sun the day revealed;
Scarce had his heat the pearly dews dispelled;
When from the woods there bolts, before our sight,
Somewhat betwixt a mortal and a sprite,
So thin, so ghastly meagre, and so wan,
So bare of flesh, he scarce resembled man.
This thing, all tattered, seemed from far to implore
Our pious aid, and pointed to the shore.
We look behind; then view his shaggy beard:
His clothes were tagged with thorns, and filth his limbs
     besmeared;

The rest, in mien, in habit, and in face,
Appeared a Greek : and such indeed he was.
He cast on us, from far, a frightful view,
Whom soon for Trojans and for foes he knew :
Stood still, and paused ; then all at once began
To stretch his limbs, and trembled as he ran.
Soon as approached, upon his knees he falls,
And thus with tears and sighs for pity calls :
"Now, by the powers above, and what we share
From nature's common gift, this vital air,
O Trojans, take me hence ! I beg no more ;
But bear me far from this unhappy shore.
'Tis true I am a Greek, and farther own,
Among your foes besieged the imperial town.
For such demerits if my death be due,
No more for this abandoned life I sue :
This only favour let my tears obtain,
To throw me headlong in the rapid main :
Since nothing more than death my crime demands,
I die content, to die by human hands."

    He said ; and on his knees my knees embraced :
I bade him boldly tell, his fortune past,
His present state, his lineage, and his name,
The occasion of his fears, and whence he came.
The good Anchises raised him with his hand ;
Who thus encouraged, answered our demand :
"From Ithaca, my native soil, I came
To Troy ; and Achæmenides my name.
Me my poor father with Ulysses sent ;
(O ! had I stayed, with poverty content !)
But, fearful for themselves, my countrymen
Left me forsaken in the Cyclop's den.
The cave, though large, was dark ; the dismal floor
Was paved with mangled limbs and putrid gore.
Our monstrous host, of more than human size
Erects his head and stares within the skies :
Bellowing, his voice, and horrid is his hue.
Ye gods, remove this plague from mortal view !
The joints of slaughtered wretches are his food ;
And for his wine, he quaffs the streaming blood.

These eyes beheld, when with his spacious hand
He seized two captives of our Grecian band ;
Stretched on his back, he dashed against the stones
Their broken bodies, and their crackling bones :
With spouting blood the purple pavement swims,
While the dire glutton grinds the trembling limbs.
   Not unrevenged Ulysses bore their fate,
Nor thoughtless of his own unhappy state ;
For, gorged with flesh, and drunk with human wine,
While fast asleep the giant lay supine
(Snoring aloud, and belching from his maw
His indigested foam, and morsels raw) ;
We pray, we cast the lots, and then surround
The monstrous body stretched along the ground.
Each, as he could approach him, lends a hand
To bore his eye-ball with a flaming brand.
Beneath his frowning forehead lay his eye ;
For only one did the vast frame supply—
But that a globe so large, his front it filled,
Like the sun's disk, or like a Grecian shield.
The stroke succeeds ; and down the pupil bends.
This vengeance followed for our slaughtered friends
But haste, unhappy wretches ! haste to fly !
Your cables cut, and on your oars rely !
Such, and so vast as Polypheme appears,
A hundred more this hated island bears :
Like him, in caves they shut their woolly sheep ;
Like him, their herds on tops of mountains keep ;
Like him, with mighty strides they stalk from steep to
    steep.
And now three moons their sharpened horns renew,
Since thus in woods and wilds, obscure from view,
I drag my loathsome days with mortal fright,
And in deserted caverns lodge by night.
Oft from the rocks a dreadful prospect see
Of the huge Cyclops, like a walking tree :
From far I hear his thundering voice resound,
And trampling feet that shake the solid ground.
Cornels and savage berries of the wood,
And roots and herbs have been my meagre food.

While all around my longing eyes I cast,
I saw your happy ships appear at last.
On those I fixed my hopes, to these I run :
'Tis all I ask, this cruel race to shun :
What other death you please, yourselves bestow."
Scarce had he said, when on the mountain's brow,
We saw the giant shepherd stalk before
His following flock, and leading to the shore :
A monstrous bulk, deformed, deprived of sight ;
His staff a trunk of pine, to guide his steps aright.
His ponderous whistle from his neck descends ;
His woolly care their pensive lord attends :
This only solace his hard fortune sends.
Soon as he reached the shore and touched the waves,
From his bored eye the gutt'ring blood he laves :
He gnashed his teeth and groaned : through seas he
    strides ;
And scarce the topmost billows touched his sides.
  Seized with a sudden fear, we run to sea,
The cables cut, and silent haste away ;
The well-deserving stranger entertain ;
Then, buckling to the work, our oars divide the main.
The giant hearkened to the dashing sound ;
But, when our vessels out of reach he found,
He strided onward, and in vain essayed
The Ionian deep, and durst no farther wade.
With that he roared aloud : the dreadful cry
Shakes earth and air and seas ; the billows fly
Before the bellowing noise to distant Italy,
The neighbouring Ætna trembling all around,
The winding caverns echo to the sound.
  His brother Cyclops hear the yelling roar,
And rushing down the mountains, crowd the shore.
We saw their stern distorted looks, from far,
And one-eyed glance, that vainly threatened war—
A dreadful council ! with their heads on high
(The misty clouds about their foreheads fly)
Not yielding to the towering tree of Jove,
Or tallest cypress of Diana's grove.
New pangs of mortal fear our minds assail ;

We tug at every oar, and hoist up every sail,
And take the advantage of the friendly gale.
Forewarned by Helenus, we strive to shun
Charybdis' gulf, nor dare to Scylla run.
An equal fate on either side appears :
We, tacking to the left, are free from fears ;
For, from Pelorus' point, the north arose,
And drove us back where swift Pantagias flows.
His rocky mouth we pass ; and make our way
By Thapsus, and Megara's winding bay.
This passage Achæmenides had shown,
Tracing the course which he before had run.

  Right o'er against Plemmyrium's watery strand,
There lies an isle, once called the Ortygian land.
Alpheüs, as old fame reports, has found
From Greece a secret passage under ground ;
By love to beauteous Arethusa led ;
And, mingling here, they roll in the same sacred bed.
As Helenus enjoined, we next adore
Diana's name, protectress of the shore.
With prosperous gales we pass the quiet sounds
Of still Helorus, and his fruitful bounds.
Then, doubling cape Pachynus, we survey
The rocky shore extended to the sea.
The town of Camarine from far we see,
And fenny lake, undrained by Fate's decree.
In sight of the Geloan fields we pass,
And the large walls, where mighty Gela was ;
Then Agragas, with lofty summits crowned,
Long for the race of warlike steeds renowned.
We passed Selinus, and the palmy land ;
And widely shun the Lilybæan strand,
Unsafe, for secret rocks and moving sand.
At length on shore the weary fleet arrived,
Which Drepanum's unhappy port received.
Here, after endless labours (often tossed
By raging storms, and driven on every coast),
My dear, dear father, spent with age, I lost—
Ease of my cares, and solace of my pain,
Saved through a thousand toils, but saved in vain !

The prophet, who my future woes revealed,
Yet this, the greatest and the worst, concealed ;
And dire Celæno, whose foreboding skill
Denounced all else, was silent of this ill.
This my last labour was.   Some friendly god
From thence conveyed us to your blest abode.'

    Thus, to the listening queen, the royal guest
His wandering course and all his toils expressed ;
And here concluding, he retired to rest.

BOOK IV

THE ARGUMENT

Dido discovers to her sister her passion for Æneas, and her thoughts of marrying him. She prepares a hunting match for his entertainment. Juno, by Venus's consent, raises a storm which separates the hunters, and drives Æneas and Dido into the same cave, where their marriage is supposed to be completed. Jupiter despatches Mercury to Æneas, to warn him from Carthage. Æneas secretly prepares for his voyage. Dido finds out his design, and, to put a stop to it, makes use of her own and her sister's entreaties, and discovers all the variety of passions that are incident to a neglected lover. When nothing would prevail upon him, she contrives her own death, with which this book concludes.

But anxious cares already seized the queen ;
She fed within her veins a flame unseen :
The hero's valour, acts, and birth, inspire
Her soul with love, and fan the secret fire.
His words, his looks, imprinted in her heart,
Improve the passion, and increase the smart.
Now, when the purple morn had chased away
The dewy shadows, and restored the day,
Her sister first with early care she sought,
And thus in mournful accents eased her thought :
' My dearest Anna ! what new dreams affright
My labouring soul ! what visions of the night
Disturb my quiet, and distract my breast
With strange ideas of our Trojan guest !
His worth, his actions, and majestic air,
A man descended from the gods, declare
Fear ever argues a degenerate kind :
His birth is well asserted by his mind.
Then, what he suffered, when by fate betrayed !

212

What brave attempts for falling Troy he made !
Such were his looks, so gracefully he spoke,
That, were I not resolved against the yoke
Of hapless marriage—never to be cursed
With second love, so fatal was my first—
To this one error I might yield again ;
For, since Sichæus was untimely slain,
This only man is able to subvert
The fixed foundations of my stubborn heart.
And, to confess my frailty, to my shame,
Somewhat I find within, if not the same,
Too like the sparkles of my former flame.
But first let yawning earth a passage rend,
And let me through the dark abyss descend—
First let avenging Jove, with flames from high,
Drive down this body to the nether sky,
Condemned with ghosts in endless night to lie—
Before I break the plighted faith I gave !
No ! he who had my vows, shall ever have ;
For, whom I loved on earth, I worship in the grave.'
    She said : the tears ran gushing from her eyes,
And stopped her speech.   Her sister thus replies :
' O dearer than the vital air I breathe !
Will you to grief your blooming years bequeath,
Condemned to waste in woes your lonely life,
Without the joys of mother or of wife ?
Think you these tears, this pompous train of woe,
Are known or valued by the ghosts below ?
I grant, that, while your sorrows yet were green,
It well became a woman, and a queen,
The vows of Tyrian princes to neglect ;
To scorn Iärbas and his love reject ;
With all the Libyan lords of mighty name :
But will you fight against a pleasing flame ?
This little spot of land, which heaven bestows,
On every side is hemmed with warlike foes :
Gætulian cities here are spread around,
And fierce Numidians there your frontiers bound :
Here lies a barren waste of thirsty land,
And there the Syrtes raise the moving sand :

Barcæan troops besiege the narrow shore ;
And from the sea Pygmalion threatens more.
Propitious heaven, and gracious Juno, lead
This wandering navy to your needful aid :
How will your empire spread, your city rise,
From such a union, and with such allies !
Implore the favour of the powers above ;
And leave the conduct of the rest to love.
Continue still your hospitable way,
And still invent occasions of their stay,
Till storms and winter winds shall cease to threat,
And planks and oars repair their shattered fleet.'

These words, which from a friend and sister came
With ease resolved the scruples of her fame,
And added fury to the kindled flame.
Inspired with hope, the project they pursue ;
On every altar sacrifice renew ;
A chosen ewe of two years old they pay
To Ceres, Bacchus, and the god of day.
Preferring Juno's power (for Juno ties
The nuptial knot, and makes the marriage joys),
The beauteous queen before her altar stands,
And holds the golden goblet in her hands.
A milk-white heifer she with flowers adorns,
And pours the ruddy wine betwixt her horns ;
And, while the priests with prayer the gods invoke,
She feeds their altars with Sabæan smoke ;
With hourly care the sacrifice renews,
And anxiously the panting entrails views.
What priestly rites, alas ! what pious art,
What vows avail to cure a bleeding heart ?
A gentle fire she feeds within her veins,
Where the soft god secure in silence reigns.

Sick with desire, and seeking him she loves,
From street to street the raving Dido roves.
So, when the watchful shepherd, from the blind,
Wounds with a random shaft the careless hind,
Distracted with her pain she flies the woods,
Bounds o'er the lawn, and seeks the silent floods—
With fruitless care ; for still the fatal dart

Sticks in her side, and rankles in her heart.
And now she leads the Trojan chief along
The lofty walls, amidst the busy throng;
Displays her Tyrian wealth, and rising town,
Which love, without his labour makes his own.
This pomp she shows, to tempt her wandering guest:
Her faltering tongue forbids to speak the rest.
When day declines and feasts renew the night,
Still on his face she feeds her famished sight;
She longs again to hear the prince relate
His own adventures, and the Trojan fate.
He tells it o'er and o'er; but still in vain;
For still she begs to hear it once again.
The hearer on the speaker's mouth depends;
And thus the tragic story never ends.

Then, when they part, when Phœbe's paler light
Withdraws, and falling stars to sleep invite,
She last remains; when every guest is gone,
Sits on the bed he pressed, and sighs alone;
Absent, her absent hero sees and hears;
Or in her bosom young Ascanius bears,
And seeks the father's image in the child,
If love by likeness might be so beguiled.

Meantime the rising towers are at a stand;
No labours exercise the youthful band,
Nor use of arts, nor toils of arms they know:
The mole is left unfinished to the foe;
The mounds, the works, the walls neglected lie,
Short of their promised height, that seemed to threat
          the sky.

But when imperial Juno, from above,
Saw Dido fettered in the chains of Love,
Hot with the venom which her veins inflamed;
And by no sense of shame to be reclaimed;
With soothing words to Venus she begun:
'High praises, endless honours, you have won,
And mighty trophies, with your worthy son!
Two gods a silly woman have undone!
Nor am I ignorant, you both suspect
This rising city which my hands erect:

But shall celestial discord never cease?
'Tis better ended in a lasting peace.
You stand possessed of all your soul desired;
Poor Dido with consuming love is fired.
Your Trojan with my Tyrian let us join;
So Dido shall be yours, Æneas mine—
One common kingdom, one united line.
Eliza shall a Dardan lord obey,
And lofty Carthage for a dower convey.'
Then Venus (who her hidden fraud descried,
Which would the sceptre of the world misguide
To Libyan shores) thus artfully replied:
'Who, but a fool, would wars with Juno choose,
And such alliance and such gifts refuse;
If fortune with our joint desires comply?
The doubt is all from Jove, and destiny;
Lest he forbid, with absolute command,
To mix the people in one common land—
Or will, the Trojan and the Tyrian line
In lasting leagues, and sure succession, join.
But you, the partner of his bed and throne,
May move his mind: my wishes are your own.'
'Mine (said imperial Juno) be the care:
Time urges now:—to perfect this affair
Attend my counsel, and the secret share.
    When next the sun his rising light displays,
And gilds the world below with purple rays,
The queen, Æneas, and the Tyrian court,
Shall to the shady woods, for sylvan game, resort.
There, while the huntsmen pitch their toils around,
And cheerful horns, from side to side, resound,
A pitchy cloud shall cover all the plain
With hail, and thunder, and tempestuous rain:
The fearful train shall take their speedy flight,
Dispersed, and all involved in gloomy night:
One cave a grateful shelter shall afford
To the fair princess and the Trojan lord.
I will myself the bridal bed prepare,
If you, to bless the nuptials, will be there;
So shall their loves be crowned with due delights;

And Hymen shall be present at the rites.'
The queen of love consents, and closely smiles
At her vain project, and discovered wiles.

  The rosy morn was risen from the main ;
And horns and hounds awake the princely train :
They issue early through the city gate,
Where the more wakeful huntsmen ready wait,
With nets, and toils, and darts, beside the force
Of Spartan dogs, and swift Massylian horse.
The Tyrian peers and officers of state,
For the slow queen, in antechambers wait :
Her lofty courser, in the court below
(Who his majestic rider seems to know),
Proud of his purple trappings, paws the ground ;
And champs the golden bit, and spreads the foam around.
The queen at length appears : on either hand,
The brawny guards in martial order stand.
A flowered cymar with golden fringe she wore,
And at her back a golden quiver bore ;
Her flowing hair a golden caul restrains ;
A golden clasp the Tyrian robe sustains.
Then young Ascanius, with a sprightly grace
Leads on the Trojan youth to view the chase.
But far above the rest in beauty shines
The great Æneas, when the troop he joins ;
Like fair Apollo, when he leaves the frost
Of wintry Xanthus, and the Lycian coast ;
When to his native Delos he resorts,
Ordains the dances, and renews the sports ;
Where painted Scythians, mixed with Cretan bands,
Before the joyful altars join their hands :
Himself, on Cynthus walking, sees below
The merry madness of the sacred show.
Green wreaths of bays his length of hair inclose ;
A golden fillet binds his awful brows ;
His quiver sounds.—Not less the prince is seen
In manly presence, or in lofty mien.

  Now had they reached the hills, and stormed the seat
Of savage beasts, in dens, their last retreat.
The cry pursues the mountain-goats ; they bound

From rock to rock, and keep the craggy ground :
Quite otherwise the stags, a trembling train
In herds unsingled, scour the dusty plain,
And a long chase, in open view maintain.
The glad Ascanius, as his courser guides,
Spurs through the vale, and these and those outrides.
His horse's flanks and sides are forced to feel
The clanking lash, and goring of the steel.
Impatiently he views the feeble prey,
Wishing some nobler beast to cross his way ;
And rather would the tusky boar attend,
Or see the tawny lion downward bend.

Meantime, the gathering clouds obscure the skies ;
From pole to pole the forky lightning flies ;
The rattling thunders roll ; and Juno pours
A wintry deluge down, and sounding showers.
The company, dispersed, to coverts ride,
And seek the homely cots, or mountain's hollow side.
The rapid rains, descending from the hills,
To rolling torrents raise the creeping rills.
The queen and prince, as love or fortune guides,
One common cavern in her bosom hides,
Then first the trembling earth the signal gave ;
And flashing fires enlighten all the cave :
Hell from below, and Juno from above,
And howling nymphs, were conscious to their love.
From this ill-omened hour, in time arose
Debate and death, and all succeeding woes.

The queen, whom sense of honour could not move,
No longer made a secret of her love,
But called it marriage ; by that specious name
To veil the crime, and sanctify the shame.

The loud report through Libyan cities goes.
Fame, the great ill, from small beginnings grows—
Swift from the first ; and every moment brings
New vigour to her flights, new pinions to her wings.
Soon grows the pigmy to gigantic size ;
Her feet on earth, her forehead in the skies.
Enraged against the gods, revengeful Earth
Produced her, last of the Titanian birth :

Swift is her walk, more swift her wingèd haste :
A monstrous phantom, horrible and vast.
As many plumes as raise her lofty flight ;
So many piercing eyes enlarge her sight ;
Millions of opening mouths to fame belong,
And every mouth is furnished with a tongue ;
And round, with listening ears the flying plague is hung.
She fills the peaceful universe with cries
No slumbers ever close her wakeful eyes .
By day, from lofty towers her head she shows,
And spreads through trembling crowds disastrous news ;
With court-informers, haunts, and royal spies ;
Things done, relates ; not done, she feigns, and mingles
 truth with lies.
Talk is her business ; and her chief delight
To tell of prodigies, and cause affright.
She fills the people's ears with Dido's name,
Who, lost to honour and the sense of shame,
Admits into her throne and nuptial bed
A wandering guest, who from his country fled.
Whole days with him she passes in delights ;
And wastes in luxury long winter nights,
Forgetful of her fame, and royal trust,
Dissolved in ease, abandoned to her lust.
 The goddess widely spreads the loud report,
And flies at length to king Iärbas' court.
When first possessed with this unwelcome news,
Whom did he not of men and gods accuse ?
This prince, from ravished Garamantis born,
A hundred temples did with spoils adorn
In Ammon's honour, his celestial sire ;
A hundred altars fed with wakeful fire ;
And, through his vast dominions, priests ordained,
Whose watchful care these holy rites maintained.
The gates and columns were with garlands crowned,
And blood of victim beasts enriched the ground.
 He, when he heard a fugitive could move
The Tyrian princess, who disdained his love,
His breast with fury burned, his eyes with fire—
Mad with despair, impatient with desire—

Then on the sacred altars pouring wine,
He thus with prayers implored his sire divine :
'Great Jove ! propitious to the Moorish race,
Who feast on painted beds, with offerings grace
Thy temples, and adore thy power divine
With blood of victims, and with sparkling wine ;
Seest thou not this ! or do we fear in vain
Thy boasted thunder, and thy thoughtless reign ?
Do thy broad hands the forky lightnings lance ?
Thine are the bolts, or the blind work of chance ?
A wandering woman builds within our state,
A little town, bought at an easy rate ;
She pays me homage—(and my grants allow
A narrow space of Libyan lands to plough) ;
Yet, scorning me, by passion blindly led,
Admits a banished Trojan to her bed !
And now this other Paris, with his train
Of conquered cowards, must in Afric reign !
(Whom, what they are, their looks and garb confess,
Their locks with oil perfumed, their Lydian dress.)
He takes the spoil, enjoys the princely dame ;
And I, rejected I, adore an empty name !'
  His vows, in haughty terms, he thus preferred,
And held his altar's horns : the mighty Thunderer
    heard,
Then cast his eyes on Carthage, where he found
The lustful pair in lawless pleasure drowned,
Lost in their loves, insensible of shame,
And both forgetful of their better fame.
He calls Cyllenius ; and the god attends ;
By whom this menacing command he sends :
'Go, mount the western winds, and cleave the sky ;
Then, with a swift descent, to Carthage fly :
There find the Trojan chief, who wastes his days
In slothful riot and inglorious ease,
Nor minds the future city, given by fate.
To him this message from my mouth relate :
Nor so fair Venus hoped, when twice she won
Thy life with prayers ; nor promised such a son.
Her's was a hero, destined to command

A martial race, and rule the Latian land ;
Who should his ancient line from Teucer draw ;
And on the conquered world impose the law.
If glory cannot move a mind so mean,
Nor future praise from fading pleasure wean,
Yet why should he defraud his son of fame,
And grudge the Romans their immortal name?
What are his vain designs? what hopes he more
From his long lingering on a hostile shore,
Regardless to redeem his honour lost,
And for his race to gain the Ausonian coast?
Bid him with speed the Tyrian court forsake ;
With this command the slumbering warrior wake.'
   Hermes obeys ; with golden pinions binds
His flying feet, and mounts the western winds :
And, whether o'er the seas or earth he flies,
With rapid force they bear him down the skies.
But first he grasps within his awful hand
The mark of sovereign power, his magic wand ;
With this he draws the ghosts from hollow graves ;
With this he drives them down the Stygian waves ;
With this he seals in sleep the wakeful sight,
And eyes, though closed in death, restores to light.
Thus armed, the god begins his airy race,
And drives the racking clouds along the liquid space ;
Now sees the top of Atlas, as he flies,
Whose brawny back supports the starry skies :
Atlas, whose head with piny forests crowned,
Is beaten by the winds, with foggy vapours bound.
Snows hide his shoulders : from beneath his chin
The founts of rolling streams their race begin :
A beard of ice on his large breast depends :
Here, poised upon his wings, the god descends.
Then, rested thus, he from the towering height
Plunged downward with precipitated flight :
Lights on the seas, and skims along the flood.
As water-fowl, who seek their fishy food,
Less, and yet less, to distant prospect show ;
By turns they dance aloft, and dive below :
Like these, the steerage of his wings he plies,

And near the surface of the water flies;
Till, having passed the seas, and crossed the sands,
He closed his wings, and stooped on Libyan lands;
Where shepherds once were housed in homely sheds,
Now towers, within the clouds advance their heads.

   Arriving there, he found the Trojan prince
New ramparts raising for the town's defence.
A purple scarf, with gold embroidered o'er
(Queen Dido's gift), about his waist he wore;
A sword, with glittering gems diversified,
For ornament, not use, hung idly by his side.
Then thus, with wingèd words, the god began
(Resuming his own shape): 'Degenerate man!
Thou woman's property! what mak'st thou here,
These foreign walls and Tyrian towers to rear?—
Forgetful of thy own! All-powerful Jove,
Who sways the world below and heaven above,
Has sent me down with this severe command:
What means thy lingering in the Libyan land?
If glory cannot move a mind so mean,
Nor future praise from flitting pleasure wean,
Regard the fortunes of thy rising heir:
The promised crown let young Ascanius wear,
To whom the Ausonian sceptre, and the state
Of Rome's imperial name, is owed by fate.'
So spoke the god; and, speaking, took his flight
Involved in clouds; and vanished out of sight.

   The pious prince was seized with sudden fear:
Mute was his tongue, and upright stood his hair.
Revolving in his mind the stern command,
He longs to fly, and loathes the charming land.
What should he say, or how should he begin?
What course, alas! remains, to steer between
The offended lover and the powerful queen?
This way, and that, he turns his anxious mind;
And all expedients tries, and none can find.
Fixed on the deed, but doubtful of the means;
After long thought, to this advice he leans:
Three chiefs he calls, commands them to repair
The fleet, and ship their men, with silent care.

Some plausible pretence he bids them find,
To colour what in secret he designed.
Himself, meantime, the softest hours would choose,
Before the love-sick lady heard the news,
And move her tender mind, by slow degrees
To suffer what the sovereign power decrees:
Jove will inspire him, when, and what to say.
They hear with pleasure, and with haste obey.

But soon the queen perceives the thin disguise:
(What arts can blind a jealous woman's eyes?)
She was the first to find the secret fraud,
Before the fatal news was blazed abroad:
Love the first motions of the lover hears,
Quick to presage, and e'en in safety fears.
Nor impious Fame was wanting, to report
The ships repaired, the Trojans' thick resort,
And purpose to forsake the Tyrian court.
Frantic with fear, impatient of the wound,
And impotent of mind, she roves the city round.
Less wild the Bacchanalian dames appear,
When, from afar, their nightly god they hear,
And howl about the hills, and shake the wreathy spear
At length she finds the dear perfidious man;
Prevents his formed excuse, and thus began:
'Base and ungrateful! could you hope to fly,
And undiscovered 'scape a lover's eye?
Nor could my kindness your compassion move,
Nor plighted vows, nor dearer bands of love?
Or is the death of a despairing queen
Not worth preventing, though too well foreseen?
E'en when the wintry winds command your stay,
You dare the tempests, and defy the sea.
False as you are, suppose you were not bound
To lands unknown, and foreign coasts to sound;
Were Troy restored, and Priam's happy reign,
Now durst you tempt, for Troy, the raging main?
See, whom you fly! am I the foe you shun?
Now, by those holy vows, so late begun,
By this right hand (since I have nothing more
To challenge, but the faith you gave before),

I beg you by these tears too truly shed,
By the new pleasures of our nuptial bed;
If ever Dido, when you most were kind,
Were pleasing in your eyes, or touched your mind;
By these my prayers, if prayers may yet have place,
Pity the fortunes of a falling race!
For you I have provoked a tyrant's hate,
Incensed the Libyan and the Tyrian state,
For you alone, I suffer in my fame,
Bereft of honour, and exposed to shame!
Whom have I now to trust, ungrateful guest?
(That only name remains of all the rest!)
What have I left? or whither can I fly?
Must I attend Pygmalion's cruelty,
Or, till Iärbas shall in triumph lead
A queen that proudly scorned his proffered bed?
Had you deferred, at least, your hasty flight,
And left behind some pledge of our delight;
Some babe to bless the mother's mournful sight;
Some young Æneas to supply your place,
Whose features might express his father's face;
I should not then complain to live bereft
Of all my husband, or be wholly left.'
    Here paused the queen.   Unmoved he holds his eyes,
By Jove's command; nor suffered love to rise
Though heaving in his heart; and thus at length replies:
'Fair queen, you never can reveal repeat
Your boundless favours, or I own my debt;
Nor, can my mind forget Eliza's name
While vital breath inspires this mortal frame.
This only let me speak in my defence—
I never hoped a secret flight from hence,
Much less pretended to the lawful claim
Of sacred nuptials, or a husband's name.
For, if indulgent heaven would leave me free,
And not submit my life to fate's decree,
My choice would lead me to the Trojan shore,
Those relics to review, their dust adore;
And Priam's ruined palace to restore.
But now the Delphian oracle commands,

And fate invites me to the Latian lands.
That is the promised place to which I steer ;
And all my vows are terminated there.
If you, a Tyrian and a stranger born,
With walls and towers a Libyan town adorn,
Why may not we—like you, a foreign race—
Like you, seek shelter in a foreign place?
As often as the night obscures the skies
With humid shades, or twinkling stars arise,
Anchises' angry ghost in dreams appears,
Chides my delay, and fills my soul with fears ;
And young Ascanius justly may complain,
Defrauded of his fate and destined reign.
E'en now the herald of the gods appeared—
Waking I saw him, and his message heard.
From Jove he came commissioned, heavenly **bright**
With radiant beams, and manifest to sight
(The sender and the sent I both attest) :
These walls he entered, and those words expressed.
Fair queen, oppose not what the gods command :
Forced by my fate, I leave your happy land.'
    Thus while he spoke, already she began
With sparkling eyes to view the guilty man ;
From head to foot surveyed his person o'er ;
Nor longer these outrageous threats forbore :
' False as thou art, and more than false, forsworn *!*
Not sprung from noble blood, nor goddess born,
But hewn from hardened entrails of a rock !
And rough Hyrcanian tigers gave thee suck !
Why should I fawn? what have I worse to fear?
Did he once look, or lend a listening ear,
Sighed when I sobbed, or shed one kindly tear?
All, symptoms of a base ungrateful mind,
So foul, that which is worse, 'tis hard to find.
Of man's injustice why should I complain?
The gods, and Jove himself, behold in vain
Triumphant treason : yet no thunder flies ;
Nor Juno views my wrongs with equal eyes :
Faithless is earth, and faithless are the skies !
Justice is fled, and truth is now no more !

I saved the shipwrecked exile on my shore:
With needful food his hungry Trojans fed:
I took the traitor to my throne and bed.
Fool that I was! 'tis little to repeat
The rest: I stored and rigged his ruined fleet.
I rave, I rave! A god's command he pleads,
And makes heaven accessory to his deeds.
Now Lycian lots, and now the Delian god,
Now Hermes is employed from Jove's abode,
To warn him hence; as if the peaceful state
Of heavenly powers were touched with human fate!
But go! thy flight no longer I detain—
Go! seek thy promised kingdom through the main!
Yet, if the heavens will hear my pious vow,
The faithless waves, not half so false as thou,
Or secret sands, shall sepulchres afford
To thy proud vessels, and their perjured lord!
Then shalt thou call on injured Dido's name:
Dido shall come in a black sulphury flame,
When death has once dissolved her mortal frame—
Shall smile to see the traitor vainly weep:
Her angry ghost, arising from the deep,
Shall haunt thee waking, and disturb thy sleep!
At least my shade thy punishment shall know;
And fame shall spread the pleasing news below.'

Abruptly here she stops; then turns away
Her loathing eyes, and shuns the sight of day.
Amazed he stood, revolving in his mind
What speech to frame, and what excuse to find.
Her fearful maids their fainting mistress led,
And softly laid her on her ivory bed.

But good Æneas, though he much desired
To give that pity which her grief required
(Though much he mourned, and laboured with his love);
Resolved at length, obeys the will of Jove:
Reviews his forces: they with early care
Unmoor their vessels, and for sea prepare.
The fleet is soon afloat, in all its pride;
And well-caulked galleys in the harbour ride.
Then oaks for oars they felled; or, as they stood,

Of its green arms despoiled the growing wood,
Studious of flight. The beach is covered o'er
With Trojan bands, that blacken all the shore:
On every side are seen, descending down,
Thick swarms of soldiers laden, from the town.
Thus, in battalia, march embodied ants,
Fearful of winter, and of future wants,
T' invade the corn, and to their cells convey
The plundered forage of their yellow prey.
The sable troops, along the narrow tracks,
Scarce bear the weighty burden on their backs:
Some set their shoulders to the ponderous grain;
Some guard the spoil; some lash the lagging train;
All ply their several tasks, and equal toil sustain.

What pangs the tender breast of Dido tore,
When, from the tower, she saw the covered shore,
And heard the shouts of sailors from afar,
Mixed with the murmurs of the watery war!
All-powerful Love! what changes canst thou cause
In human hearts, subjected to thy laws!
Once more her haughty soul the tyrant bends
To prayers and mean submissions she descends.
No female arts or aids she left untried,
Nor counsels unexplored, before she died.

'Look, Anna! look! the Trojans crowd to sea;
They spread their canvas, and their anchors weigh;
The shouting crew their ships with garlands bind,
Invoke the sea-gods, and invite the wind.
Could I have thought this threatening blow so near,
My tender soul had been forewarned to bear.
But do not you my last request deny;
With yon perfidious man your interest try;
And bring me news, if I must live or die.
You are his favourite; you alone can find
The dark recesses of his inmost mind;
In all his trusted secrets you have part,
And know the soft approaches to his heart.
Haste then, and humbly seek my haughty foe;
Tell him, I did not with the Grecians go,
Nor did my fleet against his friends employ,

Nor swore the ruin of unhappy Troy,
Nor moved with hands profane his father's dust:
Why should he then reject a suit so just?
Whom does he shun? and whither would he fly?
Can he this last, this only prayer deny?
Let him at least his dangerous flight delay,
Wait better winds, and hope a calmer sea.
The nuptials he disclaims, I urge no more:
Let him pursue the promised Latian shore.
A short delay is all I ask him now—
A pause of grief, an interval from woe;
Till my soft soul be tempered to sustain
Accustomed sorrows, and inured to pain.
If you in pity grant this one request,
My death shall glut the hatred of his breast.'

This mournful message pious Anna bears,
And seconds with her own, her sister's tears:
But all her arts are still employed in vain:
Again she comes, and is refused again.
His hardened heart nor prayers nor threat'nings move;
Fate and the god, had stopped his ears to love.

As, when the winds their airy quarrel try,
Justling from every quarter of the sky;
This way and that the mountain oak they bend;
His boughs they shatter, and his branches rend;
With leaves and falling mast they spread the ground;
The hollow valleys echo to the sound;
Unmoved, the royal plant their fury mocks,
Or, shaken, clings more closely to the rocks:
Far as he shoots his towering head on high,
So deep in earth his fixed foundations lie.
No less a storm the Trojan hero bears;
Thick messages and loud complaints he hears,
And bandied words, still beating on his ears.
Sighs, groans, and tears, proclaim his inward pains;
But the firm purpose of his heart remains.

The wretched queen, pursued by cruel Fate,
Begins at length the light of heaven to hate;
And loathes to live. Then dire portents she sees,
To hasten on the death her soul decrees—

Strange to relate ! for when, before the shrine
She pours in sacrifice the purple wine,
The purple wine is turned to putrid blood ;
And the white offered milk, converts to mud.
This dire presage, to her alone revealed,
From all, and e'en her sister, she concealed.
A marble temple stood within the grove,
Sacred to death, and to her murdered love ;
That honoured chapel she had hung around
With snowy fleeces, and with garlands crowned.
Oft, when she visited this lonely dome,
Strange voices issued from her husband's tomb :
She thought she heard him summon her away,
Invite her to his grave, and chide her stay.
Hourly 'tis heard, when with a boding note
The solitary skreech-owl strains her throat,
And on a chimney's top, or turret's height,
With songs obscene, disturbs the silence of the night.
Besides, old prophecies augment her fears ;
And stern Æneas in her dreams appears,
Disdainful as by day : she seems, alone,
To wander in her sleep, through ways unknown,
Guideless and dark ; or, in a desert plain
To seek her subjects, and to seek in vain—
Like Pentheus, when, distracted with his fear
He saw two suns, and double Thebes, appear ;
Or mad Orestes, when his mother's ghost
Full in his face infernal torches tossed,
And shook her snaky locks : he shuns the sight,
Flies o'er the stage, surprised with mortal fright :
The Furies guard the door, and intercept his flight.
    Now, sinking underneath a load of grief,
From death alone she seeks her last relief :
The time and means resolved within her breast,
She to her mournful sister thus addressed
(Dissembling hope, her cloudy front she clears,
And a false vigour in her eyes appears) :
' Rejoice ! (she said) instructed from above,
My lover I shall gain, or lose my love.
Nigh rising Atlas, next the falling sun,

Long tracts of Æthiopian climates run :
There, a Massylian priestess I have found,
Honoured for age, for magic arts renowned.
The Hesperian temple was her trusted care ;
'Twas she supplied the wakeful dragon's fare :
She, poppy-seeds in honey taught to steep :
Reclaimed his rage, and soothed him into sleep :
She watched the golden fruit.   Her charms unbind
The chains of love, or fix them on the mind :
She stops the torrents, leaves the channel dry,
Repels the stars, and backward bears the sky.
The yawning earth rebellows to her call ;
Pale ghosts ascend ; and mountain ashes fall.
Witness ye gods, and thou, my better part,
How loth I am to try this impious art !
Within the secret court, with silent care,
Erect a lofty pile, exposed in air :
Hang on the topmost part, the Trojan vest,
Spoils, arms, and presents, of my faithless guest.
Next, under these, the bridal bed be placed,
Where I my ruin in his arms embraced.
All relics of the wretch are doomed to fire ;
For so the priestess and her charms require.'
   Thus far she said, and farther speech forbears.
A mortal paleness in her face appears :
Yet the mistrustless Anna could not find
The secret funeral in these rites designed ;
Nor thought so dire a rage possessed her mind.
Unknowing of a train concealed so well,
She feared no worse than when Sichæus fell ;
Therefore obeys.   The fatal pile they rear
Within the secret court, exposed in air,
The cloven holms and pines are heaped on high :
And garlands on the hollow spaces lie :
Sad cypress, vervain, yew, compose the wreath ;
And every baleful green denoting death.
The queen, determined to the fatal deed,
The spoils and sword he left, in order spread,
And the man's image on the nuptial bed.
   And now (the sacred altars placed around)

The priestess enters, with her hair unbound,
And thrice invokes the powers below the ground.
Night, Erebus, and Chaos, she proclaims,
And threefold Hecate, with her hundred names,
And three Dianas: next, she sprinkles round
With feigned Avernian drops, the hallowed ground ;
Culls hoary simples, found by Phœbe's light,
With brazen sickles reaped at noon of night ;
Then mixes baleful juices in the bowl,
And cuts the forehead of a new-born foal,
Robbing the mother's love.   The destined queen
Observes, assisting at the rites obscene :
A leavened cake in her devoted hands
She holds ; and next the highest altar stands :
One tender foot was shod, her other bare ;
Girt was her gathered gown, and loose her hair.
Thus dressed, she summoned with her dying breath
The heavens and planets conscious of her death,
And every power, if any rules above,
Who minds or who revenges injured love.
'Twas dead of night, when weary bodies close
Their eyes in balmy sleep, and soft repose :
The winds no longer whisper through the woods ;
Nor murmuring tides disturb the gentle floods.
The stars in silent order moved around ;
And Peace, with downy wings was brooding on the
   ground.
The flocks and herds, and particoloured fowl
Which haunt the woods or swim the weedy pool,
Stretched on the quiet earth, securely lay,
Forgetting the past labours of the day.
All else, of Nature's common gift partake ;
Unhappy Dido was alone awake :
Nor sleep nor ease the furious queen can find :
Sleep fled her eyes, as quiet fled her mind.
Despair, and rage, and love, divide her heart ;
Despair and rage had some, but love the greater part.
   Then thus she said within her secret mind :
' What shall I do ? what succour can I find ?
Become a suppliant to Iärbas' pride,

And take my turn to court, and be denied?
Shall I with this ungrateful Trojan go,
Forsake an empire, and attend a foe?
Himself I refuged, and his train relieved—
'Tis true—but am I sure to be received?
Can gratitude in Trojan souls have place?
Laomedon still lives in all his race!
Then shall I seek alone the churlish crew,
Or with my fleet their flying sails pursue?
What force have I but those, whom scarce before
I drew reluctant from their native shore?
Will they again embark at my desire,
Once more sustain the seas, and quit their second Tyre?
Rather with steel thy guilty breast invade,
And take the fortune thou thyself hast made.
Your pity, sister, first seduced my mind;
Or seconded too well what I designed.
These dear-bought pleasures had I never known,
Had I continued free, and still my own;
(Avoiding love), I had not found despair,
But shared with savage beasts the common air:
Like them, a lonely life I might have led;
Not mourned the living, nor disturbed the dead.'
These thoughts she brooded in her anxious breast.—
On board, the Trojan found more easy rest.
Resolved to sail, in sleep he passed the night;
And ordered all things for his early flight.
    To whom, once more the wingèd god appears:
His former youthful mien and shape he wears;
And with this new alarm invades his ears:
'Sleep'st thou, O goddess-born? and canst thou drown
Thy needful cares, so near a hostile town,
Beset with foes; nor hear'st the western gales
Invite thy passage, and inspire thy sails?
She harbours in her heart a furious hate
(And thou shalt find the dire effects too late),
Fixed on revenge, and obstinate to die.—
Haste swiftly hence, while thou hast power to fly!
The sea with ships will soon be covered o'er,
And blazing firebrands kindle all the shore.

Prevent her rage, while night obscures the skies;
And sail before the purple morn arise.
Who knows what hazards thy delay may bring?
Woman's a various and a changeful thing!'
Thus, Hermes in the dream; then took his flight
Aloft in air, unseen, and mixed with night.
　Twice warned by the celestial messenger,
The pious prince arose with hasty fear;
Then roused his drowsy train without delay:
'Haste to your banks! your crooked anchors weigh,
And spread your flying sails, and stand to sea!
A god commands! he stood before my sight,
And urged us once again to speedy flight.
O sacred power! what power soe'er thou art,
To thy blessed orders I resign my heart.
Lead thou the way; protect thy Trojan bands;
And prosper the design thy will commands.'
He said; and, drawing forth his flaming sword,
His thundering arm divides the many-twisted cord.
An emulating zeal inspires his train:
They run; they snatch; they rush into the main.
With headlong haste they leave the desert shores,
And brush the liquid seas with labouring oars.
　Aurora now had left her saffron bed,
And beams of early light the heavens o'erspread;
When, from a tower, the queen, with wakeful eyes,
Saw day point upward from the rosy skies.
She looked to seaward; but the sea was void,
And scarce in ken the sailing ships descried.
Stung with despite, and furious with despair,
She struck her trembling breast, and tore her hair.
'And shall the ungrateful traitor go (she said),
My land forsaken, and my love betrayed?
Shall we not arm? not rush from every street,
To follow, sink, and burn, his perjured fleet?
Haste! haul my galleys out! pursue the foe!
Bring flaming brands! set sail, and swiftly row!
What have I said? Where am I? Fury turns
My brain; and my distempered bosom burns.
Then, when I gave my person and my throne,

This hate, this rage, had been more timely shown.
See now the promised faith, the vaunted name,
The pious man, who, rushing through the flame,
Preserved his gods, and to the Phrygian shore
The burden of his feeble father bore !
I should have torn him piece-meal—strewed in floods
His scattered limbs, or left exposed in woods :
Destroyed his friends, and son ; and from the fire
Have set the reeking boy before the sire !
Events are doubtful, which on battle wait ;
Yet where's the doubt, to souls secure of fate ?
My Tyrians, at their injured queen's command,
Had tossed their fires amid the Trojan band :
At once extinguished all the faithless name ;
And I myself, in vengeance of my shame,
Had fall'n upon the pile, to mend the funeral flame.
Thou Sun, who view'st at once the world below !
Thou Juno, guardian of the nuptial vow !
Thou Hecate, hearken from thy dark abodes !
Ye Furies, fiends, and violated gods !
All powers invoked with Dido's dying breath,
Attend her curses, and avenge her death !
If so the Fates ordain, and Jove commands,
The ungrateful wretch should find the Latian lands,
Yet let a race untamed, and haughty foes,
His peaceful entrance with dire arms oppose :
Oppressed with numbers in the unequal field,
His men discouraged, and himself expelled,
Let him for succour sue from place to place,
Torn from his subjects, and his son's embrace.
First, let him see his friends in battle slain,
And their untimely fate lament in vain :
And when at length, the cruel war will cease,
On hard conditions may he buy his peace ;
Nor let him then enjoy supreme command ;
But fall, untimely, by some hostile hand ;
And lie unburied on the barren sand !
These are my prayers, and this my dying will ;
And you, my Tyrians, every curse fulfil :
Perpetual hate and mortal wars proclaim

Against the prince, the people, and the name.
These grateful offerings on my grave bestow;
Nor league, nor love, the hostile nations know!
Now, and from hence in every future age,
When rage excites your arms, and strength supplies
    the rage,
Rise some avenger of our Libyan blood;
With fire and sword pursue the perjured brood:
Our arms, our seas, our shores, opposed to theirs;
And the same hate descend on all our heirs!'

    This said, within her anxious mind she weighs
The means of cutting short her odious days.
Then to Sichæus' nurse she briefly said
(For, when she left her country, her's was dead),
'Go, Barce, call my sister. Let her care
The solemn rites of sacrifice prepare;
The sheep, and all the atoning offerings, bring;
Sprinkling her body from the crystal spring
With living drops: then let her come; and thou,
With sacred fillets bind thy hoary brow.
Thus will I pay my vows to Stygian Jove,
And end the cares of my disastrous love;
Then cast the Trojan image on the fire;
And, as that burns, my passion shall expire.'

    The nurse moves onward with officious care,
And all the speed her aged limbs can bear.
But furious Dido, with dark thoughts involved,
Shook at the mighty mischief she resolved.
With livid spots distinguished was her face;
Red were her rolling eyes, and discomposed her pace:
Ghastly she gazed; with pain she drew her breath;
And nature shivered at approaching death.

    Then swiftly to the fatal place she passed,
And mounts the funeral pile with furious haste;
Unsheaths the sword the Trojan left behind
(Not for so dire an enterprise designed).
But when she viewed the garments loosely spread,
Which once he wore, and saw the conscious bed,
She paused, and with a sigh, the robes embraced;
Then on the couch her trembling body cast,

Repressed her ready tears, and spoke her last:
'Dear pledges of my love, while heaven so pleased,
Receive a soul, of mortal anguish eased.
My fatal course is finished; and I go,
A glorious name, among the ghosts below.
A lofty city by my hands is raised;
Pygmalion punished, and my lord appeased.
What could my fortune have afforded more,
Had the false Trojan never touched my shore?'
Then kissed the couch; and 'Must I die (she said),
And unrevenged? 'tis doubly to be dead!
Yet e'en this death with pleasure I receive:
On any terms, 'tis better than to live.
These flames, from far, may the false Trojan view;
These boding omens his base flight pursue!'
She said, and struck: deep entered in her side
The piercing steel, with reeking purple dyed.
Clogged in the wound the cruel weapon stands;
The spouting blood came streaming on her hands.

Her sad attendants saw the deadly stroke,
And with loud cries the sounding palace shook.
Distracted, from the fatal sight they fled,
And through the town the dismal rumour spread.
First from the frighted court the yell began;
Redoubled, thence from house to house it ran:
The groans of men, with shrieks, laments, and cries
Of mixing women, mount the vaulted skies.
Not less the clamour, than if—ancient Tyre,
Or the new Carthage, set by foes on fire—
The rolling ruin, with their loved abodes,
Involved the blazing temple of their gods.

Her sister hears: and furious with despair,
She beats her breast, and rends her yellow hair;
And, calling on Eliza's name aloud,
Runs breathless to the place, and breaks the crowd,
'Was all that pomp of woe for this prepared,
These fires, this funeral pile, these altars reared?
Was all this train of plots contrived (said she),
All, only to deceive unhappy me?
Which is the worst? Didst thou in death pretend

To scorn thy sister, or delude thy friend?
Thy summoned sister and thy friend had come:
One sword had served us both, one common tomb:
Was I to raise the pile, the powers invoke,
Not to be present at the fatal stroke?
At once thou hast destroyed thyself and me,
Thy town, thy senate, and thy colony!
Bring water! bathe the wound; while I in death
Lay close my lips to hers, and catch the flying breath.'
This said, she mounts the pile with eager haste,
And in her arms the gasping queen embraced;
Her temples chafed; and her own garments tore
To stanch the streaming blood, and cleanse the gore.
Thrice Dido tried to raise her drooping head,
And, fainting, thrice fell grovelling on the bed:
Thrice oped her heavy eyes, and saw the light;
But, having found it, sickened at the sight,
And closed her lids at last in endless night.

Then Juno, grieving that she should sustain
A death so lingering, and so full of pain,
Sent Iris down to free her from the strife
Of labouring nature, and dissolve her life.
For, since she died not doomed by heaven's decree,
Or her own crime, but human casualty,
And rage of love that plunged her in despair,
The Sisters had not cut the topmost hair,
Which Proserpine and they can only know;
Nor made her sacred to the shades below.
Downward the various goddess took her flight,
And drew a thousand colours from the light.
Then stood above the dying lover's head,
And said: 'I thus devote thee to the dead:
This offering to the infernal gods I bear.'
Thus while she spoke, she cut the fatal hair:
The struggling soul was loosed, and life dissolved in air.

BOOK V

THE ARGUMENT

Æneas, setting sail from Afric, is driven by a storm on the coasts of Sicily, where he is hospitably received by his friend Acestes, king of part of the island, and born of Trojan parentage. He applies himself to celebrate the memory of his father with divine honours, and accordingly institutes funeral games, and appoints prizes for those who should conquer in them. While these ceremonies were performing, Juno sends Iris to persuade the Trojan women to burn the ships, who upon her instigation set fire to them; which burned four, and would have consumed the rest, had not Jupiter by a miraculous shower extinguished it. Upon this, Æneas, by the advice of one of his generals, and a vision of his father, builds a city for the women, old men, and others, who were either unfit for war, or weary of the voyage, and sails for Italy. Venus procures of Neptune a safe voyage for him and all his men, excepting only his pilot Palinurus, who was unfortunately lost.

MEANTIME the Trojan cuts his watery way,
Fixed on his voyage, through the curling sea;
Then, casting back his eyes, with dire amaze,
Sees on the Punic shore the mountain blaze:
The cause unknown; yet his presaging mind
The fate of Dido from the fire divined.
He knew the stormy souls of womankind;
What secret springs their eager passions move,
How capable of death for injured love.
Dire auguries from hence the Trojans draw;
Till neither fires nor shining shores they saw.

   Now seas and skies their prospects only bound:
An empty space above, a floating field around.
But soon the heavens with shadows were o'erspread;
A swelling cloud hung hovering o'er their head:

Livid it looked—the threatening of a storm ;
Then night and horror ocean's face deform.
The pilot, Palinurus, cried aloud :
'What gusts of weather from that gathering cloud
My thoughts presage ! Ere yet the tempest roars,
Stand to your tackle, mates, and stretch your oars ;
Contract your swelling sails, and luff to wind.'
The frighted crew perform the task assigned.
Then, to his fearless chief, ' not heaven (said he),
Though Jove himself should promise Italy,
Can stem the torrent of this raging sea.
Mark, how the shifting winds from west arise,
And what collected night involves the skies !
Nor can our shaken vessels live at sea,
Much less against the tempest force their way :
'Tis fate diverts our course, and fate we must obey.
Not far from hence, if I observed aright
The southing of the stars, and polar light,
Sicilia lies, whose hospitable shores
In safety we may reach, with struggling oars.'
Æneas then replied : ' Too sure I find,
We strive in vain against the seas and wind :
Now shift your sails : what place can please me more
Than what you promise, the Sicilian shore,
Whose hallowed earth Anchises' bones contains,
And where a prince of Trojan lineage reigns.'
The course resolved, before the western wind
They scud amain, and make the port assigned.
   Meantime Acestes, from a lofty stand,
Beheld the fleet descending on the land ;
And, not unmindful of his ancient race,
Down from the cliff he ran, with eager pace,
And held the hero in a strict embrace.
Of a rough Libyan bear, the spoils he wore,
And either hand a pointed javelin bore.
His mother was a dame of Dardan blood ;
His sire Crinisus, a Sicilian flood.
He welcomes his returning friends ashore
With plenteous country cates, and homely store.
   Now, when the following morn had chased away

The flying stars, and light restored the day,
Æneas called the Trojan troops around,
And thus bespoke them from a rising ground:
'Offspring of heaven, divine Dardanian race!
The sun, revolving through the ethereal space,
The shining circle of the year has filled,
Since first this isle my father's ashes held:
And now the rising day renews the year—
A day for ever sad, for ever dear.
This would I celebrate with annual games,
With gifts on altars piled, and holy flames,
Though banished to Gætulia's barren sands,
Caught on the Grecian seas, or hostile lands:
But, since this happy storm our fleet has driven
(Not, as I deem, without the will of heaven)
Upon these friendly shores and flowery plains,
Which hide Anchises and his blest remains;
Let us with joy perform his honours due,
And pray for prosperous winds, our voyage to renew—
Pray, that in towns and temples of our own,
The name of great Anchises may be known;
And yearly games may spread the god's renown.
Our sports, Acestes, of the Trojan race,
With royal gifts ordained, is pleased to grace:
Two steers on every ship the king bestows:
His gods and ours shall share your equal vows.
Besides, if, nine days hence, the rosy morn
Shall with unclouded light the skies adorn,
That day with solemn sports I mean to grace:
Light galleys on the seas shall run a watery race:
Some shall in swiftness for the goal contend,
And others try the twanging bow to bend:
The strong, with iron gauntlets armed, shall stand
Opposed in combat on the yellow sand.
Let all be present at the games prepared;
And joyful victors wait the just reward.
But now assist the rites with garlands crowned.'
He said, and first his brows with myrtle bound.
Then Helymus, by his example led,
And old Acestes, each adorned his head;

Thus young Ascanius, with a sprightly grace,
His temples tied, and all the Trojan race.
    Æneas then advanced amidst the train,
By thousands followed through the flowery plain,
To great Anchises' tomb ; which when he found,
He poured to Bacchus, on the hallowed ground
Two bowls of sparkling wine, of milk two more,
And two (from offered bulls) of purple gore.
With roses then the sepulchre he strowed,
And thus, his father's ghost bespoke aloud :
' Hail, O ye holy manes ! hail again,
Paternal ashes, now revived in vain !
The gods permitted not, that you with me
Should reach the promised shores of Italy,
Or Tiber's flood—what flood soe'er it be.'
Scarce had he finished, when, with speckled **pride**,
A serpent from the tomb began to glide ;
His hugy bulk on seven high volumes rolled ;
Blue was his breadth of back, but streaked with **scaly
gold** :
Thus riding on his curls, he seemed to pass
A rolling fire along, and singe the grass.
More various colours through his body run,
Than Iris when her bow imbibes the sun.
Betwixt the rising altars, and around,
The sacred monster shot along the ground ;
With harmless play amidst the bowls he passed,
And with his lolling tongue assayed the taste :
Thus fed with holy food, the wondrous guest
Within the hollow tomb retired to rest.
The pious prince, surprised at what he viewed,
The funeral honours with more zeal renewed ;
Doubtful if this the place's genius were,
Or guardian of his father's sepulchre.
Five sheep, according to the rites, he slew ;
As many swine, and steers of sable hue ;
New generous wine he from the goblets poured ;
And called his father's ghost, from hell restored.
The glad attendants in long order come,
Offering their gifts at great Anchises' tomb .

Some add more oxen ; some divide the spoil ;
Some place the chargers on the grassy soil ;
Some blow the fires, and offered entrails broil.
  Now came the day desired.   The skies were bright
With rosy lustre of the rising light :
The bordering people, roused by sounding fame
Of Trojan feasts and great Acestes' name,
The crowded shore with acclamations fill ;
Part to behold, and part to prove their skill.
And first the gifts in public view they place,
Green laurel-wreaths, and palm, the victors' grace.
Within the circle, arms and tripods lie,
Ingots of gold and silver heaped on high,
And vests embroidered, of the Tyrian dye.
The trumpet's clangour then the feast proclaims ;
And all prepare for their appointed games.
Four galleys first, which equal rowers bear,
Advancing, in the watery lists appear.
The speedy Dolphin, that outstrips the wind,
Bore Mnestheus, author of the Memmian kind :
Gyas the vast Chimæra's bulk commands,
Which rising like a towering city stands :
Three Trojans tug at every labouring oar ;
Three banks in three degrees the sailors bore ;
Beneath their sturdy strokes the billows roar.
Sergestus, who began the Sergian race
In the great Centaur, took the leading place :
Cloanthus on the sea-green Scylla stood ;
From whom Cluentius draws his Trojan blood.
  Far in the sea, against the foaming shore,
There stands a rock : the raging billows roar
Above his head in storms ; but when 'tis clear,
Uncurl their ridgy backs, and at his foot appear.
In peace, below, the gentle waters run ;
The cormorants, above, lie basking in the sun.
On this the hero fixed an oak in sight,
The mark to guide the mariners aright.
To bear with this, the seamen stretch their oars ;
Then round the rock they steer, and seek the former
    shores.

The lots decide their place. Above the rest,
Each leader shining in his Tyrian vest :
The common crew, with wreaths of poplar boughs
Their temples crown, and shade their sweaty brows :
Besmeared with oil, their naked shoulders shine :
All take their seats, and wait the sounding sign.
They grip their oars ; and every panting breast
Is raised by turns with hope, by turns with fear depressed.
The clangour of the trumpet gives the sign ;
At once they start, advancing in a line ;
With shouts the sailors rend the starry skies ;
Lashed with their oars, the smoky billows rise ;
Sparkles the briny main, and the vexed ocean fries.
Exact in time, with equal strokes they row :
At once the brushing oars and brazen prow
Dash up the sandy waves, and ope the depths below.
Not fiery coursers, in a chariot-race,
Invade the field with half so swift a pace :
Not the fierce driver with more fury lends
The sounding lash, and ere the stroke descends,
Low to the wheels his pliant body bends.
The partial crowd their hopes and fears divide,
And aid with eager shouts, the favoured side.
Cries, murmurs, clamours, with a mixing sound,
From woods to woods, from hills to hills rebound.
    Amidst the loud applauses of the shore,
Gyas outstripped the rest, and sprung before :
Cloanthus, better manned, pursued him fast ;
But his o'er-masted galley checked his haste.
The Centaur and the Dolphin brush the brine
With equal oars, advancing in a line :
And now the mighty Centaur seems to lead,
And now the speedy Dolphin gets a-head :
Now board to board the rival vessels row ;
The billows lave the skies, and ocean groans below.
They reached the mark. Proud Gyas and his train
In triumph rode, the victors of the main :
But, steering round, he charged his pilot : ' Stand
More close to shore, and skim along the sand !

Let others bear to sea.'   Menœtes heard ;
But secret shelves too cautiously he feared,
And, fearing, sought the deep ; and still aloof he
    steered.
With louder cries the captain called again :
' Bear to the rocky shore, and shun the main !'
He spoke, and speaking, at his stern he saw
The bold Cloanthus near the shelvings draw.
Betwixt the mark and him the Scylla stood,
And in a closer compass ploughed the flood.
He passed the mark ; and, wheeling, got before :
Gyas blasphemed the gods, devoutly swore,
Cried out for anger, and his hair he tore.
Mindless of others' lives (so high was grown
His rising rage), and careless of his own,
The trembling dotard to the deck he drew,
And hoisted up, and overboard he threw :
This done, he seized the helm ; his fellows cheered ;
Turned short upon the shelves, and madly steered.

Hardly his head the plunging pilot rears,
Clogged with his clothes, and cumbered with his years:
Now drooping wet, he climbs the cliff with pain.
The crowd that saw him fall, and float again,
Shout from the distant shore ; and loudly laughed,
To see his heaving breast disgorge the briny draught.
The following Centaur, and the Dolphin's crew,
Their vanished hopes of victory renew ;
While Gyas lags, they kindle in the race,
To reach the mark.   Sergestus takes the place ;
Mnestheus pursues ; and, while around they wind,
Comes up, not half his galley's length behind ;
Then on the deck amidst his mates, appeared,
And thus their drooping courages he cheered :
' My friends, and Hector's followers heretofore,
Exert your vigour ; tug the labouring oar ;
Stretch to your strokes, my still-unconquered crew,
Whom from the flaming walls of Troy I drew.
In this our common interest, let me find
That strength of hand, that courage of the mind,
As when you stemmed the strong Malean flood ;

And o'er the Syrtes' broken billows rowed.
I seek not now the foremost palm to gain ;
Though yet—but, ah ! that haughty wish is vain !
Let those enjoy it whom the gods ordain.
But to be last, the lags of all the race !—
Redeem yourselves and me from that disgrace.'
Now, one and all, they tug amain ; they row
At the full stretch, and shake the brazen prow.
The sea beneath them sinks ; their labouring sides
Are swelled, and sweat runs guttering down in tides.
Chance aids their daring with unhoped success :
Sergestus, eager, with his beak to press
Betwixt the rival galley and the rock,
Shuts up the unwieldy Centaur in the lock.
The vessel struck ; and, with the dreadful shock
Her oars she shivered, and her head she broke.
The trembling rowers from their banks arise,
And, anxious for themselves, renounce the prize.
With iron poles they heave her off the shores ;
And gather from the sea their floating oars.
The crew of Mnestheus, with elated minds,
Urge their success, and call the willing winds ;
Then ply their oars, and cut their liquid way
In larger compass, on the roomy sea.
As, when the dove her rocky hold forsakes,
Roused in a fright, her sounding wings she shakes ;
The cavern rings with clattering ; out she flies,
And leaves her callow care, and cleaves the skies :
At first she flutters ; but at length she springs
To smoother flight, and shoots upon her wings :
So Mnestheus in the Dolphin cuts the sea ;
And, flying with a force, that force assists his way.
Sergestus in the Centaur soon he passed,
Wedged in the rocky shoals, and sticking fast.
In vain the victor he with cries implores,
And practises to row with shattered oars.
Then Mnestheus bears with Gyas and outflies :
The ship, without a pilot, yields the prize.
Unvanquished Scylla now alone remains :
Her he pursues ; and all his vigour strains.

Shouts from the favouring multitude arise ;
Applauding Echo to the shouts replies :
Shouts, wishes, and applause, run rattling through the
    skies.
These clamours with disdain the Scylla heard ;
Much, grudged the praise, but more, the robbed reward :
Resolved to hold their own, they mend their pace ;
All obstinate to die, or gain the race.
Raised with success, the Dolphin swiftly ran ;
For they can conquer, who believe they can.
Both urge their oars ; and fortune both supplies
(And both perhaps had shared an equal prize) ;
When to the seas Cloanthus holds his hands,
And succour from the watery powers demands :
' Gods of the liquid realms on which I row !
If, given by you, the laurel bind my brow,
(Assist to make me guilty of my vow !)
A snow-white bull shall on your shores be slain ;
His offered entrails cast into the main,
And ruddy wine, from golden goblets thrown,
Your grateful gift and my return shall own.'
The choir of nymphs, and Phorcus, from below,
With virgin Panopea, heard his vow ;
And old Portunus, with his breadth of hand,
Pushed on and sped the galley to the land.
Swift as a shaft, or winged wind, she flies,
And, darting to the port, obtains the prize.
    The herald summons all, and then proclaims
Cloanthus conqueror of the naval games.
The prince with laurel, crowns the victor's head ;
And three fat steers are to his vessel led
(The ship's reward) ; with generous wine beside,
And sums of silver, which the crew divide.
The leaders are distinguished from the rest ;
The victor honoured with a nobler vest,
Where gold and purple strive in equal rows,
And needlework its happy cost bestows.
There, Ganymede is wrought with living art,
Chasing through Ida's groves the trembling hart ;
Breathless he seems, yet eager to pursue ;

When from aloft descends, in open view
The bird of Jove, and, sousing on his prey,
With crooked talons bears the boy away.
In vain, with lifted hands and gazing eyes,
His guards behold him soaring through the skies;
And dogs pursue his flight, with imitated cries.

Mnestheus, the second victor was declared;
And, summoned there, the second prize he shared—
A coat of mail, which brave Demoleus bore,
More brave Æneas from his shoulders tore,
In single combat on the Trojan shore.
This was ordained for Mnestheus to possess—
In war for his defence, for ornament in peace.
Rich was the gift, and glorious to behold,
But yet so ponderous with its plates of gold,
That scarce two servants could the weight sustain:
Yet, loaded thus, Demoleus o'er the plain
Pursued and lightly seized, the Trojan train.
The third, succeeding to the last reward,
Two goodly bowls of massy silver shared,
With figures prominent, and richly wrought,
And two brass caldrons from Dodona brought.

Thus all, rewarded by the hero's hands,
Their conquering temples bound with purple bands.
And now Sergestus, clearing from the rock,
Brought back his galley shattered with the shock.
Forlorn she looked, without an aiding oar,
And, hooted by the vulgar, made to shore.
As when a snake, surprised upon the road,
Is crushed athwart her body by the load
Of heavy wheels; or with a mortal wound
Her belly bruised, and trodden to the ground—
In vain, with loosened curls, she crawls along;
Yet, fierce above, she brandishes her tongue;
Glares with her eyes, and bristles with her scales,
But, grovelling in the dust, her parts unsound she
      trails.
So slowly to the port the Centaur tends,
But, what she wants in oars, with sails amends.
Yet, for his galley saved, the grateful prince

Is pleased the unhappy chief to recompense:
Pholoe, the Cretan slave, rewards his care,
Beauteous herself, with lovely twins as fair.
    From thence his way the Trojan hero bent
Into the neighbouring plain, with mountains pent,
Whose sides were shaded with surrounding wood.
Full in the midst of this fair valley, stood
A native theatre, which, rising slow
By just degrees, o'erlooked the ground below.
High on a sylvan throne the leader sat;
A numerous train attend in solemn state.
Here those, that in the rapid course delight,
Desire of honour, and the prize, invite.
The rival runners without order stand;
The Trojans, mixed with the Sicilian band.
First Nisus, with Euryalus, appears—
Euryalus a boy of blooming years,
With sprightly grace and equal beauty crowned—
Nisus, for friendship to the youth, renowned.
Diores next, of Priam's royal race,
Then Salius, joined with Patron, took their place;
(But Patron in Arcadia had his birth,
And Salius, his from Acarnanian earth;)
Then two Sicilian youths—the names of these
Swift Helymus, and lovely Panopes
(Both jolly huntsmen, both in forests bred,
And owning old Acestes for their head),
With several others of ignobler name,
Whom time has not delivered o'er to fame.
    To these the hero thus his thoughts explained,
In words which general approbation gained:
' One common largess is for all designed
(The vanquished and the victor shall be joined):
Two darts of polished steel and Gnossian wood,
A silver-studded axe, alike bestowed.
The foremost three have olive-wreaths decreed
The first of these obtains a stately steed
Adorned with trappings; and the next in fame,
The quiver of an Amazonian dame,
With feathered Thracian arrows well supplied:

A golden belt shall gird his manly side,
Which with a sparkling diamond shall be tied.
The third this Grecian helmet shall content.'
He said.   To their appointed base they went ;
With beating hearts the expected sign receive,
And, starting all at once, the barrier leave.
Spread out, as on the wingèd winds, they flew,
And seized the distant goal with greedy view.
Shot from the crowd, swift Nisus all o'er-passed ;
Nor storms, nor thunder, equal half his haste.
The next, but, though the next, yet far disjoined,
Came Salius ; and Euryalus behind ;
Then Helymus, whom young Diores plied,
Step after step, and almost side by side,
His shoulders pressing—and, in longer space,
Had won, or left at least a dubious race.

Now, spent, the goal they almost reach at last,
When eager Nisus, hapless in his haste,
Slipped first, and, slipping, fell upon the plain,
Soaked with the blood of oxen newly slain.
The careless victor had not marked his way ;
But, treading where the treacherous puddle lay,
His heels flew up ; and on the grassy floor
He fell, besmeared with filth and holy gore.
Not mindless then, Euryalus, of thee,
Nor of the sacred bonds of amity,
He strove the immediate rival's hope to cross,
And caught the foot of Salius as he rose :
So Salius lay extended on the plain :
Euryalus springs out, the prize to gain,
And leaves the crowd :—applauding peals attend
The victor to the goal, who vanquished by his friend.
Next Helymus ; and then Diores came,
By two misfortunes made the third in fame.

But Salius enters, and, exclaiming loud
For justice, deafens and disturbs the crowd ;
Urges his cause may in the court be heard ;
And pleads the prize is wrongfully conferred.
But favour for Euryalus appears ;
His blooming beauty, with his tender years,

Had bribed the judges for the promised prize;
Besides, Diores fills the court with cries,
Who vainly reaches at the last reward,
If the first palm on Salius be conferred.
Then thus the prince: ' Let no disputes arise:
Where Fortune placed it, I award the prize.
But Fortune's errors give me leave to mend,
At least to pity my deserving friend.'
He said, and, from among the spoils, he draws
(Ponderous with shaggy mane and golden paws)
A lion's hide: to Salius this he gives:
Nisus with envy sees the gift, and grieves.
' If such rewards to vanquished men are due
(He said), and falling is to rise by you,
What prize may Nisus from your bounty claim,
Who merited the first rewards and fame?
In falling, both an equal fortune tried;
Would Fortune for my fall so well provide!'
With this he pointed to his face, and showed
His hands and all his habit smeared with blood.
The indulgent father of the people smiled,
And caused to be produced an ample shield,
Of wondrous art, by Didymaon wrought,
Long since from Neptune's bars in triumph brought.
This given to Nisus, he divides the rest,
And equal justice in his gifts expressed.

The race thus ended, and rewards bestowed,
Once more the prince bespeaks the attentive crowd:
' If there be here, whose dauntless courage dare
In gauntlet fight, with limbs and body bare,
His opposite sustain in open view,
Stand forth the champion, and the games renew.
Two prizes I propose, and thus divide—
A bull with gilded horns, and fillets tied,
Shall be the portion of the conquering chief:
A sword and helm shall cheer the loser's grief.'
Then haughty Dares in the lists appears:
Stalking he strides, his head erected bears:
His nervous arms the weighty gauntlet wield;
And loud applauses echo through the field.

Dares alone in combat used to stand
The match of mighty Paris, hand to hand;
The same, at Hector's funerals, undertook
Gigantic Butes, of the Amycian stock,
And, by the stroke of his resistless hand,
Stretched the vast bulk upon the yellow sand.
Such Dares was; and such he strode along,
And drew the wonder of the gazing throng.
His brawny back and ample breast he shows;
His lifted arms around his head he throws,
And deals, in whistling air, his empty blows.
His match is sought; but, through the trembling band,
Not one dares answer to the proud demand.
Presuming of his force, with sparkling eyes
Already he devours the promised prize.
He claims the bull with awless insolence,
And, having seized his horns, accosts the prince:
'If none my matchless valour dares oppose,
How long shall Dares wait his dastard foes?
Permit me, chief, permit without delay,
To lead this uncontended gift away.'
The crowd assents, and, with redoubled cries,
For the proud challenger demands the prize.

Acestes, fired with just disdain, to see
The plain usurped without a victory,
Reproached Entellus thus, who sat beside,
And heard and saw, unmoved, the Trojan's pride:
'Once, but in vain, a champion of renown,
So tamely can you bear the ravished crown,
A prize in triumph borne before your sight,
And shun for fear the danger of the fight?
Where is your Eryx now, the boasted name,
The god who taught your thundering arm the game?
Where now your baffled honour? where the spoil
That filled your house, and fame that filled our isle?'
Entellus thus: 'My soul is still the same,
Unmoved with fear, and moved with martial fame;
But my chill blood is curdled in my veins;
And scarce the shadow of a man remains.
Oh! could I turn to that fair prime again,

That prime, of which this boaster is so vain,
The brave, who this decrepit age defies,
Should feel my force, without the promised prize.'
He said ; and, rising at the word, he threw
Two ponderous gauntlets down in open view—
Gauntlets, which Eryx wont in fight to wield,
And sheath his hands with, in the listed field.
With fear and wonder seized, the crowd beholds
The gloves of death, with seven distinguished folds
Of tough bull-hides ; the space within is spread
With iron, or with loads of heavy lead.
Dares himself was daunted at the sight,
Renounced his challenge, and refused to fight.
Astonished at their weight, the hero stands,
And poised the ponderous engines in his hands.
'What had your wonder (said Entellus) been,
Had you the gauntlets of Alcides seen,
Or viewed the stern debate on this unhappy green !
These, which I bear, your brother Eryx bore,
Still marked with battered brains and mingled gore.
With these he long sustained the Herculean arm ;
And these I wielded while my blood was warm,
This languished frame while better spirits fed,
Ere age unstrung my nerves, or time o'ersnowed my head,
But if the challenger these arms refuse,
And cannot wield their weight, or dare not use ;
If great Æneas and Acestes join
In his request, these gauntlets I resign ;
Let us with equal arms perform the fight ;
And let him leave to fear, since I resign my right."
This said, Entellus for the strife prepares ;
Stripped of his quilted coat, his body bares :
Composed of mighty bones and brawn, he stands,
A goodly towering object on the sands.
    Then just Æneas equal arms supplied,
Which round their shoulders to their wrists they tied.
Both on the tiptoe stand, at full extent,
Their arms aloft, their bodies inly bent ;
Their heads from aiming blows they bear afar ;
With clashing gauntlets then provoke the war.

One on his youth and pliant limbs relies;
One on his sinews, and his giant size.
The last is stiff with age, his motion slow;
He heaves for breath; he staggers to and fro;
And clouds of issuing smoke his nostrils loudly blow.
Yet equal in success, they ward, they strike;
Their ways are different, but their art alike.
Before, behind, the blows are dealt; around
Their hollow sides the rattling thumps resound
A storm of strokes, well meant, with fury flies,
And errs about their temples, ears, and eyes—
Nor always errs; for oft the gauntlet draws
A sweeping stroke along the crackling jaws.
Heavy with age, Entellus stands his ground.
But with his warping body wards the wound.
His hand and watchful eye keep even pace;
While Dares traverses, and shifts his place,
And, like a captain who beleaguers round
Some strong-built castle on a rising ground,
Views all the approaches with observing eyes;
This and that other part in vain he tries,
And more on industry than force relies.
With hands on high, Entellus threats the foe;
But Dares watched the motion from below,
And slipped aside, and shunned the long-descending
    blow.
Entellus wastes his forces on the wind,
And, thus deluded of the stroke designed,
Headlong and heavy fell: his ample breast,
And weighty limbs, his ancient mother pressed.
So falls a hollow pine, that long had stood
On Ida's height, or Erymanthus' wood,
Torn from the roots. The differing nations rise;
And shouts and mingled murmurs rend the skies.
Acestes runs with eager haste, to raise
The fallen companion of his youthful days.
Dauntless he rose, and to the fight returned;
With shame his glowing cheeks, his eyes with fury,
    burned.
Disdain and conscious virtue fired his breast;

And with redoubled force his foe he pressed.
He lays on load with either hand, amain,
And headlong drives the Trojan o'er the plain ;
Nor stops, nor stays ; nor rest nor breath allows ;
But storms of strokes descend about his brows,
A rattling tempest, and a hail of blows.
But now the prince, who saw the wild increase
Of wounds, commands the combatants to cease,
And bounds Entellus' wrath, and bids the peace.
 First to the Trojan, spent with toil, he came,
And soothed his sorrow for the suffered shame.
'What fury seized my friend ? The gods (said he),
To him propitious, and averse to thee,
Have given his arm superior force to thine.
'Tis madness to contend with strength divine.'
The gauntlet-fight thus ended, from the shore
His faithful friends unhappy Dares bore :
His mouth and nostrils poured a purple flood ;
And pounded teeth came rushing with his blood.
Faintly he staggered through the hissing throng,
And hung his head, and trailed his legs along.
The sword and casque are carried by his train ;
But with his foe the palm and ox remain.
 The champion, then, before Æneas came,
Proud of his prize, but prouder of his fame :
'O goddess-born, and you, Dardanian host,
Mark with attention, and forgive my boast :
Learn what I was, by what remains ! and know,
From what impending fate you saved my foe.'
Sternly he spoke ; and then confronts the bull ;
And, on his ample forehead aiming full,
The deadly stroke, descending, pierced the skull.
Down drops the beast, nor needs a second wound,
But sprawls in pangs of death, and spurns the ground.
Then thus : 'In Dares' stead I offer this.
Eryx ! accept a nobler sacrifice :
Take the last gift my withered arms can yield :
Thy gauntlets I resign, and here renounce the field.'
 This done, Æneas orders, for the close,
The strife of archers, with contending bows.

The mast, Sergestus' shattered galley bore,
With his own hands he raises on the shore.
A fluttering dove upon the top they tie,
The living mark at which their arrows fly.
The rival archers in a line advance,
Their turn of shooting to receive from chance:
A helmet holds their names: the lots are drawn;
On the first scroll was read Hippocoön:
The people shout.   Upon the next was found
Young Mnestheus, late with naval honours crowned.
The third contained Eurytion's noble name,
Thy brother, Pandarus, and next in fame,
Whom Pallas urged the treaty to confound,
And send among the Greeks a feathered wound.
Acestes, in the bottom, last remained,
Whom not his age from youthful sports restrained.
Soon all with vigour bend their trusty bows;
And from the quiver each his arrow chose,
Hippocoön's was the first: with forceful sway
It flew, and, whizzing, cut the liquid way.
Fixed in the mast the feathered weapon stands:
The fearful pigeon flutters in her bands;
And the tree trembled; and the shouting cries
Of the pleased people rend the vaulted skies.
Then Mnestheus to the head his arrow drove,
With lifted eyes, and took his aim above,
But made a glancing shot, and missed the dove,
Yet missed so narrow, that he cut the cord
Which fastened by the foot, the flitting bird.
The captive thus released, away she flies,
And beats with clapping wings the yielding skies.
His bow already bent, Eurytion stood;
And, having first invoked his brother-god,
His wingèd shaft with eager haste he sped.
The fatal message reached her as she fled:
She leaves her life aloft; she strikes the ground,
And renders back the weapon in the wound.
Acestes, grudging at his lot, remains
Without a prize to gratify his pains.
Yet, shooting upward, sends his shaft, to shew

An archer's art, and boast his twanging bow.
The feathered arrow gave a dire portent,
And latter augurs judge from this event.
Chafed by the speed, it fired ; and, as it flew,
A train of following flames, ascending, drew :
Kindling they mount, and mark the shiny way ;
Across the skies as falling meteors play,
And vanish into wind, or in a blaze decay.
The Trojans and Sicilians wildly stare,
And trembling, turn their wonder into prayer.
The Dardan prince put on a smiling face,
And strained Acestes with a close embrace ;
Then honouring him with gifts above the rest,
Turned the bad omen, nor his fears confessed.
' The gods (said he) this miracle have wrought,
And ordered you the prize without the lot.
Accept this goblet, rough with figured gold,
Which Thracian Cisseus gave my sire of old :
This pledge of ancient amity receive,
Which to my second sire I justly give.'
He said, and, with the trumpet's cheerful sound,
Proclaimed him victor, and with laurel crowned.
Nor good Eurytion envied him the prize,
Though he transfixed the pigeon in the skies.
Who cut the line, with second gifts was graced ;
The third was his whose arrow pierced the mast.

The chief, before the games were wholly done,
Called Periphantes, tutor to his son,
And whispered thus : ' With speed Ascanius find ;
And, if his childish troop be ready joined,
On horseback let him grace his grandsire's day,
And lead his equals armed in just array.'
He said ; and, calling out, the cirque he clears.
The crowd withdrawn, an open plain appears.
And now the noble youths, of form divine,
Advance before their fathers, in a line :
The riders grace the steeds, the steeds with glory shine.

Thus marching on in military pride,
Shouts of applause resound from side to side.
Their casques adorned with laurel wreaths they wear,

Each brandishing aloft a cornel spear.
Some at their backs their gilded quivers bore ;
Their chains of burnished gold hung down before.
Three graceful troops they formed upon the green ;
Three graceful leaders at their head were seen ;
Twelve followed every chief, and left a space between.
The first, young Priam led—a lovely boy,
Whose grandsire was the unhappy king of Troy ;
(His race in after-times was known to fame,
New honours adding to the Latian name)—
And well the royal boy his Thracian steed became.
White were the fetlocks of his feet before ;
And on his front a snowy star he bore.
Then beauteous Atys, with Iülus bred,
Of equal age, the second squadron led.
The last in order, but the first in place
First in the lovely features of his face,
Rode fair Ascanius, on a fiery steed,
Queen Dido's gift, and of the Tyrian breed.
Sure coursers for the rest the king ordains,
With golden bits adorned, and purple reins.

The pleased spectators peals of shouts renew,
And all the parents in the children view ;
Their make, their motions, and their sprightly grace,
And hopes and fears alternate in their face.

The unfledged commanders, and their martial train,
First make the circuit of the sandy plain
Around their sires ; and at the appointed sign,
Drawn up in beauteous order, form a line.
The second signal sounds : the troop divides
In three distinguish'd parts, with three distinguish'd
    guides.
Again they close, and once again disjoin :
In troop to troop opposed, and line to line.
They meet ; they wheel ; they throw their darts afar,
With harmless rage, and well-dissembled war.
Then in a round the mingled bodies run ;
Flying they follow, and pursuing shun ;
Broken they break ; and rallying, they renew
In other forms the military show.

At last, in order undiscerned they join,
And march together in a friendly line.
And, as the Cretan labyrinth of old,
With wandering ways, and many a winding fold,
Involved the weary feet without redress,
In a round error which denied recess ;
So fought the Trojan boys in warlike play,
Turned and returned, and still a different way.
Thus, dolphins in the deep each other chase
In circles, when they swim around the watery race.
This game, these carousals, Ascanius taught ;
And, building Alba, to the Latins brought,
Shewed what he learned : the Latin sires impart
To their succeeding sons the graceful art :
From these imperial Rome received the game,
Which Troy, the youths, the Trojan troop, they name.

Thus far the sacred sports they celebrate ;
But Fortune soon resumed her ancient hate ;
For, while they pay the dead his annual dues,
Those envied rites Saturnian Juno views ;
And sends the goddess of the various bow,
To try new methods of revenge below :
Supplies the winds to wing her airy way,
Where in the port secure the navy lay.
Swiftly fair Iris down her arch descends,
And undiscerned, her fatal voyage ends.

She saw the gathering crowd ; and, gliding thence,
The desert shore, and fleet without defence.
The Trojan matrons, on the sands alone,
With sighs and tears Anchises' death bemoan :
Then, turning to the sea their weeping eyes,
Their pity to themselves renews their cries.
' Alas ! (said one) what oceans yet remain
For us to sail ! what labours to sustain !'
All take the word, and, with a general groan
Implore the gods for peace, and places of their own.
The goddess, great in mischief, views their pains,
And in a woman's form her heavenly limbs restrains.
In face and shape, old Beroë she became,
Doryclus' wife, a venerable dame ;

Once blessed with riches, and a mother's name.
Thus changed, amidst the crying crowd she ran,
Mixed with the matrons, and these words began:
'O wretched we! whom not the Grecian power
Nor flames destroyed, in Troy's unhappy hour!
O wretched we! reserved by cruel Fate
Beyond the ruins of the sinking state!
Now, seven revolving years are wholly run,
Since this improsperous voyage we begun;
Since, tossed from shores to shores, from lands to
    lands,
Inhospitable rocks and barren sands.
Wandering in exile, through the stormy sea,
We search in vain for flying Italy.
Now cast by Fortune on this kindred land,
What should our rest and rising walls withstand;
Or hinder, here, to fix our banished band?
O country lost, and gods redeemed in vain,
If still in endless exile we remain!
Shall we no more the Trojan walls renew.
Or streams of some dissembled Simoïs view?
Haste! join with me! the unhappy fleet consume!
Cassandra bids; and I declare her doom.
In sleep I saw her; she supplied my hands
(For this I more than dreamt) with flaming brands:
"With these (said she) these wandering ships destroy:
These are your fatal seats, and this your Troy."
Time calls you now; the precious hour employ;
Slack not the good presage, while heaven inspires
Our minds to dare, and gives the ready fires.
See! Neptune's altars minister their brands;
The God is pleased; the god supplies our hands.'
    Then from the pile a flaming fir she drew,
And, tossed in air, amidst the galleys threw.
Rapt in amaze, the matrons wildly stare:
Then Pyrgo, reverenced for her hoary hair—
Pyrgo, the nurse of Priam's numerous race:
'No Beroë this, though she belies her face!
What terrors from her frowning front arise!
Behold a goddess in her ardent eyes!

What rays around her heavenly face are seen !
Mark her majestic voice, and more than mortal mien !
Beroë but now I left, whom, pined with pain,
Her age and anguish from these rites detain.'
She said. The matrons, seized with new amaze,
Roll their malignant eyes, and on the navy gaze.
They fear, and hope, and neither part obey :
They hope the fated land, but fear the fatal way.

    The goddess, having done her task below,
Mounts up on equal wings, and bends her painted bow.
Struck with the sight, and seized with rage divine,
The matrons prosecute their mad design :
They shriek aloud : they snatch with impious hands
The food of altars : firs and flaming brands,
Green boughs and saplings, mingled in their haste,
And smoking torches, on the ships they cast.
The flame, unstopped at first, more fury gains ;
And Vulcan rides at large with loosened reins :
Triumphant to the painted stern he soars,
And seizes in his way the banks and crackling oars.

    Eumelus was the first the news to bear,
While yet they crowd the rural theatre.
Then what they hear is witnessed by their eyes :
A storm of sparkles and of flames arise.
Ascanius took the alarm, while yet he led
His early warriors on his prancing steed ;
And, spurring on, his equals soon o'erpassed ;
Nor could his frightened friends reclaim his haste.
Soon as the royal youth appeared in view,
He sent his voice before him as he flew :
' What madness moves you, matrons ! to destroy
The last remainders of unhappy Troy ?
Not hostile fleets, but your own hopes, you burn,
And on your friends your fatal fury turn.
Behold your own Ascanius !'—While he said,
He drew his glittering helmet from his head,
In which the youths to sportful arms he led.
By this, Æneas and his train appear ;
And now the women, seized with shame and fear,
Dispersed, to woods and caverns take their flight ;

Abhor their actions, and avoid the light;
Their friends acknowledge, and their error find;
And shake the goddess from their altered mind.
   Not so the raging fires their fury cease,
But, lurking in the seams, with seeming peace
Work on their way amid the smouldering tow;
Sure in destruction, but in motion slow.
The silent plague through the green timber eats,
And vomits out a tardy flame by fits.
Down to the keels, and upward to the sails,
The fire descends or mounts, but still prevails;
Nor buckets poured, nor strength of human hand,
Can the victorious element withstand.
   The pious hero rends his robe, and throws
To heaven his hands, and, with his hands, his vows.
'O Jove! (he cried) if prayers can yet have place;
If thou abhorr'st not all the Dardan race;
If any spark of pity still remain;
If gods are gods, and not invoked in vain;
Yet spare the relics of the Trojan train!
Yet from the flames our burning vessels free!
Or let thy fury fall alone on me:
At this devoted head thy thunder throw,
And send the willing sacrifice below.'
   Scarce had he said, when southern storms arise:
From pole to pole the forky lightning flies:
Loud rattling shakes the mountains and the plain:
Heaven bellies downward, and descends in rain:
Whole sheets of water from the clouds are sent,
Which, hissing through the planks, the flames prevent,
And stop the fiery pest.   Four ships alone
Burn to the waist, and for the fleet atone.
   But doubtful thoughts the hero's heart divide,
If he should still in Sicily reside,
Forgetful of his fates,—or tempt the main,
In hope the promised Italy to gain.
Then Nautes, old and wise—to whom alone
The will of Heaven by Pallas was foreshown;
Versed in portents, experienced, and inspired
To tell events, and what the Fates required—

Thus, while he stood to neither part inclined,
With cheerful words relieved his labouring mind:
'O goddess-born! resigned in every state,
With patience bear, with prudence push your fate.
By suffering well, our fortune we subdue;
Fly when she frowns, and when she calls, pursue.
Your friend Acestes is of Trojan kind;
To him disclose the secrets of your mind;
Trust in his hands your old and useless train,
Too numerous for the ships which yet remain—
The feeble, old, indulgent of their ease,
The dames, who dread the dangers of the seas,
With all the dastard crew, who dare not stand
The shock of battle with your foes by land.
Here you may build a common town for all,
And, from Acestes' name, Acesta call.'
The reasons, with his friend's experience joined,
Encouraged much, but more disturbed his mind,

    'Twas dead of night; when, to his slumbering eyes
His father's shade, descended from the skies,
And thus he spoke: 'O, more than vital breath
Loved while I lived, and dear e'en after death!
O son, in various toils and troubles tossed!
The king of heaven employs my careful ghost
On his commands—the god who saved from fire
Your flaming fleet, and heard your just desire.
The wholesome counsel of your friend receive,
And here, the coward train and women, leave.
The chosen youth, and those who nobly dare,
Transport, to tempt the dangers of the war:
The stern Italians will their courage try:
Rough are their manners, and their minds are high.
But first to Pluto's palace you shall go,
And seek my shade among the blest below;
For not with impious ghosts my soul remains;
Nor suffers, with the damned, perpetual pains;
But breathes the living air and soft Elysian plains.
The chaste Sibylla shall your steps convey,
And blood of offered victims free the way.
There shall you know what realms the gods assign,

And learn the fates and fortunes of your line.
But now farewell ! I vanish with the night,
And feel the blast of heaven's approaching light.'
He said, and mixed with shades, and took his airy
    flight.
'Whither so fast ? (the filial duty cried)
And why, ah ! why the wished embrace denied ?'
  He said, and rose ; as holy zeal inspires,
He rakes hot embers, and renews the fires ;
His country gods and Vesta then adores
With cakes and incense, and their aid implores.
Next, for his friends and royal host he sent,
Revealed his vision, and the god's intent,
With his own purpose. All, without delay,
The will of Jove, and his desires, obey.
They list with women, each degenerate name
Who dares not hazard life for future fame.
These they cashier. The brave remaining few,
Oars, banks, and cables, half-consumed, renew.
The prince designs a city with the plough :
The lots their several tenements allow.
This part, is named from Ilium, that, from Troy ;
And the new king ascends the throne with joy ;
A chosen senate from the people draws ;
Appoints the judges, and ordains the laws.
Then, on the top of Eryx, they begin
A rising temple to the Paphian queen.
Anchises, last, is honoured as a god :
A priest is added ; annual gifts bestowed ;
And groves are planted round his blest abode.
Nine days they pass in feasts, their temples crowned ;
And fumes of incense in the fanes abound.
Then from the south arose a gentle breeze,
That curled the smoothness of the glassy seas ;
The rising winds a ruffling gale afford,
And call the merry mariners aboard.
  Now loud laments along the shores resound,
Of parting friends in close embraces bound.
The trembling women, the degenerate train
Who shunned the frightful dangers of the main ;

E'en those desire to sail, and take their share
Of the rough passage, and the promised war:
Whom good Æneas cheers; and recommends
To their new master's care his fearful friends.
On Eryx' altars three fat calves he lays;
A lamb, new-fallen, to the stormy seas;
Then slips his halsers, and his anchors weighs.
High on the deck, the godlike hero stands
With olive crowned, a charger in his hands;
Then cast the reeking entrails in the brine,
And poured the sacrifice of purple wine.
Fresh gales arise: with equal strokes they vie,
And brush the buxom seas, and o'er the billows fly.

    Meantime the mother goddess, full of fears,
To Neptune thus addressed, with tender tears:
'The pride of Jove's imperious queen, the rage,
The malice, which no sufferings can assuage,
Compel me to these prayers; since neither fate,
Nor time, nor pity, can remove her hate.
E'en Jove is thwarted by his haughty wife:
Still vanquished, yet she still renews the strife.
As if 'twere little to consume the town
Which awed the world, and wore the imperial crown,
She prosecutes the ghost of Troy with pains,
And gnaws e'en to the bones the last remains.
Let her, the causes of her hatred tell;
But you, can witness its effects too well.
You saw the storm she raised on Libyan floods,
That mixed the mounting billows with the clouds;
When, bribing Æolus, she shook the main,
And moved rebellion in your watery reign.
With fury she possessed the Dardan dames,
To burn their fleet with execrable flames,
And forced Æneas, when his ships were lost,
To leave his followers on a foreign coast.
For what remains, your godhead I implore;
And trust my son to your protecting power.
If neither Jove's nor Fate's decree withstand,
Secure his passage to the Latian land.'

    Then thus, the mighty ruler of the main:

'What may not Venus hope from Neptune's reign?
My kingdom claims your birth; my late defence
Of your endangered fleet may claim your confidence.
Nor less by land than sea my deeds declare,
How much your loved Æneas is my care.
Thee, Xanthus! and thee, Simoïs! I attest—
Your Trojan troops when proud Achilles pressed,
And drove before him headlong on the plain;
And dashed against the walls the trembling train;
When floods were filled with bodies of the slain;
When crimson Xanthus, doubtful of his way,
Stood up on ridges to behold the sea
(New heaps came tumbling in, and choked his way);
When your Æneas fought, but fought with odds
Of force unequal, and unequal gods;
I spread a cloud before the victor's sight,
Sustained the vanquished, and secured his flight:
E'en then secured him, when I sought with joy
The vowed destruction of ungrateful Troy.
My will's the same: fair goddess! fear no more,
Your fleet shall safely gain the Latian shore:
Their lives are given: one destined head alone
Shall perish, and for multitudes atone.'
   Thus having armed with hopes her anxious mind,
His finny team Saturnian Neptune joined;
Then adds the foamy bridle to their jaws,
And to the loosened reins permits the laws.
High on the waves his azure car he guides;
Its axles thunder, and the sea subsides;
And the smooth ocean rolls her silent tides.
The tempests fly before their father's face;
Trains of inferior gods his triumph grace;
And monster whales before their master play;
And choirs of Tritons crowd the watery way.
The marshalled powers in equal troops divide
To right and left: the gods his better side
Inclose; and, on the worse, the Nymphs and Nereids
   ride.
  Now smiling hope, with sweet vicissitude,
Within the hero's mind his joys renewed.

He calls to raise the masts, the sheets display;
The cheerful crew with diligence obey:
They scud before the wind, and sail in open sea.
Ahead of all, the master-pilot steers;
And as he leads, the following navy veers.
   The steeds of Night had travelled half the sky:
The drowsy rowers on their benches lie;
When the soft god of sleep, with easy flight
Descends, and draws behind a trail of light.
Thou, Palinurus, art his destined prey;
To thee alone he takes his fatal way.
Dire dreams to thee, and iron sleep, he bears;
And, lighting on thy prow, the form of Phorbas wears.
Then thus the traitor-god began his tale:
'The winds, my friend, inspire a pleasing gale;
The ships, without thy care securely sail.
Now steal an hour of sweet repose; and I
Will take the rudder, and thy room supply.'
To whom, the yawning pilot, half asleep:
'Me dost thou bid to trust the treacherous deep,
The harlot-smiles of her dissembling face,
And to her faith commit the Trojan race?
Shall I believe the Siren South again,
And, oft betrayed, not know the monster main!'
He said: his fastened hands the rudder keep;
And, fixed on heaven, his eyes repel invading sleep.
The god was wroth, and at his temples threw
A branch in Lethe dipped, and drunk with Stygian
    dew:
The pilot, vanquished by the power divine,
Soon closed his swimming eyes, and lay supine.
Scarce were his limbs extended at their length;
The god, insulting, with superior strength
Fell heavy on him, plunged him in the sea;
And, with the stern, the rudder tore away.
Headlong he fell, and, struggling in the main,
Cried out for helping hands, but cried in vain.
The victor dæmon mounts obscure in air;
While the ship sails without the pilot's care.
On Neptune's faith the floating fleet relies;

But what the man forsook, the god supplies;
And, o'er the dangerous deep, secure the navy flies:
Glides by the Sirens' cliffs, a shelfy coast,
Long infamous, for ships and sailors lost;
And white with bones. The impetuous ocean roars,
And rocks rebellow from the sounding shores.
The watchful hero felt the knocks, and found
The tossing vessel sailed on shoaly ground.
Sure of his pilot's loss, he takes himself
The helm, and steers aloof, and shuns the shelf.
Inly he grieved, and, groaning from the breast,
Deplored his death; and thus his pain expressed:
'For faith reposed on seas, and on the flattering sky,
Thy naked corpse is doom'd on shores unknown to lie.'

BOOK VI

THE ARGUMENT

The Sibyl foretells Æneas the adventures he should meet with in Italy. She attends him to hell; describing to him the various scenes of that place, and conducting him to his father Anchises, who instructs him in those sublime mysteries of the soul of the world, and the transmigration; and shows him that glorious race of heroes, which was to descend from him and his posterity.

He said, and wept; then spread his sails before
The winds, and reached at length the Cuman shore:
Their anchors dropped, his crew the vessels moor.
They turn their heads to sea, their sterns to land;
And greet with greedy joy the Italian strand.
Some strike from clashing flints their fiery seed;
Some gather sticks, the kindled flames to feed,
Or search for hollow trees, and fell the woods,
Or trace through valleys the discovered floods.
  Thus while their several charges they fulfil,
The pious prince ascends the sacred hill
Where Phœbus is adored; and seeks the shade
Which hides from sight his venerable maid
(Deep in a cave the Sibyl makes abode):
Thence full of fate returns; and of the god.
Through Trivia's grove they walk; and now behold,
And enter now, the temple roofed with gold.
When Dædalus, to fly the Cretan shore,
His heavy limbs on jointed pinions bore
(The first who sailed in air), 'tis sung by Fame,
To the Cumæan coast at length he came;
And here alighting, built this costly frame.
Inscribed to Phœbus, here, he hung on high

The steerage of his wings, that cut the sky :
Then, o'er the lofty gate, his art embossed
Androgeos' death, and (offerings to his ghost)
Seven youths from Athens yearly sent, to meet
The fate appointed by revengeful Crete.
And next to these the dreadful urn was placed,
In which the destined names by lots were cast :
The mournful parents stand around in tears ;
And rising Crete against their shore appears.
There too, in living sculpture, might be seen
The mad affection of the Cretan queen ;
Then how she cheats her bellowing lover's eye :
The rushing leap, the doubtful progeny—
The lower part a beast, a man above—
The monument of their polluted love.
Not far from thence he graved the wonderous maze,
A thousand doors, a thousand winding ways :
Here dwells the monster, hid from human view ;
Not to be found but by the faithful clue ;
Till the kind artist, moved with pious grief,
Lent to the loving maid this last relief ;
And all those erring paths described so well,
That Theseus conquered, and the monster fell.
Here, hapless Icarus had found his part,
Had not the father's grief restrained his art :
He twice essayed to cast his son in gold ;
Twice from his hands he dropped the forming mould.

　　All this, with wondering eyes Æneas viewed ;
Each varying object his delight renewed.
Eager to read the rest——Achates came,
And by his side the mad divining dame,
The priestess of the god, Deïphobe her name.
'Time suffers not (she said), to feed your eyes
With empty pleasures : haste the sacrifice.
Seven bullocks, yet unyoked, for Phœbus choose,
And for Diana, seven unspotted ewes.'
This said, the servants urge the sacred rites ;
While to the temple she the prince invites.
A spacious cave, within its farmost part,
Was hewed and fashioned by laborious art,

Through the hill's hollow sides : before the place,
A hundred doors a hundred entries grace ;
As many voices issue, and the sound
Of Sibyl's words as many times rebound.
Now to the mouth they come.   Aloud she cries :
' This is the time ! inquire your destinies !
He comes ! behold the god !'   Thus while she said
(And shivering at the sacred entry stayed),
Her colour changed ; her face was not the same ;
And hollow groans from her deep spirit came.
Her hair stood up ; convulsive rage possessed
Her trembling limbs, and heaved her labouring breast.
Greater than human kind she seemed to look ;
And with an accent more than mortal, spoke :
Her staring eyes with sparkling fury roll ;
When all the god came rushing on her soul.
Swiftly she turned, and, foaming as she spoke :
' Why this delay ? (she cried) the powers invoke !
Thy prayers alone can open this abode ;
Else vain are my demands, and dumb the god.'
    She said no more.   The trembling Trojans hear,
O'erspread with a damp sweat, and holy fear.
The prince himself, with awful dread possessed,
His vows to great Apollo thus addressed :
' Indulgent god ! propitious power to Troy,
Swift to relieve, unwilling to destroy !
Directed by whose hand, the Dardan dart
Pierced the proud Grecian's only mortal part !
Thus far, by Fate's decrees and thy commands,
Through ambient seas and through devouring sands,
Our exiled crew has sought the Ausonian ground ;
And now, at length, the flying coast is found.
Thus far the fate of Troy, from place to place,
With fury has pursued her wandering race.
Here cease, ye powers, and let your vengeance end,
Troy is no more, and can no more offend.
And thou, O sacred maid, inspired to see
The event of things in dark futurity !
Give me, what heaven has promised to my fate,
To conquer and command the Latian state ;

To fix my wandering gods, and find a place
For the long exiles of the Trojan race.
Then shall my grateful hands a temple rear
To the twin gods, with vows and solemn prayer ;
And annual rites, and festivals, and games,
Shall be performed to their auspicious names.
Nor shalt thou want thy honours in my land ;
For there thy faithful oracles shall stand,
Preserved in shrines ; and every sacred lay,
Which by thy mouth, Apollo shall convey ;
All shall be treasured by a chosen train
Of holy priests, and ever shall remain.
But, oh ! commit not thy prophetic mind
To flitting leaves, the sport of every wind,
Lest they disperse in air our empty fate :
Write not, but, what the powers ordain, relate.'

Struggling in vain, impatient of her load,
And labouring underneath the ponderous god,
The more she strove to shake him from her breast,
With more, and far superior force he pressed ;
Commands his entrance, and, without control,
Usurps her organs, and inspires her soul.
Now, with a furious blast, the hundred doors
Ope of themselves ; a rushing whirlwind roars
Within the cave, and Sibyl's voice restores :
' Escaped the dangers of the watery reign,
Yet more and greater ills by land remain.
The coast so long desired (nor doubt the event),
Thy troops shall reach, but, having reached, repent.
Wars ! horrid wars, I view !—a field of blood,
And Tiber rolling with a purple flood.
Simoïs nor Xanthus shall be wanting there :
A new Achilles shall in arms appear ;
And he too, goddess-born. Fierce Juno's hate
Added to hostile force, shall urge thy fate.
To what strange nations shalt not thou resort ;
Driven to solicit aid at every court !
The cause, the same which Ilium once oppressed :
A foreign mistress, and a foreign guest.
But thou, secure of soul, unbent with woes,

The more thy fortune frowns, the more oppose.
The dawnings of thy safety shall be shown,
From whence thou least shalt hope—a Grecian town.'
　　Thus, from the dark recess, the Sibyl spoke;
And the resisting air the thunder broke;
The cave rebellowed, and the temple shook.
The ambiguous god, who ruled her labouring breast,
In these mysterious words his mind expressed:
Some truth revealed, in terms involved the rest.
At length her fury fell: her foaming ceased,
And, ebbing in her soul, the god decreased.
　　Then thus the chief: 'No terror to my view,
No frightful face of danger, can be new.
Inured to suffer, and resolved to dare,
The Fates, without my power, shall be without my care.
This let me crave—since near your grove the road
To hell lies open, and the dark abode
Which Acheron surrounds, the innavigable flood—
Conduct me through the regions void of light,
And lead me longing to my father's sight.
For him, a thousand dangers I have sought,
And, rushing where the thickest Grecians fought,
Safe on my back the sacred burden brought.
He, for my sake, the raging ocean tried,
And wrath of heaven (my still auspicious guide),
And bore, beyond the strength decrepit age supplied.
Oft, since he breathed his last, in dead of night,
His reverend image stood before my sight;
Enjoined to seek, below, his holy shade—
Conducted there by your unerring aid.
But you, if pious minds by prayers are won,
Oblige the father, and protect the son.
Yours is the power; nor Proserpine in vain
Has made you priestess of her nightly reign.
If Orpheus, armed with his enchanting lyre,
The ruthless king with pity could inspire,
And from the shades below redeem his wife;
If Pollux, offering his alternate life,
Could free his brother, and can daily go
By turns aloft, by turns descend below;—

Why name I Theseus, or his greater friend,
Who trod the downward path, and upward could ascend?
Not less than theirs, from Jove my lineage came ;
My mother greater, my descent the same.'
  So prayed the Trojan prince, and, while he prayed,
His hand upon the holy altar laid.
Then, thus replied the prophetess divine :
' O goddess-born, of great Anchises' line !
The gates of hell are open night and day ;
Smooth the descent, and easy is the way :
But to return, and view the cheerful skies,
In this, the task and mighty labour lies.
To few, great Jupiter imparts this grace,
And those of shining worth, and heavenly race.
Betwixt those regions and our upper light,
Deep forests and impenetrable night
Possess the middle space : the infernal bounds,
Cocytus, with his sable waves surrounds.
But, if so dire a love your soul invades,
As twice below to view the trembling shades ;
If you so hard a toil will undertake,
As twice to pass the innavigable lake ;
Receive my counsel. In the neighbouring grove
There stands a tree : the queen of Stygian Jove
Claims it her own ; thick woods and gloomy night
Conceal the happy plant from human sight.
One bough it bears ; but (wondrous to behold !)
The ductile rind and leaves of radiant gold :
This, from the vulgar branches must be torn,
And to fair Proserpine, the present borne,
Ere leave be given to tempt the nether skies.
The first thus rent, a second will arise ;
And the same metal the same room supplies.
Look round the wood, with lifted eyes, to see
The lurking gold upon the fatal tree ;
Then rend it off, as holy rites command :
The willing metal will obey thy hand,
Following with ease, if, favoured by thy fate,
Thou art foredoomed to view the Stygian state ;
If not, no labour can the tree constrain ;

And strength of stubborn arms and steel, are vain.
Besides, you know not, while you here attend,
The unworthy fate of your unhappy friend :
Breathless he lies ; and his unburied ghost,
Deprived of funeral rites, pollutes your host.
Pay first his pious dues ; and, for the dead,
Two sable sheep around his hearse be led ;
Then, living turfs upon his body lay :
This done, securely take the destined way,
To find the regions destitute of day.'
　　She said, and held her peace.—Æneas went
Sad from the cave, and full of discontent,
Unknowing whom the sacred Sibyl meant.
Achates, the companion of his breast,
Goes grieving by his side, with equal cares oppressed.
Walking they talked, and fruitlessly divined,
What friend the priestess by those words designed.
　　But soon they found an object to deplore :
Misenus lay extended on the shore—
Son of the god of winds :—none so renowned,
The warrior-trumpet in the field to sound,
With breathing brass to kindle fierce alarms,
And rouse to dare their fate in honourable arms.
He served great Hector, and was ever near,
Not with his trumpet only, but his spear.
But, by Pelides' arms when Hector fell,
He chose Æneas ; and he chose as well.
Swoln with applause, and aiming still at more,
He now provokes the sea-gods from the shore.
With envy, Triton heard the martial sound,
And the bold champion, for his challenge, drowned ;
Then cast his mangled carcase on the strand :
The gazing crowd around the body stand.
All weep ; but most Æneas mourns his fate ;
And hastens to perform the funeral state.
In altar-wise, a stately pile they rear ;
The basis broad below, and top advanced in air.
An ancient wood, fit for the work designed
(The shady covert of the savage kind),
The Trojans found : the sounding axe is plied :

Firs, pines, and pitch-trees, and the towering pride
Of forest ashes, feel the fatal stroke;
And piercing wedges cleave the stubborn oak.
Huge trunks of trees, felled from the steepy crown
Of the bare mountains, roll with ruin down.
Armed like the rest the Trojan prince appears,
And, by his pious labour, urges theirs.
    Thus while he wrought, involving in his mind
The ways to compass what his wish designed,
He cast his eyes upon the gloomy grove,
And then with vows implored the queen of love:
'O! may thy power, propitious still to me,
Conduct my steps to find the fatal tree,
In this deep forest; since the Sibyl's breath
Foretold, alas! too true, Misenus' death.'
Scarce had he said, when, full before his sight,
Two doves, descending from their airy flight,
Secure upon the grassy plain alight.
He knew his mother's birds; and thus he prayed:
'Be you my guides, with your auspicious aid,
And lead my footsteps, till the branch be found,
Whose glittering shadow gilds the sacred ground.
And thou, great parent! with celestial care,
In this distress, be present to my prayer.'
Thus having said, he stopped, with watchful sight
Observing still the motions of their flight,
What course they took, what happy signs they show.
They fed, and, fluttering, by degrees withdrew
Still farther from the place, but still in view:
Hopping and flying, thus they led him on
To the slow lake, whose baleful stench to shun,
They winged their flight aloft; then, stooping low,
Perched on the double tree that bears the golden bough.
Through the green leaves the glittering shadows glow;
As, on the sacred oak, the wintry misletoe,
Where the proud mother views her precious brood,
And happier branches, which she never sowed.
Such was the glittering; such the ruddy rind,
And dancing leaves, that wantoned in the wind.
He seized the shining bough with griping hold,

And rent away with ease, the lingering gold ;
Then to the Sibyl's palace bore the prize.

Meantime, the Trojan troops, with weeping eyes,
To dead Misenus pay his obsequies.
First, from the ground, a lofty pile they rear,
Of pitch-trees, oaks, and pines, and unctuous fir :
The fabric's front with cypress twigs they strew,
And stick the sides with boughs of baleful yew.
The topmost part his glittering arms adorn ;
Warm waters, then, in brazen caldrons borne,
Are poured to wash his body, joint by joint ;
And fragrant oils the stiffened limbs anoint.
With groans and cries Misenus they deplore ;
Then on a bier, with purple covered o'er,
The breathless body, thus bewailed, they lay,
And fire the pile, their faces turned away :
Such reverent rites their fathers used to pay.
Pure oil and incense on the fire they throw,
And fat of victims, which his friends bestow.
These gifts the greedy flames to dust devour ;
Then, on the living coals, red wine they pour ;
And, last, the relics by themselves dispose,
Which in a brazen urn the priests inclose.
Old Corynæus compassed thrice the crew,
And dipped an olive-branch in holy dew,
Which thrice he sprinkled round ; and thrice aloud
Invoked the dead, and then dismissed the crowd.

But good Æneas ordered on the shore
A stately tomb, whose top a trumpet bore,
A soldier's falchion, and a seaman's oar.
Thus was his friend interred ; and deathless fame
Still to the lofty cape consigns his name.

These rites performed, the prince, without delay,
Hastes to the nether world, his destined way.
Deep was the cave ; and, downward as it went
From the wide mouth, a rocky, rough descent :
And here the access a gloomy grove defends ;
And here the innavigable lake extends,
O'er whose unhappy waters, void of light,
No bird presumes to steer his airy flight :

Such deadly stenches from the depth arise,
And steaming sulphur, that infects the skies.
From hence, the Grecian bards their legends make,
And give the name Avernus, to the lake.
Four sable bullocks, in the yoke untaught,
For sacrifice the pious hero brought.
The priestess pours the wine betwixt their horns ;
Then cuts the curling hair ; that first oblation burns,
Invoking Hecate hither to repair—
A powerful name in hell and upper air,
The sacred priests, with ready knives bereave
The beasts of life, and in full bowls receive
The streaming blood ; a lamb to Hell and Night
(The sable wool without a streak of white),
Æneas offers ; and, by Fate's decree,
A barren heifer, Proserpine, to thee !
With holocausts he Pluto's altar fills ;
Seven brawny bulls with his own hand he kills ;
Then, on the broiling entrails, oil he pours ;
Which, ointed thus, the raging flame devours.
Late the nocturnal sacrifice begun,
Nor ended till the next returning sun.
Then earth began to bellow, trees to dance,
And howling dogs in glimmering light advance,
Ere Hecate came : ' Far hence be souls profane !
(The Sibyl cried) and from the grove abstain !
Now, Trojan, take the way thy fates afford ;
Assume thy courage, and unsheath thy sword.'
She said, and passed along the gloomy space ;
The prince pursued her steps with equal pace.
  Ye realms yet unrevealed to human sight !
Ye gods who rule the regions of the night !
Ye gliding ghosts ! permit me to relate
The mystic wonders of your silent state.
  Obscure they went through dreary shades, that led
Along the waste dominions of the dead.
Thus wander travellers in woods by night,
By the moon's doubtful and malignant light,
When Jove in dusky clouds involves the skies,
And the faint crescent shoots by fits before their eyes.

Just in the gate, and in the jaws of hell,
Revengeful Cares and sullen Sorrows dwell ;
And pale Diseases, and repining Age,
Want, Fear, and Famine's unresisted rage ;
Here Toils, and Death, and Death's half-brother Sleep
(Forms terrible to view), their sentry keep ;
With anxious Pleasures of a guilty mind ;
Deep Frauds before, and open Force behind ;
The Furies' iron beds ; and Strife, that shakes
Her hissing tresses, and unfolds her snakes.
Full in the midst of this infernal road,
An elm displays her dusky arms abroad :
The god of sleep there hides his heavy head,
And empty dreams on every leaf are spread.
Of various forms unnumbered spectres more,
Centaurs, and double shapes, besiege the door.
Before the passage, horrid Hydra stands,
And Briareus with all his hundred hands ;
Gorgons, Geryon with his triple frame,
And vain Chimæra vomits empty flame.
The chief unsheathed his shining steel, prepared,
Though seized with sudden fear, to force the guard,
Offering his brandished weapon at their face,
Had not the Sibyl stopped his eager pace,
And told him what those empty phantoms were—
Forms without bodies, and impassive air.
    Hence to deep Acheron they take their way,
Whose troubled eddies, thick with ooze and clay,
Are whirled aloft, and in Cocytus lost :
There, Charon stands, who rules the dreary coast—
A sordid god : down from his hoary chin
A length of beard descends, uncombed, unclean :
His eyes, like hollow furnaces on fire ;
A girdle foul with grease, binds his obscene attire.
He spreads his canvas ; with his pole he steers ;
The freights of flitting ghosts in his thin bottom bears
He looked in years ; yet, in his years were seen
A youthful vigour, and autumnal green.
An airy crowd came rushing where he stood,
Which filled the margin of the fatal flood :

Husbands and wives, boys and unmarried maids,
And mighty heroes' more majestic shades:
And youths, intombed before their fathers' eyes,
With hollow groans, and shrieks, and feeble cries.
Thick as the leaves in autumn strew the woods,
Or fowls by winter forced, forsake the floods,
And wing their hasty flight to happier lands—
Such, and so thick, the shivering army stands,
And press for passage, with extended hands.
  Now these, now those, the surly boatman bore:
The rest he drove to distance from the shore.
The hero, who beheld with wondering eyes,
The tumult mixed with shrieks, laments, and cries,
Asked of his guide, what the rude concourse meant?
Why to the shore the thronging people bent?
What forms of law among the ghosts were used?
Why some were ferried o'er, and some refused?
'Son of Anchises! offspring of the gods!
(The Sibyl said) you see the Stygian floods!
The sacred streams which heaven's imperial state
Attests in oaths, and fears to violate.
The ghosts rejected are the unhappy crew
Deprived of sepulchres and funeral due:
The boatman, Charon: those, the buried host,
He ferries over to the farther coast;
Nor dares his transport vessel cross the waves
With such whose bones are not composed in graves.
A hundred years they wander on the shore;
At length, their penance done, are wafted o'er.'
  The Trojan chief his forward pace repressed,
Revolving anxious thoughts within his breast.
He saw his friends, who, whelmed beneath the waves,
Their funeral honours claimed, and asked their quiet
    graves.
The lost Leucaspis in the crowd he knew,
And the brave leader of the Lycian crew,
Whom, on the Tyrrhene seas, the tempests met;
The sailors mastered, and the ship o'erset.
Amidst the spirits, Palinurus pressed,
Yet fresh from life, a new-admitted guest.

Who, while he steering viewed the stars, and bore
His course from Afric to the Latian shore,
Fell headlong down. The Trojan fixed his view,
And scarcely through the gloom the sullen shadow
knew.
Then thus the prince : ' What envious power, O friend !
Brought your loved life to this disastrous end ?
For Phœbus, ever true in all he said,
Has in your fate alone, my faith betrayed.
The god foretold you should not die before
You reached, secure from seas, the Italian shore.
Is this the unerring power ?' The ghost replied :
' Nor Phœbus flattered, nor his answers lied ;
Nor envious gods have sent me to the deep ;
But, while the stars and course of heaven I keep,
My wearied eyes were seized with fatal sleep.
I fell ; and with my weight the helm, constrained,
Was drawn along, which yet my gripe retained.
Now by the winds and raging waves I swear,
Your safety, more than mine, was then my care ;
Lest, of the guide bereft, the rudder lost,
Your ship should run against the rocky coast.
Three blustering nights, borne by the southern blast,
I floated, and discovered land at last :
High on a mounting wave my head I bore,
Forcing my strength, and gathering to the shore :
Panting, but past the danger, now I seized
The craggy cliffs, and my tired members eased.
While, cumbered with my dropping clothes I lay,
The cruel nation, covetous of prey,
Stained with my blood the unhospitable coast ;
And now, by winds and waves, my lifeless limbs are
tossed ;
Which, O ! avert, by yon ethereal light,
Which I have lost for this eternal night.
Or, if by dearer ties you may be won,
By your dead sire, and by your living son,
Redeem from this reproach my wandering ghost.
Or with your navy seek the Velin coast,
And in a peaceful grave my corpse compose ;

Or, if a nearer way your mother shows
(Without whose aid, you durst not undertake
This frightful passage o'er the Stygian lake),
Lend to this wretch your hand, and waft him o'er
To the sweet banks of yon forbidden shore.'
Scarce had he said ; the prophetess began :
' What hopes delude thee, miserable man ?
Thinkest thou, thus unintombed to cross the floods,
To view the Furies and infernal gods,
And visit without leave, the dark abodes ?
Attend the term of long revolving years ;
Fate, and the dooming gods, are deaf to tears.
This comfort of thy dire misfortune take—
The wrath of heaven, inflicted for thy sake,
With vengeance shall pursue the inhuman coast,
Till they propitiate thy offended ghost ;
And raise a tomb, with vows and solemn prayer ;
And Palinurus' name the place shall bear.'
This calmed his cares—soothed with his future fame,
And pleased to hear his propagated name.
  Now nearer to the Stygian lake they draw :
Whom, from the shore the surly boatman saw ;
Observed this passage through the shady wood,
And marked their near approaches to the flood :
Then thus he called aloud, inflamed with wrath :
' Mortal, whate'er, who this forbidden path
In arms presum'st to tread ! I charge thee, stand,
And tell thy name, and business in the land !
Know, this the realm of night—the Stygian shore :
My boat conveys no living bodies o'er :
Nor was I pleased great Theseus once to bear
(Who forced a passage with his pointed spear),
Nor strong Alcides—men of mighty fame ;
And from the immortal gods their lineage came.
In fetters, one, the barking porter tied,
And took him trembling from his sovereign's side :
Two, sought by force to seize his beauteous bride.'
To whom the Sibyl thus : ' Compose thy mind :
Nor frauds are here contrived, nor force designed.
Still may the dog the wandering troops constrain

Of airy ghosts, and vex the guilty train ;
And with her grisly lord his lovely queen remain.
The Trojan chief, whose lineage is from Jove,
Much famed for arms, and more for filial love,
Is sent to seek his sire in your Elysian grove.
If neither piety, nor heaven's command,
Can gain his passage to thy Stygian strand,
This fatal present shall prevail at least '—
Then showed the shining bough, concealed within her
  vest.
No more was needful ; for the gloomy god
Stood mute with awe, to see the golden rod ;
Admired the destined offering to his queen—
A venerable gift, so rarely seen.
His fury thus appeased, he puts to land :
The ghosts forsake their seats at his command :
He clears the deck, receives the mighty freight ;
The leaky vessel groans beneath the weight.
Slowly she sails, and scarcely stems the tides ;
The pressing water pours within her sides.
His passengers at length are wafted o'er,
Exposed, in muddy weeds upon the miry shore.
 No sooner landed, in his den they found
The triple porter of the Stygian sound,
Grim Cerberus ; who soon began to rear
His crested snakes, and armed his bristling hair.
The prudent Sibyl had before prepared
A sop, in honey steeped, to charm the guard ;
Which, mixed with powerful drugs, she cast before
His greedy grinning jaws, just oped to roar.
With three enormous mouths he gapes, and straight,
With hunger pressed, devours the pleasing bait.
Long draughts of sleep his monstrous limbs enslave ;
He reels, and falling, fills the spacious cave.
The keeper charmed, the chief without delay
Passed on, and took the irremeable way.
Before the gates, the cries of babes new-born,
Whom Fate had from their tender mothers torn,
Assault his ears : then, those whom form of laws
Condemned to die, when traitors judged their cause.

Nor want they lots, nor judges to review
The wrongful sentence, and award a new.
Minos, the strict inquisitor, appears ;
And lives and crimes, with his assessors, hears.
Round, in his urn, the blended balls he rolls,
Absolves the just, and dooms the guilty souls.
The next, in place and punishment, are they
Who prodigally threw their souls away :
Fools, who, repining at their wretched state,
And loathing anxious life, suborned their fate.
With late repentance, now they would retrieve
The bodies they forsook, and wish to live ;
Their pains and poverty desire to bear,
To view the light of heaven, and breathe the vital air :
But Fate forbids ; the Stygian floods oppose,
And, with nine circling streams, the captive souls inclose.
   Not far from thence, the Mournful Fields appear,
So called from lovers that inhabit there.
The souls whom that unhappy flame invades,
In secret solitude and myrtle shades
Make endless moans, and, pining with desire,
Lament too late their unextinguished fire.
Here Procris, Eriphyle here he found
Baring her breast, yet bleeding with the wound
Made by her son.   He saw Pasiphaë there,
With Phædra's ghost ; a foul incestuous pair.
There Laodamia, with Evadne, moves :
Unhappy both, but loyal in their loves :
Cæneus, a woman once, and once a man,
But ending in the sex she first began.
Not far from these Phœnician Dido stood,
Fresh from her wound, her bosom bathed in blood ;
Whom when the Trojan hero hardly knew,
Obscure in shades, and with a doubtful view
(Doubtful as he who sees, through dusky night,
Or thinks he sees, the moon's uncertain light),
With tears he first approached the sullen shade ;
And as his love inspired him, thus he said :
'Unhappy queen ! then is the common breath
Of rumour true, in your reported death,

And I, alas! the cause?—By Heaven, I vow,
And all the powers that rule the realms below,
Unwilling I forsook your friendly state,
Commanded by the gods, and forced by Fate!
Those gods, that Fate, whose unresisted might
Have sent me to these regions void of light,
Through the vast empire of eternal night!
Nor dared I to presume, that, pressed with grief,
My flight should urge you to this dire relief.
Stay, stay your steps, and listen to my vows!
'Tis the last interview that Fate allows!'
In vain he thus attempts her mind to move
With tears and prayers, and late repenting love.
Disdainfully she looked; then turning round,
She fixed her eyes unmoved upon the ground;
And, what he says and swears, regards no more
Than the deaf rocks, when the loud billows roar:
But whirled away, to shun his hateful sight,
Hid in the forest, and the shades of night:
Then sought Sichæus through the shady grove,
Who answered all her cares, and equalled all her love.
  Some pious tears the pitying hero paid,
And followed with his eyes the flitting shade;
Then took the forward way, by Fate ordained,
And, with his guide, the farther fields attained,
Where, severed from the rest, the warrior souls re-
      mained.
Tydeus he met, with Meleager's race,
The pride of armies, and the soldiers' grace;
And pale Adrastus with his ghastly face.
Of Trojan chiefs he viewed a numerous train,
All much lamented, all in battle slain:
Glaucus and Medon, high above the rest,
Antenor's sons and Ceres' sacred priest,
And proud Idæus, Priam's charioteer,
Who shakes his empty reins, and aims his airy spear.
The gladsome ghosts, in circling troops, attend,
And with unwearied eyes behold their friend;
Delight to hover near, and long to know
What business brought him to the realms below.

But Argive chiefs, and Agamemnon's train,
When his refulgent arms flashed through the shady
    plain,
Fled from his well-known face with wonted fear;
As when his thundering sword and pointed spear
Drove headlong to their ships, and gleaned the routed
    rear.
They raised a feeble cry, with trembling notes,
But the weak voice deceived their gasping throats.
Here Priam's son, Deïphobus, he found,
Whose face and limbs were one continued wound;
Dishonest, with lopped arms, the youth appears,
Spoiled of his nose, and shortened of his ear.
He scarcely knew him, striving to disown
His blotted form, and blushing to be known;
And therefore first began : ' O Teucer's race!
Who durst thy faultless figure thus deface?
What heart could wish, what hand inflict this dire dis-
    grace?
'Twas famed, that in our last and fatal night,
Your single prowess long sustained the fight;
Till tired, not forced, a glorious fate you chose,
And fell upon a heap of slaughtered foes.
But, in remembrance of so brave a deed,
A tomb and funeral honours I decreed;
Thrice called your manes on the Trojan plains:
The place your armour and your name retains.
Your body too I sought, and, had I found,
Designed for burial in your native ground.'
    The ghost replied : ' Your piety has paid
All needful rites to rest my wandering shade;
But cruel Fate, and my more cruel wife,
To Grecian swords betrayed my sleeping life.
These are the monuments of Helen's love:
The shame I bear below, the marks I bore above.
You know in what deluding joys, we past
The night that was by heaven decreed our last.
For, when the fatal horse, descending down
Pregnant with arms o'erwhelmed the unhappy town,
She feigned nocturnal orgies; left my bed;

And, mixed with Trojan dames, the dances led ;
Then, waving high her torch, the signal made,
Which roused the Grecians from their ambuscade.
With watching over-worn, with cares oppressed,
Unhappy I had laid me down to rest ;
And heavy sleep my weary limbs possessed.
Meantime my worthy wife our arms mislaid,
And, from beneath my head, my sword conveyed ;
The door unlatched, and, with repeated calls
Invites her former lord within my walls.
Thus, in her crime her confidence she placed,
And with new treasons would redeem the past.
What need I more ?   Into the room they ran,
And meanly murdered a defenceless man.
Ulysses, basely born, first led the way.—
Avenging powers ! with justice if I pray,
That fortune be their own another day !
But answer you ; and in your turn relate
What brought you, living, to the Stygian state :
Driven by the winds and errors of the sea,
Or did you heaven's superior doom obey ?
Or tell what other chance conducts your way,
To view with mortal eyes, our dark retreats,
Tumults and torments of the infernal seats.'
    While thus, in talk the flying hours they pass,
The sun had finished more than half his race ;
And they, perhaps, in words and tears had spent
The little time of stay which heaven had lent :
But thus the Sibyl chides their long delay :
' Night rushes down, and headlong drives the day :
'Tis here, in different paths, the way divides ;
The right to Pluto's golden palace guides ;
The left to that unhappy region tends,
Which to the depth of Tartarus descends :
The seat of night profound, and punished fiends.'
Then thus Deïphobus : ' O sacred maid !
Forbear to chide ; and be your will obeyed.
Lo ! to the secret shadows I retire,
To pay my penance till my years expire.
Proceed, auspicious prince, with glory crowned,

And born to better fates than I have found.'
He said ; and, while he said, his steps he turned
To secret shadows, and in silence mourned.

   The hero, looking on the left, espied
A lofty tower, and strong on every side
With treble walls, which Phlegethon surrounds,
Whose fiery flood the burning empire bounds ;
And, pressed betwixt the rocks, the bellowing noise
    resounds.
Wide is the fronting gate, and raised on high
With adamantine columns, threats the sky.
Vain is the force of man, and heaven's as vain,
To crush the pillars which the pile sustain.
Sublime on these, a tower of steel is reared ;
And dire Tisiphonè there keeps the ward,
Girt in her sanguine gown, by night and day
Observant of the souls that pass the downward way.
From hence are heard the groans of ghosts, the pains
Of sounding lashes, and of dragging chains.
The Trojan stood astonished at their cries ;
And asked his guide, from whence those yells arise,
And what the crimes, and what the tortures were,
And loud laments that rent the liquid air?

   She thus replied : ' The chaste and holy race
Are all forbidden this polluted place.
But Hecate, when she gave to rule the woods,
Then led me trembling through these dire abodes,
And taught the tortures of the avenging gods.
These are the realms of unrelenting Fate ;
And awful Rhadamanthus rules the state :
He hears and judges each committed crime ;
Inquires into the manner, place, and time.
The conscious wretch must all his acts reveal
(Loth to confess, unable to conceal),
From the first moment of his vital breath,
To his last hour of unrepenting death.
Straight o'er the guilty ghost, the Fury shakes
The sounding whip, and brandishes her snakes,
And the pale sinner, with her sisters, takes.'

   Then, of itself, unfolds the eternal door ;

With dreadful sounds the brazen hinges roar.
' You see, before the gate, what stalking ghost
Commands the guard, what sentries keep the post.
More formidable Hydra stands within,
Whose jaws with iron teeth severely grin.
The gaping gulf low to the centre lies,
And twice as deep, as earth is distant from the skies.
The rivals of the gods, the Titan race,
Here, singed with lightning, roll within the unfathomed
    space.
Here lie the Aloëan twins (I saw them both) :
Enormous bodies, of gigantic growth,
Who dared in fight the Thunderer to defy,
Affect his heaven, and force him from the sky.
Salmoneus, suffering cruel pains, I found,
For emulating Jove, the rattling sound
Of mimic thunder, and the glittering blaze
Of pointed lightnings, and their forky rays.
Through Elis, and the Grecian towns, he flew,
The audacious wretch four fiery coursers drew :
He waved a torch aloft, and, madly vain,
Sought godlike worship from a servile train.
Ambitious fool ! with horny hoofs to pass
O'er hollow arches of resounding brass ;
To rival thunder in its rapid course,
And imitate inimitable force !
But he, the king of heaven, obscure on high,
Bared his red arm, and launching from the sky
His writhen bolt, not shaking empty smoke,
Down to the deep abyss the flaming felon struck.
    There Tityus was to see, who took his birth
From heaven, his nursing from the foodful earth.
Here his gigantic limbs, with large embrace,
Infold nine acres of infernal space.
A ravenous vulture, in his opened side,
Her crooked beak and cruel talons tried ;
Still for the growing liver digged his breast :
The growing liver still supplied the feast ;
Still are his entrails fruitful to their pains :
The immortal hunger lasts, the immortal food remains.

Ixion and Pirithoüs I could name,
And more Thessalian chiefs of mighty fame.
High o'er their heads a mouldering rock is placed,
That promises a fall, and shakes at every blast.
They lie below, on golden beds displayed ;
And genial feasts with regal pomp are made.
The queen of Furies by their sides is set,
And snatches from their mouths the untasted meat ;
Which if they touch, her hissing snakes she rears,
Tossing her torch, and thundering in their ears.

   Then they, who brothers' better claim disown,
Expel their parents, and usurp the throne ;
Defraud their clients, and, to lucre sold,
Sit brooding on unprofitable gold—
Who dare not give, and e'en refuse to lend,
To their poor kindred, or a wanting friend.
Vast is the throng of these ; nor less the train
Of lustful youths, for foul adultery slain :
Hosts of deserters, who their honour sold,
And basely broke their faith for bribes of gold.
All these within the dungeon's depth remain,
Despairing pardon, and expecting pain.
Ask not what pains ; nor farther seek to know
Their process, or the forms of law below.
Some roll a mighty stone ; some, laid along
And bound with burning wires, on spokes of wheels are
     hung.
Unhappy Theseus doomed for ever, there
Is fixed by Fate, on his eternal chair ;
And wretched Phlegyas warns the world with cries
(Could warning make the world more just or wise):
' Learn righteousness, and dread the avenging deities.'
To tyrants others have their country sold,
Imposing foreign lords for foreign gold :
Some have old laws repealed, new statutes made ;
Not as the people pleased, but as they paid.
With incest some their daughters' bed profaned :
All dared the worst of ills, and, what they dared,
     attained.
Had I a hundred mouths, a hundred tongues,

And throats of brass, inspired with iron lungs,
I could not half those horrid crimes repeat,
Nor half the punishments those crimes have met.
    But let us haste our voyage to pursue :
The walls of Pluto's palace are in view ;
The gate, and iron arch above it, stands,
On anvils laboured by the Cyclops' hands.
Before our farther way the Fates allow,
Here must we fix on high the golden bough.'
She said : and through the gloomy shades they past,
And chose the middle path.—Arrived at last,
The prince, with living water sprinkled o'er
His limbs and body ; then approached the door,
Possessed the porch, and on the front above
He fixed the fatal bough, required by Pluto's love.
    These holy rites performed, they took their way,
Where long extended plains of pleasure lay.
The verdant fields with those of heaven may vie,
With ether vested, and a purple sky—
The blissful seats of happy souls below :
Stars of their own, and their own suns, they know.
Their airy limbs in sports they exercise,
And, on the green, contend the wrestler's prize.
Some, in heroic verse, divinely sing ;
Others in artful measures lead the ring.
The Thracian bard, surrounded by the rest,
There stands conspicuous in his flowing vest.
His flying fingers, and harmonious quill,
Strike seven distinguished notes, and seven at once
    they fill.
Here found they Teucer's old heroic race,
Born better times and happier years to grace.
Assaracus and Ilus here enjoy
Perpetual fame, with him who founded Troy.
The chief beheld their chariots from afar,
Their shining arms, and coursers trained to war.
Their lances fixed in earth, their steeds around,
Free from their harness, graze the flowery ground.
The love of horses which they had, alive,
And care of chariots, after death survive.

Some cheerful souls were feasting on the plain ;
Some did the song, and some the choir, maintain,
Beneath a laurel shade, where mighty Po
Mounts up to woods above, and hides his head below.
Here patriots live, who, for their country's good,
In fighting fields, were prodigal of blood :
Priests of unblemished lives here make abode,
And poets worthy their inspiring god ;
And searching wits, of more mechanic parts,
Who graced their age with new invented arts ;
Those who, to worth their bounty did extend,
And those who knew that bounty to commend.
The heads of these with holy fillets bound,
And all their temples were with garlands crowned.
  To these the Sibyl thus her speech addressed,
And first to him surrounded by the rest
(Towering his height, and ample was his breast) :
'Say, happy souls ! divine Musæus ! say
Where lives Anchises, and where lies our way
To find the hero, for whose only sake
We sought the dark abodes, and crossed the bitter
    lake ? '
To this the sacred poet thus replied :
'In no fixed place the happy souls reside :
In groves we live, and lie on mossy beds,
By crystal streams, that murmur through the meads,
But pass yon easy hill, and thence descend ;
The path conducts you to your journey's end.'
This said, he led them up the mountain's brow,
And shews them all the shining fields below :
They wind the hill, and through the blissful meadows
    go.
But old Anchises, in a flowery vale,
Reviewed his mustered race, and took the tale—
Those happy spirits, which, ordained by Fate,
For future being and new bodies wait :
With studious thought observed the illustrious throng,
In nature's order, as they passed along :
Their names, their fates, their conduct, and their care,
In peaceful senates, and successful war.

He, when Æneas on the plain appears,
Meets him with open arms, and falling tears:
' Welcome (he said), the gods, undoubted race !
O long expected, to my dear embrace !
Once more 'tis given me to behold your face !
The love and pious duty which you pay,
Have passed the perils of so hard a way.
'Tis true, computing times, I now believed
The happy day approached, nor are my hopes deceived.
What length of lands, what oceans have you passed,
What storms sustained, and on what shores been cast !
How have I feared your fate ! but feared it most,
When love assailed you on the Libyan coast.'
To this, the filial duty thus replies :
' Your sacred ghost, before my sleeping eyes
Appeared, and often urged this painful enterprise.
After long tossing on the Tyrrhene sea,
My navy rides at anchor in the bay.
But reach your hand, oh parent shade ! nor shun
The dear embraces of your longing son !'
He said ; and falling tears his face bedew ;
Then thrice, around his neck, his arms he threw ;
And thrice the flitting shadow slipped away,
Like winds, or empty dreams, that fly the day.

Now, in a secret vale, the Trojan sees
A separate grove, through which a gentle breeze
Plays with a passing breath, and whispers through the
          trees ;
And, just before the confines of the wood,
The gliding Lethe leads her silent flood.
About the boughs an airy nation flew,
Thick as the humming bees, that hunt the golden dew
In summer's heat ; on tops of lilies feed,
And creep within their bells, to suck the balmy seed :
The wingèd army roams the field around ;
The rivers and the rocks remurmur to the sound.
Æneas wondering stood, then asked the cause
Which to the stream the crowding people draws.
Then thus the sire : ' The souls that throng the flood,
Are those to whom, by Fate, are other bodies owed ;

In Lethe's lake they long oblivion taste,
Of future life secure, forgetful of the past.
Long has my soul desired this time and place,
To set before your sight your glorious race ;
That this presaging joy may fire your mind,
To seek the shores by destiny designed.'
' O father ! can it be, that souls sublime
Return, to visit our terrestrial clime ;
And that the generous mind, released by death,
Can covet lazy limbs, and mortal breath ?'
Anchises, then, in order, thus begun
To clear those wonders to his godlike son :
' Know, first, that heaven and earth's compacted frame,
And flowing waters, and the starry flame,
And both the radiant lights, one common soul
Inspires and feeds, and animates the whole.
This active mind, infused through all the space,
Unites and mingles with the mighty mass.
Hence men and beasts the breath of life obtain,
And birds of air, and monsters of the main.
The ethereal vigour is in all the same ;
And every soul is filled with equal flame :
As much as earthly limbs, and gross allay
Of mortal members, subject to decay,
Blunt not the beams of heaven and edge of day.
From this coarse mixture of terrestrial parts,
Desire and fear by turns possess their hearts,
And grief, and joy ! nor can the grovelling mind,
In the dark dungeon of the limbs confined,
Assert the native skies, or own its heavenly kind :
Nor death itself can wholly wash their stains ;
But long-contracted filth e'en in the soul remains.
The relics of inveterate vice they wear ;
And spots of sin obscene in every face appear.
For this are various penances enjoined ;
And some are hung to bleach upon the wind ;
Some plunged in waters, others purged in fires,
Till all the dregs are drained, and all the rust expires.
All have their manes, and those manes bear :
The few, so cleansed, to these abodes repair,

And breathe, in ample fields, the soft Elysian air.
Then are they happy, when by length of time
The scurf is worn away, of each committed crime;
No speck is left of their habitual stains;
But the pure ether of the soul remains.
But, when a thousand rolling years are past
(So long their punishments and penance last),
Whole droves of minds, are by the driving god
Compelled to drink the deep Lethæan flood;
In large forgetful draughts to steep the cares
Of their past labours, and their irksome years;
That, unremembering of its former pain,
The soul may suffer mortal flesh again.

Thus having said, the father-spirit leads
The priestess and his son through swarms of shades,
And takes a rising ground, from thence to see
The long procession of his progeny.
'Survey (pursued the sire) this airy throng,
As, offered to the view, they pass along.
These are the Italian names, which Fate will join
With ours, and graff upon the Trojan line.
Observe, the youth who first appears in sight,
And holds the nearest station to the light,
Already seems to snuff the vital air,
And leans just forward on a shining spear:
Silvius is he, thy last-begotten race,
But first in order sent, to fill thy place—
An Alban name, but mixed with Dardan blood;
Born in the covert of a shady wood.
Him fair Lavinia, thy surviving wife,
Shall breed in groves, to lead a solitary life.
In Alba he shall fix his royal seat,
And, born a king, a race of kings beget;
Then Procas, honour of the Trojan name,
Capys, and Numitor, of endless fame.
A second Silvius after these appears
(Silvius Æneas, for thy name he bears);
For arms and justice equally renowned;
Who, late restored, in Alba shall be crowned.
How great they look! how vigorously they wield

Their weighty lances, and sustain the shield !
But they, who crowned with oaken wreaths appear,
Shall Gabian walls and strong Fidenæ rear ;
Nomentum, Bola, with Pometia, found ;
And raise Collatian towers on rocky ground.
All these shall then be towns of mighty fame,
Though now they lie obscure, and lands without a name.
  See Romulus the great ! born to restore
The crown that once his injured grandsire wore.
This prince, a priestess of our blood shall bear ;
And like his sire in arms he shall appear.
Two rising crests his royal head adorn :
Born from a god, himself to godhead born ;
His sire already signs him for the skies,
And marks his seat amidst the deities.
Auspicious chief ! thy race, in times to come,
Shall spread the conquests of imperial Rome—
Rome, whose ascending towers shall heaven invade,
Involving earth and ocean in her shade ;
High as the mother of the gods in place,
And proud, like her, of an immortal race.
Then, when in pomp she makes the Phrygian round,
With golden turrets on her temples crowned :
A hundred gods her sweeping train supply,
Her offspring all ; and all command the sky.
  Now fix your sight, and stand intent, to see
Your Roman race, and Julian progeny !
There mighty Cæsar waits his vital hour,
Impatient for the world, and grasps his promised power.
But next behold the youth of form divine—
Cæsar himself, exalted in his line—
Augustus, promised oft, and long foretold,
Sent to the realm that Saturn ruled of old ;
Born to restore a better age of gold.
Afric and India shall his power obey ;
He shall extend his propagated sway
Beyond the solar year ; without the starry way,
Where Atlas turns the rolling heavens around,
And his broad shoulders with their lights are crowned.
At his foreseen approach, already quake

The Caspian kingdoms and Mæotian lake.
Their seers behold the tempest from afar ;
And threatening oracles denounce the war.
Nile hears him knocking at his seven-fold gates,
And seeks his hidden spring, and fears his nephew's
    fates.
Nor Hercules more lands or labours knew,
Not though the brazen-footed hind he slew,
Freed Erymanthus from the foaming boar,
And dipped his arrows in Lernæan gore ;
Nor Bacchus, turning from his Indian war,
By tigers drawn triumphant in his car,
From Nysa's top descending on the plains,
With curling vines around his purple reins.
And doubt we, yet through dangers to pursue
The paths of honour, and a crown in view ?
    But what's the man who from afar appears,
His head with olive crowned, his hand a censer bears?
His hoary beard and holy vestments bring
His lost idea back : I know the Roman king.
He shall to peaceful Rome new laws ordain,
Called from his mean abode, a sceptre to sustain.
Him, Tullus next in dignity succeeds ;
An active prince, and prone to martial deeds.
He shall his troops for fighting-fields prepare,
Disused to toils, and triumphs of the war.
By dint of sword his crown he shall increase,
And scour his armour from the rust of peace.
Whom Ancus follows, with a fawning air,
But vain within, and proudly popular.
    Next view the Tarquin kings, the avenging sword
Of Brutus, justly drawn, and Rome restored.
He first renews the rods and axe severe,
And gives the consuls royal robes to wear.
His sons, who seek the tyrant to sustain,
And long for arbitrary lords again,
With ignominy scourged in open sight,
He dooms to death deserved, asserting public right.
Unhappy man ! to break the pious laws
Of nature, pleading in his children's cause !

Howe'er the doubtful fact is understood,
'Tis love of honour, and his country's good:
The consul, not the father, sheds the blood.
Behold Torquatus the same tract pursue;
And, next, the two devoted Decii view:
The Drusian line, Camillus loaded home
With standards well redeemed, and foreign foes o'er-
 come.
  The pair you see in equal armour shine,
Now, friends below, in close embraces join;
But, when they leave the shady realms of night,
And, clothed in bodies, breathe your upper light,
With mortal hate each other shall pursue:
What wars, what wounds, what slaughter, shall ensue!
From Alpine heights the father first descends;
His daughter's husband in the plain attends:
His daughter's husband arms his eastern friends.
Embrace again, my sons! be foes no more;
Nor stain your country with her children's gore!
And thou, the first, lay down thy lawless claim,
Thou, of my blood, who bear'st the Julian name!
Another comes, who shall in triumph ride,
And to the Capitol his chariot guide,
From conquered Corinth, rich with Grecian spoils.
And yet another, famed for warlike toils,
On Argos shall impose the Roman laws,
And on the Greeks, revenge the Trojan cause;
Shall drag in chains their Achillean race;
Shall vindicate his ancestors' disgrace,
And Pallas, for her violated place.
Great Cato there, for gravity renowned;
And conquering Cossus goes with laurels crowned.
Who can omit the Gracchi? who declare
The Scipios' worth, those thunderbolts of war,
The double bane of Carthage! Who can see,
Without esteem for virtuous poverty,
Severe Fabricius; or can cease to admire
The ploughman consul in his coarse attire?
Tired as I am, my praise the Fabii claim;
And thou, great hero, greatest of thy name,

Ordained in war to save the sinking state,
And, by delays, to put a stop to fate !
   Let others better mould the running mass
Of metals, and inform the breathing brass,
And soften into flesh a marble face ;
Plead better at the bar ; describe the skies,
And when the stars descend, and when they rise.
But, Rome ! 'tis thine alone, with awful sway,
To rule mankind, and make the world obey :
Disposing peace and war thy own majestic way.
To tame the proud, the fettered slave to free,
These are imperial arts, and worthy thee.'
   He paused—and, while with wondering eyes they
      viewed
The passing spirits, thus his speech renewed :
' See great Marcellus ! how, untired in toils,
He moves with manly grace, how rich with regal
      spoils !
He, when his country (threatened with alarms)
Requires his courage and his conquering arms,
Shall more than once the Punic bands affright ;
Shall kill the Gaulish king in single fight ;
Then to the Capitol in triumph move ;
And the third spoils shall grace Feretrian Jove.'
   Æneas here beheld, of form divine,
A godlike youth in glittering armour shine ;
With great Marcellus keeping equal pace ;
But gloomy were his eyes, dejected was his face.
He saw, and, wondering, asked his airy guide,
What, and of whence, was he who pressed the hero's
      side ?
' His son, or one of his illustrious name ?
How like the former, and almost the same !
Observe the crowds that compass him around :
All gaze and all admire, and raise a shouting sound :
But hovering mists around his brows are spread ;
And night, with sable shades, involves his head.'
' Seek not to know (the ghost replied with tears)
The sorrows of thy sons in future years.
This youth, the blissful vision of a day,

Shall just be shewn on earth, and snatched away.
The gods, too high had raised the Roman state:
Were but their gifts as permanent as great!
What groans of men shall fill the Martian field!
How fierce a blaze his flaming pile shall yield!
What funeral pomp shall floating Tiber see,
When, rising from his bed, he views the sad solemnity!
No youth shall equal hopes of glory give;
No youth afford so great a cause to grieve.
The Trojan honour, and the Roman boast;
Admired when living, and adored when lost!
Mirror of ancient faith in early youth!
Undaunted worth, inviolable truth!
No foe, unpunished, in the fighting field
Shall dare thee, foot to foot, with sword and shield;
Much less in arms oppose thy matchless force,
When thy sharp spurs shall urge thy foaming horse.
Ah! couldst thou break through Fate's severe decree,
A new Marcellus shall arise in thee!
Full canisters of fragrant lilies bring,
Mixed with the purple roses of the spring:
Let me with funeral flowers his body strow;
This gift which parents to their children owe,
This unavailing gift, at least, I may bestow!'
   Thus having said, he led the hero round
The confines of the blest Elysian ground;
Which when Anchises to his son had shown,
And fired his mind to mount the promised throne,
He tells the future wars, ordained by Fate;
The strength and customs of the Latian state;
The prince and people; and fore-arms his care
With rules, to push his fortune, or to bear.
   Two gates the silent house of Sleep adorn;
Of polished ivory this, that of transparent horn
True visions through transparent horn arise;
Through polished ivory pass deluding lies.
Of various things discoursing as he passed,
Anchises hither bends his steps at last;
Then, through the gate of ivory, he dismissed
His valiant offspring, and divining guest.

Straight to the ships Æneas took his way,
Embarked his men, and skimmed along the sea;
Still coasting, till he gained Caieta's bay.
At length on oozy ground his galleys moor:
Their heads are turned to sea, their sterns to shore.

BOOK VII

THE ARGUMENT

King Latinus entertains Æneas, and promises him his only daughter
Lavinia, the heiress of his crown. Turnus, being in love with
her, favoured by her mother, and stirred up by Juno and Alecto,
breaks the treaty which was made, and engages in his quarrel
Mezentius, Camilla, Messapus, and many other of the neighbouring
princes; whose forces, and the names of their commanders, are
particularly related.

AND thou, O matron of immortal fame !
Here dying, to the shore hast left thy name :
Caieta still the place is called from thee,
The nurse of great Æneas' infancy.
Here rest thy bones in rich Hesperia's plains :
Thy name ('tis all a ghost can have) remains.

    Now, when the prince her funeral rites had paid,
He ploughed the Tyrrhene seas with sails displayed.
From land a gentle breeze arose by night ;
Serenely shone the stars ; the moon was bright,
And the sea trembled with her silver light.
Now near the shelves of Circe's shores they run
(Circe the rich, the daughter of the sun) :
A dangerous coast !—The goddess wastes her days
In joyous songs ; the rocks resound her lay.
In spinning, or the loom, she spends the night ;
And cedar-brands supply her father's light.
From hence were heard, rebellowing to the main,
The roars of lions that refuse the chain,
The grunts of bristled boars, and groans of bears,
And herds of howling wolves that stun the sailors' ears
These from their caverns, at the close of night,
Fill the sad isle with horror and affright.

Darkling they mourn their fate, whom Circe's power
(That watched the moon, and planetary hour),
With words and wicked herbs, from human kind
Had altered, and in brutal shapes confined.
Which monsters, lest the Trojans' pious host
Should bear, or touch upon the enchanted coast,
Propitious Neptune steered their course by night,
With rising gales, that sped their happy flight.
Supplied with these, they skim the sounding shore,
And hear the swelling surges vainly roar.
Now, when the rosy morn began to rise,
And waved her saffron streamer through the skies;
When Thetis blushed in purple, not her own,
And from her face the breathing winds were blown,
A sudden silence sate upon the sea,
And sweeping oars, with struggling, urge their way.
  The Trojan, from the main, beheld a wood,
Which thick with shades, and a brown horror, stood:
Betwixt the trees the Tiber took his course,
With whirlpools dimpled; and with downward force
That drove the sand along, he took his way,
And rolled his yellow billows to the sea.
About him, and above, and round the wood,
The birds that haunt the borders of his flood,
That bathed within, or basked upon his side,
To tuneful songs their narrow throats applied.
The captain gives command; the joyful train
Glide through the gloomy shade, and leave the main.
  Now, Erato! thy poet's mind inspire,
And fill his soul with thy celestial fire.
Relate what Latium was; her ancient kings:
Declare the past and present state of things;
When first the Trojan fleet Ausonia sought,
And how the rivals loved, and how they fought.
These are my theme; and how the war began,
And how concluded by the godlike man;
For I shall sing of battles, blood, and rage,
Which princes and their people did engage;
And haughty souls, that, moved with mutual hate,
In fighting fields pursued and found their fate;

That roused the Tyrrhene realm with loud alarms,
And peaceful Italy involved in arms.
A larger scene of action is displayed;
And, rising hence, a greater work is weighed.
    Latinus, old and mild, had long possessed
The Latian sceptre, and his people blessed:
His father Faunus: a Laurentian dame
His mother; fair Marica was her name.
But Faunus came from Picus: Picus drew
His birth from Saturn, if records be true.
Thus king Latinus, in the third degree,
Had Saturn author of his family.
But this old peaceful prince, as heaven decreed,
Was blessed with no male issue to succeed:
His sons in blooming youth were snatched by fate;
One only daughter heired the royal state.
Fired with her love, and with ambition led,
The neighbouring princes court her nuptial bed.
Among the crowd, but far above the rest,
Young Turnus to the beauteous maid addressed.
Turnus, for high descent and graceful mien
Was first, and favoured by the Latian queen:
With him she strove to join Lavinia's hand;
But dire portents the purposed match withstand.
    Deep in the palace, of long growth there stood
A laurel's trunk, a venerable wood;
Where rites divine were paid; whose holy hair
Was kept and cut with superstitious care.
This plant, Latinus, when his town he walled
Then found, and from the tree Laurentum called;
And last, in honour of his new abode,
He vowed the laurel to the laurel's god.
It happened once (a boding prodigy!)
A swarm of bees, that cut the liquid sky
(Unknown from whence they took their airy flight),
Upon the topmost branch in clouds alight;
There, with their clasping feet, together clung,
And a long cluster from the laurel hung.
An ancient augur prophesied from hence:
'Behold! on Latian shores a foreign prince;

From the same parts of heaven his navy stands,
To the same parts on earth : his army lands ;
The town he conquers, and the tower commands.'
  Yet more ; when fair Lavinia fed the fire
Before the gods, and stood beside her sire,
(Strange to relate !) the flames, involved in smoke
Of incense, from the sacred altar broke,
Caught her dishevelled hair, and rich attire ;
Her crown and jewels crackled in the fire :
From thence the fuming trail began to spread,
And lambent glories danced about her head.
This new portent the seer with wonder views,
Then pausing, thus his prophecy renews :
' The nymph who scatters flaming fires around,
Shall shine with honour, shall herself be crowned ;
But, caused by her irrevocable fate,
War shall the country waste, and change the state.
  Latinus, frightened with this dire ostent,
For counsel to his father Faunus went ;
And sought the shades renowned for prophecy,
Which near Albunea's sulphurous fountain lie.
To those, the Latian and the Sabine land
Fly when distressed ; and thence relief demand.
The priest on skins of offerings takes his ease,
And nightly visions in his slumber sees ;
A swarm of thin aërial shapes appears,
And, fluttering round his temples, deafs his ears.
These he consults, the future fates to know,
From powers above, and from the fiends below.
Here, for the god's advice, Latinus flies,
Offering a hundred sheep for sacrifice :
Their woolly fleeces, as the rites required,
He laid beneath him, and to rest retired.
No sooner were his eyes in slumber bound,
When, from above, a more than mortal sound
Invades his ears ; and thus the vision spoke :
' Seek not, my seed, in Latian bands to yoke
Our fair Lavinia, nor the gods provoke.
A foreign son upon the shore descends,
Whose martial fame from pole to pole extends.

His race, in arms and arts of peace renowned,
Not Latium shall contain, nor Europe bound :
'Tis theirs, whate'er the sun surveys around.'
These answers, in the silent night received,
The king himself divulged, the land believed :
The fame through all the neighbouring nations flew,
When now the Trojan navy was in view.

Beneath a shady tree, the hero spread
His table on the turf, with cakes of bread ;
And, with his chiefs, on forest fruits he fed.
They sat ; and (not without the god's command),
Their homely fare despatched ; the hungry band
Invade their trenchers next, and soon devour,
To mend the scanty meal—their cakes of flour.
Ascanius this observed, and, smiling, said :
' See ! we devour the plates on which we fed.'
The speech had omen, that the Trojan race
Should find repose ; and this the time and place.

Æneas took the word, and thus replies
(Confessing fate with wonder in his eyes) :
' All hail, O earth ! all hail, my household gods !
Behold the destined place of your abodes !
For thus Anchises prophesied of old,
And this our fatal place of rest foretold :
" When, on a foreign shore, instead of meat,
By famine forced, your trenchers you shall eat,
Then ease your weary Trojans will attend,
And the long labours of your voyage end.
Remember on that happy coast to build ;
And with a trench inclose the fruitful field."
This, was that famine, this the fatal place ;
Which ends the wandering of our exiled race.
Then, on to-morrow's dawn, your care employ
To search the land, and where the cities lie,
And what the men ; but give this day to joy.
Now pour to Jove ; and after Jove is blest,
Call great Anchises to the genial feast :
Crown high the goblets with a cheerful draught ;
Enjoy the present hour ; adjourn the future thought.'

Thus having said, the hero bound his brows

With leafy branches, then performed his vows :
Adoring first the genius of the place ;
Then Earth, the mother of the heavenly race ;
The nymphs, and native godheads yet unknown ;
And Night, and all the stars that gild her sable throne.
And ancient Cybel, and Idæan Jove ;
And last his sire below, and mother-queen above.
    Then heaven's high monarch thundered thrice aloud;
And thrice he shook aloft a golden cloud.
Soon through the joyful camp a rumour flew,
The time was come their city to renew :
Then every brow with cheerful green is crowned ;
The feasts are doubled, and the bowls go round.
    When next the rosy morn disclosed the day,
The scouts to several parts divide their way,
To learn the natives' names, their towns explore,
The coasts, and trendings of the crooked shore :
Here Tiber flows, and here Numicus stands ;
Here warlike Latins hold the happy lands.
    The pious chief, who sought by peaceful ways
To found his empire, and his town to raise,
A hundred youths from all his train selects,
And to the Latian court their course directs
(The spacious palace where their prince resides),
And all their heads with wreaths of olive hides.
They go, commissioned to require a peace ;
And carry presents, to procure access.
Thus while they speed their pace, the prince designs
The new-elected seat, and draws the lines :
The Trojans round the place a rampire cast,
And palisades about the trenches placed.
    Meantime, the train, proceeding on their way,
From far the town and lofty towers, survey ;
At length approach the walls.   Without the gate,
They see the boys and Latian youth, debate
The martial prizes on the dusty plain :
Some drive the cars, and some the coursers rein ;
Some bend the stubborn bow for victory ;
And some with darts their active sinews try.
A posting messenger, despatched from hence,

Of this fair troop, advised their aged prince
That foreign men of mighty stature, came ;
Uncouth their habit, and unknown their name.
    The king ordains their entrance, and ascends
His regal seat, surrounded by his friends.
The palace, built by Picus, vast and proud,
Supported by a hundred pillars stood,
And round encompassed with a rising wood.
The pile o'erlooked the town, and drew the sight,
Surprised at once with reverence and delight.
There, kings received the marks of sovereign power :
In state the monarchs marched ; the lictors bore
Their awful axes, and the rods, before.
Here the tribunal stood, the house of prayer ;
And here the sacred senators repair ;
All at large tables, in long order set,
A ram their offering, and a ram their meat.
Above the portal, carved in cedar wood,
Placed in their ranks, their godlike grandsires stood :
Old Saturn, with his crooked scythe, on high ;
And Italus, that led the colony ;
And ancient Janus, with his double face,
And bunch of keys, the porter of the place.
There stood Sabinus, planter of the vines ;
On a short pruning-hook his head reclines,
And studiously surveys his generous wines :
Then warlike kings, who for their country fought,
And honourable wounds from battle brought.
Around the posts, hung helmets, darts, and spears,
And captive chariots, axes, shields, and bars,
And broken beaks of ships, the trophies of their wars.
Above the rest, as chief of all the band,
Was Picus placed, a buckler in his hand,
His other waved a long divining wand.
Girt in his Gabine gown the hero sat,
Yet could not with his art avoid his fate ;
For Circe, long had loved the youth in vain,
Till love, refused, converted to disdain :
Then, mixing powerful herbs, with magic art ;
She changed his form, who could not change his heart :

Constrained him in a bird, and made him fly,
With particoloured plumes, a chattering pie.
   In this high temple, on a chair of state,
The seat of audience, old Latinus sat ;
Then gave admission to the Trojan train ;
And thus with pleasing accents he began :
' Tell me, ye Trojans—for that name you own ;
Nor is your course upon our coasts unknown—
Say what you seek, and whither were you bound ;
Were you by stress of weather cast aground ?
(Such dangers of the sea are often seen,
And oft befall to miserable men),
Or come your shipping in our ports to lay,
Spent and disabled in so long a way ?
Say what you want ? the Latians you shall find
Not forced to goodness, but by will inclined ;
For, since the time of Saturn's holy reign,
His hospitable customs we retain.
I call to mind (but time the tale has worn)
The Aurunci told that Dardanus, though born
On Latian plains, yet sought the Phrygian shore,
And Samothracia, Samos called, before.
From Tuscan Corythum he claimed his birth ;
But after, when exempt from mortal earth,
From thence ascended to his kindred skies,
A god, and, as a god, augments their sacrifice.'
   He said.—Ilioneus made this reply :
' O king, of Faunus' royal family !
Nor wintry winds to Latium forced our way,
Nor did the stars our wandering course betray.
Willing we sought your shores ; and, hither bound,
The port, so long desired, at length we found ;
From our sweet homes and ancient realms expelled—
Great as the greatest that the sun beheld.
The god began our line, who rules above ;
And, as our race, our king descends from Jove :
And hither are we come, by his command,
To crave admission in your happy land.
How dire a tempest, from Mycenæ poured,
Our plains, our temples, and our town, devoured ;

What was the waste of war, what fierce alarms
Shook Asia's crown with European arms ;
E'en such have heard, if any such there be,
Whose earth is bounded by the frozen sea ;
And such as, born beneath the burning sky
And sultry sun, betwixt the tropics lie.
From that dire deluge, through the watery waste
(Such length of years, such various perils, past),
At last escaped, to Latium we repair,
To beg what you without your want may spare—
The common water, and the common air ;
Sheds which ourselves will build, and mean abodes,
Fit to receive and serve our banished gods.
Nor our admission shall your realm disgrace,
Nor length of time our gratitude efface ;
Besides what endless honour you shall gain,
To save and shelter Troy's unhappy train.
Now, by my sovereign, and his fate, I swear
(Renowned for faith in peace, for force in war),
Oft our alliance other lands desired,
And, what we seek of you, of us required.
Despise not then, that in our hands we bear
These holy boughs, and sue with words of prayer.
Fate and the gods, by their supreme command,
Have doomed our ships to seek the Latian land.
To these abodes our fleet Apollo sends ;
Here Dardanus was born, and hither tends ;
Where Tuscan Tiber rolls with rapid force,
And where Numicus opes his holy source.
Besides, our prince presents with his request,
Some small remains of what his sire possessed :
This golden charger, snatched from burning Troy,
Anchises did in sacrifice employ :
This royal robe and this tiara wore
Old Priam, and this golden sceptre bore
In full assemblies, and in solemn games :
These purple vests were weaved by Dardan dames.
  Thus while he spoke, Latinus rolled around
His eyes, and fixed awhile upon the ground :
Intent he seemed, and anxious in his breast ;

Not by the sceptre moved, or kingly vest,
But pondering future things of wondrous weight—
Succession, empire, and his daughter's fate.
On these he mused within his thoughtful mind ;
And then revolved what Faunus had divined.
This was the foreign prince, by fate decreed
To share his sceptre, and Lavinia's bed ;
This was the race that sure portents foreshow
To sway the world, and land and sea subdue.
At length he raised his cheerful head, and spoke :
'The powers (said he) the powers we both invoke,
To you, and yours, and mine, propitious be,
And firm our purpose with their augury !
Have what you ask : your presents I receive :
Land, where and when you please, with ample leave :
Partake and use my kingdom as your own :
All shall be yours, while I command the crown.
And, if my wished alliance please your king,
Tell him he should not send the peace, but bring :
Then let him not a friend's embraces fear ;
The peace is made when I behold him here.
Besides this answer, tell my royal guest
I add to his commands my own request :
Only one daughter heirs my crown and state,
Whom not our oracles, nor heaven, nor fate,
Nor frequent prodigies, permit to join
With any native of the Ausonian line.
A foreign son-in-law shall come from far
(Such is our doom), a chief renowned in war,
Whose race shall bear aloft the Latian name,
And through the conquered world diffuse our fame.
Himself to be the man the fates require,
I firmly judge, and what I judge, desire.'
He said ; and then on each bestowed a steed.
Three hundred horses, in high stables fed,
Stood ready, shining all, and smoothly dressed :
Of these, he chose the fairest and the best
To mount the Trojan troop.   At his command,
The steeds caparisoned with purple stand,
With golden trappings, glorious to behold,

And champ betwixt their teeth the foaming gold.
Then to his absent guest the king decreed
A pair of coursers born of heavenly breed ;
Who from their nostrils breathed ethereal fire ;
Whom Circe stole from her celestial sire,
By substituting mares produced on earth,
Whose wombs conceived a more than mortal birth.
These draw the chariot which Latinus sends,
And the rich present to the prince commends.
Sublime on stately steeds the Trojans borne,
To their expecting lord with peace return.

But jealous Juno, from Pachynus' height,
As she from Argos took her airy flight,
Beheld, with envious eyes this hateful sight.
She saw the Trojan and his joyful train
Descend upon the shore ; desert the main ;
Design a town ; and, with unhoped success,
The ambassadors return with promised peace.
Then, pierced with pain, she shook her haughty head,
Sighed from her inward soul, and thus she said :
' O hated offspring of my Phrygian foes !
O fates of Troy, which Juno's fates oppose !
Could they not fall unpitied on the plain ?
But, slain, revive, and, taken, 'scape again !
When execrable Troy in ashes lay,
Through fires and swords and seas they forced their
          way !
Then vanquished Juno must in vain contend ;
Her rage disarmed, her empire at an end !
Breathless and tired, is all my fury spent ?
Or does my glutted spleen at length relent ?
As if 'twere little from their town to chase,
I through the seas pursued their exiled race ;
Engaged the heavens, opposed the stormy main ;
But billows roared and tempests raged in vain.
What have my Scyllas and my Syrtes done,
When these they overpass, and those they shun ?
On Tiber's shores they land, secure of fate,
Triumphant o'er the storms and Juno's hate !
Mars could in mutual blood the Centaurs bathe ;

And Jove himself gave way to Cynthia's wrath,
Who sent the tusky boar to Calydon ;
(What great offence had either people done ?)
But I, the consort of the Thunderer,
Have waged a long and unsuccessful war ;
With various arts and arms in vain have toiled ;
And by a mortal man at length am foiled !
If native power prevail not, shall I doubt
To seek for needful succour from without?
If Jove and heaven my just desires deny,
Hell shall the power of heaven and Jove supply !
Grant that the Fates have firmed, by their decree,
The Trojan race to reign in Italy :
At least I can defer the nuptial day,
And, with protracted wars, the peace delay :
With blood the dear alliance shall be bought,
And both the people near destruction brought.
So shall the son-in-law and father join,
With ruin, war, and waste of either line.
O fatal maid ! thy marriage is endowed
With Phrygian, Latian, and Rutulian blood.
Bellona leads thee to thy lover's hand :
Another queen brings forth another brand,
To burn with foreign fires another land :
A second Paris, differing but in name,
Shall fire his country with a second flame.'

  Thus having said, she sinks beneath the ground
With furious haste, and shoots the Stygian sound,
To rouse Alecto from the infernal seat
Of her dire sisters, and their dark retreat.
This Fury, fit for her intent, she chose ;
One who delights in wars, and human woes.
E'en Pluto hates his own mis-shapen race ;
Her sister Furies fly her hideous face ;
So frightful are the forms the monster takes,
So fierce the hissings of her speckled snakes.
Her, Juno finds, and thus inflames her spite :
' O virgin daughter of eternal Night !
Give me this once thy labour, to sustain
My right, and execute my just disdain.

Let not the Trojans with a feigned pretence
Of proffered peace, delude the Latian prince:
Expel from Italy that odious name,
And let not Juno suffer in her fame.
'Tis thine to ruin realms, o'erturn a state,
Betwixt the dearest friends to raise debate,
And kindle kindred blood to mutual hate.
Thy hand o'er towns the funeral torch displays,
And forms a thousand ills ten thousand ways.
Now, shake from out thy fruitful breast, the seeds
Of envy, discord, and of cruel deeds:
Confound the peace established, and prepare
Their souls to hatred, and their hands to war.'

  Smeared as she was with black Gorgonean blood,
The Fury sprang above the Stygian flood;
And on her wicker wings, sublime, through night,
She to the Latian palace took her flight;
There sought the queen's apartment, stood before
The peaceful threshold, and besieged the door.
Restless Amata lay, her swelling breast
Fired with disdain for Turnus dispossessed,
And the new nuptials of the Trojan guest.
From her black bloody locks, the Fury shakes
Her darling plague, the favourite of her snakes.
With her full force she threw the poisonous dart,
And fixed it deep within Amata's heart;
That, thus envenomed, she might kindle rage,
And sacrifice to strife her house and husband's age.
Unseen, unfelt, the fiery serpent skims
Betwixt her linen and her naked limbs;
His baneful breath inspiring as he glides:
Now like a chain around her neck he rides;
Now like a fillet to her head repairs,
And with his circling volumes folds her hairs.
At first the silent venom slid with ease,
And seized her cooler senses by degrees;
Then, ere the infected mass was fired too far,
In plaintive accents she began the war,
And thus bespoke her husband: 'Shall (she said)
A wandering prince enjoy Lavinia's bed?

If nature plead not in a parent's heart,
Pity my tears, and pity her desert.
I know, my dearest lord, the time will come,
You would, in vain, reverse your cruel doom :
The faithless pirate soon will set to sea,
And bear the royal virgin far away !
A guest like him (a Trojan guest) before,
In show of friendship sought the Spartan shore,
And ravished Helen from her husband bore.
Think on a king's inviolable word ;
And think on Turnus, her once plighted lord.
To this false foreigner you give your throne,
And wrong a friend, a kinsman, and a son.
Resume your ancient care ; and, if the god
Your sire, and you, resolve on foreign blood,
Know all are foreign, in a larger sense,
Not born your subjects, or derived from hence.
Then, if the line of Turnus you retrace,
He springs from Inachus of Argive race.'
But, when she saw her reasons idly spent,
And could not move him from his fixed intent,
She flew to rage ; for now the snake possessed
Her vital parts, and poisoned all her breast.
She raves, she runs with a distracted pace,
And fills with horrid howls, the public place.
And, as young striplings whip the top for sport,
On the smooth pavement of an empty court ;
The wooden engine flies and whirls about,
Admired with clamours, of the beardless rout :
They lash aloud ; each other they provoke,
And lend their little souls at every stroke :
Thus fares the queen ; and thus her fury blows
Amidst the crowd, and kindles as she goes.

  Not yet content, she strains her malice more,
And adds new ills to those contrived before :
She flies the town, and, mixing with the throng
Of madding matrons, bears the bride along ;
Wandering through woods and wilds, and devious
        ways,
And with these arts the Trojan match delays.

She feigned the rites of Bacchus, cried aloud,
And to the buxom god the virgin vowed.
' Evœ ! O Bacchus !' thus began the song ;
And ' Evœ !' answered all the female throng.
' O virgin worthy thee alone !' she cried ;
' O worthy thee alone !' the crew replied.
' For thee she feeds her hair, she leads thy dance,
And with thy winding ivy wreathes her lance.'
Like fury seized the rest : the progress known,
All seek the mountains, and forsake the town ;
All, clad in skins of beasts, the javelin bear,
Give to the wanton winds their flowing hair ;
And shrieks and shoutings rend the suffering air.
The queen herself, inspired with rage divine,
Shook high above her head a flaming pine ;
Then rolled her haggard eyes around the throng,
And sung in Turnus' name the nuptial song :
' Io ! ye Latian dames, if any here
Hold your unhappy queen, Amata, dear ;
If there be here (she said), who dare maintain
My right, nor think the name of mother vain ;
Unbind your fillets, loose your flowing hair,
And orgies and nocturnal rites prepare.'
    Amata's breast the Fury thus invades,
And fires with rage, amid the sylvan shades.
Then, when she found her venom spread so far,
The royal house embroiled in civil war,
Raised on her dusky wings, she cleaves the skies,
And seeks the palace where young Turnus lies.
His town (as fame reports) was built of old
By Danaë, pregnant with almighty gold ;
Who fled her father's rage, and, with a train
Of following Argives, through the stormy main
Driven by the southern blasts, was fated here to reign.
    'Twas Ardua once ; now Ardea's name it bears ;
Once a fair city, now consumed with years.
Here, in his lofty palace, Turnus lay,
Betwixt the confines of the night and day,
Secure in sleep.—The Fury laid aside
Her looks and limbs, and with new methods tried

The foulness of the infernal form to hide.
Propped on a staff, she takes a trembling mien ;
Her face is furrowed, and her front obscene ;
Deep-dinted wrinkles on her cheek she draws ;
Sunk are her eyes, and toothless are her jaws ;
Her hoary hair with holy fillets bound ;
Her temples with an olive wreath are crowned
Old Chalybe, who kept the secret fane
Of Juno, now she seemed, and thus began
(Appearing in a dream) to rouse the careless man :
'Shall Turnus then such endless toil sustain
In fighting-fields, and conquer towns in vain ?
Win, for a Trojan head to wear the prize,
Usurp thy crown, enjoy thy victories ?
The bride and sceptre, which thy blood has bought,
The king transfers ; and foreign heirs are sought !
Go now, deluded man, and seek again
New toils, new dangers, on the dusty plain !
Repel the Tuscan foes, their city seize :
Protect the Latians in luxurious ease !
This dream all-powerful Juno sends : I bear
Her mighty mandates, and her words you hear.
Haste ! arm your Ardeans ; issue to the plain ;
With faith to friend, assault the Trojan train :
Their thoughtless chiefs ; their painted ships that lie
In Tiber's mouth, with fire and sword destroy.
The Latian king, unless he shall submit,
Own his old promise, and his new forget—
Let him, in arms the power of Turnus prove ;
And learn to fear whom he disdains to love.
For such is heaven's command.'   The youthful prince
With scorn replied, and made this bold defence :
'You tell me, mother, what I knew before,
The Phrygian fleet is landed on the shore.
I neither fear nor will provoke the war ;
My fate is Juno's most peculiar care.
But time has made you dote, and vainly tell
Of arms imagined in your lonely cell.
Go ! be the temple and the gods your care :
Permit to men the thought of peace and war.'

These haughty words Alecto's rage provoke,
And frightened Turnus trembled as she spoke.
Her eyes grow stiffened, and with sulphur burn;
Her hideous looks and hellish form return;
Her curling snakes with hissings fill the place,
And open all the furies of her face:
Then, darting fire from her malignant eyes,
She cast him backward as he strove to rise,
And lingering sought to frame some new replies.
High on her head she rears two twisted snakes;
Her chains she rattles, and her whip she shakes;
And churning bloody foam, thus loudly speaks:
' Behold whom time has made to dote and tell
Of arms imagined in her lonely cell!
Behold the Fates' infernal minister!
War, death, destruction, in my hand I bear.'
    Thus having said, her smouldering torch, impressed
With her full force, she plunged into his breast.
Aghast he waked; and starting from his bed,
Cold sweat, in clammy drops, his limbs o'erspread.
' Arms! arms! (he cries): my sword and shield pre-
    pare!'
He breathes defiance, blood, and mortal war.
So, when with crackling flames a caldron fries,
The bubbling waters from the bottom rise;
Above the brims they force their fiery way;
Black vapours climb aloft, and cloud the day.
    The peace polluted thus, a chosen band
He first commissions to the Latian land,
In threatening embassy; then raised the rest
To meet in arms the intruding Trojan guest;
To force the foes from the Lavinian shore,
And Italy's endangered peace restore.
Himself alone an equal match he boasts,
To fight the Phrygian and Ausonian hosts.
The gods invoked, the Rutuli prepare
Their arms, and warm each other to the war.
His beauty these, and those his blooming age,
The rest, his house and his own fame engage.
    While Turnus urges thus his enterprise,

The Stygian Fury to the Trojans flies ;
New frauds invents, and takes a steepy stand,
Which overlooks the vale with wide command ;
Where fair Ascanius and his youthful train,
With horns and hounds a hunting match ordain,
And pitch their toils around the shady plain.
The Fury fires the pack ; they snuff, they vent,
And feed their hungry nostrils with the scent.
'Twas of a well-grown stag, whose antlers rise
High o'er his front, his beams invade the skies.
From this light cause, the infernal maid prepares
The country churls to mischief, hate, and wars.

The stately beast the two Tyrrhidæ bred,
Snatched from his dam, and the tame youngling fed.
Their father, Tyrrheus, did his fodder bring—
Tyrrheus chief ranger to the Latian king :
Their sister Silvia, cherished with her care
The little wanton, and did wreaths prepare
To hang his budding horns ; with ribbons tied
His tender neck, and combed his silken hide,
And bathed his body.   Patient of command
In time he grew, and, growing used to hand,
He waited at his master's board for food ;
Then sought his savage kindred in the wood,
Where grazing all the day ; at night he came
To his known lodgings, and his country dame.
This household beast, that used the woodland grounds,
Was viewed at first by the young hero's hounds,
As down the stream he swam, to seek retreat
In the cool waters, and to quench his heat.
Ascanius, young and eager of his game,
Soon bent his bow, uncertain in his aim ;
But the dire fiend the fatal arrow guides,
Which pierced his bowels through his panting sides.
The bleeding creature issues from the floods,
Possessed with fear, and seeks his known abodes,
His old familiar hearth, and household gods.
He falls ; he fills the house with heavy groans ;
Implores their pity, and his pain bemoans.
Young Silvia beats her breast, and cries aloud

For succour from the clownish neighbourhood.
The churls assemble ; for the fiend who lay
In the close woody covert, urged their way.
One with a brand yet burning from the flame ;
Armed with a knotty club another came :
Whate'er they catch or find, without their care,
Their fury makes an instrument of war.
Tyrrheus, the foster-father of the beast,
Then clenched a hatchet in his horny fist,
But held his hand from the descending stroke,
And left his wedge within the cloven oak,
To whet their courage, and their rage provoke.

And now the goddess, exercised in ill,
Who watched an hour to work her impious will,
Ascends the roof, and to her crooked horn,
Such as was then by Latian shepherds borne,
Adds all her breath.   The rocks and woods around,
And mountains, tremble at the infernal sound.
The sacred lake of Travia from afar ;
The Véline fountains, and sulphureous Nar,
Shake at the baleful blast, the signal of the war.
Young mothers wildly stare, with fear possessed,
And strain their helpless infants to their breast.

The clowns, a boisterous, rude, ungoverned crew,
With furious haste to the loud summons flew.
The powers of Troy, then issuing on the plain,
With fresh recruits their youthful chief sustain :
Nor theirs a raw and unexperienced train,
But a firm body of embattled men.
At first, while fortune favoured neither side,
The fight with clubs and burning brands was tried ;
But now, both parties reinforced, the fields
Are bright with flaming swords and brazen shields.
A shining harvest either host displays,
And shoots against the sun with equal rays.

Thus, when a black-browed gust begins to rise,
White foam at first on the curled ocean fries ;
Then roars the main, the billows mount the skies ;
Till, by the fury of the storm full blown,
The muddy bottom o'er the clouds is thrown.

First Almon falls, old Tyrrheus' eldest care,
Pierced with an arrow from the distant war ;
Fixed in his throat the flying weapon stood,
And stopped his breath, and drank his vital blood.
Huge heaps of slain around the body rise ;
Among the rest, the rich Galesus lies—
A good old man, while peace he preached in vain,
Amidst the madness of the unruly train :
Five herds, five bleating flocks, his pastures filled ;
His lands a hundred yoke of oxen tilled.
Thus, while in equal scales their fortune stood,
The Fury bathed them in each other's blood ;
Then, having fixed the fight, exulting flies,
And bears fulfilled her promise to the skies.

To Juno thus she speaks : ' Behold ! 'tis done,
The blood already drawn, the war begun ;
The discord is complete ; nor can they cease
The dire debate, nor you command the peace.
Now, since the Latian and the Trojan brood
Have tasted vengeance, and the sweets of blood ;
Speak, and my power shall add this office more :
The neighbouring nations of the Ausonian shore
Shall hear the dreadful rumour from afar,
Of armed invasion, and embrace the war.'
Then Juno thus : ' The grateful work is done,
The seeds of discord sowed, the war begun :
Frauds, fears, and fury, have possessed the state,
And fixed the causes of a lasting hate.
A bloody Hymen shall the alliance join
Betwixt the Trojan and the Ausonian line :
But thou with speed to night and hell repair ;
For not the gods, nor angry Jove, will bear
Thy lawless wandering walks in upper air.
Leave what remains to me.' Saturnia said :
The sullen fiend her sounding wings displayed,
Unwilling left the light, and sought the nether shade.

In midst of Italy, well known to fame,
There lies a lake (Amsanctus is the name),
Below the lofty mounts : on either side
Thick forests the forbidden entrance hide.

Full in the centre of the sacred wood
An arm arises of the Stygian flood,
Which, breaking from beneath with bellowing sound,
Whirls the black waves and rattling stones around.
Here Pluto pants for breath from out his cell ;
And opens wide the grinning jaws of hell.
To this infernal lake the Fury flies ;
Here hides her hated head, and frees the labouring skies.
  Saturnian Juno, now, with double care,
Attends the fatal process of the war.
The clowns, returned from battle, bear the slain ;
Implore the gods, and to their king complain.
The corpse of Almon, and the rest, are shown :
Shrieks, clamours, murmurs, fill the frighted town.
Ambitious Turnus in the press appears,
And, aggravating crimes, augments their fears ;
Proclaims his private injuries aloud—
A solemn promise made, and disavowed ;
A foreign son is sought, and a mixed mongrel brood.
Then they, whose mothers, frantic with their fear,
In woods and wilds the flags of Bacchus bear,
And lead his dances with dishevelled hair,
Increase the clamour, and the war demand
(Such was Amata's interest in the land),
Against the public sanctions of the peace,
Against all omens of their ill success.
  With fates averse, the rout in arms resort
To force their monarch, and insult the court.
But, like a rock unmoved, a rock that braves
The raging tempest and the rising waves,
Propped on himself he stands : his solid sides
Wash off the sea-weeds, and the sounding tides—
So stood the pious prince unmoved ; and long
Sustained the madness of the noisy throng.
But, when he found that Juno's power prevailed,
And all the methods of cool counsel failed,
He calls the gods to witness their offence ;
Disclaims the war, asserts his innocence.
' Hurried by fate (he cries), and borne before
A furious wind, we leave the faithful shore !

37   M

O more than madmen ! you yourselves shall bear
The guilt of blood and sacrilegious war :
Thou, Turnus, shall atone it by thy fate,
And pray to Heaven for peace, but pray too late.
For me, my stormy voyage at an end,
I to the port of death securely tend.
The funeral pomp which to your kings you pay,
Is all I want, and all you take away.'
He said no more, but, in his walls confined,
Shut out the woes which he too well divined ;
Nor with the rising storm would vainly strive,
But left the helm, and let the vessel drive.

A solemn custom was observed of old,
Which Latium held, and now the Romans hold ;
Their standard when in fighting-fields they rear
Against the fierce Hyrcanians, or declare
The Scythian, Indian, or Arabian war ;
Or from the boasting Parthians would regain
Their eagles, lost in Carræ's bloody plain.
Two gates of steel (the name of Mars they bear,
And still are worshipped with religious fear)
Before his temple stand : the dire abode,
And the feared issues of the furious god,
Are fenced with brazen bolts ; without the gates,
The wary guardian Janus doubly waits.
Then, when the sacred senate votes the wars,
The Roman consul their decree declares,
And in his robes the sounding gates unbars.
The youth in military shouts arise,
And the loud trumpets break the yielding skies.
These rites, of old by sovereign princes used,
Were the king's office : but the king refused,
Deaf to their cries ; nor would the gates unbar
Of sacred peace, or loose the imprisoned war ;
But hid his head, and, safe from loud alarms,
Abhorred the wicked ministry of arms.
Then, heaven's imperious queen shot down from high ;
At her approach the brazen hinges fly ;
The gates are forced, and every falling bar ;
And like a tempest, issues out the war.

The peaceful cities of the Ausonian shore,
Lulled in their ease, and undisturbed before,
Are all on fire ; and some, with studious care,
Their restive steeds in sandy plains prepare ;
Some their soft limbs in painful marches try ;
And war is all their wish, and arms the general cry.
Part scour their rusty shields with seam ; and part
New-grind the blunted axe, and point the dart ;
With joy they view the waving ensigns fly,
And hear the trumpet's clangour pierce the sky.
Five cities forge their arms—the Atinian powers,
Antemnæ, Tibur with her lofty towers,
Ardea the proud, the Crustumerian town :
All these of old were places of renown.
Some hammer helmets for the fighting field ;
Some twine young sallows to support the shield ;
The corselet some, and some the cuishes mould,
With silver plated, and with ductile gold.
The rustic honours of the scythe and share,
Give place to swords and plumes, the pride of war.
Old falchions are new-tempered in the fires :
The sounding trumpet every soul inspires.
The word is given ; with eager speed they lace
The shining head-piece, and the shield embrace.
The neighing steeds are to the chariots tied ;
The trusty weapon sits on every side.
    And now the mighty labour is begun :
Ye muses, open all your Helicon !
Sing you the chiefs that swayed the Ausonian land,
Their arms, and armies under their command ;
What warriors in our ancient clime were bred ;
What soldiers followed, and what heroes led.
For well you know, and can record alone,
What fame to future times conveys but darkly down.
    Mezentius first appeared upon the plain :
Scorn sat upon his brows, and sour disdain,
Defying earth and heaven.   Etruria lost,
He brings to Turnus' aid his baffled host.
The charming Lausus, full of youthful fire,
Rode in the rank, and next his sullen sire ;

To Turnus only second in the grace
Of manly mien, and features of the face.
A skilful horseman, and a huntsman bred ;
With fates averse, a thousand men he led :
His sire unworthy of so brave a son ;
Himself well worthy of a happier throne.

Next Aventinus drives his chariot round
The Latian plains, with palms and laurels crowned ;
Proud of his steeds, he smokes along the field ;
His father's hydra fills his ample shield ;
A hundred serpents hiss about the brims ;
The son of Hercules he justly seems,
By his broad shoulders and gigantic limbs—
Of heavenly, part, and part, of earthly blood,
A mortal woman mixing with a god.
For strong Alcides, after he had slain
The triple Geryon, drove from conquered Spain
His captive herds ; and, thence in triumph led,
On Tuscan Tiber's flowery banks they fed.
Then, on mount Aventine, the son of Jove
The priestess Rhea found, and forced to love.

For arms, his men long piles and javelins bore,
And poles with pointed steel their foes in battle gore.
Like Hercules himself, his son appears
In savage pomp ; a lion's hide he wears ;
About his shoulders hangs the shaggy skin ;
The teeth and gaping jaws severely grin.
Thus, like the god his father, homely drest,
He strides into the hall, a horrid guest.

Then two twin-brothers from fair Tibur came
(Which from their brother Tiburs took the name),
Fierce Coras and Catillus, void of fear :
Armed Argive horse they led, and in the front appear.
Like cloud-born Centaurs, from the mountain's height
With rapid course descending to the fight
They rush along ; the rattling woods give way ;
The branches bend before their sweepy sway.

Nor was Præneste's founder wanting there,
Whom fame reports the son of Mulciber :
Found in the fire, and fostered in the plains,

A shepherd and a king at once he reigns;
And leads to Turnus' aid his country swains.
His own Præneste sends a chosen band,
With those who plough Saturnia's Gabine land;
Besides the succour which cold Anien yields,
The rocks of Hernicus, and dewy fields,
Anagnia fat, and father Amasene—
A numerous rout, but all of naked men:
Nor arms they wear, nor swords and bucklers wield,
Nor drive the chariot through the dusty field;
But whirl from leathern slings huge balls of lead;
And spoils of yellow wolves adorn their head:
The left foot naked, when they march to fight;
But in a bull's raw hide they sheath the right.
   Messapus next (great Neptune was his sire),
Secure of steel, and fated from the fire,
In pomp appears; and with his ardour warms
A heartless train, unexercised in arms:
The just Faliscans he to battle brings;
And those who live where lake Ciminius springs;
And where Feronia's grove and temple stands,
Who till Fescennian or Flavinian lands:
All these in order march, and marching, sing
The warlike actions of their sea-born king:
Like a long team of snowy swans on high,
Which clap their wings, and cleave the liquid sky,
When, homeward from their watery pastures borne,
They sing, and Asia's lakes their notes return.
Not one who heard their music from afar,
Would think these troops an army trained to war,
But flocks of fowl, that, when the tempests roar,
With their hoarse gabbling seek the silent shore.
   Then Clausus came, who led a numerous band
Of troops embodied from the Sabine land;
And, in himself alone, an army brought.
'Twas he the noble Claudian race begot—
The Claudian race, ordained, in times to come,
To share the greatness of imperial Rome.
He led the Cures forth of old renown,
Mutuscans from their olive-bearing town,

And all the Eretian powers ; besides a band
That followed from Velinum's dewy land ;
And Amiternian troops, of mighty fame,
And mountaineers, that from Severus came,
And from the craggy cliffs of Tetrica ;
And those where yellow Tiber takes his way,
And where Himella's wanton waters play.
Casperia sends her arms, with those that lie
By Fabaris, and fruitful Foruli :
The warlike aids of Horta next appear ;
And the cold Nursians come to close the rear,
Mixed with the natives born of Latine blood ;
Whom Allia washes with her fatal flood.
Not thicker billows beat the Libyan main,
When pale Orion sets in wintry rain ;
Nor thicker harvests on rich Hermus rise,
Or Lycian fields, when Phœbus burns the skies,
Than stand these troops : their bucklers ring around :
Their trampling turns the turf, and shakes the solid
      ground.
   High in his chariot then Halesus came,
A foe by birth to Troy's unhappy name :
From Agamemnon born : to Turnus' aid,
A thousand men the youthful hero led,
Who till the Massic soil, for wine renowned ;
And fierce Auruncans from their hilly ground ;
And those who live by Sidicinian shores ;
And where with shoaly fords Vulturnus roars ;
Cales' and Osca's old inhabitants ;
And rough Saticulans, inured to wants.
Light demi-lances from afar they throw,
Fastened with leathern thongs, to gall the foe :
Short crooked swords in closer fight they wear ;
And on their warding arm light bucklers bear.
   Nor, Œbalus, shalt thou be left unsung ;
From nymph Sebethis and old Telon sprung,
Who then in Teleboan Capri reigned ;
But that short isle the ambitious youth disdained,
And o'er Campania stretched his ample sway,
Where swelling Sarnus seeks the Tyrrhene sea—

O'er Batulum, and where Abella sees
From her high towers, the harvest of her trees.
And these (as was the Teuton use of old)
Wield brazen swords, and brazen bucklers hold;
Sling weighty stones when from afar they fight—
Their casques are cork, a covering thick and light.

Next these in rank, the warlike Ufens went,
And led the mountain troops that Nursia sent.
The rude Æquiculæ his rule obeyed;
Hunting their sport, and plundering was their trade.
In arms they ploughed, to battle still prepared;
Their soil was barren, and their hearts were hard.

Umbro the priest the proud Marrubians led,
By king Archippus sent to Turnus' aid;
And peaceful olives crowned his hoary head.
His wand and holy words, the viper's rage
And venomed wounds of serpents, could assuage.
He, when he pleased with powerful juice to steep
Their temples, shut their eyes in pleasing sleep.
But vain were Marsian herbs, and magic art,
To cure the wound given by the Dardan dart.
Yet his untimely fate, the Angitian woods
In sighs remurmured to the Fucine floods.

The son of famed Hippolytus was there,
Famed as his sire, and, as his mother, fair;
Whom in Egerian groves Aricia bore,
And nursed his youth along the marshy shore,
Where great Diana's peaceful altars flame,
In fruitful fields; and Virbius was his name.
Hippolytus, as old records have said,
Was by his stepdame sought to share her bed;
But, when no female arts his mind could move,
She turned to furious hate her impious love.
Torn by wild horses on the sandy shore,
Another's crimes the unhappy hunter bore,
Glutting his father's eyes with guiltless gore.
But chaste Diana, who his death deplored,
With Æsculapian herbs his life restored:
When Jove, who saw from high, with just disdain,
The dead inspired with vital breath again,

Struck to the centre, with his flaming dart,
The unhappy founder of the godlike art.
But Trivia kept in secret shades alone
Her care, Hippolytus, to fate unknown ;
And called him Virbius in the Egerian grove
Where then he lived obscure, but safe from Jove.
For this, from Trivia's temple and her wood,
Are coursers driven who shed their master's blood—
Affrighted by the monsters of the flood.
His son, the second Virbius, yet retained
His father's art ; and warrior steeds he reined.

Amid the troops, and like the leading god,
High o'er the rest in arms, the graceful Turnus rode ;
A triple pile of plumes his crest adorned,
On which with belching flames Chimæra burned :
The more the kindled combat rises higher,
The more with fury burns the blazing fire.
Fair Iö graced his shield ; but Iö now
With horns exalted stands, and seems to low—
A noble charge ! Her keeper by her side,
To watch her, walks, his hundred eyes applied ;
And on the brims her sire, the watery god,
Rolled from his silver urn his crystal flood.

A cloud of foot succeeds, and fills the fields
With swords, and pointed spears, and clattering shields;
Of Argive, and of old Sicanian bands,
And those who plough the rich Rutulian lands ;
Auruncan youth, and those Sacrana yields ;
And the proud Labicans, with painted shields ;
And those who near Numician streams reside ;
And those whom Tiber's holy forests hide,
Or Circe's hills from the main land divide ;
Where Ufens glides along the lowly lands,
Or the black water of Pomptina stands.

Last, from the Volscians fair Camilla came,
And led her warlike troops—a warrior dame ;
Unbred to spinning, in the loom unskilled ;
She chose the nobler Pallas of the field.
Mixed with the first, the fierce virago fought ;
Sustained the toils of arms, the danger sought ;

Outstripped the winds in speed upon the plain,
Flew o'er the field, nor hurt the bearded grain :
She swept the seas, and, as she skimmed along,
Her flying feet unbathed on billows hung.
Men, boys, and women, stupid with surprise,
Where'er she passes, fixed their wondering eyes :
Longing they look, and gaping at the sight,
Devour her o'er and o'er with vast delight.
Her purple habit sits with such a grace
On her smooth shoulders, and so suits her face ;
Her head with ringlets of her hair is crowned ;
And in a golden caul the curls are bound.
She shakes her myrtle javelin ; and, behind,
Her Lycian quiver dances in the wind.

BOOK VIII

THE ARGUMENT

The war being now begun, both the generals make all possible preparations. Turnus sends to Diomedes. Æneas goes in person to beg succours from Evander and the Tuscans. Evander receives him kindly, furnishes him with men, and sends his son Pallas with him. Vulcan, at the request of Venus, makes arms for her son Æneas, and draws on his shield the most memorable actions of his posterity.

WHEN Turnus had assembled all his powers,
His standard planted on Laurentum's towers,
When now the sprightly trumpet, from afar,
Had given the signal of approaching war,
Had roused the neighing steeds to scour the fields,
While the fierce riders clattered on their shields,
Trembling with rage, the Latian youth prepare
To join the allies, and headlong rush to war.
Fierce Ufens, and Messapus, led the crowd,
With bold Mezentius, who blasphemed aloud.
These through the country took their wasteful course,
The fields to forage, and to gather force.
Then Venulus to Diomede they send,
To beg his aid, Ausonia to defend,
Declare the common danger, and inform
The Grecian leader of the growing storm :
' Æneis, landed on the Latian coast,
With banished gods, and with a baffled host,
Yet now aspired to conquest of the state.
And claimed a title from the gods and fate ;
What numerous nations in his quarrel came
And how they spread his formidable name.

What he designed, what mischiefs might arise
If fortune favoured his first enterprise,
Was left for him to weigh, whose equal fears
And common interest was involved in theirs.'
  While Turnus and the allies thus urge the war,
The Trojan, floating in a flood of care,
Beholds the tempest which his foes prepare.
This way, and that, he turns his anxious mind;
Thinks, and rejects the counsels he designed;
Explores himself in vain in every part,
And gives no rest to his distracted heart.
So, when the sun by day, or moon by night,
Strike on the polished brass their trembling light,
The glittering species here and there divide,
And cast their dubious beams from side to side;
Now on the walls, now on the pavement play,
And to the ceiling flash the glaring day.
  'Twas night; and weary nature lulled asleep
The birds of air, and fishes of the deep,
And beasts, and mortal men. The Trojan chief
Was laid on Tiber's banks, oppressed with grief,
And found in silent slumber, late relief.
Then, through the shadows of the poplar wood,
Arose the father of the Roman flood;
An azure robe was o'er his body spread,
A wreath of shady reeds adorned his head:
Thus, manifest to sight, the god appeared,
And with these pleasing words his sorrow cheered:
' Undoubted offspring of ethereal race,
O long expected in this promised place!
Who, through the foes, hast borne thy banished gods,
Restored them to their hearths, and old abodes;
This is thy happy home, the clime where fate
Ordains thee to restore the Trojan state.
Fear not! The war shall end in lasting peace,
And all the rage of haughty Juno cease.
And that this nightly vision may not seem
The effect of fancy, or an idle dream,
A sow beneath an oak shall lie along,
All white herself, and white her thirty young.

When thirty rolling years have run their race,
Thy son Ascanius, on this empty space,
Shall build a royal town, of lasting fame,
Which from this omen shall receive the name.
Time shall approve the truth.—For what remains,
And how with sure success to crown thy pains,
With patience next attend.   A banished band,
Driven with Evander from the Arcadian land,
Have planted here, and placed on high their walls :
Their town the founder, Pallanteum calls,
Derived from Pallas, his great grandsire's name :
But the fierce Latians old possession claim,
With war infesting the new colony :
These make thy friends, and on their aid rely.
To thy free passage I submit my streams.
Wake, son of Venus, from thy pleasing dreams !
And when the setting stars are lost in day,
To Juno's power thy just devotion pay ;
With sacrifice the wrathful queen appease :
Her pride at length shall fall, her fury cease.
When thou return'st victorious from the war,
Perform thy vows to me with grateful care.
The god am I, whose yellow water flows
Around these fields, and fattens as it goes :
Tiber my name—among the rolling floods
Renowned on earth, esteemed among the gods.
This is my certain seat.   In times to come,
My waves shall wash the walls of mighty Rome !

　　He said ; and plunged below.   While yet he spoke,
His dream Æneas and his sleep forsook.
He rose, and looking up, beheld the skies
With purple blushing, and the day arise.
Then water in his hollow palm he took
From Tiber's flood, and thus the powers bespoke :
' Laurentian nymphs, by whom the streams are fed,
And father Tiber, in thy sacred bed
Receive Æneas, and from danger keep !
Whatever fount, whatever holy deep,
Conceals thy watery stores—where'er they rise,
And, bubbling from below, salute the skies—

Thou, king of horned floods, whose plenteous urn
Suffices fatness to the fruitful corn,
For this, thy kind compassion of our woes,
Shalt share my morning song, and evening vows.
But, oh ! be present to thy people's aid,
And firm the gracious promise thou hast made.'
    Thus having said, two galleys from his stores
With care he chooses, mans, and fits with oars.
Now on the shore the fatal swine is found—
Wondrous to tell !—She lay along the ground :
Her well-fed offspring at her udders hung ;
She white herself, and white her thirty young.
Æneas takes the mother and her brood,
And all on Juno's altar are bestowed.
The following night, and the succeeding day,
Propitious Tiber smoothed his watery way ;
He rolled his river back, and poised he stood,
A gentle swelling, and a peaceful flood.
The Trojans mount their ships ; they put from shore,
Borne on the waves, and scarcely dip an oar.
Shouts from the land give omen to their course ;
And the pitched vessels glide with easy force.
The woods and waters wonder at the gleam
Of shields, and painted ships that stem the stream.
One summer's night and one whole day they pass
Betwixt the green-wood shades, and cut the liquid glass.
The fiery sun had finished half his race,
Looked back and doubted in the middle space,
When they from far beheld the rising towers,
The tops of sheds, and shepherds' lowly bowers,
Thin as they stood, which then of homely clay,
Now rise in marble, from the Roman sway.
These cots (Evander's kingdom, mean and poor)
The Trojan saw, and turned his ships to shore.
    'Twas on a solemn day : the Arcadian states,
The king and prince, without the city gates,
Then paid their offerings in a sacred grove
To Hercules, the warrior son of Jove.
Thick clouds of rolling smoke involve the skies ;
And fat of entrails on his altar fries.

But when they saw the ships that stemmed the flood,
And glittered through the covert of the wood,
They rose with fear, and left the unfinished feast,
Till dauntless Pallas reassured the rest
To pay the rites.   Himself without delay
A javelin seized, and singly took his way;
Then gained a rising ground, and called from far:
'Resolve me, strangers, whence and what you are;
Your business here; and bring you peace or war?'
High on the stern Æneas took his stand,
And held a branch of olive in his hand,
While thus he spoke: 'The Phrygians' arms you see;
Expelled from Troy, provoked in Italy
By Latian foes, with war unjustly made—
At first affianced, and at last betrayed.
This message bear: The Trojans and their chief
Bring holy peace, and beg the king's relief.'
Struck with so great a name, and all on fire,
The youth replies: 'Whatever you require,
Your fame exacts. Upon our shores descend
A welcome guest, and, what you wish, a friend.'
He said, and downward hasting to the strand,
Embraced the stranger-prince, and joined his hand.
Conducted to the grove, Æneas broke
The silence first, and thus the king bespoke:
'Best of the Greeks! to whom, by Fate's command,
I bear these peaceful branches in my hand:
Undaunted I approach you, though I know
Your birth is Grecian, and your land my foe:
From Atreus though your ancient lineage came,
And both the brother-kings your kindred claim;
Yet, my self-conscious worth, your high renown,
Your virtue, through the neighbouring nations blown;
Our fathers' mingled blood, Apollo's voice,
Have led me hither; less by need than choice.
Our father Dardanus, as fame has sung
And Greeks acknowledge, from Electra sprung:
Electra from the loins of Atlas came—
Atlas, whose head sustains the starry frame.
Your sire is Mercury, whom long before

On cold Cyllene's top fair Maia bore.
Maia the fair, on fame if we rely,
Was Atlas' daughter, who sustains the sky.
Thus from one common source our streams divide ;
Ours is the Trojan, yours the Arcadian side,
Raised by these hopes, I sent no news before,
Nor asked your leave, nor did your faith implore ;
But come without a pledge, my own ambassador.
The same Rutulians, who with arms pursue
The Trojan race, are equal foes to you.
Our host expelled, what further force can stay
The victor troops from universal sway?
Then will they stretch their power athwart the land,
And either sea from side to side command.
Receive our offered faith, and give us thine ;
Ours is a generous and experienced line :
We want not hearts nor bodies for the war ;
In council cautious, and in fields we dare.'
He said ; and, while he spoke, with piercing eyes
Evander viewed the man with vast surprise—
Pleased with his action, ravished with his face ;
Then answered briefly with a royal grace :
'O valiant leader of the Trojan line,
In whom the features of thy father shine !
How I recall Anchises ! how I see
His motions, mien, and all my friend, in thee !
Long though it be, 'tis fresh within my mind,
When Priam to his sister's court designed
A welcome visit, with a friendly stay ;
And through the Arcadian kingdom took his way.
Then, past a boy, the callow down began
To shade my chin, and call me first a man.
I saw the shining train with vast delight ;
And Priam's goodly person pleased my sight ;
But great Anchises, far above the rest,
With awful wonder fired my youthful breast.
I longed to join in friendship's holy bands
Our mutual hearts, and plight our mutual hands.
I first accosted him : I sued, I sought,
And with a loving force, to Pheneus brought.

He gave me, when at length constrained to go,
A Lycian quiver and a Gnossian bow ;
A vest embroidered, glorious to behold,
And two rich bridles, with their bits of gold,
Which my son's coursers in obedience hold.
The league you ask, I offer as your right ;
And, when to-morrow's sun reveals the light,
With swift supplies you shall be sent away.
Now celebrate, with us, this solemn day,
Whose holy rites admit no long delay.
Honour our annual feast ; and take your seat
With friendly welcome, at a homely treat.'
 Thus having said, the bowls (removed for fear)
The youths replaced, and soon restored the cheer.
On sods of turf he set the soldiers round :
A maple throne, raised higher from the ground,
Received the Trojan chief ; and, o'er the bed
A lion's shaggy hide, for ornament, they spread.
The loaves were served in canisters ; the wine
In bowls ; the priest renewed the rites divine :
Broiled entrails are their food, and beef's continued
  chine.
But, when the rage of hunger was repressed,
Thus spoke Evander to his royal guest :
 ' These rites, these altars, and this feast, O king !
From no vain fears or superstition spring ;
Or blind devotion, or from blinder chance,
Or heady zeal, or brutal ignorance :
But, saved from danger, with a grateful sense,
The labours of a god we recompense.
See, from afar, yon rock that mates the sky ;
About whose feet such heaps of rubbish lie ;
Such indigested ruin ; bleak and bare,
How desert now it stands, exposed in air !
'Twas once a robber's den, enclosed around
With living stone, and deep beneath the ground.
The monster Cacus, more than half a beast,
This hold, impervious to the sun, possessed.
The pavement ever foul with human gore ;
Heads, and their mangled members, hung the door.

Vulcan this plague begot ; and, like his sire,
Black clouds he belched, and flakes of livid fire.
Time, long expected, eased us of our load,
And brought the needful presence of a god.
The avenging force of Hercules, from Spain
Arrived in triumph ; from Geryon slain :—
Thrice lived the giant, and thrice lived in vain.
His prize, the lowing herds, Alcides drove
Near Tiber's banks, to graze the shady grove.
Allured with hope of plunder, and intent
By force to rob, by fraud to circumvent,
The brutal Cacus, as by chance they strayed,
Four oxen thence, and four fair kine, conveyed.
And, lest the printed footsteps might be seen,
He dragged them backwards to his rocky den.
The tracks averse a lying notice gave,
And led the searcher backward from the cave.
Meantime the herdsman hero shifts his place,
To find fresh pasture, and untrodden grass.
The beasts, who missed their mates, filled all around
With bellowings ; and the rocks restored the sound.
One heifer, who had heard her love complain,
Roared from the cave, and made the project vain.
Alcides found the fraud ; with rage he shook,
And tossed about his head his knotted oak.
Swift as the winds, or Scythian arrows' flight,
He clomb with eager haste, the aërial height.
Then first we saw the monster mend his pace :
Fear in his eyes, and paleness in his face,
Confessed the god's approach. Trembling he springs,
As terror had increased his feet with wings ;
Nor stayed for stairs ; but down the depth he threw
His body : on his back the door he drew ;
(The door, a rib of living rock ; with pains
His father hewed it out, and bound with iron chains :)
He broke the heavy links ; the mountain closed,
And bars and levers to his foe opposed.
The wretch had hardly made his dungeon fast ;
The fierce avenger came with bounding haste ;
Surveyed the mouth of the forbidden hold ;

And here and there his raging eyes he rolled.
He gnashed his teeth; and thrice he compassed
    round
With wingèd speed the circuit of the ground.
Thrice at the cavern's mouth he pulled in vain;
And, panting, thrice desisted from his pain.
  A pointed flinty rock, all bare and black,
Grew gibbous from behind the mountain's back:
Owls, ravens, all ill omens of the night,
Here built their nests, and hither winged their flight.
The leaning head hung threatening o'er the flood,
And nodded to the left. The hero stood
Averse, with planted feet, and from the right
Tugged at the solid stone with all his might.
Thus heaved, the fixed foundations of the rock
Gave way: heaven echoed at the rattling shock.
Tumbling, it choked the flood: on either side
The banks leap backward, and the streams divide:
The sky shrunk upward with unusual dread;
And trembling Tiber dived beneath his bed.
The court of Cacus stands revealed to sight;
The cavern glares with new-admitted light.
So the pent vapours, with a rumbling sound,
Heave from below, and rend the hollow ground.
A sounding flaw succeeds; and, from on high,
The gods with hate behold the nether sky:
The ghosts repine at violated night,
And curse the invading sun, and sicken at the sight.
The graceless monster, caught in open day,
Enclosed, and in despair to fly away.
Howls horrible from underneath, and fills
His hollow palace with unmanly yells.
The hero stands above, and from afar
Plies him with darts, and stones, and distant war.
He, from his nostrils and huge mouth, expires
Black clouds of smoke, amidst his father's fires;
Gathering, with each repeated blast, the night,
To make uncertain aim, and erring sight.
The wrathful god then plunges from above,
And, where in thickest waves the sparkles drove,

There lights ; and wades through fumes ; and gropes
    his way,
Half singed, half stifled, till he grasps his prey.
The monster, spewing fruitless flames, he found ;
He squeezed his throat ; he writhed his neck around,
And in a knot his crippled members bound ;
Then, from their sockets tore his burning eyes :
Rolled on a heap the breathless robber lies.
The doors, unbarred, received the rushing day ;
And thorough lights disclose the ravished prey.
The bulls, redeemed, breathe open air again
Next, by the feet, they drag him from his den.
The wondering neighbourhood, with glad surprise,
Beheld his shagged breast, his giant size,
His mouth that flames no more, and his extinguished
    eyes.
   From that auspicious day, with rites divine,
We worship at the hero's holy shrine.
Potitius first ordained these annual vows :
As priests, were added the Pinarian house,
Who raised this altar in the sacred shade,
Where honours, ever due, for ever shall be paid.
For these deserts, and this high virtue shown,
Ye warlike youths, your heads with garlands crown :
Fill high the goblets with a sparkling flood ;
And with deep draughts invoke our common god.'
This said, a double wreath Evander twined ;
And poplars black and white his temples bind :
Then brims his ample bowl.   With like design
The rest invoke the gods, with sprinkled wine.
   Meantime the sun descended from the skies,
And the bright evening-star began to rise.
And now the priests, Potitius at their head,
In skins of beasts involved, the long procession led ;
Held high the flaming tapers in their hands,
As custom had prescribed their holy bands ;
Then with a second course the tables load,
And with full chargers, offer to the god.
The Salii sing, and 'cense his altars round
With Saban smoke, their heads with poplar bound—

One choir of old, another of the young,
To dance, and bear the burden of the song.
The lay records the labours, and the praise,
And all the immortal acts of Hercules.
First, how the mighty babe, when swathed in bands,
The serpents strangled with his infant hands ;
Then, as in years and matchless force he grew,
The Œchalian walls, and Trojan, overthrew.
Besides, a thousand hazards they relate,
Procured by Juno's and Eurystheus' hate.
'Thy hands, unconquered hero, could subdue
The cloud-born Centaurs, and the monster-crew :
Nor thy resistless arm the bull withstood,
Nor he, the roaring terror of the wood :
The triple porter of the Stygian seat,
With lolling tongue, lay fawning at thy feet ;
And, seized with fear, forgot his mangled meat.
The infernal waters trembled at thy sight ;
Thee, god ! no face of danger could affright ;
No huge Typhöeus, nor the unnumbered snake,
Increased with hissing heads, in Lerna's lake.
Hail, Jove's undoubted son ! an added grace
To heaven and the great author of thy race !
Receive the grateful offerings which we pay,
And smile propitious on thy solemn day !'
    In numbers thus they sung : above the rest,
The den and death of Cacus crown the feast.
The woods to hollow vales convey the sound ;
The vales to hills ; and hills the notes rebound.
    The rites performed, the cheerful train retire.
Betwixt young Pallas and his aged sire,
The Trojan passed, the city to survey ;
And pleasing talk beguiled the tedious way.
The stranger cast around his curious eyes,
New objects viewing still with new surprise ;
With greedy joy inquires of various things,
And acts and monuments of ancient kings.
Then thus the founder of the Roman towers :
'These woods were first the seat of sylvan powers,
Of nymphs and fauns, and savage men who took

Their birth from trunks of trees and stubborn oak.
Nor laws they knew, nor manners, nor the care
Of labouring oxen, nor the shining share,
Nor arts of gain, nor what they gained to spare.
Their exercise the chase : the running flood
Supplied their thirst ; the trees supplied their food.
Then Saturn came, who fled the power of Jove,
Robbed of his realms, and banished from above.
The men dispersed on hills, to towns he brought ;
And laws ordained, and civil customs taught ;
And Latium called the land where safe he lay
From his unduteous son, and his usurping sway.
With his mild empire, peace and plenty came ;
And hence the golden times derived their name.
A more degenerate and discoloured age
Succeeded this, with avarice and rage.
The Ausonians then, and bold Sicanians, came ;
And Saturn's empire often changed the name.
Then kings (gigantic Tibris, and the rest)
With arbitrary sway the land oppressed :
For Tiber's flood was Albula before,
Till, from the tyrant's fate, his name it bore.
I last arrived, driven, from my native home
By fortune's power, and fate's resistless doom.
Long tossed on seas, I sought this happy land,
Warned by my mother-nymph, and called by heaven's
    command.'
   Thus, walking on, he spoke, and showed the gate,
Since called Carmental by the Roman state ;
Where stood an altar, sacred to the name
Of old Carmenta ; the prophetic dame
Who to her son foretold the Ænean race,
Sublime in fame, and Rome's imperial place.
Then shows the forests, which, in after-times,
Fierce Romulus, for perpetrated crimes,
A sacred refuge made :—with this, the shrine
Where Pan below the rock had rites divine.
Then tells of Argus' death, his murdered guest,
Whose grave and tomb his innocence attest.
Thence, to the steep Tarpeian rock he leads—

Now roofed with gold, then thatched with homely
    reeds.
A reverent fear (such superstition reigns
Among the rude) e'en then possessed the swains:
Some god, they knew (what god, they could not tell)
Did there amidst the sacred horror dwell.
The Arcadians thought him Jove; and said they saw
The mighty Thunderer with majestic awe;
Who shook his shield, and dealt his bolts around,
And scattered tempests on the teeming ground.
Then saw two heaps of ruins (once they stood
Two stately towns, on either side the flood),
Saturnia's and Janiculum's remains;
And either place the founder's name retains.

 Discoursing thus together, they resort
Where poor Evander kept his country court.
They viewed the ground of Rome's litigious hall:
(Once oxen lowed, where now the lawyers bawl),
Then, stooping, through the narrow gate they pressed,
When thus the king bespoke his Trojan guest:
' Mean as it is, this palace, and this door,
Received Alcides, then a conqueror.
Dare to be poor: accept our homely food,
Which feasted him; and emulate a god.'
Then underneath a lowly roof he led
The weary prince, and laid him on a bed;
The stuffing leaves with hides of bears o'erspread.

 Now night had shed her silver dews around,
And with her sable wings embraced the ground,
When love's fair goddess, anxious for her son
(New tumults rising, and new wars begun),
Couched with her husband in his golden bed,
With these alluring words invokes his aid—
And, that her pleasing speech his mind may move,
Inspires each accent with the charms of love:
' While cruel fate conspired with Grecian powers,
To level with the ground the Trojan towers,
I asked not aid the unhappy to restore;
Nor did the succour of thy skill implore;
Nor urged the labours of my lord in vain,

A sinking empire longer to sustain :
Though much I owed to Priam's house, and more
The danger of Æneas did deplore.
But now by Jove's command, and fate's decree,
His race is doomed to reign in Italy ;
With humble suit I beg thy needful art,
O still propitious power, that rul'st my heart !
A mother kneels a suppliant for her son.
By Thetis and Aurora thou wert won
To forge impenetrable shields, and grace
With fated arms a less illustrious race.
Behold, what haughty nations are combined
Against the relics of the Phrygian kind !
With fire and sword my people to destroy,
And conquer Venus twice, in conquering Troy.'
  She said ; and straight, her arms of snowy hue
About her unresolving husband threw.
Her soft embraces soon infuse desire ;
His bones and marrow sudden warmth inspire ;
And all the godhead feels the wonted fire.
Not half so swift the rattling thunder flies,
Or forky lightnings flash along the skies.
The goddess, proud of her successful wiles,
And conscious of her form, in secret smiles.
Then thus the power, obnoxious to her charms,
Panting, and half dissolving in her arms :
' Why seek you reasons for a cause so just ;
Or your own beauties or my love distrust ?
Long since, had you required my helpful hand,
The artificer, and art, you might command,
To labour arms for Troy : nor Jove, nor Fate,
Confined their empire to so short a date.
And, if you now desire new wars to wage,
My skill I promise, and my pains engage :
Whatever melting metals can conspire,
Or breathing bellows, or the forming fire,
Is freely yours : your anxious fears remove,
And think no task is difficult to love.'
Trembling he spoke ; and, eager of her charms,
He snatched the willing goddess to his arms ;

Till, in her lap infused, he lay possessed
Of full desire, and sunk to pleasing rest.
    Now when the night her middle race had rode,
And his first slumber had refreshed the god—
The time when early housewives leave the bed;
When living embers on the hearth they spread:
Supply the lamp, and call the maids to rise;
With yawning mouths, and with half-opened eyes,
They ply the distaff by the winking light,
And to their daily labour add the night:
Thus frugally they earn their children's bread,
And uncorrupted keep their nuptial bed:
Not less concerned, nor at a later hour,
Rose from his downy couch the forging Power.
    Sacred to Vulcan's name, an isle there lay,
Betwixt Sicilia's coasts and Lipare,
Raised high on smoking rocks; and, deep below,
In hollow caves the fires of Ætna glow.
The Cyclops here their heavy hammers deal:
Loud strokes, and hissing of tormented steel,
Are heard around: the boiling waters roar;
And smoky flames through fuming tunnels soar.
Hither the father of the fire, by night,
Through the brown air precipitates his flight.
On their eternal anvils here he found
The brethren beating, and the blows go round;
A load of pointless thunder now there lies
Before their hands, to ripen for the skies:
These darts, for angry Jove, they daily cast—
Consumed on mortals with prodigious waste.
Three rays of writhen rain, of fire three more;
Of wingèd southern winds and cloudy store
As many parts, the dreadful mixture frame;
And fears are added, and avenging flame.
Inferior ministers, for Mars, repair
His broken axle-trees, and blunted war;
And send him forth again with furbished arms,
To wake the lazy war, with trumpet's loud alarms.
The rest refresh the scaly snakes that fold
The shield of Pallas, and renew their gold:

Full on the crest the Gorgon's head they place,
With eyes that roll in death, and with distorted face.
  ' My sons ! (said Vulcan), set your tasks aside ;
Your strength and master-skill must now be tried.
Arms for a hero forge—arms that require
Your force, your speed, and all your forming fire.'
He said.   They set their former work aside,
And their new toils with eager haste divide.
A flood of molten silver, brass, and gold,
And deadly steel, in the large furnace rolled :
Of this, their artful hands a shield prepare,
Alone sufficient to sustain the war.
Seven orbs within a spacious round they close.
One stirs the fire, and one the bellows blows.
The hissing steel is in the smithy drowned ;
The grot with beaten anvils groans around.
By turns, their arms advance in equal time ;
By turns, their hands descend, and hammers chime.
They turn the glowing mass with crooked tongs ;
The fiery work proceeds with rustic songs.
  While, at the Lemnian god's command they urge
Their labours thus, and ply the Æolian forge,
The cheerful morn salutes Evander's eyes ;
And songs of chirping birds invite to rise.
He leaves his lowly bed : his buskins meet
Above his ankles ; sandals sheath his feet :
He sets his trusty sword upon his side,
And o'er his shoulder throws a panther's hide.
Two menial dogs before their master pressed.
Thus clad, and guarded thus, he seeks his kingly guest.
Mindful of promised aid, he mends his pace,
But meets Æneas in the middle space.
Young Pallas did his father's steps attend ;
And true Achates waited on his friend.
They join their hands : a secret seat they choose ;
The Arcadian first their former talk renews :
  ' Undaunted prince ! I never can believe
The Trojan empire lost, while you survive.
Command the assistance of a faithful friend :
But feeble are the succours I can send.

Our narrow kingdom here the Tiber bounds:
That other side the Latian state surrounds,
Insults our walls, and wastes our fruitful grounds.
But mighty nations I prepare, to join
Their arms with yours, and aid your just design.
You come, as by your better genius sent;
And Fortune seems to favour your intent.
Not far from hence there stands a hilly town,
Of ancient building, and of high renown,
Torn from the Tuscans by the Lydian race,
Who gave the name of Cære to the place—
Once Agyllina called.   It flourished long,
In pride of wealth and warlike people strong;
Till cursed Mezentius, in a fatal hour
Assumed the crown, with arbitrary power.
What words can paint those execrable times,
The subjects' sufferings, and the tyrant's crimes?
That blood, those murders, O ye gods! replace
On his own head, and on his impious race!
The living and the dead, at his command
Were coupled face to face, and hand to hand;
Till, choked with stench, in loathed embraces tied,
The lingering wretches pined away and died.
Thus plunged in ills, and meditating more—
The people's patience, tried, no longer bore
The raging monster; but with arms beset
His house, and vengeance and destruction threat.
They fire his palace: while the flame ascends,
They force his guards and execute his friends.
He cleaves the crowd, and, favoured by the night,
To Turnus' friendly court directs his flight.
By just revenge the Tuscans set on fire,
With arms, their king to punishment require:
Their numerous troops, now mustered on the strand,
My counsel shall submit to your command.
Their navy swarms upon the coasts; they cry
To hoist their anchors; but the gods deny.
An ancient augur, skilled in future fate,
With these foreboding words restrains their hate:
"Ye brave in arms, ye Lydian blood, the flower

Of Tuscan youth, and choice of all their power,
Whom just revenge against Mezentius arms,
To seek your tyrant's death by lawful arms!
Know this: no native of our land may lead
This powerful people: seek a foreign head."
Awed with these words, in camps they still abide;
And wait with longing looks their promised guide.
Tarchon, the Tuscan chief, to me has sent
Their crown, and every regal ornament:
The people join their own with his desire;
And all, my conduct as their king, require.
But the chill blood that creeps within my veins,
And age, and listless limbs unfit for pains;
And a soul conscious of its own decay,
Have forced me to refuse imperial sway.
My Pallas were more fit to mount the throne
And should; but he's a Sabine mother's son,
And half a native: but, in you combine
A manly vigour, and a foreign line.
Where Fate and smiling Fortune show the way,
Pursue the ready path to sovereign sway.
The staff of my declining days, my son,
Shall make your good or ill success his own;
In fighting-fields, from you shall learn to dare,
And serve the hard apprenticeship of war;
Your matchless courage and your conduct view;
And early shall begin t' admire and copy you.
Besides, two hundred horse he shall command—
Though few, a warlike and well-chosen band.
These in my name are listed; and my son
As many more has added in his own.'
  Scarce had he said; Achates and his guest,
With downcast eyes, their silent grief expressed;
Who, short of succours, and in deep despair,
Shook at the dismal prospect of the war.
But his bright mother, from a breaking cloud,
To cheer her issue, thundered thrice aloud:
Thrice forky lightning flashed along the sky;
And Tyrrhene trumpets thrice were heard on high.
Then, gazing up, repeated peals they hear;

And, in a heaven serene, refulgent arms appear:
Reddening the skies, and glittering all around,
The tempered metals clash, and yield a silver sound.
The rest stood trembling: struck with awe divine:
Æneas only, conscious to the sign,
Presaged the event, and joyful viewed, above,
The accomplished promise of the queen of love.
Then to the Arcadian king: 'This prodigy
(Dismiss your fear) belongs alone to me.
Heaven calls me to the war: the expected sign
Is given of promised aid, and arms divine.
My goddess-mother, whose indulgent care
Foresaw the dangers of the growing war,
This omen gave; when bright Vulcanian arms,
Fated from force of steel by Stygian charms,
Suspended, shone on high: she then foreshowed
Approaching fights, and fields to float in blood.
Turnus shall dearly pay for faith forsworn:
And corpse, and swords, and shields on Tiber borne,
Shall choke his flood: now sound the loud alarms;
And, Latian troops, prepare your perjured arms!'
  He said, and, rising from his homely throne,
The solemn rites of Hercules begun;
And on his altars waked the sleeping fires;
Then cheerful to his household gods retires:
There offers chosen sheep. The Arcadian king
And Trojan youth the same oblations bring.
Next, of his men and ships he makes review;
Draws out the best and ablest of the crew.
Down with the falling stream the refuse run,
To raise with joyful news his drooping son.
Steeds are prepared to mount the Trojan band,
Who wait their leader to the Tyrrhene land.
A sprightly courser, fairer than the rest,
The king himself presents his royal guest.
A lion's hide his back and limbs infold,
Precious with studded work, and paws of gold.
Fame through the little city spreads aloud
The intended march: amid the fearful crowd,
The matrons beat their breasts, dissolve in tears,

And double their devotion in their fears.
The war at hand appears with more affright,
And rises every moment to the sight.
Then old Evander, with a close embrace,
Strained his departing friend; and tears o'erflow his face.
'Would heaven (said he) my strength and youth recall,
Such as I was beneath Præneste's wall—
Then when I made the foremost foes retire,
And set whole heaps of conquered shields on fire;
When Herilus in single fight I slew,
Whom with three lives Feronia did endue;
And thrice I sent him to the Stygian shore,
Till the last ebbing soul returned no more—
Such if I stood renewed; not these alarms
Nor death, should rend me from my Pallas' arms;
Nor proud Mezentius thus, unpunished, boast
His rapes and murders on the Tuscan coast.
Ye gods! and mighty Jove! in pity bring
Relief, and hear a father and a king!
If fate and you reserve these eyes, to see
My son returned with peace and victory;
If the loved boy shall bless his father's sight;
If we shall meet again with more delight;
Then draw my life in length; let me sustain,
In hopes of his embrace, the worst of pain.
But, if your hard decrees—which, O! I dread—
Have doomed to death his undeserving head;
This, O! this very moment let me die,
While hopes and fears in equal balance lie;
While, yet possessed of all his youthful charms,
I strain him close within these aged arms:
Before that fatal news my soul shall wound!'
He said; and swooning, sunk upon the ground.
His servants bore him off, and softly laid
His languished limbs upon his homely bed.

The horsemen march; the gates are opened wide;
Æneas at their head, Achates by his side.
Next these the Trojan leaders rode along:
Last, follows in the rear the Arcadian throng.
Young Pallas shone conspicuous o'er the rest:

Gilded his arms, embroidered was his vest.
So, from the seas, exerts his radiant head
The star by whom the lights of heaven are led ;
Shakes from his rosy locks the pearly dews ;
Dispels the darkness, and the day renews.
The trembling wives, the walls and turrets crowd,
And follow with their eyes the dusty cloud,
Which winds disperse by fits, and shew from far
The blaze of arms, and shields, and shining war.
The troops, drawn up in beautiful array,
O'er heathy plains pursue the ready way.
Repeated peals of shouts are heard around ;
The neighing coursers answer to the sound ;
And shake with horny hoofs the solid ground.

A green-wood shade, long for religion known,
Stands by the streams that wash the Tuscan town ;
Encompassed round with gloomy hills above,
Which add a holy horror to the grove.
The first inhabitants, of Grecian blood,
That sacred forest to Silvanus vowed
(The guardian of their flocks and fields), and pay
Their due devotions on his annual day.
Not far from hence, along the river side
In tents secure, the Tuscan troops abide,
By Tarchon led.   Now, from a rising ground,
Æneas cast his wondering eyes around,
And all the Tyrrhene army had in sight,
Stretched on the spacious plain from left to right.
Thither his warlike train the Trojan led,
Refreshed his men, and wearied horses fed.

Meantime the mother-goddess, crowned with charms,
Breaks through the clouds, and brings the fated arms.
Within a winding vale she finds her son,
On the cool river's banks retired, alone.
She shews her heavenly form without disguise,
And gives herself to his desiring eyes.
' Behold ! (she said) performed in every part,
My promise made, and Vulcan's laboured art.
Now seek, secure, the Latian enemy ;
And haughty Turnus to the field defy.'

She said : and, having first her son embraced,
The radiant arms beneath an oak she placed.
Proud of the gift, he rolled his greedy sight
Around the work, and gazed with vast delight.
He lifts, he turns, he poises, and admires
The crested helm, that vomits radiant fires :
His hands the fatal sword and corslet hold—
One keen with tempered steel, one stiff with gold—
Both ample, flaming both, and beamy bright :
So shines a cloud, when edged with adverse light.
He shakes the pointed spear ; and longs to try
The plaited cuishes on his manly thigh ;
But most admires the shield's mysterious mould,
And Roman triumphs rising on the gold :
For there, embossed, the heavenly smith had wrought
(Not in the rolls of future fate untaught)
The wars in order ; and the race divine
Of warriors issuing from the Julian line.
The cave of Mars was dressed with mossy greens :
There, by the wolf, were laid the martial twins.
Intrepid on her swelling dugs they hung :
The foster dam lolled out her fawning tongue :
They sucked secure, while, bending back her head,
She licked their tender limbs, and formed them as they fed.
Not far from thence new Rome appears ; with games
Projected for the rape of Sabine dames.
The pit resounds with shrieks ; a war succeeds,
For breach of public faith, and unexampled deeds.
Here, for revenge the Sabine troops contend ;
The Romans there, with arms the prey defend :
Wearied with tedious war, at length they cease ;
And both the kings and kingdoms plight the peace.
The friendly chiefs before Jove's altar stand,
Both armed, with each a charger in his hand :
A fatted sow for sacrifice is led,
With imprecations on the perjured head.
Near this, the traitor Metius, stretched between
Four fiery steeds, is dragged along the green,
By Tullus' doom : the brambles drink his blood ;
And his torn limbs are left, the vulture's food.

There, Porsena to Rome, proud Tarquin brings ;
And would by force restore the banished kings :
One tyrant for his fellow-tyrant fights :
The Roman youth assert their native rights.
Before the town the Tuscan army lies,
To win by famine, or by fraud surprise.
Their king, half threatening, half disdaining, stood,
While Cocles broke the bridge, and stemmed the flood.
The captive maids there tempt the raging tide ;
'Scaped from their chains, with Clœlia for their guide.

  High on a rock, heroic Manlius stood
To guard the temple, and the temple's god.
Then Rome was poor ; and there you might behold
The palace thatched with straw, now roofed with gold.
The silver goose before the shining gate
There flew, and by her cackle saved the state.
She told the Gaul's approach : the approaching Gauls,
Obscure in night, ascend and seize the walls.
The gold dissembled well their yellow hair ;
And golden chains on their white necks they wear.
Gold are their vests ; long Alpine spears they wield ;
And their left arm sustains a length of shield.
Hard by, the leaping Salian priests advance ;
And naked through the streets the mad Luperci dance,
In caps of wool : the targets drop from heaven.
Here modest matrons, in soft litters driven,
To pay their vows in solemn pomp appear ;
And odorous gums in their chaste hands they bear.

  Far hence removed, the Stygian seats are seen ;
Pains of the damned ; and punished Cataline
Hung on a rock—the traitor ; and, around,
The Furies hissing from the nether ground.
Apart from these, the happy souls he draws ;
And Cato's holy ghost dispensing laws.

  Betwixt the quarters, flows a golden sea ;
But foaming surges there in silver play.
The dancing dolphins with their tails divide
The glittering waves, and cut the precious tide.
Amid the main, two mighty fleets engage :
Their brazen beaks opposed with equal rage.

Actium surveys the well-disputed prize :
Leucate's watery plain with foamy billows fries.
Young Cæsar, on the stern in armour bright,
Here leads the Romans and their gods to fight :
His beamy temples shoot their flames afar ;
And o'er his head is hung the Julian star.
Agrippa seconds him, with prosperous gales,
And, with propitious gods, his foes assails.
A naval crown, that binds his manly brows,
The happy fortune of the fight foreshows.

Ranged on the line opposed, Antonius brings
Barbarian aids, and troops of eastern kings,
The Arabians near, and Bactrians from afar,
Of tongues discordant, and a mingled war :
And, rich in gaudy robes, amidst the strife,
His ill fate follows him—the Egyptian wife.
Moving they fight : with oars and forky prows
The froth is gathered and the water glows.
It seems as if the Cyclades again
Were rooted up, and justled in the main ;
Or floating mountains floating mountains meet ;
Such is the fierce encounter of the fleet.
Fire-balls are thrown, and pointed javelins fly ;
The fields of Neptune take a purple dye.
The queen herself, amidst the loud alarms,
With cymbal tossed, her fainting soldiers warms—
Fool as she was ! who had not yet divined
Her cruel fate ; nor saw the snakes behind.
Her country gods, the monsters of the sky,
Great Neptune, Pallas, and love's queen, defy.
The dog Anubis barks, but barks in vain,
Nor longer dares oppose the ethereal train.
Mars, in the middle of the shining shield
Is graved, and strides along the liquid field.
The Diræ souse from heaven with swift descent ;
And Discord, dyed in blood, with garments rent,
Divides the press : her steps Bellona treads,
And shakes her iron rod above their heads.

This seen, Apollo, from his Actian height
Pours down his arrows ; at whose wingèd flight

The trembling Indians and Egyptians yield,
And soft Sabæans quit the watery field.
The fatal mistress hoists her silken sails,
And shrinking from the fight, invokes the gales.
Aghast she looks, and heaves her breast for breath,
Panting, and pale with fear of future death.
The god had figured her, as driven along
By winds and waves, and scudding through the throng.
Just opposite, sad Nilus opens wide
His arms and ample bosom to the tide,
And spreads his mantle o'er the winding coast;
In which, he wraps his queen and hides the flying host.

 The victor to the gods his thanks expressed;
And Rome triumphant with his presence blessed.
Three hundred temples in the town he placed;
With spoils and altars every temple graced.
Three shining nights, and three succeeding days,
The fields resound with shouts, the streets with praise,
The domes with songs, the theatres with plays.
All altars flame : before each altar lies,
Drenched in his gore, the destined sacrifice.
Great Cæsar sits sublime upon his throne,
Before Apollo's porch of Parian stone;
Accepts the presents vowed for victory;
And hangs the monumental crowns on high.
Vast crowds of vanquished nations march along,
Various in arms, in habit, and in tongue.
Here, Mulciber assigns the proper place
For Carians, and the ungirt Numidian race;
Then ranks the Thracians in the second row,
With Scythians, expert in the dart and bow.
And here the tamed Euphrates humbly glides;
And there the Rhine submits her swelling tides;
And proud Araxes, whom no bridge could bind.
The Danes' unconquered offspring march behind;
And Morini, the last of human kind.

 These figures, on the shield divinely wrought,
By Vulcan laboured, and by Venus brought,
With joy and wonder fill the hero's thought.
Unknown the names, he yet admires the grace;
And bears aloft the fame and fortune of his race.

BOOK IX

THE ARGUMENT

Turnus takes advantage of Æneas' absence, fires some of his ships (which are transformed into sea-nymphs), and assaults his camp. The Trojans, reduced to the last extremities, send Nisus and Euryalus to recall Æneas; which furnishes the poet with that admirable episode of their friendship, generosity, and the conclusion of their adventures.

WHILE these affairs in distant places passed,
The various Iris Juno sends with haste
To find bold Turnus; who, with anxious thought,
The secret shade of his great grandsire sought.
Retired alone she found the daring man,
And oped her rosy lips, and thus began:
'What none of all the gods, could grant thy vows—
That, Turnus, this auspicious day bestows.
Æneas, gone to seek the Arcadian prince,
Has left the Trojan camp without defence;
And, short of succours there, employs his pains
In parts remote, to raise the Tuscan swains.
Now snatch an hour that favours thy designs;
Unite thy forces, and attack their lines.'
This said, on equal wings she poised her weight,
And formed a radiant rainbow in her flight.
The Daunian hero lifts his hands and eyes,
And thus invokes the goddess as she flies:
'Iris, the grace of heaven! what power divine
Has sent thee down, through dusky clouds to shine?
See, they divide: immortal day appears,
And glittering planets dancing in their spheres!
With joy these happy omens I obey,
And follow, to the war the god that leads the way.'

Thus having said, as by the brook he stood,
He scooped the water from the crystal flood;
Then with his hands the drops to heaven he throws,
And loads the powers above with offered vows.

Now march the bold confederates through the plain,
Well horsed, well clad, a rich and shining train.
Messapus leads the van; and, in the rear,
The sons of Tyrrheus in bright arms appear.
In the main battle, with his flaming crest,
The mighty Turnus towers above the rest.
Silent they move, majestically slow,
Like ebbing Nile, or Ganges in his flow.
The Trojans view the dusty cloud from far,
And the dark menace of the distant war.
Caïcus from the rampire saw it rise,
Black'ning the fields, and thick'ning through the skies:
Then to his fellows thus aloud he calls:
'What rolling clouds, my friends, approach the walls?
Arm! arm! and man the works! prepare your spears,
And pointed darts! the Latian host appears.'

Thus warned, they shut their gates; with shouts
ascend
The bulwarks, and, secure, their foes attend:
For their wise general, with foreseeing care,
Had charged them not to tempt the doubtful war,
Nor, though provoked, in open fields advance,
But close within their lines attend their chance.
Unwilling, yet they keep the strict command,
And sourly wait in arms the hostile band.
The fiery Turnus flew before the rest:
A piebald steed of Thracian strain he pressed;
His helm of massy gold; and crimson was his crest.
With twenty horse to second his designs,
An unexpected foe, he faced the lines.
'Is there (he said), in arms who bravely dare
His leader's honour and his danger share?'
Then spurring on, his brandished dart he threw
In sign of war: applauding shouts ensue.

Amazed to find a dastard race that run
Behind the rampires, and the battle shun,

He rides around the camp, with rolling eyes,
And stops at every post, and every passage tries.
So roams the nightly wolf about the fold :
Wet with descending showers, and stiff with cold,
He howls for hunger, and he grins for pain
(His gnashing teeth are exercised in vain) ;
And, impotent of anger, finds no way
In his distended paws to grasp the prey.
The mothers listen ; but the bleating lambs
Securely swig the dug, beneath the dams.
Thus ranges eager Turnus o'er the plain,
Sharp with desire, and furious with disdain ;
Surveys each passage with a piercing sight,
To force his foes in equal field to fight.
Thus while he gazes round, at length he spies,
Where, fenced with strong redoubts, their navy lies
Close underneath the walls : the washing tide
Secures from all approach this weaker side.
He takes the wished occasion, fills his hand
With ready fires, and shakes a flaming brand.
Urged by his presence, every soul is warmed,
And every hand with kindled fires is armed ;
From the fired pines the scattering sparkles fly ;
Fat vapours, mixed with flames, involve the sky.
What power, O Muses ! could avert the flame,
Which threatened, in the fleet, the Trojan name ?
Tell : for the fact, through length of time obscure,
Is hard to faith ; yet shall the fame endure.
  'Tis said, that when the chief prepared his flight,
And felled his timber from mount Ida's height,
The grandame goddess then approached her son,
And with a mother's majesty begun :
' Grant me (she said) the sole request I bring,
Since conquered heaven has owned you for its king.
On Ida's brows, for ages past, there stood,
With firs and maples filled, a shady wood ;
And on the summit rose a sacred grove,
Where I was worshipped with religious love.
These woods, that holy grove, my long delight,
I gave the Trojan prince, to speed his flight.

Now, filled with fear, on their behalf I come ;
Let neither winds o'erset, nor waves entomb,
The floating forests of the sacred pine ;
But let it be their safety to be mine.'
Then thus replied her awful son, who rolls
The radiant stars, and heaven and earth controls:
'How dare you, mother, endless date demand
For vessels moulded by a mortal hand ?
What then is fate ? Shall bold Æneas ride,
Of safety certain, on the uncertain tide ?
Yet, what I can, I grant : when, wafted o'er,
The chief is landed on the Latian shore,
Whatever ships escape the raging storms,
At my command shall change their fading forms
To nymphs divine, and plough the watery way,
Like Doto and the daughters of the sea.'

To seal his sacred vow, by Styx he swore,
The lake of liquid pitch, the dreary shore,
And Phlegethon's innavigable flood,
And the black regions of his brother-god.
He said ; and shook the skies with his imperial nod.

And now at length the numbered hours were come,
Prefixed by fate's irrevocable doom,
When the great mother of the gods was free
To save her ships, and finish Jove's decree.
First, from the quarter of the morn, there sprung
A light that signed the heavens, and shot along ;
Then from a cloud, fringed round with golden fires,
Were timbrels heard, and Berecynthian choirs ;
And, last, a voice with more than mortal sounds,
Both hosts, in arms opposed, with equal horror wounds:
'O Trojan race ! your needless aid forbear ;
And know, my ships are my peculiar care.
With greater ease, the bold Rutulian may
With hissing brands attempt to burn the sea,
Than singe my sacred pines. But you, my charge,
Loosed from your crooked anchors, launch at large,
Exalted each a nymph : forsake the sand,
And swim the seas, at Cybele's command.'
No sooner had the goddess ceased to speak,

When, lo ! the obedient ships their halsers break ;
And strange to tell, like dolphins, in the main
They plunge their prows, and dive, and spring again :
As many beauteous maids the billows sweep,
As rode before tall vessels on the deep.
The foes, surprised with wonder, stood aghast ;
Messapus curbed his fiery courser's haste ;
Old Tiber roared, and, raising up his head,
Called back his waters to their oozy bed.
Turnus alone, undaunted, bore the shock,
And with these words his trembling troops bespoke :
' These monsters for the Trojans' fate are meant,
And are by Jove for black presages sent.
He takes the cowards' last relief away ;
For fly they cannot, and, constrained to stay,
Must yield unfought, a base inglorious prey.
The liquid half of all the globe is lost ;
Heaven shuts the seas, and we secure the coast.
Theirs is no more than that small spot of ground,
Which myriads of our martial men surround.
Their fates I fear not, or vain oracles.
Twas given to Venus, they should cross the seas,
And land secure upon the Latian plains :
Their promised hour is passed, and mine remains.
Tis in the fate of Turnus, to destroy
With sword and fire, the faithless race of Troy.
Shall such affronts as these, alone, inflame
The Grecian brothers, and the Grecian name?
My cause and theirs is one ; a fatal strife,
And final ruin, for a ravished wife.
Was't not enough, that, punished for the crime,
They fell—but will they fall a second time?
One would have thought they paid enough before,
To curse the costly sex, and durst offend no more.
Can they securely trust their feeble wall,
A slight partition, a thin interval
Betwixt their fate and them ; when Troy, though built
By hands divine, yet perished by their guilt?
Lend me for once, my friends, your valiant hands,
To force from out their lines these dastard bands.

Less than a thousand ships will end this war;
Nor Vulcan needs his fated arms prepare.
Let all the Tuscans, all the Arcadians, join;
Nor these, nor those, shall frustrate my design.
Let them not fear the treasons of the night,
The robbed Palladium, the pretended flight:
Our onset shall be made in open light.
No wooden engine shall their town betray:
Fires they shall have around, but fires by day.
No Grecian babes before their camp appear,
Whom Hector's arms detained to the tenth tardy
    year.
Now, since the sun is rolling to the west,
Give we the silent night to needful rest:
Refresh your bodies, and your arms prepare:
The morn shall end the small remains of war.'
    The post of honour to Messapus falls,
To keep the nightly guard, to watch the walls,
To pitch the fires at distances around,
And close the Trojans in their scanty ground.
Twice seven Rutulian captains ready stand;
And twice seven hundred horse these chiefs command
All clad in shining arms the works invest,
Each with a radiant helm, and waving crest.
Stretched at their length, they press the grassy
    ground;
They laugh; they sing (the jolly bowls go round);
With lights and cheerful fires renew the day;
And pass the wakeful night in feasts and play.
    The Trojans, from above, their foes beheld,
And with armed legions all the rampires filled.
Seized with affright, their gates they first explore;
Join works to works with bridges, tower to tower:
Thus all things needful for defence abound:
Mnestheus and brave Serestus walk the round,
Commissioned by their absent prince to share
The common danger, and divide the care.
The soldiers draw their lots, and, as they fall,
By turns relieve each other on the wall.
    Nigh where the foes their utmost guards advance,

To watch the gate was warlike Nisus' chance.
His father Hyrtacus, of noble blood ;
His mother was a huntress of the wood,
And sent him to the wars.   Well could he bear
His lance in fight, and dart the flying spear ;
But better skilled unerring shafts to send.
Beside him stood Euryalus, his friend—
Euryalus, than whom, the Trojan host
No fairer face, or sweeter air, could boast :
Scarce had the down to shade his cheeks begun.
One was their care, and their delight was one :
One common hazard in the war they shared ;
And now were both by choice upon the guard.
    Then Nisus thus : ' Or do the gods inspire
This warmth, or make we gods of our desire?
A generous ardour boils within my breast,
Eager of action, enemy to rest :
This urges me to fight, and fires my mind
To leave a memorable name behind.
Thou seest the foe secure : how faintly shine
Their scattered fires : the most, in sleep supine
Along the ground, an easy conquest lie :
The wakeful few the fuming flagon ply :
All hushed around.   Now hear what I revolve—
A thought unripe—and scarcely yet resolve.
Our absent prince both camp and council mourn ;
By message both would hasten his return :
If they confer what I demand, on thee
(For fame is recompense enough for me),
Methinks, beneath yon hill, I have espied
A way that safely will my passage guide.'
Euryalus stood listening while he spoke ;
With love of praise and noble envy struck ;
Then to his ardent friend exposed his mind :
All this, alone, and leaving me behind !
Am I unworthy, Nisus, to be joined ?
Think'st thou I can my share of glory yield,
Or send thee, unassisted, to the field ?
Not so my father taught my childhood arms—
Born in a siege, and bred among alarms.

Nor is my youth unworthy of my friend,
Nor of the heaven-born hero I attend.
The thing called life with ease I can disclaim,
And think it over-sold to purchase fame.'
   Then Nisus thus : ' Alas ! thy tender years
Would minister new matter to my fears.
So may the gods who view this friendly strife,
Restore me to thy loved embrace with life,
Condemned to pay my vows (as sure I trust),
This thy request is cruel and unjust.
But if some chance—as many chances are,
And doubtful hazards, in the deeds of war—
If one should reach my head, there let it fall,
And spare thy life : I would not perish all.
Thy blooming youth deserves a longer date :
Live thou to-mourn thy love's unhappy fate,
To bear my mangled body from the foe,
Or buy it back, and funeral rites bestow.
Or, if hard fortune shall those dues deny,
Thou canst at least an empty tomb supply.
O ! let not me the widow's tears renew ;
Nor let a mother's curse my name pursue—
Thy pious parent, who, for love of thee,
Forsook the coasts of friendly Sicily ;
Her age committing to the seas and wind,
When every weary matron stayed behind.'
To this, Euryalus : ' You plead in vain,
And but protract the cause you cannot gain.
No more delays ! but haste !'   With that, he wakes
The nodding watch : each to his office takes.
   The guard relieved, the generous couple went
To find the council at the royal tent.
All creatures else forgot their daily care,
And sleep, the common gift of nature, share ;
Except the Trojan peers, who wakeful sat
In nightly council for the endangered state.
They vote a message to their absent chief,
Shew their distress, and beg a swift relief.
Amid the camp a silent seat they chose,
Remote from clamour, and secure from foes.

On their left arms their ample shields they bear,
Their right reclined upon the bending spear.
  Now Nisus and his friend approach the guard,
And beg admission, eager to be heard—
The affair important, not to be deferred.
Ascanius bids them be conducted in,
Ordering the more experienced to begin.
Then Nisus thus : ' Ye fathers, lend your ears ;
Nor judge our bold attempt beyond our years.
The foe, securely drenched in sleep and wine,
Neglect their watch ; the fires but thinly shine ;
And where the smoke in cloudy vapours flies,
Covering the plain, and curling to the skies,
Betwixt two paths which at the gate divide,
Close by the sea, a passage we have spied,
Which will our way to great Æneas guide.
Expect each hour to see him safe again,
Loaded with spoils of foes in battle slain.
Snatch we the lucky minute while we may ;
Nor can we be mistaken in the way ;
For, hunting in the vales, we both have seen
The rising turrets, and the stream between ;
And know the winding course, with every ford.'
He ceased ; and old Aletes took the word :
' Our country gods, in whom our trust we place,
Will yet from ruin save the Trojan race,
While we behold such dauntless worth appear
In dawning youth, and souls so void of fear.'
Then into tears of joy the father broke :
Each in his longing arms by turns he took ;
Panted and paused ; and thus again he spoke :
' Ye brave young men, what equal gifts caɴ we,
In recompense of such desert, decree ?
The greatest, sure, and best you can receive,
The gods and your own conscious worth will give.
The rest our grateful general will bestow,
And young Ascanius, till his manhood, owe.'
' And I, whose welfare in my father lies,
(Ascanius adds) by the great deities,
By my dear country, by my household gods,

By hoary Vesta's rites and dark abodes,
Adjure you both (on you my fortune stands :
That and my faith I plight into your hands) :
Make me but happy in his safe return,
Whose wanted presence I can only mourn ;
Your common gift shall two large goblets be
Of silver, wrought with curious imagery,
And high embossed, which, when old Priam reigned,
My conquering sire at sacked Arisba gained ;
And, more, two tripods cast in antique mould,
With two great talents of the finest gold ;
Beside a costly bowl, engraved with art,
Which Dido gave, when first she gave her heart.
But, if in conquered Italy we reign,
When spoils by lot the victor shall obtain—
Thou saw'st the courser by proud Turnus pressed,
That, Nisus ! and his arms, and nodding crest,
And shield, from chance exempt, shall be thy share ;
Twelve labouring slaves, twelve handmaids young and
        fair,
All clad in rich attire, and trained with care ;
And, last, a Latian field with fruitful plains,
And a large portion of the king's domains.
But thou, whose years are more to mine allied,
No fate my vowed affection shall divide
From thee, heroic youth !   Be wholly mine :
Take full possession : all my soul is thine.
One faith, one fame, one fate, shall both attend :
My life's companion, and my bosom friend—
My peace shall be committed to thy care ;
And, to thy conduct, my concerns in war.'
    Then thus the young Euryalus replied :
' Whatever fortune, good or bad, betide,
The same shall be my age, as now my youth ;
No time shall find me wanting to my truth,
This only from your goodness let me gain
(And, this ungranted, all rewards are vain) :
Of Priam's royal race my mother came—
And sure the best that ever bore the name—
Whom neither Troy nor Sicily could hold

From me departing, but, o'erspent and old,
My fate she followed.   Ignorant of this
(Whatever) danger, neither parting kiss
Nor pious blessing taken, her I leave,
And in this only act of all my life deceive.
By this right hand, and conscious night, I swear,
My soul so sad a farewell could not bear.
Be you her comfort ; fill my vacant place
(Permit me to presume so great a grace) ;
Support her age, forsaken and distressed.
That hope alone will fortify my breast
Against the worst of fortunes and of fears.'
He said.   The moved assistants melt in tears.
Then thus Ascanius, wonder-struck to see
That image of his filial piety :
'So great beginnings, in so green an age,
Exact the faith which I again engage.
Thy mother all the dues shall justly claim,
Creüsa had, and only want the name.
Whate'er event thy bold attempt shall have,
'Tis merit to have borne a son so brave.
Now by my head, a sacred oath, I swear
(My father used it), what, returning here
Crowned with success, I for thyself prepare ;
That, if thou fail, shall thy loved mother share.'

   He said, and, weeping while he spoke the word,
From his broad belt he drew a shining sword,
Magnificent with gold.   Lycaon made,
And in an ivory scabbard sheathed the blade.
This was his gift.   Great Mnestheus gave his friend
A lion's hide, his body to defend ;
And good Aletes furnished him, beside,
With his own trusty helm, of temper tried.
   Thus armed they went.   The noble Trojans wait
Their issuing forth, and follow to the gate
With prayers and vows.   Above the rest appears
Ascanius, manly far beyond his years,
And messages committed to their care,
Which all in winds were lost, and flitting air.
The trenches first they passed ; then took their way

Where their proud foes in pitched pavilions lay:
To many fatal, ere themselves were slain.
They found the careless host dispersed upon the plain,
Who, gorged, and drunk with wine, supinely snore.
Unharnessed chariots stand along the shore:
Amidst the wheels and reins, the goblet by,
A medley of debauch and war, they lie.
Observing Nisus shewed his friend the sight:
' Behold a conquest gained without a fight.
Occasion offers; and I stand prepared:
There lies our way: be thou upon the guard,
And look around, while I securely go,
And hew a passage through the sleeping foe.'
Softly he spoke; then, striding took his way,
With his drawn sword, where haughty Rhamnes lay;
His head raised high on tapestry beneath,
And heaving from his breast, he drew his breath—
A king and prophet, by king Turnus loved;
But fate by prescience cannot be removed.
Him and his sleeping slaves he slew; then spies
Where Remus, with his rich retinue, lies.
His armour-bearer first, and next he kills
His charioteer, intrenched betwixt the wheels
And his loved horses: last invades their lord;
Full on his neck he drives the fatal sword;
The gasping head flies off; a purple flood
Flows from the trunk, that welters in the blood,
Which, by the spurning heels dispersed around,
The bed besprinkles, and bedews the ground.
Lamus the bold and Lamyrus the strong,
He slew, and then Sarranus fair and young.
From dice and wine the youth retired to rest,
And puffed the fumy god from out his breast:
E'en then he dreamt of drink and lucky play—
More lucky, had it lasted till the day.
   The famished lion thus, with hunger bold,
O'erleaps the fences of the nightly fold,
And tears the peaceful flocks: with silent awe
Trembling they lie, and pant beneath his paw.
Nor with less rage Euryalus employs

The wrathful sword, or fewer foes destroys :
But on the ignoble crowd his fury flew :
He Fadus, Hebesus, and Rhœtus, slew.
Oppressed with heavy sleep the former fall,
But Rhœtus wakeful, and observing all :
Behind a spacious jar he slinked for fear :
The fatal iron found and reached him there ;
For, as he rose, it pierced his naked side,
And, reeking, thence returned in crimson dyed.
The wound pours out a stream of wine and blood ;
The purple soul comes floating in the flood.

Now, where Messapus quartered, they arrive.
The fires were fainting there, and just alive ;
The warrior-horses, tied in order, fed :
Nisus observed the discipline, and said :
' Our eager thirst of blood may both betray :
And see, the scattered streaks of dawning day,
Foe to nocturnal thefts ! No more, my friend :
Here let our glutted execution end.
A lane through slaughtered bodies we have made.'
The bold Euryalus, though loth, obeyed.
Of arms, and arras, and of plate, they find
A precious load ; but these they leave behind.
Yet, fond of gaudy spoils, the boy would stay
To make the rich caparison his prey,
Which on the steed of conquered Rhamnes lay.
Nor did his eyes less longingly behold
The girdle-belt, with nails of burnished gold.
This present Cædicus the rich bestowed
On Remulus, when friendship first they vowed,
And, absent, joined in hospitable ties ;
He, dying, to his heir bequeathed the prize ;
Till, by the conquering Ardean troops oppressed,
He fell ; and they the glorious gift possessed.
These glittering spoils (now made the victor's gain)
He to his body suits, but suits in vain.
Messapus' helm he finds among the rest,
And laces on, and wears the waving crest.
Proud of their conquest, prouder of their prey,
They leave the camp, and take the ready way.

But far they had not passed, before they spied
Three hundred horse, with Volscens for their guide.
The queen a legion to king Turnus sent;
But the swift horse the slower foot prevent,
And now, advancing, sought the leader's tent.
They saw the pair; for, through the doubtful shade,
His shining helm Euryalus betrayed,
On which the moon with full reflection played.
' 'Tis not for nought (cried Volscens from the crowd),
These men go there (then raised his voice aloud):
Stand! stand! why thus in arms? and whither bent
From whence, to whom, and on what errand sent?'
Silent they scud away, and haste their flight
To neighbouring woods, and trust themselves to night.
The speedy horse all passages belay,
And spur their smoking steeds to cross their way,
And watch each entrance of the winding wood.
Black was the forest: thick with beech it stood,
Horrid with fern, and intricate with thorn:
Few paths of human feet, or tracks of beasts, were worn.
The darkness of the shades, his heavy prey,
And fear, misled the younger from his way.
But Nisus hit the turns with happier haste,
And thoughtless of his friend, the forest passed,
And Alban plains (from Alba's name so called)
Where king Latinus then his oxen stalled;
Till, turning at the length, he stood his ground,
And missed his friend, and cast his eyes around.
' Ah wretch! (he cried) where have I left behind
The unhappy youth? where shall I hope to find?
Or what way take?'   Again he ventures back,
And treads the mazes of his former track.
He winds the wood, and, listening, hears the noise
Of trampling coursers, and the riders' voice.
The sound approached; and suddenly he viewed
The foes inclosing, and his friend pursued,
Forelaid and taken, while he strove in vain
The shelter of the friendly shades to gain.
What should he next attempt? what arms employ,
What fruitless force, to free the captive boy?

Or desperate should he rush and lose his life,
With odds oppressed, in such unequal strife?
Resolved at length, his pointed spear he shook;
And, casting on the moon a mournful look:
'Guardian of groves, and goddess of the night!
Fair queen! (he said) direct my dart aright.
If e'er my pious father, for my sake,
Did grateful off'rings on thy altars make,
Or I increased them with my sylvan toils,
And hung thy holy roofs with savage spoils,
Give me to scatter these.' Then from his ear
He poised, and aimed, and launched the trembling spear.
The deadly weapon, hissing from the grove,
Impetuous on the back of Sulmo drove;
Pierced his thin armour, drank his vital blood,
And in his body left the broken wood.
He staggers round; his eyeballs roll in death;
And with short sobs he gasps away his breath.
All stand amazed:—a second javelin flies
With equal strength, and quivers through the skies.
This through thy temples, Tagus, forced the way,
And in the brain-pan warmly buried lay.
Fierce Volscens foams with rage, and gazing round,
Descried not him who gave the deadly wound,
Nor knew to fix revenge: 'But thou (he cries),
Shalt pay for both,' and at the prisoner flies
With his drawn sword. Then, struck with deep despair,
That cruel sight the lover could not bear;
But from his covert rushed in open view.
And sent his voice before him as he flew:
  Me! me! (he cried) turn all your swords alone
On me—the fact confessed, the fault my own.
He neither could nor durst, the guiltless youth—
Ye moon and stars, bear witness to the truth!
His only crime (if friendship can offend)
Is too much love to his unhappy friend.'
Too late he speaks: the sword, which fury guides,
Driven with full force, had pierced his tender sides.
Down fell the beauteous youth: the yawning wound
Gushed out a purple stream, and stained the ground.

His snowy neck reclines upon his breast,
Like a fair flower by the keen share oppressed—
Like a white poppy sinking on the plain,
Whose heavy head is overcharged with rain.

Despair, and rage, and vengeance justly vowed,
Drove Nisus headlong on the hostile crowd.
Volscens he seeks; on him alone he bends:
Borne back and bored by his surrounding friends,
Onward he pressed, and kept him still in sight,
Then whirled aloft his sword with all his might:
The unerring steel descended while he spoke,
Pierced his wide mouth, and through his weazon
  broke.
Dying, he slew; and staggering on the plain,
With swimming eyes he sought his lover slain;
Then quiet on his bleeding bosom fell,
Content, in death, to be revenged so well.

O happy friends! for, if my verse can give
Immortal life, your fame shall ever live,
Fixed as the Capitol's foundation lies,
And spread, where'er the Roman eagle flies!

The conquering party first divide the prey,
Then their slain leader to the camp convey.
With wonder, as they went, the troops were filled,
To see such numbers whom so few had killed.
Sarranus, Rhamnes, and the rest, they found:
Vast crowds the dying and the dead surround;
And the yet reeking blood overflows the ground.
All knew the helmet which Messapus lost,
But mourned a purchase that so dear had cost.

Now rose the ruddy morn from Tithon's bed,
And with the dawn of day the skies o'erspread;
Nor long the sun his daily course withheld,
But added colours to the world revealed;
When, early, Turnus, wakening with the light,
All clad in armour, calls his troops to fight.
His martial men with fierce harangues he fired,
And his own ardour in their souls inspired.
This done—to give new terror to his foes,
The heads of Nisus and his friend he shows,

Raised high on pointed spears—a ghastly sight !
Loud peals of shouts ensue, and barbarous delight.
  Meantime the Trojans run where danger calls ;
They line their trenches, and they man their walls.
In front extended to the left they stood :
Safe was the right, surrounded by the flood.
But, casting from their towers a frightful view,
They saw the faces, which too well they knew,
Though then disguised in death, and smeared all
    o'er
With filth obscene, and dropping putrid gore.
  Soon, hasty fame through the sad city bears
The mournful message to the mother's ears.
An icy cold benumbs her limbs ; she shakes ;
Her cheeks the blood, her hand the web, forsakes.
She runs the rampires round, amidst the war,
Nor fears the flying darts : she rends her hair,
And fills with loud laments the liquid air.
' Thus, then, my loved Euryalus appears !
Thus looks the prop of my declining years !
Was't on this face my famished eyes I fed ?
Ah ! how unlike the living is the dead !
And couldst thou leave me, cruel, thus alone !
Not one kind kiss from a departing son !
No look, no last adieu, before he went,
In an ill-boding hour to slaughter sent !
Cold on the ground, and pressing foreign clay,
To Latian dogs and fowls he lies a prey !
Nor was I near to close his dying eyes,
To wash his wounds, to weep his obsequies,
To call about his corpse his crying friends,
Or spread the mantle (made for other ends)
On his dear body, which I wove with care,
Nor did my daily pains or nightly labour spare.
Where shall I find his corpse ? what earth sustains
His trunk dismembered, and his cold remains ?
For this, alas ! I left my needful ease,
Exposed my life to winds, and winter seas !
If any pity touch Rutulian hearts,
Here empty all your quivers, all your darts :

Or, if they fail, thou, Jove, conclude my woe,
And send me thunder-struck to shades below!'

Her shrieks and clamours pierce the Trojans' ears,
Unman their courage, and augment their fears:
Nor young Ascanius could the sight sustain,
Nor old Ilioneus his tears restrain,
But Actor and Idæus jointly sent,
To bear the madding mother to her tent.

And now the trumpets terribly, from far,
With rattling clangour, rouse the sleepy war.
The soldiers' shouts succeed the brazen sounds;
And heaven, from pole to pole, the noise rebounds.
The Volscians bear their shields upon their head,
And, rushing forward, form a moving shed.
These fill the ditch; those pull the bulwarks down;
Some raise the ladders; others scale the town.
But, where void spaces on the walls appear,
Or thin defence, they pour their forces there.
With poles and missive weapons, from afar,
The Trojans keep aloof the rising war.
Taught, by their ten years' siege, defensive fight,
They roll down ribs of rocks, an unresisted weight,
To break the penthouse with the ponderous blow,
Which yet the patient Volscians undergo—
But could not bear the unequal combat long;
For, where the Trojans find the thickest throng,
The ruin falls: their shattered shields give way,
And their crushed heads become an easy prey.
They shrink for fear, abated of their rage,
Nor longer dare in a blind fight engage—
Contented now to gall them from below
With darts and slings, and with the distant bow.

Elsewhere Mezentius, terrible to view,
A blazing pine within the trenches threw.
But brave Messapus, Neptune's warlike son,
Broke down the palisades, the trenches won,
And loud for ladders calls, to scale the town.

Calliope, begin! Ye sacred Nine,
Inspire your poet in his high design,
To sing what slaughter manly Turnus made,

What souls he sent below the Stygian shade,
What fame the soldiers with their captain share,
And the vast circuit of the fatal war :
For you, in singing martial facts, excel ;
You best remember, and alone can tell.

There stood a tower, amazing to the sight,
Built up of beams, and of stupendous height :
Art, and the nature of the place, conspired
To furnish all the strength that war required.
To level this, the bold Italians join :
The wary Trojans obviate their design ;
With weighty stones o'erwhelm their troops below,
Shoot through the loop-holes, and sharp javelins throw.
Turnus, the chief, tossed from his thundering hand,
Against the wooden walls, a flaming brand :
It stuck, the fiery plague ; the winds were high ;
The planks were seasoned, and the timber dry.
Contagion caught the posts ; it spread along,
Scorched, and to distance drove, the scattered throng.
The Trojans fled ; the fire pursued amain,
Still gathering fast upon the trembling train ;
Till, crowding to the corners of the wall,
Down, the defence and the defenders fall.
The mighty flaw makes heaven itself resound :
The dead and dying Trojans strew the ground.
The tower, that followed on the falling crew,
Whelmed o'er their heads, and buried whom it slew :
Some stuck upon the darts themselves had sent ;
All the same equal ruin underwent.

Young Lycus and Helenor only 'scape ;
Saved—how, they know not—from the steepy leap.
Helenor, elder of the two ; by birth,
On one side royal, one a son of earth,
Whom, to the Lydian king, Licymnia bare,
And sent her boasted bastard to the war
(A privilege which none but freemen share).
Slight were his arms, a sword and silver shield ;
No marks of honour charged its empty field.
Light as he fell, so light the youth arose,
And, rising, found himself amidst his foes ;

Nor flight was left, nor hopes to force his way.
Emboldened by despair, he stood at bay;
And, like a stag, whom all the troops surrounds
Of eager huntsmen and invading hounds—
Resolved on death, he dissipates his fears,
And bounds aloft against the pointed spears:
So dares the youth, secure of death; and throws
His dying body on his thickest foes.

　But Lycus, swifter of his feet by far,
Runs, doubles, winds, and turns, amidst the war;
Springs to the walls, and leaves his foes behind,
And snatches at the beam he first can find;
Looks up, and leaps aloft at all the stretch,
In hopes the helping hand of some kind friend to reach.
But Turnus followed hard his hunted prey—
His spear had almost reached him in the way,
Short of his reins, and scarce a span behind:
'Fool (said the chief) though fleeter than the wind,
Could'st thou presume to 'scape when I pursue?'
He said, and downward by the feet he drew
The trembling dastard: at the tug he falls:
Vast ruins come along, rent from the smoking walls.
Thus on some silver swan, or timorous hare,
Jove's bird comes sousing down from upper air;
Her crooked talons truss the fearful prey;
Then out of sight she soars, and wings her way.
So seizes the grim wolf the tender lamb,
In vain lamented by the bleating dam.

　Then rushing onward with a barbarous cry,
The troops of Turnus to the combat fly.
The ditch with faggots filled, the daring foe
Tossed firebrands to the steepy turrets throw.

　Ilioneus, as bold Lucetius came
To force the gate, and feed the kindling flame,
Rolled down the fragment of a rock so right,
It crushed him double underneath the weight.
Two more, young Liger and Asylas slew:
To bend the bow young Liger better knew;
Asylas best the pointed javelin threw.
Brave Cæneus laid Ortygius on the plain;

The victor Cæneus was by Turnus slain.
By the same hand, Clonius and Itys fall,
Sagar, and Idas standing on the wall.
From Capys' arms his fate Privernus found :
Hurt by Temilla first—but slight the wound—
His shield thrown by, to mitigate the smart,
He clapped his hand upon the wounded part :
The second shaft came swift and unespied,
And pierced his hand, and nailed it to his side,
Transfixed his breathing lungs, and beating heart :
The soul came hissing out, and hissed against the dart.

    The son of Arcens shone amid the rest,
In glittering armour and a purple vest :
Fair was his face, his eyes inspiring love—
Bred by his father in the Martian grove,
Where the fat altars of Palicus flame,
And sent in arms to purchase early fame.
Him when he spied from far, the Tuscan king
Laid by the lance, and took him to the sling ;
Thrice whirled the thong around his head, and threw ;
The heated lead half melted as it flew :
It pierced his hollow temples and his brain ;
The youth came tumbling down, and spurned the plain.

    Then young Ascanius, who, before this day,
Was wont in woods to shoot the savage prey,
First bent in martial strife the twanging bow,
And exercised against a human foe—
With this bereft Numanus of his life,
Who Turnus' younger sister took to wife.
Proud of his realm, and of his royal bride,
Vaunting before his troops, and lengthened with a
    stride,
In these insulting terms the Trojans he defied :
' Twice-conquered cowards ! now your shame is shown—
Cooped up a second time within your town !
Who dare not issue forth in open field,
But hold your walls before you for a shield.
Thus threat you war ? thus our alliance force ?
What gods, what madness, hither steered your course ?
You shall not find the sons of Atreus here,

Nor need the frauds of sly Ulysses fear,
Strong from the cradle, of a sturdy brood,
We bear our new-born infants to the flood ;
There bathed amid the stream, our boys we hold,
With winter hardened, and inured to cold.
They wake before the day to range the wood.
Kill ere they eat, nor taste unconquered food.
No sports, but what belong to war, they know—
To break the stubborn colt, to bend the bow.
Our youth, of labour patient, earn their bread ;
Hardly they work, with frugal diet fed.
From ploughs and harrows sent to seek renown,
They fight in fields, and storm the shaken town.
No part of life from toils of war is free,
No change in age, or difference in degree.
We plough and till in arms : our oxen feel,
Instead of goads, the spur and pointed steel :
The inverted lance makes furrows in the plain.
E'en time, that changes all, yet changes us in vain—
The body, not the mind—nor can control
The immortal vigour, or abate the soul.
Our helms defend the young, disguise the gray ;
We live by plunder, and delight in prey.
Your vests embroidered with rich purple shine ;
In sloth you glory, and in dances join.
Your vests have sweeping sleeves : with female pride,
Your turbans underneath your chins are tied.
Go, Phrygians, to your Dindymus again !
Go, less than women, in the shapes of men !
Go ! mixed with eunuchs in the mother's rites
(Where with unequal sound the flute invites),
Sing, dance, and howl, by turns, in Ida's shade :
Resign the war to men, who know the martial trade.'
     This foul reproach Ascanius could not hear
With patience, or a vowed revenge forbear.
At the full stretch of both his hands, he drew
And almost joined, the horns of the tough yew.
But, first, before the throne of Jove he stood,
And thus with lifted hands invoked the god :
' My first attempt, great Jupiter, succeed !

An annual offering in thy grove shall bleed,
A snow-white steer, before thy altar led,
Who, like his mother, bears aloft his head,
Butts with his threatening brows, and bellowing stands,
And dares the fight, and spurns the yellow sands.'

    Jove bowed the heavens, and lent a gracious ear,
And thundered on the left, amidst the clear.
Sounded at once the bow ; and swiftly flies
The feathered death, and hisses through the skies.
The steel through both his temples forced the way :
Extended on the ground, Numanus lay.
' Go now, vain boaster ! and true valour scorn !
The Phrygians, twice subdued, yet make this third
    return.'
Ascanius said no more.   The Trojans shake
The heavens with shouting, and new vigour take.

    Apollo then bestrode a golden cloud,
To view the feats of arms, and fighting crowd ;
And thus the beardless victor he bespoke aloud :
' Advance, illustrious youth ! increase in fame,
And wide from east to west extend thy name—
Offspring of gods thyself ; and Rome shall owe
To thee a race of demigods below.
This is the way to heaven : the powers divine
From this beginning date the Julian line.
To thee, to them, and their victorious heirs,
The conquered war is due, and the vast world is theirs.
Troy is too narrow for thy name.'   He said,
And plunging downward shot his radiant head ;
Dispelled the breathing air, that broke his flight :
Shorn of his beams, a man to mortal sight :
Old Butes' form he took, Anchises' squire,
Now left, to rule Ascanius, by his sire :
His wrinkled visage, and his hoary hairs,
His mien, his habit, and his arms, he wears,
And thus salutes the boy, too forward for his years :
' Suffice it thee, thy father's worthy son,
The warlike prize thou hast already won.
The god of archers gives thy youth a part
Of his own praise, nor envies equal art.

Now tempt the war no more.'   He said, and flew
Obscure in air, and vanished from their view.
The Trojans, by his arms, their patron know,
And hear the twanging of his heavenly bow.

   Then duteous force they use, and Phœbus' name,
To keep from fight the youth too fond of fame.
Undaunted, they themselves no danger shun:
From wall to wall the shouts and clamours run:
They bend their bows; they whirl their slings
     around:
Heaps of spent arrows fall, and strew the ground;
And helms, and shields, and rattling arms, resound.
The combat thickens, like the storm that flies
From westward, when the showery Kids arise;
Or pattering hail comes pouring on the main,
When Jupiter descends in hardened rain;
Or bellowing clouds burst with a stormy sound,
And with an armèd winter strew the ground.

   Pandarus and Bitias, thunderbolts of war,
Whom Hiera to bold Alcanor bare
On Ida's top (two youths of height and size
Like firs that on their mother-mountain rise):
Presuming on their force, the gates unbar,
And of their own accord invite the war,
With fates averse, against their king's command.
Armed, on the right and on the left they stand,
And flank the passage: shining steel they wear,
And waving crests above their heads appear.
Thus two tall oaks, that Padus' banks adorn,
Lift up to heaven their leafy heads unshorn,
And overpressed with nature's heavy load,
Dance to the whistling winds, and at each other nod.

   In flows a tide of Latians, when they see
The gate set open and the passage free:
Bold Quercens, with rash Tmarus, rushing on,
Aquicolus, that in bright armour shone,
And Hæmon first: but soon repulsed they fly,
Or in the well-defended pass they die.
These with success are fired, and those with rage;
And each on equal terms at length engage.

Drawn from their lines, and issuing from the plain,
The Trojans hand to hand the fight maintain.

Fierce Turnus in another quarter fought,
When suddenly the unhoped-for news was brought,
The foes had left the fastness of their place,
Prevailed in fight, and had his men in chase.
He quits the attack, and, to prevent their fate,
Runs, where the giant brothers guard the gate.
The first he met, Antiphates the brave
(But base-begotten on a Theban slave—
Sarpedon's son), he slew : the deadly dart
Found passage through his breast, and pierced his
    heart.
Fixed in the wound the Italian cornel stood,
Warmed in his lungs, and in his vital blood.
Aphidnus next, and Erymanthus dies,
And Meropes, and the gigantic size
Of Bitias, threatening with his ardent eyes.
Not by the feeble dart he fell oppressed
(A dart were lost within that roomy breast),
But from a knotted lance, large, heavy, strong,
Which roared like thunder as it whirled along :
Not two bull-hides the impetuous force withhold,
Nor coat of double mail, with scales of gold.
Down sunk the monster-bulk, and pressed the ground
(His arms and clattering shield on the vast body
    sound).
Not with less ruin than the Baian mole,
Raised on the seas, the surges to control—
At once comes tumbling down the rocky wall ;
Prone to the deep, the stones disjointed fall
Of the vast pile ; the scattered ocean flies ;
Black sands, discoloured froth, and mingled mud, arise:
The frighted billows roll, and seek the shores :
Then trembles Prochyta, then Ischia roars :
Typhœus, thrown beneath by Jove's command,
Astonished at the flaw that shakes the land,
Soon shifts his weary side, and scarce awake,
With wonder feels the weight press lighter on his back.

The warrior-god the Latian troops inspired,

New strung their sinews, and their courage fired,
But chills the Trojan hearts with cold affright:
Then black despair precipitates their flight.

When Pandarus beheld his brother killed,
The town with fear and wild confusion filled,
He turns the hinges of the heavy gate
With both his hands, and adds his shoulders to the
    weight;
Some happier friends within the walls inclosed;
The rest shut out, to certain death exposed:
Fool as he was, and frantic in his care,
To admit young Turnus, and include the war!
He thrust amid the crowd, securely bold,
Like a fierce tiger pent amid the fold.
Too late his blazing buckler they descry,
And sparkling fires that shot from either eye,
His mighty members, and his ample breast,
His rattling armour, and his crimson crest.

Far from that hated face the Trojans fly,
All but the fool who sought his destiny.
Mad Pandarus steps forth, with vengeance vowed
For Bitias' death, and threatens thus aloud:
'These are not Ardea's walls, nor this the town
Amata proffers with Lavinia's crown:
'Tis hostile earth you tread. Of hope bereft,
No means of safe return by flight are left.'
To whom, with count'nance calm, and soul sedate,
Thus Turnus: 'Then begin, and try thy fate:
My message to the ghost of Priam bear;
Tell him a new Achilles sent thee there.'

A lance of tough ground-ash the Trojan threw,
Rough in the rind, and knotted as it grew:
With his full force he whirled it first around,
But the soft yielding air received the wound:
Imperial Juno turned the course before,
And fixed the wandering weapon in the door.

'But hope not thou (said Turnus), when I strike,
To shun thy fate: our force is not alike,
Nor thy steel tempered by the Lemnian god.'
Then rising, on his utmost stretch he stood,

And aimed from high : the full descending blow
Cleaves the broad front and beardless cheeks in two,
Down sinks the giant with a thundering sound :
His ponderous limbs oppress the trembling ground ;
Blood, brains, and foam, gush from the gaping wound.
Scalp, face, and shoulders, the keen steel divides ;
And the shared visage hangs on equal sides.
   The Trojans fly from their approaching fate :
And, had the victor then secured the gate,
And to his troops without, unclosed the bars,
One lucky day had ended all his wars.
But boiling youth, and blind desire of blood,
Push on his fury, to pursue the crowd.
Hamstringed behind, unhappy Gyges died ;
Then Phalaris is added to his side.
The pointed javelins from the dead he drew,
And their friend's arms against their fellows threw.
Strong Halius stands in vain ; weak I'hegeus flies ;
Saturnia, still at hand, new force and fire supplies.
Then Halius, Prytanis, Alcander fall—
Engaged against the foes who scaled the wall :
But, whom they feared without, they found within.
At last, though late, by Lynceus he was seen.
He calls new succours, and assaults the prince :
But weak his force, and vain is their defence.
Turned to the right, his sword the hero drew,
And at one blow the bold aggressor slew—
He joints the neck, and, with a stroke so strong,
The helm flies off, and bears the head along.
Next him, the huntsman Amycus he killed,
In darts envenomed, and in poison, skilled.
Then Clytius fell beneath his fatal spear,
And Cretheus, whom the Muses held so dear :
He fought with courage, and he sung the fight :
Arms were his business, verses his delight.
   The Trojan chiefs behold, with rage and grief,
Their slaughtered friends, and hasten their relief.
Bold Mnestheus rallies first the broken train,
Whom brave Serestus and his troop sustain.
To save the living, and revenge the dead,

Against one warrior's arms all Troy they led.
'O, void of sense and courage! (Mnestheus cried)
Where can you hope your coward heads to hide?
Ah! where beyond these rampires can you run?
One man, and in your camp inclosed, you shun!
Shall then a single sword such slaughter boast,
And pass unpunished from a numerous host?
Forsaking honour, and renouncing fame,
Your gods, your country, and your king, you shame!'
　　This just reproach their virtue does excite:
They stand, they join, they thicken to the fight.

　　Now Turnus doubts, and yet disdains to yield,
But with slow paces measures back the field,
And inches to the walls, where Tiber's tide,
Washing the camp, defends the weaker side.
The more he loses, they advance the more,
And tread in every step he trod before.
They shout; they bear him back; and, whom by might
They cannot conquer, they oppress with weight.

　　As, compassed with a wood of spears around,
The lordly lion stills maintains his ground;
Grins horrible, retires, and turns again;
Threats his distended paws, and shakes his mane;
He loses while in vain he presses on,
Nor will his courage let him dare to run:
So Turnus fares, and unresolved of flight,
Moves tardy back, and just recedes from fight.
Yet twice, enraged, the combat he renews,
Twice breaks, and twice his broken foes pursues.
But now they swarm, and with fresh troops supplied
Come rolling on, and rush from every side:
Nor Juno, who sustained his arms before,
Dares with new strength suffice the exhausted store;
For Jove, with sour commands, sent Iris down,
To force the invader from the frighted town.

　　With labour spent, no longer can he wield
The heavy falchion, or sustain the shield;
O'erwhelmed with darts, which from afar they fling;
The weapons round his hollow temples ring:
His golden helm gives way, with stony blows

Battered, and flat, and beaten to his brows.
His crest is rashed away ; his ample shield
Is falsified, and round with javelins filled.
  The foe, now faint, the Trojans overwhelm ;
And Mnestheus lays hard load upon his helm.
Sick sweat succeeds ; he drops at every pore ;
With driving dust his cheeks are pasted o'er ;
Shorter and shorter every gasp he takes ;
And vain efforts and hurtless blows he makes.
Armed as he was, at length he leaped from high,
Plunged in the flood, and made the waters fly.
The yellow god the welcome burden bore,
And wiped the sweat, and washed away the gore ;
Then gently wafts him to the farther coast,
And sends him safe to cheer his anxious host.

BOOK X

THE ARGUMENT

Jupiter, calling a council of the gods, forbids them to engage in either party. At Æneas' return there is a bloody battle; Turnus killing Pallas; Æneas, Lausus and Mezentius. Mezentius is described as an atheist; Lausus as a pious and virtuous youth. The different actions and death of these two are the subject of a noble episode.

THE gates of heaven unfold : Jove summons all
The gods to council in the common hall.
Sublimely seated, he surveys from far
The fields, the camp, the fortune of the war,
And all the inferior world. From first to last,
The sovereign senate in degrees are placed.
   Then thus the almighty sire began : ' Ye gods,
Natives or denizens of blest abodes !
From whence these murmurs, and this change of mind,
This backward fate from what was first designed ?
Why this protracted war, when my commands
Pronounced a peace, and gave the Latian lands ?
What fear or hope on either part divides
Our heavens, and arms our powers on different sides ?
A lawful time of war at length will come
(Nor need your haste anticipate the doom),
When Carthage shall contend the world with Rome ;
Shall force the rigid rocks and Alpine chains,
And, like a flood, come pouring on the plains.
Then is your time for faction and debate,
For partial favour, and permitted hate.
Let now your immature dissension cease ;
Sit quiet, and compose your souls to peace.'

Thus Jupiter in few unfolds the charge;
But lovely Venus thus replies at large:
'O power immense! eternal energy!
(For to what else protection can we fly?)
Seest thou the proud Rutulians, how they dare
In fields, unpunished, and insult my care?
How lofty Turnus vaunts amidst his train,
In shining arms triumphant on the plain?
E'en in their lines and trenches they contend:
And scarce their walls the Trojan troops defend
The town is filled with slaughter, and o'erfloats,
With a red deluge, their increasing moats.
Æneas, ignorant, and far from thence,
Has left a camp exposed, without defence.
This endless outrage shall they still sustain?
Shall Troy renewed be forced and fired again?
A second siege my banished issue fears;
And a new Diomede in arms appears.
One more audacious mortal will be found;
And I, thy daughter, wait another wound.
Yet if, with fates averse, without thy leave,
The Latian lands my progeny receive,
Bear they the pains of violated law,
And thy protection from their aid withdraw.
But, if the gods their sure success foretell—
If those of heaven consent with those of hell,
To promise Italy; who dare debate
The power of Jove, or fix another fate?
What should I tell of tempests on the main,
Of Æolus usurping Neptune's reign?
Of Iris sent, with Bacchanalian heat
T' inspire the matrons and destroy the fleet?
Now Juno to the Stygian sky descends,
Solicits hell for aid, and arms the fiends.
That new example wanted yet above—
An act that well became the wife of Jove!
Alecto, raised by her, with rage inflames
The peaceful bosoms of the Latian dames.
Imperial sway no more exalts my mind;
Such hopes I had indeed, while heaven was kind,

Now let my happier foes possess my place,
Whom Jove prefers before the Trojan race ;
And conquer they, whom you with conquest grace.
Since you can spare from all your wide command,
No spot of earth, no hospitable land,
Which may my wandering fugitives receive
(Since haughty Juno will not give you leave) ;
Then, father (if I still may use that name),
By ruined Troy, yet smoking from the flame,
I beg you, let Ascanius, by my care,
Be freed from danger, and dismissed the war :
Inglorious let him live, without a crown :
The father may be cast on coasts unknown,
Struggling with fate ; but let me save the son.
Mine is Cythera, mine the Cyprian towers :
In those recesses, and those sacred bowers,
Obscurely let him rest ; his right resign
To promised empire, and his Julian line.
Then Carthage may the Ausonian towns destroy,
Nor fear the race of a rejected boy.
What profits it my son, to 'scape the fire,
Armed with his gods, and loaded with his sire ;
To pass the perils of the seas and wind ;
Evade the Greeks, and leave the war behind ;
To reach the Italian shores ; if, after all,
Our second Pergamus is doomed to fall?
Much better had he curbed his high desires,
And hovered o'er his ill-extinguished fires.
To Simoïs' banks the fugitives restore,
And give them back to war, and all the woes before.'
    Deep indignation swelled Saturnia's heart :
' And must I own (she said) my secret smart—
What with more decence were in silence kept.
And, but for this unjust reproach, had slept?
Did god or man your favourite son advise,
With war unhoped the Latians to surprise?
By fate, you boast, and by the gods' decree,
He left his native land for Italy !
Confess the truth ; by mad Cassandra, more
Than heaven, inspired, he sought a foreign shore.

Did I persuade to trust his second Troy
To the raw conduct of a beardless boy,
With walls unfinished, which himself forsakes,
And through the waves a wandering voyage takes?
When have I urged him meanly to demand
The Tuscan aid, and arm a quiet land?
Did I or Iris give this mad advice?
Or made the fool himself the fatal choice?
You think it hard, the Latians should destroy
With swords your Trojans, and with fires your Troy!
Hard and unjust indeed, for men to draw
Their native air, nor take a foreign law!
That Turnus is permitted still to live,
To whom his birth a god and goddess give!
But yet 'tis just and lawful for your line
To drive their fields, and force, with fraud to join;
Realms, not your own, among your clans divide,
And from the bridegroom tear the promised bride;
Petition, while you public arms prepare;
Pretend a peace, and yet provoke a war!
'Twas given to you, your darling son to shroud
To draw the dastard from the fighting crowd,
And, for a man, obtend an empty cloud.
From flaming fleets you turned the fire away,
And changed the ships to daughters of the sea.
But 'tis my crime—the queen of heaven offends,
If she presume to save her suffering friends!
Your son, not knowing what his foes decree,
You say, is absent: absent let him be.
Yours is Cythera, yours the Cyprian towers,
The soft recesses, and the sacred bowers.
Why do you then these needless arms prepare,
And thus provoke a people prone to war?
Did I with fire the Trojan town deface,
Or hinder from return your exiled race?
Was I the cause of mischief, or the man
Whose lawless lust the fatal war began?
Think on whose faith the adulterous youth relied;
Who promised, who procured, the Spartan bride?
When all the united states of Greece combined,

To purge the world of the perfidious kind,
Then was your time to fear the Trojan fate :—
Your quarrels and complaints are now too late.'
   Thus Juno.   Murmurs rise with mixed applause,
Just as they favour or dislike the cause.
So winds, when yet unfledged in woods they lie,
In whispers first their tender voices try,
Then issue on the main with bellowing rage,
And storms to trembling mariners presage.
   Then thus to both replied the imperial god,
Who shakes heaven's axles with his awful nod.
(When he begins, the silent senate stand,
With reverence listening to the dread command :
The clouds dispel ; the winds their breath restrain ;
And the hushed waves lie flatted on the main.)
' Celestials ! your attentive ears incline !
Since (said the god) the Trojans must not join
In wished alliance with the Latian line—
Since endless jarrings, and immortal hate,
Tend but to discompose our happy state—
The war henceforward be resigned to fate :
Each to his proper fortune stand or fall ;
Equal and unconcerned I look on all.
Rutulians, Trojans, are the same to me ;
And both shall draw the lots their fates decree.
Let these assault, if Fortune be their friend ;
And, if she favours those, let those defend :
The fates will find their way.'   The Thunderer said ;
And shook the sacred honours of his head,
Attesting Styx, the inviolable flood,
And the black regions of his brother-god.
Trembled the poles of heaven ; and earth confessed the
      nod.
This end the sessions had : the senate rise,
And to his palace wait their sovereign through the skies.
   Meantime, intent upon their siege, the foes
Within their walls the Trojan host inclose :
They wound, they kill, they watch at every gate ;
Renew the fires, and urge their happy fate.
   The Æneans wish in vain their wanted chief,

Hopeless of flight, more hopeless of relief.
Thin on the towers they stand ; and e'en those few,
A feeble, fainting, and dejected crew.
Yet in the face of danger some there stood :
The two bold brothers of Sarpedon's blood,
Asius, Acmon : both the Assaraci ;
Young Hæmon, and, though young, resolved to die.
With these were Clarus and Thymœtes joined ;
Thymbris and Castor, both of Lycian kind.
From Acmon's hands a rolling stone there came,
So large, it half deserved a mountain's name !
Strong-sinewed was the youth, and big of bone :
His brother Mnestheus could not more have done,
Or the great father of the intrepid son.
Some firebrands throw, some flights of arrows send ;
And some with darts, and some with stones, defend.
Amid the press appears the beauteous boy,
The care of Venus, and the hope of Troy.
His lovely face unarmed, his head was bare ;
In ringlets o'er his shoulders hung his hair.
His forehead circled with a diadem ;
Distinguished from the crowd, he shines a gem,
Enchased in gold, or polished ivory set,
Amidst the meaner foil of sable jet.

Nor Ismarus was wanting to the war,
Directing ointed arrows from afar,
And death with poison armed—in Lydia born,
Where plenteous harvests the fat fields adorn ;
Where proud Pactolus floats the fruitful lands,
And leaves a rich manure of golden sands.
There Capys, author of the Capuan name,
And there was Mnestheus too, increased in fame,
Since Turnus from the camp he cast with shame.

Thus mortal war was waged on either side.
Meantime the hero cuts the nightly tide ;
For, anxious, from Evander when he went,
He sought the Tyrrhene camp, and Tarchon's tent ;
Exposed the cause of coming to the chief ;
His name and country told, and asked relief ;
Proposed the terms ; his own small strength declared :

What vengeance proud Mezentius had prepared ;
What Turnus, bold and violent, designed ;
Then showed the slippery state of human kind,
And fickle fortune ; warned him to beware,
And to his wholesome counsel added prayer.
Tarchon, without delay, the treaty signs,
And to the Trojan troops the Tuscan joins.

They soon set sail ; nor now the Fates withstand ;
Their forces trusted with a foreign hand.
Æneas leads ; upon his stern appear
Two lions carved, which rising Ida bear—
Ida, to wandering Trojans ever dear.
Under their grateful shade Æneas sat,
Revolving war's events, and various fate.
His left young Pallas kept, fixed to his side,
And oft of winds inquired, and of the tide ;
Oft of the stars, and of their watery way ;
And what he suffered both by land and sea.

Now, sacred sisters, open all your spring !
The Tuscan leaders, and their army, sing,
Which followed great Æneas to the war :
Their arms, their numbers, and their names, declare.

A thousand youths brave Massicus obey,
Borne in the Tiger through the foaming sea ;
From Clusium brought, and Cosa, by his care :
For arms, light quivers, bows and shafts, they bear.
Fierce Abas next : his men bright armour wore :
His stern Apollo's golden statue bore.
Six hundred, Populonia sent along,
All skilled in martial exercise, and strong.
Three hundred more, for battle, Ilva joins,
An isle renowned for steel, and unexhausted mines.
Asylas on his prow the third appears,
Who heaven interprets, and the wandering stars ;
From offered entrails, prodigies expounds,
And peals of thunder, with presaging sounds.
A thousand spears in warlike order stand,
Sent by the Pisans under his command.
Fair Astur follows in the watery field,
Proud of his managed horse and painted shield.

Gravisca, noisome from the neighbouring fen,
And his own Cære, sent three hundred men,
With those which Minio's fields, and Pyrgi gave ;
All bred in arms, unanimous and brave.
    Thou, muse, the name of Cinyras renew,
And brave Cupavo followed but by few ;
Whose helm confessed the lineage of the man,
And bore, with wings displayed, a silver swan.
Love was the fault of his famed ancestry,
Whose forms and fortunes in his ensign fly.
For Cycnus loved unhappy Phaëthon,
And sung his loss in poplar groves, alone,
Beneath the sister-shades, to soothe his grief.
Heaven heard his song, and hastened his relief,
And changed to snowy plumes his hoary hair,
And winged his flight, to chant aloft in air.
His son Cupavo brushed the briny flood ;
Upon his stern a brawny Centaur stood,
Who heaved a rock, and, threatening still to throw,
With lifted hands alarmed the seas below :
They seemed to fear the formidable sight,
And rolled their billows on, to speed his flight.
    Ocnus was next, who led his native train
Of hardy warriors through the watery plain—
The son of Manto, by the Tuscan stream,
From whence the Mantuan town derives the name—
An ancient city, but of mixed descent ;
Three several tribes compose the government ;
Four towns are under each ; but all obey
The Mantuan laws, and own the Tuscan sway.
    Hate to Mezentius armed five hundred more,
Whom Mincius from his sire Benacus bore—
Mincius, with wreaths of reeds his forehead covered o'er.
These grave Aulestes leads : a hundred sweep
With stretching oars at once the glassy deep.
Him, and his martial train, the Triton bears ;
High on his poop the sea-green god appears :
Frowning he seems his crooked shell to sound,
And at the blast the billows dance around.
A hairy man above the waist he shows ;

A porpoise-tail beneath his belly grows;
And ends a fish: his breast the waves divides,
And froth and foam augment the murmuring tides.
    Full thirty ships transport the chosen train,
For Troy's relief, and scour the briny main.
    Now was the world forsaken by the sun,
And Phœbe half her nightly race had run.
The careful chief, who never closed his eyes,
Himself the rudder holds, the sails supplies.
A choir of Nereids meet him on the flood,
Once his own galleys, hewn from Ida's wood;
But now, as many nymphs, the sea they sweep,
As rode, before, tall vessels on the deep.
They know him from afar; and in a ring
Inclose the ship that bore the Trojan king.
Cymodoce, whose voice excelled the rest,
Above the waves advanced her snowy breast;
Her right hand stops the stern; her left divides
The curling ocean, and corrects the tides.
She spoke for all the choir; and thus began
With pleasing words to warn the unknowing man:
'Sleeps our loved lord? O goddess-born! awake!
Spread every sail, pursue your watery track,
And haste your course. Your navy once were we,
From Ida's height descending to the sea;
Till Turnus—as at anchor fixed we stood,
Presumed to violate our holy wood.
Then, loosed from shore, we fled his fires profane
(Unwillingly we broke our master's chain),
And since have sought you through the Tuscan main.
The mighty Mother changed our forms to these,
And gave us life immortal in the seas.
But young Ascanius, in his camp distressed,
By your insulting foes is hardly pressed.
The Arcadian horsemen, and Etrurian host,
Advance in order on the Latian coast:
To cut their way the Daunian chief designs,
Before their troops can reach the Trojan lines.
Thou, when the rosy morn restores the light,
First arm thy soldiers for the ensuing fight;

Thyself the fated sword of Vulcan wield,
And bear aloft the impenetrable shield.
To-morrow's sun, unless my skill be vain,
Shall see huge heaps of foes in battle slain.'
Parting, she spoke ; and with immortal force
Pushed on the vessel in her watery course ;
For well she knew the way.   Impelled behind,
The ship flew forward, and outstript the wind.
The rest make up.   Unknowing of the cause,
The chief admires their speed, and happy omens draws.
   Then thus he prayed, and fixed on heaven his eyes :
'Hear thou, great Mother of the deities,
With turrets crowned ! (on Ida's holy hill,
Fierce tigers, reined and curbed, obey thy will.)
Firm thy own omens ; lead us on to fight ;
And let thy Phrygians conquer in thy right.'
   He said no more.   And now renewing day
Had chased the shadows of the night away.
He charged the soldiers, with preventing care,
Their flags to follow, and their arms prepare ;
Warned of the ensuing fight, and bade them hope the
      war.
   Now, from his lofty poop, he viewed below
His camp encompassed, and the inclosing foe.
His blazing shield, embraced, he held on high ;
The camp receive the sign, and with loud shouts reply.
Hope arms their courage : from their towers they throw
Their darts with double force, and drive the foe.
Thus, at the signal given, the cranes arise
Before the stormy south, and blacken all the skies.
   King Turnus wondered at the fight renewed,
Till, looking back, the Trojan fleet he viewed,
The seas with swelling canvas covered o'er,
And the swift ships descending on the shore.
The Latians saw from far, with dazzled eyes,
The radiant crest that seemed in flames to rise,
And dart diffusive fires around the field,
And the keen glittering of the golden shield.
Thus threatening comets, when by night they rise,
Shoot sanguine streams, and sadden all the skies :

So Sirius, flashing forth sinister lights,
Pale human kind with plagues and with dry famine
　　frights.
Yet Turnus, with undaunted mind, is bent
To man the shores, and hinder their descent,
And thus awakes the courage of his friends :
' What you so long have wished, kind Fortune sends—
In ardent arms to meet the invading foe :
You find, and find him at advantage now.
Yours is the day : you need but only dare ;
Your swords will make you masters of the war.
Your sires, your sons, your houses, and your lands,
And dearest wives, are all within your hands :
Be mindful of the race from whence you came,
And emulate in arms your fathers' fame.
Now take the time, while staggering yet they stand
With feet unfirm, and prepossess the strand :
Fortune befriends the bold.'　No more he said,
But balanced, whom to leave, and whom to lead ;
Then these elects, the landing to prevent ;
And those he leaves, to keep the city pent.
　　Meantime the Trojan sends his troops ashore :
Some are by boats exposed, by bridges more.
With labouring oars they bear along the strand,
Where the tide languishes, and leap a-land.
Tarchon observes the coast with careful eyes,
And, where no ford he finds, no water fries,
Nor billows with unequal murmurs roar,
But smoothly slide along, and swell the shore,
That course he steered, and thus he gave command :
' Here ply your oars, and at all hazard land :
Force on the vessel, that her keel may wound
This hated soil, and furrow hostile ground.
Let me securely land—I ask no more ;
Then sink my ships, or shatter on the shore.'
　　This fiery speech inflames his fearful friends :
They tug at every oar, and every stretcher bends ;
They run their ships aground ; the vessels knock
(Thus forced ashore), and tremble with the shock.
Tarchon's alone was lost, and stranded stood ;

Stuck on a bank, and beaten by the flood,
She breaks her back ; the loosened sides give way,
And plunge the Tuscan soldiers in the sea.
Their broken oars and floating planks withstand
Their passage, while they labour to the land ;
And ebbing tides bear back upon the uncertain sand.
　　Now Turnus leads his troops without delay,
Advancing to the margin of the sea.
The trumpets sound : Æneas first assailed
The clowns new-raised and raw, and soon prevailed.
Great Theron fell, an omen of the fight—
Great Theron, large of limbs, of giant height.
He first in open fields defied the prince :
But armour scaled with gold was no defence
Against the fated sword, which opened wide
His plated shield, and pierced his naked side.
　　Next Lichas fell, who, not like others born,
Was from his wretched mother ripped and torn ;
Sacred, O Phœbus ! from his birth to thee ;
For his beginning life from biting steel was free.
Not far from him was Gyas laid along,
Of monstrous bulk ; with Cisseus fierce and strong :
Vain bulk and strength ! for, when the chief assailed,
Nor valour nor Herculean arms availed,
Nor their famed father, wont in war to go
With great Alcides, while he toiled below.
The noisy Pharos next received his death :
Æneas writhed his dart, and stopped his bawling breath.
Then wretched Cydon had received his doom,
Who courted Clytius in his beardless bloom,
And sought with lust obscene polluted joys—
The Trojan sword had cured his love of boys,
Had not his seven bold brethren stopped the course
Of the fierce champion, with united force.
Seven darts were thrown at once ; and some rebound
From his bright shield, some on his helmet sound :
The rest had reached him ; but his mother's care
Prevented those, and turned aside in air.
　　The prince then called Achates, to supply
The spears, that knew the way to victory :

'Those fatal weapons, which, inured to blood,
In Grecian bodies under Ilium stood :
Not one of those my hand shall toss in vain
Against our foes, on this contended plain.'
He said ; then seized a mighty spear, and threw ;
Which, winged with fate, through Mæon's buckler flew,
Pierced all the brazen plates, and reached his heart :
He staggered with intolerable smart.
Alcanor saw ; and reached, but reached in vain,
His helping hand, his brother to sustain.
A second spear, which kept the former course,
From the same hand, and sent with equal force,
His right arm pierced, and, holding on, bereft
His use of both, and pinioned down his left.
Then Numitor from his dead brother drew
The ill-omened spear, and at the Trojan threw :
Preventing fate directs the lance awry,
Which, glancing, only marked Achates' thigh.

In pride of youth the Sabine Clausus came,
And, from afar, at Dryops took his aim.
The spear flew hissing through the middle space,
And pierced his throat, directed at his face :
It stopped at once the passage of his wind,
And the free soul to flitting air resigned :
His forehead was the first that struck the ground ;
Life-blood and life rushed mingled through the wound.
He slew three brothers of the Borean race,
And three, whom Ismarus, their native place,
Had sent to war, but all the sons of Thrace.
Halesus, next, the bold Aurunci leads :
The son of Neptune to his aid succeeds,
Conspicuous on his horse. On either hand,
These fight to keep, and those to win, the land.
With mutual blood the Ausonian soil is dyed,
While on its borders each their claim decide.

As wintry winds, contending in the sky,
With equal force of lungs their titles try :
They rage, they roar ; the doubtful rack of heaven
Stands without motion, and the tide undriven :
Each bent to conquer, neither side to yield,

They long suspend the fortune of the field.
Both armies thus perform what courage can ;
Foot set to foot, and mingled, man to man.
   But, in another part, the Arcadian horse
With ill success engage the Latian force :
For, where the impetuous torrent, rushing down,
Huge craggy stones and rooted trees had thrown,
They left their coursers, and, unused to fight
On foot, were scattered in a shameful flight.
Pallas, who, with disdain and grief, had viewed
His foes pursuing and his friends pursued,
Used threatenings mixed with prayers, his last resource,
With these to move their minds, with those to fire their
     force.
' Which way, companions, whither would you run ?
By you yourselves, and mighty battles won,
By my great sire, by his established name,
And early promise of my future fame ;
By my youth, emulous of equal right
To share his honours—shun ignoble flight !
Trust not your feet : your hands must hew your way
Through yon black body, and that thick array :
'Tis through that forward path that we must come ;
There lies our way, and that our passage home.
Nor powers above, nor destinies below,
Oppress our arms : with equal strength we go,
With mortal hands to meet a mortal foe.
See on what foot we stand ! a scanty shore—
The sea behind, our enemies before :
No passage left, unless we swim the main ;
Or, forcing these, the Trojan trenches gain.'
This said, he strode with eager haste along,
And bore amidst the thickest of the throng.
Lagus, the first he met, with fate to foe,
Had heaved a stone of mighty weight, to throw :
Stooping, the spear descended on his chine,
Just where the bone distinguished either loin ;
It stuck so fast, so deeply buried lay,
That scarce the victor forced the steel away.
   Hisbo came on ; but, while he moved too slow

To wished revenge, the prince prevents his blow ;
For, warding his at once, at once he pressed,
And plunged the fatal weapon in his breast.
Then lewd Anchemolus he laid in dust,
Who stained his stepdame's bed with impious lust.
And, after him, the Daunian twins were slain,
Laris and Thymbrus, on the Latian plain ;
So wondrous like in feature, shape, and size,
As caused an error in their parents' eyes—
Grateful mistake ! but soon the sword decides
The nice distinction, and their fate divides :
For Thymbrus' head was lopped ; and Laris' hand,
Dismembered, sought its owner on the strand :
The trembling fingers yet the falchion strain,
And threaten still the extended stroke in vain.

Now, to renew the charge, the Arcadians came :
Sight of such acts, and sense of honest shame,
And grief, with anger mixed, their minds inflame.
Then, with a casual blow was Rhœteus slain,
Who chanced, as Pallas threw, to cross the plain :
The flying spear was after Ilus sent ;
But Rhœteus happened on a death unmeant :
From Teuthras and from Tyres while he fled,
The lance, athwart his body, laid him dead :
Rolled from his chariot with a mortal wound,
And intercepted fate, he spurned the ground.

As when, in summer, welcome winds arise,
The watchful shepherd to the forest flies,
And fires the midmost plants ; contagion spreads,
And catching flames infect the neighbouring heads ;
Around the forest flies the furious blast,
And all the leafy nation sinks at last ;
And Vulcan rides in triumph o'er the waste ;
The pastor, pleased with his dire victory,
Beholds the satiate flames in sheets ascend the sky :
So Pallas' troops their scattered strength unite,
And, pouring on their foes, their prince delight.

Halesus came, fierce with desire of blood ;
But first collected in his arms he stood :
Advancing then, he plied the spear so well,

Ladon, Demodocus, and Pheres, fell.
Around his head he tossed his glittering brand,
And from Strymonius hewed his better hand,
Held up to guard his throat; then hurled a stone
At Thoas' ample front, and pierced the bone:
It struck beneath the space of either eye;
And blood, and mingled brains, together fly.
Deep skilled in future fates, Halesus' sire
Did with the youth to lonely groves retire;
But, when the father's mortal race was run,
Dire destiny laid hold upon the son,
And hauled him to the war, to find, beneath
The Evandrian spear, a memorable death.
Pallas the encounter seeks, but, ere he throws,
To Tuscan Tiber thus addressed his vows:
' O sacred stream! direct my flying dart,
And give to pass the proud Halesus' heart:
His arms and spoils thy holy oak shall bear.'
Pleased with the bribe, the god received his prayer:
For, while his shield protects a friend distressed,
The dart came driving on, and pierced his breast.

But Lausus, no small portion of the war,
Permits not panic fear to reign too far,
Caused by the death of so renowned a knight;
But by his own example cheers the fight.
Fierce Abas first he slew—Abas, the stay
Of Trojan hopes, and hindrance of the day.
The Phrygian troops escaped the Greeks in vain:
They, and their mixed allies, now load the plain.

To the rude shock of war both armies came;
Their leaders equal, and their strength the same.
The rear so pressed the front, they could not wield
Their angry weapons, to dispute the field.
Here Pallas urges on, and Lausus there:
Of equal youth and beauty both appear,
But both by fate forbid to breathe their native air.
Their congress in the field great Jove withstands—
Both doomed to fall, but fall by greater hands.

Meantime Juturna warns the Daunian chief
Of Lausus' danger, urging swift relief.

With his driven chariot he divides the crowd,
And, making to his friends, thus calls aloud :
' Let none presume his needless aid to join :
Retire, and clear the field ; the fight is mine :
To this right hand is Pallas only due :
Oh ! were his father here, my just revenge to view !'
From the forbidden space his men retired.
Pallas their awe, and his stern words, admired ;
Surveyed him o'er and o'er with wondering sight,
Struck with his haughty mien and towering height.
Then to the king : ' Your empty vaunts forbear :
Success I hope and fate I cannot fear.
Alive, or dead, I shall deserve a name :
Jove is impartial, and to both the same.'
He said, and to the void advanced his pace :
Pale horror sat on each Arcadian face.
Then Turnus, from his chariot leaping light,
Addressed himself on foot to single fight.
And, as a lion—when he spies from far
A bull that seems to meditate the war,
Bending his neck, and spurning back the sand—
Runs roaring downward from his hilly stand :
Imagine eager Turnus not more slow
To rush from high on his unequal foe.

Young Pallas, when he saw the chief advance
Within due distance of his flying lance,
Prepares to charge him first—resolved to try
If Fortune would his want of force supply ;
And thus to heaven and Hercules addressed :
' Alcides, once on earth Evander's guest !
His son adjures thee by those holy rights,
That hospitable board, those genial nights ;
Assist my great attempt to gain this prize,
And let proud Turnus view, with dying eyes,
His ravished spoils.' 'Twas heard, the vain request ;
Alcides mourned, and stifled sighs within his breast.
Then Jove, to soothe his sorrow, thus began :
' Short bounds of life are set to mortal man :
'Tis virtue's work alone to stretch the narrow span.
So many sons of gods, in bloody fight

Around the walls of Troy, have lost the light:
My own Sarpedon fell beneath his foe;
Nor I, his mighty sire, could ward the blow.
E'en Turnus shortly shall resign his breath,
And stands already on the verge of death.'
This said, the god permits the fatal fight,
But from the Latian fields averts his sight.

Now with full force his spear young Pallas threw;
And, having thrown, his shining falchion drew.
The steel just grazed along the shoulder-joint,
And marked it slightly with the glancing point.
Fierce Turnus first to nearer distance drew,
And poised his pointed spear, before he threw:
Then, as the wingèd weapon whizzed along,
'See now (said he), whose arm is better strung.'
The spear kept on the fatal course unstayed
By plates of iron, which o'er the shield were laid:
Through folded brass, and tough bull-hides, it passed,
His corselet pierced, and reached his heart at last.
In vain the youth tugs at the broken wood;
The soul comes issuing with the vital blood:
He falls; his arms upon his body sound;
And with his bloody teeth he bites the ground.

Turnus bestrode the corpse: 'Arcadians, hear
(Said he), my message to your master bear:
Such as the sire deserved, the son I send;
It costs him dear to be the Phrygian's friend.
The lifeless body, tell him, I bestow
Unasked, to rest his wandering ghost below.'
He said, and trampled down, with all the force
Of his left foot, and spurned the wretched corpse;
Then snatched the shining belt, with gold inlaid—
The belt Eurytion's artful hands had made,
Where fifty fatal brides, expressed to sight,
All, in the compass of one mournful night,
Deprived their bridegrooms of returning light.

In an ill hour insulting Turnus tore
Those golden spoils, and in a worse he wore.
O mortals! blind in fate, who never know
To bear high fortune, or endure the low!

The time shall come, when Turnus, but in vain,
Shall wish untouched the trophies of the slain
Shall wish the fatal belt were far away,
And curse the dire remembrance of the day.
   The sad Arcadians, from the unhappy field,
Bear back the breathless body on a shield.
O grace and grief of war ! at once restored,
With praises, to thy sire, at once deplored.
One day first sent thee to the fighting-field,
Beheld whole heaps of foes in battle killed ;
One day behold thee dead, and borne upon thy shield.
This dismal news, not from uncertain fame,
But sad spectators, to the hero came :
His friends upon the brink of ruin stand,
Unless relieved by his victorious hand.
He whirls his sword around, without delay,
And hews through adverse foes an ample way,
To find fierce Turnus, of his conquest proud.
Evander, Pallas, all that friendship owed
To large deserts, are present to his eyes—
His plighted hand, and hospitable ties.
   Four sons of Sulmo, four whom Ufens bred,
He took in fight, and living victims led,
To please the ghost of Pallas, and expire,
In sacrifice, before his funeral fire.
At Magus next he threw : he stooped below
The flying spear, and shunned the promised blow,
Then, creeping, clasped the hero's knees, and prayed :
' By young Iulus, by thy father's shade,
O ! spare my life, and send me back to see
My longing sire, and tender progeny,
A lofty house I have, and wealth untold,
In silver ingots, and in bars of gold :
All these, and sums besides, which see no day,
The ransom of this one poor life shall pay.
If I survive, will Troy the less prevail ?
A single soul's too light to turn the scale.'
He said.   The hero sternly thus replied :
' Thy bars and ingots, and the sums beside,
Leave for thy children's lot.   Thy Turnus broke

All rules of war by one relentless stroke,
When Pallas fell: so deems, nor deems alone,
My father's shadow, but my living son.'
Thus having said, of kind remorse bereft,
He seized his helm, and dragged him with his left;
Then with his right hand, while his neck he wreathed,
Up to the hilts his shining falchion sheathed.

Apollo's priest, Hæmonides, was near;
His holy fillets on his front appear;
Glittering in arms, he shone amidst the crowd,
Much of his god, more of his purple, proud.
Him the fierce Trojan followed through the field:
The holy coward fell; and, forced to yield,
The prince stood o'er the priest, and, at one blow,
Sent him an offering to the shades below.
His arms Serestus on his shoulders bears,
Designed a trophy to the god of wars.

Vulcanian Cæculus renews the fight,
And Umbro born upon the mountain's height.
The champion cheers his troops t' encounter those,
And seeks revenge himself on other foes.
At Anxur's shield he drove; and, at the blow,
Both shield and arm to ground together go.
Anxur had boasted much of magic charms,
And thought he wore impenetrable arms,
So made by muttered spells; and, from the spheres,
Had life secured, in vain, for length of years.
Then Tarquitus the field in triumph trod;
A nymph his mother, and his sire a god.
Exulting in bright arms, he braves the prince:
With his protended lance he makes defence;
Bears back his feeble foe; then, pressing on,
Arrests his better hand, and drags him down;
Stands o'er the prostrate wretch, and (as he lay,
Vain tales inventing, and prepared to pray)
Mows off his head: the trunk a moment stood,
Then sunk, and rolled along the sand in blood.

The vengeful victor thus upbraids the slain:
'Lie there, proud man, unpitied on the plain:
Lie there, inglorious, and without a tomb,

Far from thy mother and thy native home ;
Exposed to savage beasts, and birds of prey,
Or thrown for food to monsters of the sea.'

On Lucas and Antæus next he ran,
Two chiefs of Turnus, and who led his van.
They fled for fear ; with these, he chased along
Camers the yellow-locked, and Numa strong ;
Both great in arms, and both were fair and young.
Camers was son to Volscens lately slain,
In wealth surpassing all the Latian train.
And in Amyclæ fixed his silent easy reign.

And, as Ægæon, when with heaven he strove,
Stood opposite in arms to mighty Jove ;
Moved all his hundred hands, provoked the war,
Defied the forky lightning from afar ;
At fifty mouths his flaming breath expires,
And flash for flash returns, and fires for fires ;
In his right hand as many swords he wields,
And takes the thunder on as many shields :
With strength like this, the Trojan hero stood ;
And soon the fields with falling corpse were strewed,
When once his falchion found the taste of blood.

With fury scarce to be conceived, he flew
Against Niphæus, whom four coursers drew.
They, when they see the fiery chief advance,
And pushing at their chests his pointed lance,
Wheeled with so swift a motion, mad with fear,
They threw their master headlong from the chair.
They stare, they start, nor stop their course, before,
They bear the bounding chariot to the shore.

Now Lucagus and Liger scour the plains,
With two white steeds ; but Liger holds the reins,
And Lucagus the lofty seat maintains—
Bold brethren both.   The former waved in air
His flaming sword : Æneas couched his spear,
Unused to threats, and more unused to fear.
Then Liger thus : ' Thy confidence is vain
To 'scape from hence, as from the Trojan plain ;
Nor these the steeds which Diomede bestrode,
Nor this the chariot where Achilles rode :

Nor Venus' veil is here, nor Neptune's shield ;
Thy fatal hour is come ; and this the field.'
Thus Liger vainly vaunts : the Trojan peer
Returned his answer with his flying spear.
As Lucagus, to lash his horses, bends,
Prone to the wheels, and his left foot protends,
Prepared for fight : the fatal dart arrives,
And through the border of his buckler drives ;
Passed through, and pierced his groin.   The deadly
  wound,
Cast from his chariot, rolled him on the ground ;
Whom thus the chief upbraids with scornful spite :
'Blame not the slowness of your steeds in flight :
Vain shadows did not force their swift retreat ;
But you yourself forsake your empty seat.'
He said, and seized at once the loosened rein ;
For Liger lay already on the plain
By the same shock ; then, stretching out his hands,
The recreant thus his wretched life demands :
'Now, by thyself, O more than mortal man !
By her and him from whom thy breath began,
Who formed thee thus divine, I beg thee, spare
This forfeit life, and hear thy suppliant's prayer.'
Thus much he spoke, and more he would have said ;
But the stern hero turned aside his head,
And cut him short : 'I hear another man :
You talked not thus before the fight began.
Now take your turn ; and, as a brother should,
Attend your brother to the Stygian flood.'
Then through his breast his fatal sword he sent ;
And the soul issued at the gaping vent.
As storms the skies, and torrents tear the ground,
Thus raged the prince, and scattered deaths around.

 At length, Ascanius and the Trojan train
Broke from the camp, so long besieged in vain.
Meantime the king of gods and mortal man
Held conference with his queen, and thus began :
'My sister-goddess, and well-pleasing wife,
Still think you Venus' aid supports the strife—
Sustains her Trojans—or themselves, alone,

With inborn valour force their fortune on?
How fierce in fight, with courage undecayed!
Judge if such warriors want immortal aid.'
To whom the goddess with the charming eyes,
Soft in her tone, submissively replies:
'Why, O my sovereign lord, whose frown I fear,
And cannot, unconcerned, your anger bear—
Why urge you thus my grief? when, if I still
(As once I was) were mistress of your will,
From your almighty power your pleasing wife
Might gain the grace of lengthening Turnus' life,
Securely snatch him from the fatal fight,
And give him to his aged father's sight.
Now let him perish, since you hold it good,
And glut the Trojans with his pious blood!
Yet, from our lineage he derives his name,
And, in the fourth degree, from god Pilumnus came;
Yet he devoutly pays you rites divine,
And offers daily incense at your shrine.'
    Then shortly thus the sovereign god replied:
'Since in my power and goodness you confide,
If, for a little space, a lengthened span,
You beg reprieve for this expiring man,
I grant you leave to take your Turnus hence
From instant fate, and can so far dispense.
But, if some secret meaning lies beneath,
To save the short-lived youth from destined death;
Or, if a farther thought you entertain,
To change the fates; you feed your hopes in vain.'
    To whom the goddess thus, with weeping eyes:
'And what if that request your tongue denies,
Your heart should grant—and not a short reprieve,
But length of certain life, to Turnus give?
Now speedy death attends the guiltless youth,
If my presaging soul divines with truth;
Which, O! I wish might err, through causeless fears,
And you (for you have power) prolong his years!'
    Thus having said, involved in clouds, she flies,
And drives a storm before her through the skies.
Swift she descends, alighting on the plain,

Where the fierce foes a dubious fight maintain.
Of air condensed, a spectre soon she made ;
And, what Æneas was, such seemed the shade.
Adorned with Dardan arms, the phantom bore
His head aloft ; a plumy crest he wore :
This hand appeared a shining sword to wield,
And that sustained an imitated shield.
With manly mien he stalked along the ground,
Nor wanted voice belied, nor vaunting sound.
(Thus haunting ghosts appear to waking sight,
Or dreadful visions in our dreams by night.)
The spectre seems the Daunian chief to dare,
And flourishes his empty sword in air.
At this, advancing, Turnus hurled his spear :
The phantom wheeled, and seemed to fly for fear.
Deluded Turnus thought the Trojan fled,
And with vain hopes his haughty fancy fed.
' Whither, O coward ? (thus he calls aloud,
Nor found he spoke to wind, and chased a cloud),
Why thus forsake your bride !   Receive from me
The fated land you sought so long by sea.'
He said, and, brandishing at once his blade,
With eager pace pursued the flying shade.
By chance a ship was fastened to the shore,
Which from old Clusium king Osinius bore :
The plank was ready laid for safe ascent ;
For shelter there the trembling shadow bent,
And skipped and skulked, and under hatches went.
Exulting Turnus, with regardless haste,
Ascends the plank, and to the galley passed.
Scarce had he reached the prow ; Saturnia's hand
The halsers cuts, and shoots the ship from land.
With wind in poop, the vessel ploughs the sea,
And measures back with speed her former way.
Meantime Æneas seeks his absent foe,
And sends his slaughtered troops to shades below.
  The guileful phantom now forsook the shroud,
And flew sublime, and vanished in a cloud.
Too late young Turnus the delusion found,
Far on the sea, still making from the ground.

Then, thankless for a life redeemed by shame,
With sense of honour stung, and forfeit fame,
Fearful besides of what in fight had passed,
His hands and haggard eyes to heaven he cast :
' O Jove ! (he cried) for what offence have I
Deserved to bear this endless infamy ?
Whence am I forced, and whither am I borne ?
How, and with what reproach, shall I return ?
Shall ever I behold the Latian plain,
Or see Laurentum's lofty towers again ?
What will they say of their deserting chief ?
The war was mine : I fly from their relief !
I led to slaughter, and in slaughter leave ;
And e'en from hence their dying groans receive.
Here, over-matched in fight, in heaps they lie ;
There, scattered o'er the fields, ignobly fly.
Gape wide, O earth, and draw me down alive !
Or, oh ! ye pitying winds, a wretch relieve !
On sands or shelves the splitting vessel drive ;
Or set me shipwrecked on some desert shore,
Where no Rutulian eyes may see me more—
Unknown to friends, or foes, or conscious fame,
Lest she should follow, and my flight proclaim.'

Thus Turnus raved, and various fates revolved :
The choice was doubtful, but the death resolved.
And now the sword, and now the sea, took place—
That to revenge, and this to purge disgrace.
Sometimes he thought to swim the stormy main,
By stretch of arms the distant shore to gain.
Thrice he the sword essayed, and thrice the flood ;
But Juno, moved with pity, both withstood,
And thrice repressed his rage ; strong gales supplied,
And pushed the vessel o'er the swelling tide.
At length she lands him on his native shores,
And to his father's longing arms restores.

Meantime, by Jove's impulse, Mezentius armed,
Succeeding Turnus, with his ardour warmed
His fainting friends, reproached their shameful flight,
Repelled the victors, and renewed the fight.
Against their king the Tuscan troops conspire ;

Such is their hate, and such their fierce desire
Of wished revenge—on him, and him alone,
All hands employed, and all their darts are thrown.
He, like a solid rock by seas inclosed,
To raging winds and roaring waves opposed,
From his proud summit looking down, disdains
Their empty menace, and unmoved remains.
   Beneath his feet fell haughty Hebrus dead,
Then Latagus, and Palmus as he fled.
At Latagus a weighty stone he flung:
His face was flatted, and his helmet rung.
But Palmus from behind receives his wound :
Hamstringed he falls, and grovels on the ground :
His crest and armour, from his body torn,
Thy shoulders, Lausus, and thy head, adorn.
Evas and Mimas, both of Troy, he slew.
Mimas his birth from fair Theano drew—
Born on that fatal night, when, big with fire,
The queen produced young Paris to his sire.
But Paris in the Phrygian fields was slain,
Unthinking Mimas on the Latian plain.
   And, as a savage boar, on mountains bred,
With forest mast and fattening marshes fed,
When once he sees himself in toils inclosed,
By huntsmen and their eager hounds opposed,
He whets his tusks, and turns, and dares the war :
The invaders dart their javelins from afar :
All keep aloof, and safely shout around ;
But none presumes to give a nearer wound :
He frets and froths, erects his bristled hide,
And shakes a grove of lances from his side :
Not otherwise the troops, with hate inspired,
And just revenge against the tyrant fired,
Their darts with clamour at a distance drive,
And only keep the languished war alive.
   From Corythus came Acron to the fight,
Who left his spouse betrothed, and unconsummate night.
Mezentius sees him through the squadron ride,
Proud of the purple favours of his bride.
Then, as a hungry lion, who beholds

A gamesome goat, who frisks about the folds,
Or beamy stag, that grazes on the plain—
He runs, he roars, he shakes his rising mane ;
He grins, and opens wide his greedy jaws :
The prey lies panting underneath his paws :
He fills his famished maw ; his mouth runs o'er
With unchewed morsels, while he churns the gore :
So proud Mezentius rushes on his foes,
And first unhappy Acron overthrows :
Stretched at his length, he spurns the swarthy ground ;
The lance, besmeared with blood, lies broken in the
    wound.
Then with disdain the haughty victor viewed
Orodes flying, nor the wretch pursued,
Nor thought the dastard's back deserved a wound,
But, running, gained the advantage of the ground :
Then turning short, he met him face to face,
To give his victory the better grace.
Orodes falls, in equal fight oppressed :
Mezentius fixed his foot upon his breast,
And rested lance ; and thus aloud he cries :
' Lo ! here the champion of my rebels lies !'
The fields around with ' Iö Pæan !' ring ;
And peals of shouts applaud the conquering king.
At this the vanquished, with his dying breath,
Thus faintly spoke, and prophesied in death :
' Nor thou, proud man, unpunished shalt remain ;
Like death attends thee on this fatal plain.'
Then, sourly smiling, thus the king replied :
' For what belongs to me, let Jove provide ;
But die thou first, whatever chance ensue.'
He said, and from the wound the weapon drew.
A hovering mist came swimming o'er his sight,
And sealed his eyes in everlasting night.
  By Cædicus, Alcathöus was slain :
Sacrator laid Hydaspes on the plain :
Orses the strong to greater strength must yield ;
He, with Parthenius, were by Rapo killed.
Then brave Messapus Ericetes slew,
Who from Lycaon's blood his lineage drew ;

But from his headstrong horse his fate he found,
Who threw his master, as he made a bound :
The chief, alighting, stuck him to the ground ;
Then Clonius, hand to hand, on foot assails :
The Trojan sinks, and Neptune's son prevails

Agis the Lycian, stepping forth with pride,
To single fight the boldest foe defied ;
Whom Tuscan Valerus by force o'ercame,
And not belied his mighty father's fame.
Salius to death the great Authronius sent :
But the same fate the victor underwent,
Slain by Nealces' hand, well skilled to throw
The flying dart, and draw the far-deceiving bow.

Thus equal deaths are dealt with equal chance :
By turns they quit their ground, by turns advance,
Victors and vanquished in the various field,
Nor wholly overcome, nor wholly yield.
The gods from heaven survey the fatal strife,
And mourn the miseries of human life.
Above the rest, two goddesses appear
Concerned for each : here Venus, Juno there.
Amidst the crowd, infernal Atè shakes
Her scourge aloft, and crest of hissing snakes.

Once more the proud Mezentius, with disdain,
Brandished his spear, and rushed into the plain,
Where towering in the midmost ranks he stood,
Like tall Orion stalking o'er the flood ;
(When with his brawny breast he cuts the waves,
His shoulders scarce the topmost billow laves),
Or like a mountain-ash, whose roots are spread,
Deep fixed in earth—in clouds he hides his head.

The Trojan prince beheld him from afar,
And dauntless undertook the doubtful war.
Collected in his strength, and like a rock
Poised on his base, Mezentius stood the shock.
He stood, and, measuring first with careful eyes
The space his spear could reach, aloud he cries :
' My strong right hand, and sword, assist my stroke !
(Those only gods Mezentius will invoke),
His armour from the Trojan pirate torn,

By my triumphant Lausus shall be worn.'
He said ; and with his utmost force he threw
The massy spear, which, hissing as it flew,
Reached the celestial shield : that stopped the course ;
But, glancing thence, the yet unbroken force
Took a new bent obliquely, and, betwixt
The side and bowels, famed Antores fixed.
Antores had from Argos travelled far,
Alcides' friend, and brother of the war ;
Till, tired with toils, fair Italy he chose,
And in Evander's palace sought repose.
Now falling by another's wound, his eyes
He casts to heaven, on Argos thinks, and dies.

The pious Trojan then his javelin sent :
The shield gave way : through triple plates it went
Of solid brass, of linen triply rolled,
And three bull hides which round the buckler rolled.
All these it passed, resistless in the course,
Transpierced his thigh, and spent its dying force.
The gaping wound gushed out a crimson flood.
The Trojan, glad with sight of hostile blood,
His falchion drew, to closer fight addressed,
And with new force his fainting foe oppressed.

His father's peril Lausus viewed with grief ;
He sighed, he wept, he ran to his relief.
And here, heroic youth, 'tis here I must
To thy immortal memory be just,
And sing an act so noble and so new,
Posterity will scarce believe 'tis true.
Pained with his wound, and useless for the fight,
The father sought to save himself by flight :
Encumbered, slow he dragged the spear along,
Which pierced his thigh, and in his buckler hung.
The pious youth, resolved on death, below
The lifted sword, springs forth to face the foe ;
Protects his parent, and prevents the blow.
Shouts of applause ran ringing through the field,
To see the son the vanquished father shield.
All, fired with generous indignation, strive,
And, with a storm of darts, to distance drive

The Trojan chief, who, held at bay from far,
On his Vulcanian orb sustained the war.
  As, when thick hail comes rattling in the wind,
The ploughman, passenger, and labouring hind,
For shelter to the neighbouring covert fly,
Or housed, or safe in hollow caverns, lie;
But that o'erblown, when heaven above them smiles,
Return to travail, and renew their toils:
Æneas thus, o'erwhelmed on every side,
The storm of darts, undaunted, did abide;
And thus to Lausus, loud, with friendly threatening cried:
'Why wilt thou rush to certain death, and rage
In rash attempts, beyond thy tender age,
Betrayed by pious love?'—Nor, thus forborne,
The youth desists, but with insulting scorn
Provokes the lingering prince, whose patience, tired,
Gave place; and all his breast with fury fired.
For now the Fates prepared their sharpened shears;
And lifted high the flaming sword appears,
Which, full descending with a frightful sway,
Through shield and corselet forced the impetuous way,
And buried deep in his fair bosom lay.
The purple streams through the thin armour strove,
And drenched the embroidered coat his mother wove;
And life at length forsook his heaving heart,
Loth from so sweet a mansion to depart.
  But when, with blood and paleness all o'erspread,
The pious prince beheld young Lausus dead,
He grieved; he wept (the sight an image brought
Of his own filial love—a sadly-pleasing thought),
Then stretched his hand to hold him up, and said:
'Poor hapless youth! what praises can be paid
To love so great, to such transcendent store
Of early worth, and sure presage of more?
Accept whate'er Æneas can afford:
Untouched thy arms, untaken be thy sword;
And all that pleased thee living, still remain
Inviolate, and sacred to the slain.
Thy body on thy parents I bestow,
To rest thy soul, at least, if shadows know,

Or have a sense of human things below.
There to thy fellow-ghosts with glory tell,
'Twas by the great Æneas' hand I fell.'
With this, his distant friends he beckons near,
Provokes their duty, and prevents their fear :
Himself assists to lift him from the ground,
With clotted locks, and blood that welled from out the
    wound.

Meantime, his father (now no father) stood,
And washed his wounds, by Tiber's yellow flood :
Oppressed with anguish, panting, and o'erspent,
His fainting limbs against an oak he leant.
A bough his brazen helmet did sustain ;
His heavier arms lay scattered on the plain :
A chosen train of youth around him stand ;
His drooping head was rested on his hand ;
His grisly beard his pensive bosom sought ;
And all on Lausus ran his restless thought.
Careful, concerned his danger to prevent,
He much inquired, and many a message sent
To warn him from the field—alas ! in vain !
Behold ! his mournful followers bear him slain :
O'er his broad shield still gushed the yawning wound,
And drew a bloody trail along the ground.
Far off he heard their cries, far off divined
The dire event with a foreboding mind.
With dust he sprinkled first his hoary head ;
Then both his lifted hands to heaven he spread ;
Last, the dear corpse embracing, thus he said :
' What joys, alas ! could this frail being give,
That I have been so covetous to live ?
To see my son, and such a son, resign
His life a ransom for preserving mine ?
And am I then preserved, and art thou lost ?
How much too dear has that redemption cost !
'Tis now my bitter banishment I feel :
This is a wound too deep for time to heal.
My guilt thy growing virtues did defame :
My blackness blotted thy unblemished name.
Chased from a throne, abandoned, and exiled

For foul misdeeds, were punishments too mild .
I owed my people these, and, from their hate,
With less resentment could have borne my fate.
And yet I live, and yet sustain the sight
Of hated men, and of more hated light—
But will not long.'   With that he raised from ground
His fainting limbs that staggered with his wound ;
Yet, with a mind resolved, and unappalled
With pains or perils, for his courser called—
Well-mouthed, well-managed, whom himself did dress
With daily care, and mounted with success—
His aid in arms, his ornament in peace.
    Soothing his courage with a gentle stroke,
The steed seemed sensible, while thus he spoke :
' O Rhœbus ! we have lived too long for me—
If life and long were terms that could agree.
This day thou either shalt bring back the head
And bloody trophies of the Trojan dead—
This day thou either shalt revenge my woe,
For murdered Lausus, on his cruel foe ;
Or, if inexorable Fate deny
Our conquest, with thy conquered master die :
For, after such a lord, I rest secure,
Thou wilt no foreign reins, or Trojan load, endure.'
He said ; and straight the officious courser kneels,
To take his wonted weight.   His hands he fills
With pointed javelins ; on his head he laced
His glittering helm, which terribly was graced
With waving horse-hair, nodding from afar ;
Then spurred his thundering steed amidst the war.
Love, anguish, wrath, and grief, to madness wrought,
Despair, and secret shame, and conscious thought
Of inborn worth, his labouring soul oppressed,
Rolled in his eyes, and raged within his breast.
Then loud he called Æneas thrice by name :
The loud repeated voice to glad Æneas came.
' Great Jove (he said), and the far-shooting god,
Inspire thy mind to make thy challenge good !'
He spoke no more, but hastened, void of fear,
And threatened with his long protended spear.

　　To whom Mezentius thus : ' Thy vaunts are vain.
My Lausus lies extended on the plain :
He's lost ! thy conquest is already won ;
The wretched sire is murdered in the son.
Nor fate I fear, but all the gods defy.
Forbear thy threats : my business is to die ;
But first receive this parting legacy.'
He said ; and straight a whirling dart he sent ;
Another after, and another, went.
Round in a spacious ring he rides the field,
And vainly plies the impenetrable shield.
Thrice rode he round ; and thrice Æneas wheeled,
Turned as he turned : the golden orb withstood
The strokes, and bore about an iron wood.
Impatient of delay, and weary grown,
Still to defend, and to defend alone,
To wrench the darts which in his buckler light,
Urged and o'erlaboured in unequal fight—
At length resolved, he throws, with all his force,
Full at the temples of the warrior-horse.
Just where the stroke was aimed, the unerring spear
Made way, and stood transfixed through either ear.
Seized with unwonted pain, surprised with fright,
The wounded steed curvets, and raised upright,
Lights on his feet before ; his hoofs behind
Spring up in air aloft, and lash the wind.
Down comes the rider headlong from his height ;
His horse came after with unwieldy weight,
And, floundering forward, pitching on his head,
His lord's encumbered shoulder overlaid.
　　From either host, the mingled shouts and cries
Of Trojans and Rutulians rend the skies :
Æneas, hastening, waved his fatal sword
High o'er his head, with this reproachful word :
' Now ! where are now thy vaunts, the fierce disdain
Of proud Mezentius, and the lofty strain ? '
　　Struggling, and wildly staring on the skies
With scarce recovered sight, he thus replies :
' Why these insulting words, this waste of breath,
To souls undaunted, and secure of death ?

'Tis no dishonour for the brave to die !
Nor came I here with hopes of victory ;
Nor ask I life, nor fought with that design :
As I had used my fortune, use thou thine.
My dying son contracted no such band ;
The gift is hateful from his murderer's hand.
For this, this only favour, let me sue ;
If pity can to conquered foes be due,
Refuse it not ; but let my body have
The last retreat of human-kind, a grave.
Too well I know the insulting people's hate :
Protect me from their vengeance after fate :
This refuge for my poor remains provide ;
And lay my much-loved Lausus by my side.'
He said, and to the sword his throat applied :
The crimson stream distained his arms around,
And the disdainful soul came rushing through the
    wound.

BOOK XI

THE ARGUMENT

Æneas erects a trophy of the spoils of Mezentius, grants a truce for
burying the dead, and sends home the body of Pallas with great
solemnity. Latinus calls a council, to propose offers of peace to
Æneas; which occasions great animosity betwixt Turnus and
Drances. In the meantime there is a sharp engagement of the
horse, wherein Camilla signalizes herself, is killed, and the
Latin troops are entirely defeated.

SCARCE had the rosy morning raised her head
Above the waves, and left her watery bed:
The pious chief, whom double cares attend
For his unburied soldiers and his friend,
Yet first to heaven performed a victor's vows:
He bared an ancient oak of all her boughs;
Then on a rising ground the trunk he placed,
Which with the spoils of his dead foe he graced.
The coat of arms by proud Mezentius worn,
Now on a naked snag in triumph borne,
Was hung on high, and glittered from afar,
A trophy sacred to the god of war.
Above his arms, fixed on the leafless wood,
Appeared his plumy crest, besmeared with blood.
His brazen buckler on the left was seen:
Truncheons of shivered lances hung between;
And on the right was placed his corselet, bored;
And to the neck was tied his unavailing sword.
A crowd of chiefs inclose the godlike man,
Who thus, conspicuous in the midst, began:
'Our toils, my friends, are crowned with sure success:
The greater part performed, achieve the less.
Now follow cheerful to the trembling town:

Press but an entrance, and presume it won.
Fear is no more : for fierce Mezentius lies,
As the firstfruits of war, a sacrifice.
Turnus shall fall extended on the plain,
And, in this omen, is already slain.
Prepared in arms, pursue your happy chance ;
That none unwarned may plead his ignorance,
And I, at heaven's appointed hour, may find
Your warlike ensigns waving in the wind.
Meantime the rites and funeral pomps prepare,
Due to your dead companions of the war—
The last respect the living can bestow,
To shield their shadows from contempt below.
That conquered earth be theirs, for which they fought,
And which for us with their own blood they bought.
But first the corpse of our unhappy friend,
To the sad city of Evander send,
Who, not inglorious, in his age's bloom
Was hurried hence by too severe a doom.'

    Thus, weeping while he spoke, he took his way,
Where, new in death, lamented Pallas lay.
Accœtes watched the corpse ; whose youth deserved
The father's trust ; and now the son he served
With equal faith, but less auspicious care.
The attendants of the slain his sorrow share.
A troop of Trojans mixed with these appear,
And mourning matrons with dishevelled hair.
Soon as the prince appears, they raise a cry ;
All beat their breasts, and echoes rend the sky.
They rear his drooping forehead from the ground :
But, when Æneas viewed the grisly wound
Which Pallas in his manly bosom bore,
And the fair flesh distained with purple gore,
First, melting into tears, the pious man
Deplored so sad a sight, then thus began :
'Unhappy youth ! when Fortune gave the rest
Of my full wishes, she refused the best !
She came ; but brought not thee along, to bless
My longing eyes, and share in my success :
She grudged thy safe return, the triumphs due

To prosperous valour, in the public view.
Not thus I promised, when thy father lent
Thy needless succour with a sad consent;
Embraced me, parting for the Etrurian land,
And sent me to possess a large command.
He warned, and from his own experience told,
Our foes were warlike, disciplined, and bold.
And now, perhaps, in hopes of thy return,
Rich odours on his loaded altars burn,
While we, with vain officious pomp, prepare
To send him back his portion of the war,
A bloody breathless body, which can owe
No farther debt, but to the powers below.
The wretched father, ere his race is run,
Shall view the funeral honours of his son!
These are my triumphs of the Latian war,
Fruits of my plighted faith and boasted care!
And yet, unhappy sire, thou shalt not see
A son, whose death disgraced his ancestry:
Thou shalt not blush, old man, however grieved:
Thy Pallas no dishonest wound received.
He died no death to make thee wish, too late,
Thou hadst not lived to see his shameful fate.
But what a champion has the Ausonian coast,
And what a friend hast thou, Ascanius, lost!'
　　Thus having mourned, he gave the word around,
To raise the breathless body from the ground;
And chose a thousand horse, the flower of all
His warlike troops, to wait the funeral,
To bear him back, and share Evander's grief—
A well-becoming, but a weak relief.
Of oaken twigs they twist an easy bier,
Then on their shoulders the sad burden rear.
The body on this rural hearse is borne:
Strewed leaves and funeral greens the bier adorn.
All pale he lies, and looks a lovely flower,
New cropt by virgin hands, to dress the bower:
Unfaded yet, but yet, unfed below,
No more to mother earth or the green stem shall owe.
Then two fair vests, of wondrous work and cost,

Of purple woven, and with gold embossed,
For ornament the Trojan hero brought,
Which with her hands Sidonian Dido wrought.
One vest arrayed the corpse ; and one they spread
O'er his closed eyes, and wrapped around his head,
That, when the yellow hair in flame should fall,
The catching fire might burn the golden caul.
Besides, the spoils of foes in battle slain,
When he descended on the Latian plain—
Arms, trappings, horses, by the hearse are led
In long array—the achievements of the dead.
Then, pinioned with their hands behind, appear
The unhappy captives, marching in the rear,
Appointed offerings in the victor's name,
To sprinkle with their blood the funeral flame.
Inferior trophies by the chiefs are borne :
Gauntlets and helms their loaded hands adorn ;
And fair inscriptions fixed, and titles read
Of Latian leaders conquered by the dead.
  Accœtes on his pupil's corpse attends,
With feeble steps, supported by his friends ;
Pausing at every pace, in sorrow drowned,
Betwixt their arms he sinks upon the ground ;
Where grovelling while he lies in deep despair,
He beats his breast, and rends his hoary hair.
The champion's chariot next is seen to roll,
Besmeared with hostile blood, and honourably foul.
To close the pomp, Æthon, the steed of state,
Is led, the funerals of his lord to wait.
Stripped of his trappings, with a sullen pace
He walks ; and the big tears run rolling down his face.
The lance of Pallas, and the crimson crest,
Are borne behind : the victor seized the rest.
The march begins : the trumpets hoarsely sound :
The pikes and lances trail along the ground.
Thus while the Trojan and Arcadian horse
To Palantean towers direct their course,
In long procession ranked ; the pious chief
Stopped in the rear, and gave a vent to grief.
' The public care (he said) which war attends,

Diverts our present woes, at least suspends.
Peace with the manes of great Pallas dwell!
Hail, holy relics! and a last farewell!'
He said no more, but, inly though he mourned,
Restrained his tears, and to the camp returned.

  Now suppliants, from Laurentum sent, demand
A truce, with olive-branches in their hand;
Obtest his clemency, and from the plain
Beg leave to draw the bodies of their slain.
They plead, that none those common rites deny
To conquered foes, that in fair battle die.
All cause of hate was ended in their death;
Nor could he war with bodies void of breath.
A king, they hoped, would hear a king's request,
Whose son he once was called, and once his guest.

  Their suit, which was too just to be denied,
The hero grants, and farther thus replied:
'O Latian princes! how severe a fate
In causeless quarrels has involved your state,
And armed against an unoffending man,
Who sought your friendship ere the war began!
You beg a truce, which I would gladly give,
Not only for the slain, but those who live.
I came not hither but by heaven's command,
And sent by fate to share the Latian land.
Nor wage I wars unjust: your king denied
My proffered friendship and my promised bride:
Left me for Turnus. Turnus then should try
His cause in arms, to conquer or to die.
My right and his are in dispute: the slain
Fell without fault, our quarrel to maintain.
In equal arms let us alone contend;
And let him vanquish, whom his fates befriend.
This is the way (so tell him) to possess
The royal virgin, and restore the peace.
Bear this my message back—with ample leave
That your slain friends may funeral rites receive.'

  Thus having said—the ambassadors, amazed,
Stood mute awhile, and on each other gazed.
Drances, their chief, who harboured in his breast

Long hate to Turnus, as his foe professed,
Broke silence first, and to the godlike man,
With graceful action bowing, thus began :
   ' Auspicious prince, in arms a mighty name,
But yet whose actions far transcend your fame !
Would I your justice or your force express,
Thought can but equal ; and all words are less.
Your answer we shall thankfully relate,
And favours granted to the Latian state.
If wished success our labours shall attend,
Think peace concluded, and the king your friend ;
Let Turnus leave the realm to your command ;
And seek alliance in some other land :
Build you the city which your fates assign ;
We shall be proud in the great work to join.'
Thus Drances ; and his words so well persuade
The rest empowered, that soon a truce is made.
Twelve days the term allowed ; and, during those,
Latians and Trojans, now no longer foes,
Mixed in the woods, for funeral piles prepare
To fell the timber, and forget the war.
Loud axes through the groaning groves resound :
Oak, mountain-ash, and poplar, spread the ground ;
Firs fall from high ; and some the trunks receive
In laden wains ; with wedges some they cleave.

   And now the fatal news by Fame is blown
Through the short circuit of the Arcadian town,
Of Pallas slain—by Fame, which just before
His triumph on distended pinions bore.
Rushing from out the gate, the people stand,
Each with a funeral flambeau in his hand.
Wildly they stare, distracted with amaze :
The fields are lightened with a fiery blaze,
That casts a sullen splendour on their friends—
The marching troop which their dead prince attends.
Both parties meet : they raise a doleful cry :
The matrons from the walls with shrieks reply ;
And their mixed mourning rends the vaulted sky.
The town is filled with tumult and with tears,
Till the loud clamours reach Evander's ears :

Forgetful of his state, he runs along,
With a disordered pace, and cleaves the throng;
Falls on the corpse; and groaning there he lies,
With silent grief, that speaks but at his eyes.
Short sighs and sobs succeed; till sorrow breaks
A passage, and at once he weeps and speaks:
  'O Pallas! thou hast failed thy plighted word!
To fight with caution, not to tempt the sword,
I warned thee, but in vain; for well I knew
What perils youthful ardour would pursue—
That boiling blood would carry thee too far,
Young as thou wert in dangers, raw to war!
O curst essay of arms! disastrous doom!
Prelude of bloody fields, and fights to come!
Hard elements of inauspicious war!
Vain vows to heaven, and unavailing care!
Thrice happy thou, dear partner of my bed!
Whose holy soul the stroke of Fortune fled—
Prescious of ills, and leaving me behind,
To drink the dregs of life by fate assigned.
Beyond the goal of nature I have gone:
My Pallas late set out, but reached too soon.
If, for my league against the Ausonian state,
Amidst their weapons I had found my fate
(Deserved from them), then I had been returned
A breathless victor, and my son had mourned.
Yet will I not my Trojan friend upbraid,
Nor grudge the alliance I so gladly made.
'Twas not his fault, my Pallas fell so young,
But my own crime for having lived too long.
Yet, since the gods had destined him to die,
At least, he led the way to victory:
First for his friends he won the fatal shore,
And sent whole herds of slaughtered foes before—
A death too great, too glorious to deplore.
Nor will I add new honours to thy grave,
Content with those the Trojan hero gave—
That funeral pomp thy Phrygian friends designed,
In which the Tuscan chiefs and army joined.
Great spoils and trophies, gained by thee, they bear:

Then let thy own achievements be thy share.
E'en thou, O Turnus, hadst a trophy stood,
Whose mighty trunk had better graced the wood,
If Pallas had arrived, with equal length
Of years, to match thy bulk with equal strength.
But why, unhappy man ! dost thou detain
These troops, to view the tears thou shedd'st in vain ?
Go, friends ! this message to your lord relate :
Tell him, that, if I bear my bitter fate,
And, after Pallas' death, live lingering on,
'Tis to behold his vengeance for my son.
I stay for Turnus, whose devoted head
Is owing to the living and the dead.
My son and I expect it from his hand ;
'Tis all that he can give, or we demand.
Joy is no more : but I would gladly go,
To greet my Pallas with such news below.'
  The morn had now dispelled the shades of night,
Restoring toils, when she restored the light.
The Trojan king, and Tuscan chief, command
To raise the piles along the winding strand.
Their friends convey the dead to funeral fires ;
Black smouldering smoke from the green wood expires ;
The light of heaven is choked, and the new day retires.
Then thrice around the kindled piles they go
(For ancient custom had ordained it so) :
Thrice horse and foot about the fires are led ;
And thrice with loud laments they hail the dead.
Tears, trickling down their breasts, bedew the ground ;
And drums and trumpets mix their mournful sound.
Amid the blaze, their pious brethren throw
The spoils, in battle taken from the foe—
Helms, bits embossed, and swords of shining steel ;
One casts a target, one a chariot wheel ;
Some to their fellows their own arms restore—
The falchions which in luckless fight they bore,
Their bucklers pierced, their darts bestowed in vain,
And shivered lances gathered from the plain.
Whole herds of offered bulls, about the fire,
And bristled boars, and woolly sheep, expire.

Around the piles a careful troop attends,
To watch the wasting flames, and weep their burning
    friends—
Lingering along the shore, till dewy night
New decks the face of heaven with starry light.
  The conquered Latians, with like pious care,
Piles without number for their dead prepare.
Part, in the places where they fell, are laid ;
And part are to the neighbouring fields conveyed.
The corpse of kings, and captains of renown,
Borne off in state, are buried in the town ;
The rest, unhonoured, and without a name,
Are cast a common heap to feed the flame.
Trojans and Latians vie with like desires
To make the field of battle shine with fires ;
And the promiscuous blaze to heaven aspires.
  Now had the morning thrice renewed the light,
And thrice dispelled the shadows of the night,
When those who round the wasted fires remain,
Perform the last sad office to the slain.
They rake the yet warm ashes from below ;
These, and the bones unburned, in earth bestow :
These relics with their country rites they grace,
And raise a mount of turf to mark the place.
  But, in the palace of the king, appears
A scene more solemn, and a pomp of tears.
Maids, matrons, widows, mix their common moans :
Orphans their sires, and sires lament their sons.
All in that universal sorrow share,
And curse the cause of this unhappy war—
A broken league, a bride unjustly sought,
A crown usurped, which with their blood is bought.
These are the crimes, with which they load the name
Of Turnus, and on him alone exclaim :
' Let him, who lords it o'er the Ausonian land,
Engage the Trojan hero hand to hand :
His is the gain ; our lot is but to serve :
'Tis just, the sway he seeks, he should deserve.'
This Drances aggravates ; and adds, with spite,
' His foe expects, and dares him to the fight.'

Nor Turnus wants a party, to support
His cause and credit in the Latian court.
His former acts secure his present fame ;
And the queen shades him with her mighty name.

    While thus their factious minds with fury burn,
The legates from the Ætolian prince return :
Sad news they bring, that, after all the cost
And care employed, their embassy is lost ;
That Diomede refused his aid in war,
Unmoved with presents, and as deaf to prayer.
Some new alliance must elsewhere be sought,
Or peace with Troy on hard conditions bought.

    Latinus, sunk in sorrow, finds too late,
A foreign son is pointed out by fate ;
And, till Æneas shall Lavinia wed,
The wrath of heaven is hovering o'er his head.
The gods, he saw, espoused the juster side,
When late their titles in the field were tried :
Witness the fresh laments, and funeral tears undried.

    Thus full of anxious thought, he summons all
The Latian senate to the council-hall.
The princes come, commanded by their head,
And crowd the paths that to the palace lead.
Supreme in power, and reverenced for his years,
He takes the throne, and in the midst appears.
Majestically sad, he sits in state,
And bids his envoys their success relate.

    When Venulus began, the murmuring sound
Was hushed, and sacred silence reigned around.
' We have (said he) performed your high command,
And passed with peril a long tract of land :
We reached the place desired ; with wonder filled,
The Grecian tents and rising towers beheld.
Great Diomede has compassed round with walls
The city, which Argyripa he calls,
From his own Argos named.   We touched, with joy,
The royal hand that razed unhappy Troy.
When introduced, our presents first we bring,
Then crave an instant audience from the king.
His leave obtained, our native soil we name,

And tell the important cause for which we came.
Attentively he heard us, while we spoke ;
Then, with soft accents, and a pleasing look,
Made this return : " Ausonian race, of old
Renowned for peace, and for an age of gold,
What madness has your altered minds possessed,
To change for war hereditary rest,
Solicit arms unknown, and tempt the sword—
A needless ill, your ancestors abhorred ?
We—for myself I speak, and all the name
Of Grecians, who to Troy's destruction came
(Omitting those who were in battle slain,
Or borne by rolling Simoïs to the main)—
Not one but suffered, and too dearly bought
The prize of honour which in arms he sought.
Some doomed to death, and some in exile driven,
Outcasts, abandoned by the care of Heaven—
So worn, so wretched, so despised a crew,
As e'en old Priam might with pity view.
Witness the vessels by Minerva tossed
In storms—the vengeful Capharean coast—
The Eubœan rocks—the prince, whose brother led
Our armies to revenge his injured bed,
In Egypt lost. Ulysses, with his men,
Have seen Charybdis, and the Cyclop's den.
Why should I name Idomeneus, in vain
Restored to sceptres, and expelled again?
Or young Achilles, by his rival slain?
E'en he, the king of men, the foremost name
Of all the Greeks, and most renowned by fame,
The proud revenger of another's wife,
Yet by his own adulteress lost his life—
Fell at his threshold : and the spoils of Troy
The foul polluters of his bed enjoy.
The gods have envied me the sweets of life,
My much-loved country, and my more loved wife :
Banished from both, I mourn ; while in the sky,
Transformed to birds, my lost companions fly ;
Hovering about the coasts they make their moan,
And cuff the cliffs with pinions not their own.

What squalid spectres, in the dead of night,
Break my short sleep, and skim before my sight !
I might have promised to myself those harms,
Mad as I was, when I, with mortal arms,
Presumed against immortal powers to move,
And violate with wounds the queen of love.
Such arms this hand shall never more employ.
No hate remains with me to ruined Troy,
I war not with its dust ; nor am I glad
To think of past events, or good or bad.
Your presents I return ; whate'er you bring
To buy my friendship, send the Trojan king.
We met in fight : I know him, to my cost :
With what a whirling force his lance he tossed !
Heavens ! what a spring was in his arm, to throw !
How high he held his shield, and rose at every blow !
Had Troy produced two more his match in might,
They would have changed the fortune of the fight :
The invasion of the Greeks had been returned,
Our empire wasted, and our cities burned.
The long defence the Trojan people made,
The war protracted, and the siege delayed,
Were due to Hector's and this hero's hand :
Both brave alike, and equal in command ;
Æneas, not inferior in the field,
In pious reverence to the gods, excelled.
Make peace, ye Latians, and avoid with care
The impending dangers of a fatal war."
He said no more ; but with this cold excuse,
Refused the alliance, and advised a truce.'

    Thus Venulus concluded his report.
A jarring murmur filled the factious court :
As, when a torrent rolls with rapid force,
And dashes o'er the stones that stop the course,
The flood, constrained within a scanty space,
Roars horrible along the uneasy race ;
White foam in gathering eddies floats around ;
The rocky shores rebellow to the sound.

    The murmur ceased : then from his lofty throne
The king invoked the gods, and thus begun :

'I wish, ye Latians, what ye now debate
Had been resolved before it was too late.
Much better had it been for you and me,
Unforced by this our last necessity,
To have been earlier wise, than now to call
A council, when the foe surrounds the wall.
O citizens! we wage unequal war,
With men, not only Heaven's peculiar care,
But Heaven's own race—unconquered in the field,
Or, conquered, yet unknowing how to yield.
What hopes you had in Diomede, lay down;
Our hopes must centre on ourselves alone.
Yet those how feeble, and, indeed, how vain,
You see too well; nor need my words explain—
Vanquished without resource—laid flat by fate—
Factions within, a foe without the gate!
Not but I grant that all performed their parts
With manly force, and with undaunted hearts:
With our united strength the war we waged;
With equal numbers, equal arms, engaged:
You see the event.—Now hear what I propose,
To save our friends, and satisfy our foes.

A tract of land the Latians have possessed
Along the Tiber, stretching to the west,
Which now Rutulians and Auruncans till;
And their mixed cattle graze the fruitful hill.
Those mountains filled with firs, that lower land,
If you consent, the Trojans shall command,
Called into part of what is ours; and there,
On terms agreed, the common country share.
There let them build and settle, if they please;
Unless they choose once more to cross the seas,
In search of seats remote from Italy,
And from unwelcome inmates set us free.
Then twice ten galleys let us build with speed,
Or twice as many more, if more they need.
Materials are at hand: a well-grown wood
Runs equal with the margin of the flood:
Let them the number and the form assign:
The care and cost of all the stores be mine.

To treat the peace, a hundred senators
Shall be commissioned hence with ample powers,
With olive crowned : the presents they shall bear,
A purple robe, a royal ivory chair,
And all the marks of sway that Latian monarchs wear,
And sums of gold.   Among yourselves debate
This great affair, and save the sinking state.'
   Then Drances took the word, who grudged long since,
The rising glories of the Daunian prince.
Factious and rich, bold at the council board,
But cautious in the field, he shunned the sword—
A close caballer, and tongue-valiant lord.
Noble his mother was, and near the throne :
But, what his father's parentage, unknown.
He rose, and took the advantage of the times,
To load young Turnus with invidious crimes.
' Such truths, O king (said he), your words contain,
As strike the sense, and all replies are vain ;
Nor are your loyal subjects now to seek
What common needs require, but fear to speak.
Let him give leave of speech, that haughty man,
Whose pride this inauspicious war began ;
For whose ambition (let me dare to say,
Fear set apart, though death is in my way),
The plains of Latium run with blood around ;
So many valiant heroes bite the ground ;
Dejected grief in every face appears ;
A town in mourning, and a land in tears ;
While he, the undoubted author of our harms,
The man who menaces the gods with arms,
Yet, after all his boasts, forsook the fight,
And sought his safety in ignoble flight.
Now, best of kings, since you propose to send
Such bounteous presents to your Trojan friend ;
Add yet a greater at our joint request,
One which he values more than all the rest :
Give him the fair Lavinia for his bride :
With that alliance let the league be tied,
And for the bleeding land a lasting peace provide.
Let insolence no longer awe the throne ;

But, with a father's right, bestow your own.
For this maligner of the general good,
If still we fear his force, he must be wooed :
His haughty godhead we with prayers implore,
Your sceptre to release, and your just rites restore.
O cursed cause of all our ills ! must we
Wage wars unjust, and fall in fight, for thee ?
What right hast thou to rule the Latian state,
And send us out to meet our certain fate ?
'Tis a destructive war : from Turnus' hand
Our peace and public safety we demand.
Let the fair bride to the brave chief remain :
If not, the peace, without the pledge, is vain.
Turnus, I know you think me not your friend,
Nor will I much with your belief contend :
I beg your greatness not to give the law
In other realms, but, beaten, to withdraw.
Pity your own, or pity our estate ;
Nor twist our fortunes with your sinking fate.
Your interest is, the war should never cease ;
But we have felt enough, to wish the peace—
A land exhausted to the last remains,
Depopulated towns, and driven plains.
Yet, if desire of fame, and thirst of power,
A beauteous princess, with a crown in dower,
So fire your mind, in arms assert your right,
And meet your foe, who dares you to the fight.
Mankind, it seems, is made for you alone !
We, but the slaves who mount you to the throne—
A base ignoble crowd, without a name,
Unwept, unworthy of the funeral flame,
By duty bound to forfeit each his life,
That Turnus may possess a royal wife !
Permit not, mighty man, so mean a crew
Should share such triumphs, and detain from you
The post of honour, your undoubted due.
Rather alone your matchless force employ,
To merit what alone you must enjoy.'

  These words, so full of malice mixed with art,
Inflamed with rage the youthful hero's heart.

Then groaning from the bottom of his breast,
He heaved for wind, and thus his wrath expressed :
' You, Drances, never want a stream of words,
Then, when the public need requires our swords.
First in the council-hall to steer the state,
And ever foremost in a tongue-debate,
While our strong walls secure us from the foe,
Ere yet with blood our ditches overflow :
But let the potent orator declaim,
And with the brand of coward blot my name ;
Free leave is given him, when his fatal hand
Has covered with more corpse the sanguine strand,
And high as mine his towering trophies stand.
If any doubt remains who dares the most,
Let us decide it at the Trojans' cost,
And issue both abreast, where honour calls—
(Foes are not far to seek without the walls),
Unless his noisy tongue can only fight,
And feet were given him but to speed his flight.
I beaten from the field ! I forced away !
Who, but so known a dastard, dares to say ?
Had he but e'en beheld the fight, his eyes
Had witnessed for me what his tongue denies—
What heaps of Trojans by this hand were slain,
And how the bloody Tiber swelled the main.
All saw, but he, the Arcadian troops retire
In scattered squadrons, and their prince expire.
The giant brothers, in their camp, have found
I was not forced with ease to quit my ground.
Not such the Trojans tried me, when, inclosed,
I singly their united arms opposed—
First forced an entrance through their thick array,
Then, glutted with their slaughter, freed my way.
'Tis a destructive war ! So let it be,
But to the Phrygian pirate, and to thee !
Meantime proceed to fill the people's ears
With false reports, their minds with panic fears :
Extol the strength of a twice-conquered race ;
Our foes encourage, and our friends debase.
Believe thy fables, and the Trojan town

Triumphant stands ; the Grecians are o'erthrown ;
Suppliant at Hector's feet Achilles lies ;
And Diomede from fierce Æneas flies !
Say, rapid Aufidus with awful dread
Runs backward from the sea, and hides his head,
When the great Trojan on his bank appears ;
For that's as true as thy dissembled fears
Of my revenge : dismiss that vanity :
Thou, Drances, art below a death from me.
Let that vile soul in that vile body rest,
The lodging is well worthy of the guest.
Now, royal father, to the present state
Of our affairs, and of this high debate—
If in your arms thus early you diffide,
And think your fortune is already tried ;
If one defeat has brought us down so low,
As never more in fields to meet the foe ;
Then I conclude for peace : 'tis time to treat,
And lie like vassals at the victor's feet.
But, oh ! if any ancient blood remains,
One drop of all our father's, in our veins,
That man would I prefer before the rest,
Who dared his death with an undaunted breast ;
Who comely fell by no dishonest wound,
To shun that sight, and, dying, gnawed the ground.
But, if we still have fresh recruits in store,
If our confederates can afford us more ;
If the contended field we bravely fought,
And not a bloodless victory was bought ;
Their losses equalled ours ; and, for their slain,
With equal fires they filled the shining plain ;
Why thus, unforced, should we so tamely yield,
And, ere the trumpet sounds, resign the field ?
Good unexpected, evils unforeseen,
Appear by turns, as Fortune shifts the scene.
Some, raised aloft, come tumbling down amain ;
Then fall so hard, they bound and rise again.
If Diomede refuse his aid to lend,
The great Messapus yet remains our friend :
Tolumnius, who foretells events, is ours ;

The Italian chiefs, and princes, join their powers ;
Nor least in number, nor in name the last,
Your own brave subjects have our cause embraced.
Above the rest, the Volscian Amazon
Contains an army in herself alone,
And heads a squadron, terrible to sight,
With glittering shields, in brazen armour bright.
Yet, if the foe a single fight demand,
And I alone the public peace withstand ;
If you consent, he shall not be refused,
Nor find a hand to victory unused.
This new Achilles, let him take the field,
With fated armour, and Vulcanian shield !
For you, my royal father, and my fame,
I, Turnus, not the least of all my name,
Devote. my soul.   He calls me hand to hand ;
And I alone will answer his demand.
Drances shall rest secure, and neither share
The danger, nor divide the prize, of war.'
     While they debate, nor these nor those will yield,
Æneas draws his forces to the field,
And moves his camp.   The scouts with flying speed
Return, and through the frighted city spread
The unpleasing news : ' The Trojans are described,
In battle marching by the river-side,
And bending to the town.'   They take the alarm :
Some tremble ; some are bold ; all in confusion arm.
The impetuous youth press forward to the field ;
They clash the sword, and clatter on the shield :
The fearful matrons raise a screaming cry ;
Old feeble men with fainter groans reply ;
A jarring sound results, and mingles in the sky,
Like that of swans remurmuring to the floods,
Or birds of differing kinds in hollow woods.
Turnus the occasion takes, and cries aloud :
' Talk on, ye quaint haranguers of the crowd ;
Declaim in praise of peace, when danger calls,
And the fierce foes in arms approach the walls.'
He said, and, turning short with speedy pace,
Casts back a scornful glance, and quits the place.

'Thou, Volusus, the Volscian troops command
To mount ; and lead thyself our Ardean band.
Messapus, and Catillus, post your force
Along the fields, to charge the Trojan horse.
Some guard the passes ; others man the wall ;
Drawn up in arms, the rest attend my call.'

They swarm from every quarter of the town,
And with disordered haste the rampires crown.
Good old Latinus, when he saw, too late,
The gathering storm just breaking on the state,
Dismissed the council till a fitter time,
And owned his easy temper as his crime,
Who, forced against his reason, had complied
To break the treaty for the promised bride.

Some help to sink new trenches ; others aid
To ram the stones, or raise the palisade.
Hoarse trumpets sound the alarm : around the walls
Runs a distracted crew, whom their last labour calls.
A sad procession in the streets is seen,
Of matrons, that attend the mother queen :
High in her chair she sits, and, at her side,
With downcast eyes, appears the fatal bride.
They mount the cliff, where Pallas' temple stands ;
Prayers in their mouths, and presents in their hands.
With censers first they fume the sacred shrine,
Then in this common supplication join :
'O patroness of arms ! unspotted maid !
Propitious hear, and lend thy Latins aid !
Break short the pirate's lance ; pronounce his fate,
And lay the Phrygian low before the gate.'

Now Turnus arms for fight. His back and breast
Well-tempered steel and scaly brass invest :
The cuishes, which his brawny thighs infold,
Are mingled metal damasked o'er with gold.
His faithful falchion sits upon his side ;
Nor casque, nor crest, his manly features hide
But, bare to view, amid surrounding friends,
With godlike grace, he from the tower descends.
Exulting in his strength, he seems to dare
His absent rival, and to promise war.

Freed from his keepers, thus, with broken reins,
The wanton courser prances o'er the plains,
Or in the pride of youth o'erleaps the mounds,
And snuffs the females in forbidden grounds;
Or seeks his watering in the well-known flood,
To quench his thirst, and cool his fiery blood:
He swims luxuriant in the liquid plain,
And o'er his shoulder flows his waving mane:
He neighs, he snorts, he bears his head on high;
Before his ample chest the frothy waters fly.

Soon as the prince appears without the gate,
The Volscians, and their virgin leader, wait
His last commands. Then, with a graceful mien,
Lights from her lofty steed the warrior-queen:
Her squadron imitates, and each descends;
Whose common suit Camilla thus commends:
'If sense of honour, if a soul secure
Of inborn worth, that can all tests endure,
Can promise aught, or on itself rely,
Greatly to dare to conquer or to die;
Then, I alone, sustained by these, will meet
The Tyrrhene troops, and promise their defeat.
Ours be the danger, ours the sole renown:
You, general, stay behind, and guard the town.'
Turnus awhile stood mute with glad surprise,
And on the fierce virago fixed his eyes,
Then thus returned: 'O grace of Italy!
With what becoming thanks can I reply?
Not only words lie labouring in my breast,
But thought itself is by thy praise oppressed.
Yet rob me not of all; but let me join
My toils, my hazard, and my fame, with thine.
The Trojan, not in stratagem unskilled,
Sends his light horse before to scour the field:
Himself, through steep ascents and thorny brakes,
A larger compass to the city takes.
This news my scouts confirm: and I prepare
To foil his cunning, and his force to dare;
With chosen foot his passage to forelay,
And place an ambush in the winding way.

Thou, with thy Volscians, face the Tuscan horse:
The brave Messapus shall my troops inforce
With those of Tibur, and the Latian band,
Subjected all to thy supreme command.'
    This said, he warns Messapus to the war,
Then every chief exhorts with equal care.
All thus encouraged, his own troop he joins,
And hastes to prosecute his deep designs.
    Inclosed with hills, a winding valley lies,
By nature formed for fraud, and fitted for surprise.
A narrow track, by human steps untrode,
Leads, through perplexing thorns, to this obscure abode.
High o'er the vale a steepy mountain stands,
Whence the surveying sight the nether ground com-
      mands.
The top is level—an offensive seat
Of war ; and from the war a safe retreat :
For, on the right and left, is room to press
The foes at hand, or from afar distress ;
To drive them headlong downward ; and to pour,
On their descending backs, a stony shower.
Thither young Turnus took the well-known way,
Possessed the pass, and in blind ambush lay.
    Meantime, Latonian Phœbe, from the skies,
Beheld the approaching war with hateful eyes,
And called the light-foot Opis to her aid,
Her most beloved and ever-trusty maid ;
Then with a sigh began : ' Camilla goes
To meet her death amidst her fatal foes—
The nymph I loved of all my mortal train,
Invested with Diana's arms, in vain.
Nor is my kindness for the virgin new :
'Twas born with her ; and with her years it grew.
Her father Metabus, when forced away
From old Privernum for tyrannic sway,
Snatched up, and saved from his prevailing foes,
This tender babe, companion of his woes.
Casmilla was her mother ; but he drowned
One hissing letter in a softer sound,
And called Camilla.   Through the woods he flies ;

Wrapped in his robe the royal infant lies.
His foes in sight, he mends his weary pace;
With shouts and clamours they pursue the chase.
The banks of Amasene at length he gains;
The raging flood his farther flight restrains,
Raised o'er the borders with unusual rains.
Prepared to plunge into the stream, he fears,
Not for himself, but for the charge he bears.
Anxious, he stops awhile, and thinks in haste,
Then, desperate in distress, resolves at last.
A knotty lance of well-boiled oak he bore;
The middle part with cork he covered o'er:
He closed the child within the hollow space;
With twigs of bending osier bound the case,
Then poised the spear, heavy with human weight,
And thus invoked my favour for the freight:
"Accept, great goddess of the woods (he said),
Sent by her sire, this dedicated maid!
Through air she flies a suppliant to thy shrine;
And the first weapons that she knows, are thine."
He said; and with full force the spear he threw:
Above the sounding waves Camilla flew.
Then, pressed by foes, he stemmed the stormy tide,
And gained, by stress of arms, the farther side.
His fastened spear he pulled from out the ground,
And, victor of his vows, his infant nymph unbound;
Nor, after that, in towns which walls inclose,
Would trust his hunted life amidst his foes;
But, rough, in open air he chose to lie;
Earth was his couch, his covering was the sky.
On hills unshorn, or in a desert den,
He shunned the dire society of men.
A shepherd's solitary life he led;
His daughter with the milk of mares he fed.
The dugs of bears, and every savage beast,
He drew, and through her lips the liquor pressed.
The little Amazon could scarcely go—
He loads her with a quiver and a bow;
And, that she might her staggering steps command,
He with a slender javelin fills her hand.

Her flowing hair no golden fillet bound :
Nor swept her trailing robe the dusty ground.
Instead of these, a tiger's hide o'erspread
Her back and shoulders, fastened to her head.
The flying dart she first attempts to fling,
And round her tender temples tossed the sling ;
Then, as her strength with years increased, began
To pierce aloft in air the soaring swan,
And from the clouds to fetch the heron and the crane.
The Tuscan matrons with each other vied,
To bless their rival sons with such a bride :
But she disdains their love, to share with me
The sylvan shades, and vowed virginity.
And, oh ! I wish, contented with my cares
Of savage spoils, she had not sought the wars :
Then had she been of my celestial train,
And shunned the fate that dooms her to be slain.
But since, opposing heaven's decree, she goes
To find her death among forbidden foes,
Haste with these arms, and take thy steepy flight,
Where, with the gods averse, the Latins fight.
This bow to thee, this quiver, I bequeath,
This chosen arrow, to revenge her death :
By whate'er hand Camilla shall be slain,
Or of the Trojan or Italian train,
Let him not pass unpunished from the plain.
Then, in a hollow cloud, myself will aid
To bear the breathless body of my maid :
Unspoiled shall be her arms, and unprofaned
Her holy limbs with any human hand,
And in a marble tomb laid in her native land.'
    She said.   The faithful nymph descends from high
With rapid flight, and cuts the sounding sky :
Black clouds and stormy winds around her body fly.
    By this, the Trojan and the Tuscan horse,
Drawn up in squadrons, with united force
Approach the walls : the sprightly coursers bound,
Press forward on their bits, and shift their ground.
Shields, arms, and spears, flash horribly from far ;
And the fields glitter with a waving war.

Opposed to these, come on with furious force
Messapus, Coras, and the Latian horse;
These in the body placed, on either hand
Sustained and closed by fair Camilla's band.
Advancing in a line, they couch their spears;
And less and less the middle space appears.
Thick smoke obscures the field; and scarce are seen
The neighing coursers, and the shouting men.
In distance of their darts they stop their course;
Then man to man they rush, and horse to horse.
The face of heaven their flying javelins hide,
And deaths unseen are dealt on either side.
Tyrrhenus, and Aconteus void of fear,
By mettled coursers borne in full career,
Meet first opposed; and, with a mighty shock,
Their horses' heads against each other knock.
Far from his steed is fierce Aconteus cast,
As with an engine's force, or lightning's blast:
He rolls along in blood, and breathes his last.
The Latian squadrons take a sudden fright,
And sling their shields behind, to save their backs in
    flight.
Spurring at speed, to their own walls they drew:
Close in the rear the Tuscan troops pursue,
And urge their flight: Asylas leads the chase;
Till, seized with shame, they wheel about, and face,
Receive their foes, and raise a threatening cry.
The Tuscans take their turn to fear and fly.
   So swelling surges, with a thundering roar,
Driven on each other's backs, insult the shore,
Bound o'er the rocks, encroach upon the land,
And far upon the beach eject the sand;
Then backward, with a swing, they take their way,
Repulsed from upper ground, and seek their mother
    sea;
With equal hurry quit the invaded shore,
And swallow back the sand and stones they spewed
    before.
Twice were the Tuscans masters of the field,
Twice by the Latins, in their turn, repelled.

Ashamed at length, to the third charge they ran—
Both hosts resolved, and mingled man to man.
Now dying groans are heard; the fields are strewed
With falling bodies, and are drunk with blood.
Arms, horses, men, on heaps together lie;
Confused the fight, and more confused the cry.

Orsilochus, who durst not press too near
Strong Remulus, at distance drove his spear,
And stuck the steel beneath his horse's ear.
The fiery steed, impatient of the wound,
Curvets, and, springing upward with a bound,
His helpless lord cast backward on the ground.
Catillus pierced Iölas first; then drew
His reeking lance, and at Herminius threw,
The mighty champion of the Tuscan crew.
His neck and throat unarmed, his head was bare,
But shaded with a length of yellow hair:
Secure, he fought, exposed on every part,
A spacious mark for swords, and for the flying dart.
Across the shoulders came the feathered wound;
Transfixed, he fell, and doubled to the ground.

The sands with streaming blood are sanguine dyed,
And death, with honour, sought on either side.

Resistless, through the war Camilla rode,
In danger unappalled, and pleased with blood.
One side was bare for her exerted breast;
One shoulder with her painted quiver pressed.
Now from afar her fatal javelins play;
Now with her axe's edge, she hews her way:
Diana's arms upon her shoulder sound;
And when, too closely pressed, she quits the ground,
From her bent bow she sends a backward wound.
Her maids, in martial pomp, on either side,
Larina, Tulla, fierce Tarpeia, ride—
Italians all—in peace their queen's delight;
In war, the bold companions of the fight.

So marched the Thracian Amazons of old,
When Thermoden with bloody billows rolled:
Such troops as these in shining arms were seen,
When Theseus met in fight their maiden queen:

Such to the field Penthesilea led,
From the fierce virgin when the Grecians fled;
With such returned triumphant from the war.
Her maids with cries attend the lofty car;
They clash with manly force their moony shields;
With female shouts resound the Phrygian fields.
  Who foremost, and who last, heroic maid,
On the cold earth were by thy courage laid?
Thy spear, of mountain-ash, Eunæus first,
With fury driven, from side to side transpierced:
A purple stream came spouting from the wound;
Bathed in his blood he lies, and bites the ground.
Liris and Pegasus at once she slew:
The former, as the slackened reins he drew,
Of his faint steed—the latter, as he stretched
His arm to prop his friend—the javelin reached.
By the same weapon, sent from the same hand,
Both fall together, and both spurn the sand.
Amastrus next is added to the slain:
The rest in rout she follows o'er the plain:
Tereus, Harpalycus, Demophoon,
And Chromis, at full speed her fury shun.
Of all her deadly darts, not one she lost;
Each was attended with a Trojan ghost.
  Young Ornytus bestrode a hunter steed,
Swift for the chase, and of Apulian breed.
Him, from afar, she spied in arms unknown:
O'er his broad back an ox's hide was thrown;
His helm a wolf, whose gaping jaws were spread
A covering for his cheeks, and grinned around his head.
He clenched within his hand an iron prong,
And towered above the rest, conspicuous in the throng.
Him soon she singled from the flying train,
And slew with ease; then thus insults the slain:
'Vain hunter! didst thou think through woods to chase
The savage herd, a vile and trembling race?
Here cease thy vaunts, and own my victory:
A woman warrior was too strong for thee.
Yet, if the ghosts demand the conqueror's name,
Confessing great Camilla, save thy shame.'

Then Butès and Orsilochus she slew,
The bulkiest bodies of the Trojan crew—
But Butès breast to breast: the spear descends
Above the gorget, where his helmet ends,
And o'er the shield which his left side defends.
Orsilochus, and she, their coursers ply:
He seems to follow, and she seems to fly.
But in a narrower ring she makes the race;
And then he flies, and she pursues the chase.
Gathering at length on her deluded foe,
She swings her axe, and rises to the blow;
Full on the helm behind, with such a sway
The weapon falls, the riven steel gives way:
He groans, he roars, he sues in vain for grace:
Brains, mingled with his blood, besmear his face.
Astonished Aunus just arrives by chance,
To see his fall, nor farther dares advance;
But, fixing on the horrid maid his eye,
He stares, and shakes, and finds it vain to fly;
Yet, like a true Ligurian, born to cheat,
(At least while Fortune favoured his deceit),
Cries out aloud: 'What courage have you shewn,
Who trust your courser's strength, and not your own?
Forego the 'vantage of your horse, alight,
And then on equal terms begin the fight:
It shall be seen, weak woman, what you can,
When foot to foot, you combat with a man.'
He said. She glows with anger and disdain,
Dismounts with speed to dare him on the plain,
And leaves her horse at large among her train;
With her drawn sword defies him to the field,
And, marching, lifts aloft her maiden shield.
The youth, who thought his cunning did succeed,
Reins round his horse, and urges all his speed:
Adds the remembrance of the spur, and hides
The goring rowels in his bleeding sides.
'Vain fool, and coward! (said the lofty maid),
Caught in the train which thou thyself hast laid!
On others practise thy Ligurian arts:
Thin stratagems, and tricks of little hearts,

Are lost on me ; nor shalt thou safe retire,
With vaunting lies, to thy fallacious sire.'
   At this, so fast her flying feet she sped,
That soon she strained beyond his horse's head :
Then turning short, at once she seized the rein,
And laid the boaster grovelling on the plain.
Not with more ease the falcon, from above,
Trusses, in middle air, the trembling dove,
Then plumes the prey, in her strong pounces bound :
The feathers, foul with blood, come tumbling to the
     ground.
   Now mighty Jove, from his superior height,
With his broad eye surveys the unequal fight.
He fires the breast of Tarchon with disdain,
And sends him to redeem the abandoned plain.
Between the broken ranks the Tuscan rides,
And these encourages, and those he chides ;
Recalls each leader, by his name, from flight ;
Renews their ardour, and restores the fight.
' What panic fear has seized your souls ?   O shame,
O brand perpetual of the Etrurian name !
Cowards incurable ! a woman's hand
Drives, breaks, and scatters, your ignoble band !
Now cast away the sword, and quit the shield !
What use of weapons which you dare not wield ?
Not thus you fly your female foes by night,
Nor shun the feast, when the full bowls invite ;
When to fat offerings the glad augur calls,
And the shrill horn-pipe sounds to bacchanals.
These are your studied cares, your lewd delight—
Swift to debauch, but slow to manly fight.'
Thus having said, he spurs amidst the foes,
Not managing the life he meant to lose.
The first he found he seized, with headlong haste,
In his strong gripe, and clasped around the waist :
'Twas Venulus, whom from his horse he tore,
And (laid athwart his own) in triumph bore.
Loud shouts ensue ; the Latins turn their eyes,
And view the unusual sight with vast surprise.
The fiery Tarchon, flying o'er the plains,

Pressed in his arms the ponderous prey sustains,
Then, with his shortened spear, explores around
His jointed arms, to fix a deadly wound.
Nor less the captive struggles for his life:
He writhes his body to prolong the strife,
And, fencing for his naked throat, exerts
His utmost vigour, and the point averts.

So stoops the yellow eagle from on high,
And bears a speckled serpent through the sky,
Fastening his crooked talons on the prey:
The prisoner hisses through the liquid way;
Resists the royal hawk; and, though oppressed,
She fights in volumes, and erects her crest:
Turned to her foe, she stiffens every scale,
And shoots her forky tongue, and whisks her threaten-
    ing tail.
Against the victor, all defence is weak:
The imperial bird still plies her with his beak;
He tears her bowels, and her breast he gores,
Then claps his pinions, and securely soars.

Thus, through the midst of circling enemies,
Strong Tarchon snatched and bore away his prize.
The Tyrrhene troops, that shrunk before, now press
The Latins, and presume the like success.

Then Arruns, doomed to death, his arts essayed
To murder, unespied, the Volscian maid:
This way and that his winding course he bends,
And wheresoe'er she turns, her steps attends.
When she retires victorious from the chase,
He wheels about with care, and shifts his place:
When, rushing on, she seeks her foes in fight,
He keeps aloof, but keeps her still in sight;
He threats, and trembles, trying every way,
Unseen to kill, and safely to betray.

Chloreus, the priest of Cybele, from far,
Glittering in Phrygian arms amidst the war,
Was by the virgin viewed. The steed he pressed
Was proud with trappings; and his brawny chest
With scales of gilded brass was covered o'er:
A robe of Tyrian dye the rider wore.

With deadly wounds he galled the distant foe;
Gnossian his shafts, and Lycian was his bow:
A golden helm his front and head surrounds;
A gilded quiver from his shoulder sounds.
Gold, weaved with linen, on his thighs he wore,
With flowers of needle-work distinguished o'er,
With golden buckles bound, and gathered up before.
Him the fierce maid beheld with ardent eyes,
Fond and ambitious of so rich a prize,
Or that the temple might his trophies hold,
Or else to shine herself in Trojan gold.
Blind in her haste, she chases him alone,
And seeks his life, regardless of her own.
This lucky moment the sly traitor chose;
Then, starting from his ambush, up he rose,
And threw, but first to heaven addressed his vows
'O patron of Soracte's high abodes!
Phœbus, the ruling power among the gods!
Whom first we serve; whole woods of unctuous pine
Are felled for thee, and to thy glory shine;
By thee protected, with our naked soles,
Through flames unsinged we march, and tread the
        kindled coals.
Give me, propitious power, to wash away
The stains of this dishonourable day:
Nor spoils, nor triumph, from the fact I claim,
But with my future actions trust my fame.
Let me, by stealth, this female plague o'ercome,
And from the field return inglorious home.'
    Apollo heard, and, granting half his prayer,
Shuffled in winds the rest, and tossed in empty air.
He gives the death desired: his safe return
By southern tempests to the seas is borne.
    Now, when the javelin whizzed along the skies,
Both armies on Camilla turned their eyes,
Directed by the sound. Of either host,
The unhappy virgin, though concerned the most,
Was only deaf; so greedy was she bent
On golden spoils, and on her prey intent;
Till in her pap the wingèd weapon stood

Infixed, and deeply drunk the purple blood.
Her sad attendants hasten to sustain
Their dying lady drooping on the plain.
Far from their sight the trembling Arruns flies,
With beating heart, and fear confused with joys ;
Nor dares he farther to pursue his blow,
Or e'en to bear the sight of his expiring foe.
  As, when the wolf has torn a bullock's hide
At unawares, or ranched a shepherd's side,
Conscious of his audacious deed, he flies,
And claps his quivering tail between his thighs :
So, speeding once, the wretch no more attends,
But, spurring forward, herds among his friends.
She wrenched the javelin with her dying hands,
But wedged within her breast the weapon stands ;
The wood she draws, the steely point remains :
She staggers in her seat with agonizing pains
(A gathering mist o'erclouds her cheerful eyes ;
And from her cheeks the rosy colour flies) :
Then turns to her, whom, of her female train
She trusted most, and thus she speaks with pain :
' Acca, 'tis past ! he swims before my sight,
Inexorable Death ; and claims his right.
Bear my last words to Turnus : fly with speed,
And bid him timely to my charge succeed,
Repel the Trojans, and the town relieve :
Farewell ! and in this kiss my parting breath receive.'
She said, and, sliding, sunk upon the plain :
Dying, her opened hand forsakes the rein :
Short, and more short, she pants : by slow degrees
Her mind the passage from her body frees.
She drops her sword ; she nods her plumy crest,
Her drooping head declining on her breast ;
In the last sigh her struggling soul expires,
And, murmuring with disdain, to Stygian sounds retires.
  A shout, that struck the golden stars ensued ;
Despair and rage, and languished fight renewed.
The Trojan troops and Tuscans, in a line,
Advance to charge ; the mixed Arcadians join.
  But Cynthia's maid, high seated, from afar

Surveys the field, and fortune of the war,
Unmoved awhile, till, prostrate on the plain,
Weltering in blood, she sees Camilla slain,
And, round her corpse, of friends and foes a fighting
    train.
Then, from the bottom of her breast, she drew
A mournful sigh, and these sad words ensue :
' Too dear a fine, ah, much lamented maid !
For warring with the Trojans thou hast paid :
Nor aught availed, in this unhappy strife,
Diana's sacred arms, to save thy life.
Yet unrevenged thy goddess will not leave
Her votary's death, nor with vain sorrow grieve.
Branded the wretch, and be his name abhorred ;
But, after ages shall thy praise record.
The inglorious coward soon shall press the plain :
Thus vows thy queen, and thus the Fates ordain.'

    High o'er the field, there stood a hilly mound—
Sacred the place, and spread with oaks around—
Where, in a marble tomb, Dercennus lay,
A king that once in Latium bore the sway.
The beauteous Opis thither bent her flight,
To mark the traitor Arruns from the height.
Him in refulgent arms she soon espied,
Swoln with success ; and loudly thus she cried.
' Thy backward steps, vain boaster, are too late ;
Turn, like a man, at length, and meet thy fate.
Charged with my message, to Camilla go,
And say I sent thee to the shades below—
An honour undeserved from Cynthia's bow.'

    She said, and from her quiver chose with speed
The wingèd shaft, predestined for the deed ;
Then to the stubborn yew her strength applied,
Till the far-distant horns approached on either side.
The bow-string touched her breast, so strong she drew ;
Whizzing in air the fatal arrow flew.
At once the twanging bow and sounding dart
The traitor heard, and felt the point within his heart.
Him, beating with his heels in pangs of death,
His flying friends to foreign fields bequeath.

The conquering damsel, with expanded wings,
The welcome message to her mistress brings.
    Their leader lost, the Volscians quit the field ;
And, unsustained, the chiefs of Turnus yield.
The frighted soldiers, when their captains fly,
More on their speed than on their strength rely.
Confused in flight, they bear each other down,
And spur their horses headlong to the town.
Driven by their foes, and to their fears resigned,
Not once they turn, but take their wounds behind.
These drop the shield, and those the lance forego,
Or on their shoulders bear the slackened bow.
The hoofs of horses, with a rattling sound,
Beat short and thick, and shake the rotten ground.
Black clouds of dust come rolling in the sky,
And o'er the darkened walls and rampires fly.
The trembling matrons, from their lofty stands,
Rend heaven with female shrieks, and wring their
    hands.
All pressing on, pursuers and pursued,
Are crushed in crowds, a mingled multitude.
Some happy few escape : the throng too late
Rush on for entrance, till they choke the gate.
E'en in the sight of home, the wretched sire
Looks on, and sees his helpless son expire.
Then, in a fright, the folding gates they close,
But leave their friends excluded with their foes.
The vanquished cry ; the victors loudly shout :
'Tis terror all within, and slaughter all without.
Blind in their fear, they bounce against the wall,
Or, to the moats pursued, precipitate their fall.
    The Latian virgins, valiant with despair,
Armed on the towers, the common danger share :
So much of zeal their country's cause inspired ;
So much Camilla's great example fired.
Poles, sharpened in the flames, from high they throw,
With imitated darts to gall the foe.
Their lives for godlike freedom they bequeath,
And crowd each other to be first in death.
Meantime to Turnus, ambushed in the shade,

With heavy tidings came the unhappy maid :
'The Volscians overthrown—Camilla killed—
The foes entirely masters of the field,
Like a resistless flood, come rolling on :
The cry goes off the plain, and thickens to the town.'
  Inflamed with rage (for so the Furies fire
The Daunian's breast, and so the Fates require),
He leaves the hilly pass, the woods in vain
Possessed, and downward issues on the plain.
Scarce was he gone, when to the straits, now freed
From secret foes, the Trojan troops succeed.
Through the black forest and the ferny brake,
Unknowingly secure, their way they take ;
From the rough mountains to the plain descend,
And there, in order drawn, their line extend.
Both armies now in open fields are seen ;
Not far the distance of the space between.
Both to the city bend. Æneas sees,
Through smoking fields, his hastening enemies ;
And Turnus views the Trojans in array,
And hears the approaching horses proudly neigh.
Soon had their hosts in bloody battle joined ;
But westward to the sea the sun declined.
Intrenched before the town, both armies lie,
While night with sable wings involves the sky.

BOOK XII

THE ARGUMENT

Turnus challenges Æneas to a single combat: articles are agreed on, but broken by the Rutuli, who wound Æneas. He is miraculously cured by Venus, forces Turnus to a duel, and concludes the poem with his death.

WHEN Turnus saw the Latins leave the field,
Their armies broken, and their courage quelled,
Himself become the mark of public spite,
His honour questioned for the promised fight—
The more he was with vulgar hate oppressed,
The more his fury boiled within his breast:
He roused his vigour for the last debate,
And raised his haughty soul, to meet his fate.

As, when the swains the Libyan lion chase,
He makes a sour retreat, nor mends his pace;
But, if the pointed javelin pierce his side,
The lordly beast returns with double pride:
He wrenches out the steel; he roars for pain;
His sides he lashes, and erects his mane:
So Turnus fares: his eye-balls flash with fire;
Through his wide nostrils clouds of smoke expire.

Trembling with rage, around the court he ran;
At length approached the king, and thus began:
'No more excuses or delays: I stand
In arms prepared to combat, hand to hand,
This base deserter of his native land.
The Trojan, by his word, is bound to take
The same conditions which himself did make.
Renew the truce; the solemn rites prepare,
And to my single virtue trust the war.

452

The Latians unconcerned shall see the fight :
This arm unaided shall assert your right :
Then, if my prostrate body press the plain,
To him the crown and beauteous bride remain.'
  To whom the king sedately thus replied :
' Brave youth ! the more your valour has been tried,
The more becomes it us, with due respect,
To weigh the chance of war, which you neglect.
You want not wealth, or a successive throne,
Or cities which your arms have made your own :
My towns and treasures are at your command ;
And stored with blooming beauties is my land :
Laurentum more than one Lavinia sees,
Unmarried, fair, of noble families.
Now let me speak, and you with patience hear,
Things which perhaps may grate a lover's ear,
But sound advice, proceeding from a heart
Sincerely yours, and free from fraudful art.
The gods, by signs, have manifestly shown,
No prince, Italian born, should heir my throne :
Oft have our augurs, in prediction skilled,
And oft our priests, a foreign son revealed.
Yet, won by worth that cannot be withstood,
Bribed by my kindness to my kindred blood,
Urged by my wife, who would not be denied,
I promised my Lavinia for your bride :
Her from her plighted lord by force I took ;
All ties of treaties, and of honour, broke :
On your account I waged an impious war—
With what success, 'tis needless to declare ;
I and my subjects feel, and you have had your share.
Twice vanquished while in bloody fields we strive,
Scarce in our walls we keep our hopes alive :
The rolling flood runs warm with human gore ;
The bones of Latians blanch the neighbouring shore.
Why put I not an end to this debate,
Still unresolved, and still a slave to fate ?
If Turnus' death a lasting peace can give,
Why should I not procure it whilst you live ?
Should I to doubtful arms your youth betray,

What would my kinsmen, the Rutulians, say?
And, should you fall in fight (which Heaven defend!)
How curse the cause, which hastened to his end
The daughter's lover, and the father's friend?
Weigh in your mind the various chance of war;
Pity your parent's age, and ease his care.'

Such balmy words he poured, but all in vain:
The proffered med'cine but provoked the pain.
The wrathful youth, disdaining the relief,
With intermitting sobs thus vents his grief:
'The care, O best of fathers! which you take
For my concerns, at my desire forsake.
Permit me not to languish out my days,
But make the best exchange of life for praise.
This arm, this lance, can well dispute the prize;
And the blood follows where the weapon flies.
His goddess-mother is not near, to shroud
The flying coward with an empty cloud.'

But now the queen, who feared for Turnus' life,
And loathed the hard conditions of the strife,
Held him by force; and, dying in his death,
In these sad accents gave her sorrow breath:
'O Turnus! I adjure thee by these tears,
And whate'er prince Amata's honour bears
Within thy breast, since thou art all my hope,
My sickly mind's repose, my sinking age's prop—
Since on the safety of thy life alone
Depends Latinus, and the Latian throne—
Refuse me not this one, this only prayer,
To waive the combat, and pursue the war.
Whatever chance attends this fatal strife,
Think it includes, in thine, Amata's life.
I cannot live a slave, or see my throne
Usurped by strangers, or a Trojan son.'

At this, a flood of tears Lavinia shed;
A crimson blush her beauteous face o'erspread,
Varying her cheeks by turns with white and red,
The driving colours, never at a stay,
Run here and there, and flush and fade away.
Delightful change! Thus Indian ivory shows,

Which with the bordering paint of purple glows ;
Or lilies damasked by the neighbouring rose.
The lover gazed, and, burning with desire,
The more he looked, the more he fed the fire :
Revenge, and jealous rage, and secret spite,
Roll in his breast, and rouse him to the fight.
    Then fixing on the queen his ardent eyes,
Firm to his first intent, he thus replies :
' O mother ! do not by your tears prepare
Such boding omens, and prejudge the war :
Resolved on fight, I am no longer free
To shun my death, if heaven my death decree.'
Then turning to the herald, thus pursues :
' Go, greet the Trojan with ungrateful news ;
Denounce from me, that, when to-morrow's light
Shall gild the heavens, he need not urge the fight :
The Trojan and Rutulian troops no more
Shall dye, with mutual blood, the Latian shore :
Our single swords the quarrel shall decide,
And to the victor be the beauteous bride.'
    He said, and striding on, with speedy pace,
He sought his coursers of the Thracian race.
At his approach, they toss their heads on high,
And, proudly neighing, promise victory.
The sires of these Orithyia sent from far,
To grace Pilumnus, when he went to war.
The drifts of Thracian snows were scarce so white,
Nor northern winds in fleetness matched their flight.
Officious grooms stand ready by his side ;
And some with combs their flowing manes divide,
And others stroke their chests, and gently soothe their
    pride.
    He sheathed his limbs in arms ; a tempered mass
Of golden metal those, and mountain-brass.
Then to his head his glittering helm he tied,
And girt his faithful falchion to his side.
In his Ætnæan forge, the god of fire
That falchion laboured for the hero's sire,
Immortal keenness on the blade bestowed,
And plunged it hissing in the Stygian flood.

Propped on a pillar, which the ceiling bore,
Was placed the lance Auruncan Actor wore;
Which with such force he brandished in his hand,
The tough ash trembled like an osier wand:
Then cried: 'O ponderous spoil of Actor slain,
And never yet by Turnus tossed in vain!
Fail not this day thy wonted force; but go,
Sent by this hand, to pierce the Trojan foe:
Give me to tear his corselet from his breast,
And from that eunuch head to rend the crest;
Dragged in the dust, his frizzled hair to soil,
Hot from the vexing iron, and smeared with fragrant oil.'

Thus while he raves, from his wide nostrils flies
A fiery steam, and sparkles from his eyes.
So fares the bull in his loved female's sight:
Proudly he bellows, and preludes the fight:
He tries his goring horns against a tree,
And meditates his absent enemy:
He pushes at the winds; he digs the strand
With his black hoofs, and spurns the yellow sand.

Nor less the Trojan, in his Lemnian arms,
To future fight his manly courage warms:
He whets his fury, and with joy prepares
To terminate at once the lingering wars;
To cheer his chiefs and tender son, relates
What heaven had promised, and expounds the fates.
Then to the Latian king he sends, to cease
The rage of arms, and ratify the peace.

The morn ensuing, from the mountain's height,
Had scarcely spread the skies with rosy light;
The ethereal coursers, bounding from the sea,
From out their flaming nostrils breathed the day;
When now the Trojan and Rutulian guard,
In friendly labour joined, the list prepared.
Beneath the walls, they measure out the space;
Then sacred altars rear, on sods of grass,
Where, with religious rites, their common gods they
place.
In purest white, the priests their heads attire,
And living waters bear, and holy fire;

And, o'er their linen hoods and shaded hair,
Long twisted wreaths of sacred vervain wear.

   In order issuing from the town, appears
The Latian legion, armed with pointed spears ;
And from the fields, advancing on a line,
The Trojan and the Tuscan forces join :
Their various arms afford a pleasing sight :
A peaceful train they seem, in peace prepared for fight.

   Betwixt the ranks the proud commanders ride,
Glittering with gold, and vests in purple dyed—
Here Mnestheus, author of the Memmian line,
And there Messapus, born of seed divine.
The sign is given ; and round the listed space,
Each man in order fills his proper place.
Reclining on their ample shields, they stand,
And fix their pointed lances in the sand.
Now, studious of the sight, a numerous throng
Of either sex promiscuous, old and young,
Swarm from the town : by those who rest behind,
The gates and walls, and houses' tops, are lined.

   Meantime the queen of heaven beheld the sight,
With eyes unpleased, from mount Albano's height :
(Since called Albano by succeeding fame,
But then an empty hill, without a name.)
She thence surveyed the field, the Trojan powers,
The Latian squadrons, and Laurentine towers.
Then thus the goddess of the skies bespake,
With sighs and tears, the goddess of the lake,
King Turnus' sister, once a lovely maid,
Ere to the lust of lawless Jove betrayed—
Compressed by force, but, by the grateful god,
Now made the Naïs of the neighbouring flood.
' O nymph, the pride of living lakes ! (said she)
O most renowned, and most beloved by me !
Long hast thou known, nor need I to record,
The wanton sallies of my wandering lord.
Of every Latian fair, whom Jove misled
To mount by stealth my violated bed,
To thee alone I grudged not his embrace,
But gave a part of heaven, and an unenvied place.

Now learn from me thy near-approaching grief,
Nor think my wishes want to thy relief.
While Fortune favoured, nor heaven's king denied
To lend my succour to the Latian side,
I saved thy brother, and the sinking state ;
But now he struggles with unequal fate,
And goes, with gods averse, o'ermatched in might,
To meet inevitable death in fight ;
Nor must I break the truce, nor can sustain the sight.
Thou, if thou dar'st, thy present aid supply :
It well becomes a sister's care to try.'
  At this the lovely nymph, with grief oppressed,
Thrice tore her hair, and beat her comely breast.
To whom Saturnia thus : 'Thy tears are late :
Haste, snatch him, if he can be snatched, from fate :
New tumults kindle ; violate the truce.
Who knows what changeful Fortune may produce ?
'Tis not a crime to attempt what I decree ;
Or, if it were, discharge the crime on me.'
She said, and sailing on the wingèd wind,
Left the sad nymph suspended in her mind.
  And now in pomp the peaceful kings appear :
Four steeds the chariot of Latinus bear :
Twelve golden beams around his temples play,
To mark his lineage from the god of day.
Two snowy coursers Turnus' chariot yoke,
And in his hand two massy spears he shook.
Then, issued from the camp, in arms divine,
Æneas, author of the Roman line ;
And by his side Ascanius took his place,
The second hope of Rome's immortal race.
Adorned in white, a reverend priest appears,
And offerings to the flaming altars bears—
A porket, and a lamb that never suffered shears.
Then to the rising sun he turns his eyes,
And strews the beasts, designed for sacrifice,
With salt and meal : with like officious care
He marks their foreheads, and he clips their hair.
Betwixt their horns the purple wine he sheds ;
With the same generous juice the flame he feeds.

Æneas then unsheathed his shining sword,
And thus with pious prayers the gods adored :
  ' All-seeing sun ! and thou, Ausonian soil,
For which I have sustained so long a toil,
Thou, king of heaven ! and thou, the queen of air,
Propitious now, and reconciled by prayer ;
Thou, god of war, whose unresisted sway
The labours and events of arms obey !
Ye living fountains, and ye running floods !
All powers of ocean, all ethereal gods !
Hear, and bear record : if I fall in field,
Or, recreant in the fight, to Turnus yield,
My Trojans shall increase Evander's town ;
Ascanius shall renounce the Ausonian crown :
All claims, all questions of debate, shall cease ;
Nor he, nor they, with force infringe the peace.
But, if my juster arms prevail in fight
(As sure they shall, if I divine aright),
My Trojans shall not o'er the Italians reign ;
Both equal, both unconquered, shall remain,
Joined in their laws, their lands, and their abodes :
I ask but altars for my weary gods.
The care of those religious rites be mine :
The crown to king Latinus I resign :
His be the sovereign sway. Nor will I share
His power in peace, or his command in war.
For me, my friends another town shall frame,
And bless the rising towers with fair Lavinia's name.'
  Thus he. Then, with erected eyes and hands,
The Latian king before his altar stands.
' By the same heaven (said he), and earth, and main,
And all the powers that all the three contain ;
By hell below, and by that upper god,
Whose thunder signs the peace, who seals it with his
    nod ;
So let Latona's double offspring hear,
And double-fronted Janus, what I swear :
I touch the sacred altars, touch the flames,
And all those powers attest, and all their names :
Whatever chance befal on either side,

No term of time this union shall divide :
No force, no fortune, shall my vows unbind,
Or shake the steadfast tenor of my mind ;
Not, though the circling seas should break their bound,
O'erflow the shores, and sap the solid ground ;
Not, though the lamps of heaven their spheres forsake,
Hurled down, and hissing in the nether lake :
E'en as this royal sceptre (for he bore
A sceptre in his hand) shall never more
Shoot out in branches, or renew the birth—
An orphan now, cut from the mother earth
By the keen axe, dishonoured of its hair,
And cased in brass, for Latian kings to bear.'

When thus in public view the peace was tied
With solemn vows, and sworn on either side,
All dues performed which holy rites require,
The victim beasts are slain before the fire,
The trembling entrails from their bodies torn,
And to the fattened flames in chargers borne.

Already the Rutulians deemed their man
O'ermatched in arms, before the fight began.
First rising fears are whispered through the crowd ;
Then, gathering sound, they murmur more aloud.
Now, side to side, they measure with their eyes
The champions' bulk, their sinews, and their size :
The nearer they approach, the more is known
The apparent disadvantage of their own.
Turnus himself appears in public sight
Conscious of fate, desponding of the fight.
Slowly he moves, and at his altar stands
With eyes dejected, and with trembling hands :
And, while he mutters undistinguished prayers,
A livid deadness in his cheeks appears.

With anxious pleasure when Juturna viewed
The increasing fright of the mad multitude,
When their short sighs and thickening sobs she heard,
And found their ready minds for change prepared ;
Dissembling her immortal form, she took
Camertes' mien, his habit, and his look—
A chief of ancient blood :—in arms well known

Was his great sire, and he his greater son.
His shape assumed, amid the ranks she ran,
And humouring their first motions, thus began:
'For shame, Rutulians! can you bear the sight
Of one exposed for all, in single fight?
Can we, before the face of Heaven, confess
Our courage colder, or our numbers less?
View all the Trojan host, the Arcadian band,
And Tuscan army; count them as they stand:
Undaunted to the battle if we go,
Scarce every second man will share a foe.
Turnus, 'tis true, in this unequal strife,
Shall lose, with honour, his devoted life,
Or change it rather for immortal fame,
Succeeding to the gods, from whence he came:
But you, a servile and inglorious band,
For foreign lords shall sow your native land,
Those fruitful fields your fighting fathers gained,
Which have so long their lazy sons sustained.'
    With words like these, she carried her design.
A rising murmur runs along the line.
Then e'en the city troops, and Latians, tired
With tedious war, seem with new souls inspired:
Their champion's fate with pity they lament,
And of the league, so lately sworn, repent.
    Nor fails the goddess to foment the rage
With lying wonders, and a false presage;
But adds a sign, which, present to their eyes,
Inspires new courage, and a glad surprise.
For, sudden, in the fiery tracts above,
Appears in pomp the imperial bird of Jove:
A plump of fowl he spies, that swim the lakes,
And o'er their heads his sounding pinions shakes;
Then, stooping on the fairest of the train,
In his strong talons trussed a silver swan.
The Italians wonder at the unusual sight:
But while he lags, and labours in his flight,
Behold the dastard fowl return anew,
And with united force the foe pursue:
Clamorous around the royal hawk they fly,

And, thickening in a cloud, overshade the sky.
They cuff, they scratch, they cross his airy course;
Nor can the encumbered bird sustain their force;
But, vexed, not vanquished, drops the pond'rous prey,
And, lightened of his burden, wings his way.

The Ausonian bands with shouts salute the sight,
Eager of action, and demand the fight.
Then king Tolumnius, versed in augurs' arts,
Cries out, and thus his boasted skill imparts:
' At length 'tis granted, what I long desired!
This, this is what my frequent vows required.
Ye gods! I take your omen, and obey.—
Advance, my friends, and charge! I lead the way.
These are the foreign foes, whose impious band,
Like that rapacious bird, infest our land:
But soon, like him, they shall be forced to sea
By strength united, and forego the prey.
Your timely succour to your country bring;
Haste to the rescue, and redeem your king.'

He said: and pressing onward through the crew,
Poised in his lifted arm, his lance he threw.
The wingèd weapon, whistling in the wind,
Came driving on, nor missed the mark designed.
At once the cornel rattled in the skies;
At once tumultuous shouts and clamours rise.
Nine brothers in a goodly band there stood,
Born of Arcadian mixed with Tuscan blood,
Gylippus' sons: the fatal javelin flew,
Aimed at the midmost of the friendly crew.
A passage through the jointed arms it found,
Just where the belt was to the body bound,
And struck the gentle youth extended on the ground.
Then, fired with pious rage, the generous train
Run madly forward to revenge the slain.
And some with eager haste their javelins throw;
And some with sword in hand assault the foe.

The wished insult the Latine troops embrace,
And meet their ardour in the middle space.
The Trojans, Tuscans, and Arcadian line,
With equal courage obviate their design.

Peace leaves the violated fields ; and hate
Both armies urges to their mutual fate :
With impious haste their altars are o'erturned,
The sacrifice half broiled, and half unburned.
Thick storms of steel from either army fly,
And clouds of clashing darts obscure the sky :
Brands from the fire are missive weapons made,
With chargers, bowls, and all the priestly trade.
Latinus, frighted, hastens from the fray,
And bears his unregarded gods away.
These on their horses vault ; those yoke the car ;
The rest, with swords on high, run headlong to the war.

Messapus, eager to confound the peace,
Spurred his hot courser through the fighting press,
At king Aulestes, by his purple known
A Tuscan prince, and by his regal crown ;
And, with a shock encountering, bore him down.
Backward he fell ; and, as his fate designed,
The ruins of an altar were behind :
There pitching on his shoulders and his head,
Amid the scattering fires he lay supinely spread.
The beamy spear, descending from above,
His cuirass pierced, and through his body drove.
Then, with a scornful smile, the victor cries :
' The gods have found a fitter sacrifice.'
Greedy of spoils, the Italians strip the dead
Of his rich armour, and uncrown his head.

Priest Corynæus armed his better hand,
From his own altar, with a blazing brand ;
And, as Ebusus with a thundering pace
Advanced to battle, dashed it on his face :
His bristly beard shines out with sudden fires ;
The crackling crop a noisome scent expires.
Following the blow, he seized his curling crown
With his left hand ; his other cast him down.
The prostrate body with his knees he pressed,
And plunged his holy poinard in his breast.

While Podalirius, with his sword, pursued
The shepherd Alsus through the flying crowd,
Swiftly he turns, and aims a deadly blow

Full on the front of his unwary foe.
The broad axe enters with a crashing sound,
And cleaves the chin with one continued wound ;
Warm blood, and mingled brains, besmear his arms
　　around ;
And iron sleep his stupid eyes oppressed,
And sealed their heavy lids in endless rest.
But good Æneas rushed amid the bands :
Bare was his head, and naked were his hands,
In sign of truce : then thus he cries aloud :
' What sudden rage, what new desire of blood,
Inflames your altered minds ? O Trojans ! cease
From impious arms, nor violate the peace.
By human sanctions, and by laws divine,
The terms are all agreed ; the war is mine.
Dismiss your fears, and let the fight ensue ;
This hand alone shall right the gods and you :
Our injured altars, and their broken vow,
To this avenging sword the faithless Turnus owe.'

　　Thus while he spoke, unmindful of defence,
A wingèd arrow struck the pious prince.
But, whether from some human hand it came,
Or hostile god, is left unknown by fame :
No human hand, or hostile god, was found,
To boast the triumph of so base a wound.

　　When Turnus saw the Trojan quit the plain,
His chiefs dismayed, his troops a fainting train,
The unhoped event his heightened soul inspires :
At once his arms and coursers he requires ;
Then, with a leap, his lofty chariot gains,
And with a ready hand assumes the reins.
He drives impetuous, and, where'er he goes,
He leaves behind a lane of slaughtered foes.
These his lance reaches ; over those he rolls
His rapid car, and crushes out their souls.
In vain the vanquished fly : the victor sends
The dead men's weapons at their living friends.

　　Thus, on the banks of Hebrus' freezing flood,
The god of battles, in his angry mood,
Clashing his sword against his brazen shield,

Lets loose the reins, and scours along the field ;
Before the wind his fiery coursers fly ;
Groans the sad earth, resounds the rattling sky.
Wrath, Terror, Treason, Tumult, and Despair
(Dire faces, and deformed), surround the car—
Friends of the god, and followers of the war.

With fury not unlike, nor less disdain,
Exulting Turnus flies along the plain ;
His smoking horses, at their utmost speed,
He lashes on ; and urges o'er the dead.
Their fetlocks run with blood ; and, when they bound,
The gore and gathering dust are dashed around.
Thamyris and Pholus, masters of the war,
He killed at hand ; but Sthenelus afar :
From far the sons of Imbrasus he slew,
Glaucus and Lades, of the Lycian crew—
Both taught to fight on foot, in battle joined,
Or mount the courser that outstrips the wind.

Meantime Eumedes, vaunting in the field,
New fired the Trojans, and their foes repelled,
This son of Dolon bore his grandsire's name,
But emulated more his father's fame—
His guileful father, sent a nightly spy,
The Grecian camp and order to descry—
Hard enterprise ! and well he might require
Achilles' car and horses for his hire :
But, met upon the scout, the Ætolian prince
In death bestowed a juster recompense.

Fierce Turnus viewed the Trojan from afar,
And launched his javelin from his lofty car,
Then lightly leaping down, pursued the blow,
And, pressing with his foot his prostrate foe,
Wrenched from his feeble hold the shining sword,
And plunged it in the bosom of its lord.
' Possess (said he) the fruit of all thy pains,
And measure, at thy length, our Latian plains.
Thus are my foes rewarded by my hand ;
Thus may they build their town, and thus enjoy the land!'

Then Dares, Butes, Sybaris, he slew,
Whom o'er his neck the floundering courser threw.

As when loud Boreas, with his blustering train,
Stoops from above, incumbent on the main;
Where'er he flies, he drives the rack before,
And rolls the billows on the Ægean shore:
So, where resistless Turnus takes his course,
The scattered squadrons bend before his force:
His crest of horse's hair is blown behind
By adverse air, and rustles in the wind.

This haughty Phegeus saw with high disdain,
And, as the chariot rolled along the plain,
Light from the ground he leapt, and seized the rein.
Thus hung in air, he still retained his hold,
The coursers frighted, and their force controlled.
The lance of Turnus reached him as he hung,
And pierced his plated arms, but passed along,
And only razed the skin. He turned, and held
Against his threatening foe his ample shield,
Then called for aid: but, while he cried in vain,
The chariot bore him backward on the plain.
He lies reversed; the victor king descends,
And strikes so justly where his helmet ends,
He lops the head. The Latian fields are drunk
With streams that issue from his bleeding trunk.

While he triumphs, and while the Trojans yield,
The wounded prince is forced to leave the field:
Strong Mnestheus, and Achates often tried,
And young Ascanius, weeping by his side,
Conduct him to his tent. Scarce can he rear
His limbs from earth, supported on his spear.
Resolved in mind, regardless of the smart,
He tugs with both his hands, and breaks the dart.
The steel remains. No readier way he found
To draw the weapon, than t' enlarge the wound.
Eager of fight, impatient of delay,
He begs; and his unwilling friends obey.

Iäpis was at hand to prove his art,
Whose blooming youth so fired Apollo's heart,
That, for his love, he proffered to bestow
His tuneful harp, and his unerring bow:
The pious youth, more studious how to save

His aged sire, now sinking to the grave,
Preferred the power of plants, and silent praise
Of healing arts, before Phœbean bays.

Propped on his lance the pensive hero stood,
And heard and saw, unmoved, the mourning crowd.
The famed physician tucks his robes around
With ready hands, and hastens to the wound.
With gentle touches he performs his part,
This way and that, soliciting the dart,
And exercises all his heavenly art.
All softening simples, known of sovereign use,
He presses out, and pours their noble juice.
These first infused, to lenify the pain—
He tugs with pincers, but he tugs in vain.
Then to the patron of his art he prayed :
The patron of his art refused his aid.

Meantime the war approaches to the tents :
The alarm grows hotter, and the noise augments :
The driving dust proclaims the danger near ;
And first their friends and then their foes appear ;
Their friends retreat ; their foes pursue the rear.
The camp is filled with terror and affright :
The hissing shafts within the trench alight ;
An undistinguished noise ascends the sky—
The shouts of those who kill, and groans of those who die.

But now the goddess-mother, moved with grief,
And pierced with pity, hastens for relief.
A branch of healing dittany she brought,
Which in the Cretan fields with care she sought,
(Rough is the stem, which woolly leaves surround ;
The leaves with flowers, the flowers with purple crowned),
Well known to wounded goats ; a sure relief
To draw the pointed steel, and ease the grief.
This Venus brings, in clouds involved, and brews
The extracted liquor with ambrosian dews,
And odorous panacee. Unseen she stands,
Tempering the mixture with her heavenly hands,
And pours it in a bowl, already crowned
With juice of medic'nal herbs, prepared to bathe the
    wound.

The leech, unknowing of superior art
Which aids the cure, with this foments the part ;
And in a moment ceased, the raging smart.
Stanched is the blood, and in the bottom stands :
The steel, but scarcely touched with tender hands,
Moves up, and follows of its own accord,
And health and vigour are at once restored.
Iäpis first perceived the closing wound,
And first the footsteps of a god he found.
'Arms ! arms ! (he cries) the sword and shield prepare,
And send the willing chief, renewed, to war.
This is no mortal work, no cure of mine,
Nor art's effect, but done by hands divine.
Some god our general to the battle sends ;
Some god preserves his life for greater ends.'
    The hero arms in haste : his hands infold
His thighs with cuishes of refulgent gold :
Inflamed to fight, and rushing to the field,
That hand sustaining the celestial shield,
This gripes the lance, and with such vigour shakes,
That to the rest the beamy weapon quakes.
Then with a close embrace he strained his son,
And, kissing through his helmet, thus begun :
' My son ! from my example learn the war,
In camps to suffer, and in fields to dare ;
But happier chance than mine attend thy care !
This day my hand thy tender age shall shield,
And crown with honours of the conquered field :
Thou, when thy riper years shall send thee forth
To toils of war, be mindful of my worth :
Assert thy birthright ; and in arms be known
For Hector's nephew, and Æneas' son.'
    He said ; and, striding, issued on the plain.
Antheus and Mnestheus, and a numerous train,
Attend his steps : the rest their weapons take,
And, crowding to the field, the camp forsake.
A cloud of blinding dust is raised around ;
Labours beneath their feet the trembling ground.
    Now Turnus, posted on a hill, from far
Beheld the progress of the moving war :

With him the Latins viewed the covered plains ;
And the chill blood ran backward in their veins.
Juturna saw the advancing troops appear,
And heard the hostile sound, and fled for fear.
Æneas leads ; and draws a sweeping train,
Closed in their ranks, and pouring on the plain.
As when a whirlwind, rushing to the shore
From the mid ocean, drives the waves before ;
The painful hind with heavy heart foresees
The flatted fields, and slaughter of the trees :
With such impetuous rage the prince appears,
Before his doubled front ; nor less destruction bears.
And now both armies shock in open field :
Osiris, is by strong Thymbræus killed.
Archetius, Ufens, Epulon, are slain,
(All famed in arms, and of the Latian train),
By Gyas', Mnestheus' and Achates' hand.
The fatal augur falls, by whose command
The truce was broken, and whose lance, embrued
With Trojan blood, the unhappy fight renewed.
Loud shouts and clamours rend the liquid sky ;
And o'er the field the frighted Latins fly.
The prince disdains the dastards to pursue,
Nor moves to meet in arms the fighting few.
Turnus alone, amid the dusky plain,
He seeks, and to the combat calls in vain.
Juturna heard, and, seized with mortal fear,
Forced from the beam her brother's charioteer ;
Assumes his shape, his armour, and his mien,
And, like Metiscus, in his seat is seen.

As the black swallow near the palace plies ;
O'er empty courts, and under arches, flies ;
Now hawks aloft, now skims along the flood,
To furnish her loquacious nest with food :
So drives the rapid goddess o'er the plains ;
The smoking horses run with loosened reins.
She steers a various course among the foes ;
Now here, now there, her conquering brother shows ;
Now with a straight, now with a wheeling flight,
She turns and bends, but shuns the single fight.

Æneas, fired with fury, breaks the crowd,
And seeks his foe, and calls by name aloud:
He runs within a narrower ring, and tries
To stop the chariot; but the chariot flies.
If he but gain a glimpse, Juturna fears,
And far away the Daunian hero bears.

What should he do? Nor arts nor arms avail;
And various cares in vain his mind assail.
The great Messapus, thundering through the field,
In his left hand two pointed javelins held;
Encountering on the prince, one dart he drew,
And with unerring aim, and utmost vigour, threw.
Æneas saw it come, and stooping low
Beneath his buckler, shunned the threatening blow.
The weapon hissed above his head, and tore
The waving plume, which on his helm he wore.
Forced by this hostile act, and fired with spite,
That flying Turnus still declined the fight,
The prince, whose piety had long repelled
His inborn ardour, now invades the field;
Invokes the powers of violated peace,
Their rites and injured altars to redress;
Then, to his rage abandoning the rein,
With blood and slaughtered bodies fills the plain.

What god can tell, what numbers can display,
The various labours of that fatal day?
What chiefs and champions fell on either side,
In combat slain, or by what deaths they died?
Whom Turnus, whom the Trojan hero killed?
Who shared the fame and fortune of the field?
Jove! could'st thou view, and not avert thy sight,
Two jarring nations joined in cruel fight,
Whom leagues of lasting love so shortly shall unite?
Æneas first Rutulian Sucro found,
Whose valour made the Trojans quit their ground;
Betwixt his ribs the javelin drove so just,
It reached his heart, nor needs a second thrust.
Now Turnus, at two blows, two brethren slew:
First from his horse fierce Amycus he threw;
Then, leaping on the ground, on foot assailed

Diores, and in equal fight prevailed.
Their lifeless trunks he leaves upon the place ;
Their heads, distilling gore, his chariot grace.
   Three cold on earth the Trojan hero threw,
Whom without respite at one charge he slew :
Cethegus, Tanaïs, Talus, fell oppressed,
And sad Onytes, added to the rest—
Of Theban blood, whom Peridia bore.
   Turnus two brothers from the Lycian shore,
And from Apollo's fane to battle sent,
O'erthrew ; nor Phœbus could their fate prevent.
Peaceful Menœtes after these he killed,
Who long had shunned the dangers of the field :
On Lerna's lake a silent life he led,
And with his nets and angle earned his bread.
Nor pompous cares, nor palaces, he knew,
But wisely from the infectious world withdrew.
Poor was his house : his father's painful hand
Discharged his rent, and ploughed another's land.
   As flames among the lofty woods are thrown
On different sides, and both by winds are blown ;
The laurels crackle in the sputtering fire ;
The frighted sylvans from their shades retire :
Or as two neighbouring torrents fall from high,
Rapid they run ; the foamy waters fry ;
They roll to sea with unresisted force,
And down the rocks precipitate their course :
Not with less rage the rival heroes take
Their different ways ; nor less destruction make.
With spears afar, with swords at hand, they strike ;
And zeal of slaughter fires their souls alike.
Like them, their dauntless men maintain the field ;
And hearts are pierced, unknowing how to yield :
They blow for blow return, and wound for wound ;
And heaps of bodies raise the level ground.
   Murrhanus, boasting of his blood, that springs
From a long royal race of Latian kings,
Is by the Trojan from his chariot thrown,
Crushed with the weight of an unwieldy stone :
Betwixt the wheels he fell ; the wheels, that bore

His living load, his dying body tore.
His starting steeds, to shun the glittering sword,
Paw down his trampled limbs, forgetful of their lord.
    Fierce Hyllus threatened high, and, face to face,
Affronted Turnus in the middle space :
The prince encountered him in full career,
And at his temples aimed the deadly spear ;
So fatally the flying weapon sped,
That through his brazen helm it pierced his head.
Nor, Cisseus, could'st thou 'scape from Turnus' hand,
In vain the strongest of the Arcadian band :
Nor to Cupencus could his gods afford
Availing aid against the Ænean sword,
Which to his naked heart pursued the course ;
Nor could his plated shield sustain the force.
    Iölas fell, whom not the Grecian powers,
Nor great subverter of the Trojan towers,
Were doomed to kill, while Heaven prolonged his
      date :
But who can pass the bounds prefixed by Fate ?
In high Lyrnessus, and in Troy, he held
Two palaces, and was from each expelled :
Of all the mighty man, the last remains
A little spot of foreign earth contains.
    And now both hosts their broken troops unite
In equal ranks, and mix in mortal fight.
Serestus and undaunted Mnestheus join
The Trojan, Tuscan, and Arcadian line :
Sea-born Messapus, with Atinas, heads
The Latin squadrons, and to battle leads.
They strike, they push, they throng the scanty space,
Resolved on death, impatient of disgrace ;
And where one falls, another fills his place.
    The Cyprian goddess now inspires her son
To leave the unfinished fight, and storm the town ;
For, while he rolls his eyes around the plain
In quest of Turnus, whom he seeks in vain,
He views the unguarded city from afar,
In careless quiet, and secure of war.
Occasion offers, and excites his mind

To dare beyond the task he first designed.
Resolved, he calls his chiefs ; they leave the fight :
Attended thus, he takes a neighbouring height :
The crowding troops about their general stand,
All under arms, and wait his high command.
Then thus the lofty prince : ' Hear and obey,
Ye Trojan bands, without the least delay.
Jove is with us ; and what I have decreed,
Requires our utmost vigour, and our speed.
Your instant arms against the town prepare,
The source of mischief, and the seat of war.
This day the Latian towers, that mate the sky,
Shall, level with the plain, in ashes lie :
The people shall be slaves, unless in time
They kneel for pardon, and repent their crime.
Twice have our foes been vanquished on the plain :
Then shall I wait till Turnus will be slain ?
Your force against the perjured city bend ;
There it began, and there the war shall end.
The peace profaned our rightful arms requires :
Cleanse the polluted place with purging fires.'
    He finished ; and—one soul inspiring all—
Formed in a wedge, the foot approach the wall.
Without the town, an unprovided train
Of gaping gazing citizens are slain.
Some firebrands, others scaling-ladders, bear ;
And those they toss aloft, and these they rear :
The flames now launched, the feathered arrows fly ;
And clouds of missive arms obscure the sky.
Advancing to the front, the hero stands,
And, stretching out to heaven his pious hands,
Attests the gods, asserts his innocence,
Upbraids with breach of faith the Ausonian prince ;
Declares the royal honour doubly stained,
And twice the rites of holy peace profaned.
    Dissenting clamours in the town arise ;
Each will be heard, and all at once advise.
One part for peace, and one for war, contends :
Some would exclude their foes, and some admit their
    friends.

The helpless king is hurried in the throng,
And (whate'er tide prevails) is borne along.
  Thus, when the swain, within a hollow rock,
Invades the bees with suffocating smoke,
They run around, or labour on their wings,
Disused to flight, and shoot their sleepy stings;
To shun the bitter fumes, in vain they try:
Black vapours, issuing from the vent, involve the sky.
  But Fate and envious Fortune now prepare
To plunge the Latins in the last despair.
The queen, who saw the foes invade the town,
And brands on tops of burning houses thrown,
Cast round her eyes, distracted with her fear:—
No troops of Turnus in the field appear.
Once more she stares abroad, but still in vain,
And then concludes the royal youth is slain.
Mad with her anguish, impotent to bear
The mighty grief, she loathes the vital air.
She calls herself the cause of all this ill,
And owns the dire effects of her ungoverned will:
She raves against the gods; she beats her breast;
She tears with both her hands her purple vest:
Then round a beam a running noose she tied,
And, fastened by the neck, obscenely died.
  Soon as the fatal news by fame was blown,
And to her dames and to her daughter known,
The sad Lavinia rends her yellow hair,
And rosy cheeks: the rest her sorrow share:
With shrieks the palace rings, and madness of
        despair.
The spreading rumour fills the public place:
Confusion, fear, distraction, and disgrace,
And silent shame, are seen in every face.
Latinus tears his garments as he goes,
Both for his public and his private woes;
With filth his venerable beard besmears,
And sordid dust deforms his silver hairs.
And much he blames the softness of his mind,
Obnoxious to the charms of woman-kind,
And soon reduced to change what he so well designed—

To break the solemn league so long desired,
Nor finish what his fates, and those of Troy, required.
  Now Turnus rolls aloof, o'er empty plains,
And here and there some straggling foes he gleans.
His flying coursers please him less and less,
Ashamed of easy fight, and cheap success.
Thus half contented, anxious in his mind,
The distant cries come driving in the wind—
Shouts from the walls, but shouts in murmurs drowned;
A jarring mixture, and a boding sound.
'Alas! (said he) what mean these dismal cries?
What doleful clamours from the town arise?'
Confused, he stops, and backward pulls the reins.
She, who the driver's office now sustains,
Replies, 'Neglect, my lord, these new alarms:
Here fight, and urge the fortune of your arms:
There want not others to defend the wall.
If by your rival's hand the Italians fall,
So shall your fatal sword his friends oppress,
In honour equal, equal in success.'
  To this, the prince: 'O sister!—for I knew,
The peace infringed proceeded first from you:
I knew you, when you mingled first in fight:
And now in vain you would deceive my sight—
Why, goddess, this unprofitable care?
Who sent you down from heaven, involved in air,
Your share of mortal sorrows to sustain,
And see your brother bleeding on the plain?
For to what power can Turnus have recourse,
Or how resist his fate's prevailing force?
These eyes beheld Murrhanus bite the ground—
Mighty the man, and mighty was the wound.
I heard my dearest friend, with dying breath,
My name invoking to revenge his death.
Brave Ufens fell with honour on the place,
To shun the shameful sight of my disgrace.
On earth supine, a manly corpse he lies;
His vest and armour are the victor's prize.
Then, shall I see Laurentum in a flame,
Which only wanted, to complete my shame?

How will the Latins hoot their champion's flight!
How Drances will insult, and point them to the sight!
Is death so hard to bear?—Ye gods below!
(Since those above so small compassion show),
Receive a soul unsullied yet with shame,
Which not belies my great forefathers' name.'

　　He said : and while he spoke, with flying speed
Came Saces urging on his foamy steed :
Fixed on his wounded face a shaft he bore,
And, seeking Turnus, sent his voice before :
'Turnus! on you, on you alone, depends
Our last relief ;—compassionate your friends!
Like lightning, fierce Æneas, rolling on,
With arms invests, with flames invades, the town ;
The brands are tossed on high ; the winds conspire
To drive along the deluge of the fire.
All eyes are fixed on you : your foes rejoice ;
E'en the king staggers, and suspends his choice—
Doubts to deliver or defend the town,
Whom to reject, or whom to call his son.
The queen, on whom your utmost hopes were placed,
Herself suborning death, has breathed her last.
'Tis true, Messapus, fearless of his fate,
With fierce Atinas' aid, defends the gate :
On every side surrounded by the foe,
The more they kill, the greater numbers grow ;
An iron harvest mounts, and still remains to mow.
You, far aloof from your forsaken bands,
Your rolling chariot drive o'er empty sands.'

　　Stupid he sat, his eyes on earth declined,
And various cares revolving in his mind :
Rage, boiling from the bottom of his breast,
And sorrow mixed with shame, his soul oppressed ;
And conscious worth lay labouring in his thought,
And love by jealousy to madness wrought.
By slow degrees his reason drove away
The mists of passion, and resumed her sway
Then, rising on his car, he turned his look,
And saw the town involved in fire and smoke.
A wooden tower with flames already blazed,

Which his own hands on beams and rafters raised,
And bridges laid above to join the space,
And wheels below to roll from place to place.
'Sister ! the Fates have vanquished : let us go
The way which heaven and my hard fortune show.
The fight is fixed ; nor shall the branded name
Of a base coward blot your brother's fame.
Death is my choice : but suffer me to try
My force, and vent my rage before I die.'
He said : and leaping down without delay,
Through crowds of scattered foes he freed his way.
Striding he passed, impetuous as the wind,
And left the grieving goddess far behind.

As, when a fragment, from a mountain torn
By raging tempests, or by torrents borne,
Or sapped by time, or loosened from the roots—
Prone through the void the rocky ruin shoots,
Rolling from crag to crag, from steep to steep ;
Down sink, at once, the shepherds and their sheep,
Involved alike, they rush to nether ground ;
Stunned with the shock they fall, and stunned from
　　earth rebound :
So Turnus, hasting headlong to the town,
Shouldering and shoving, bore the squadrons down.
Still pressing onward, to the walls he drew,
Where shafts and spears and darts promiscuous flew,
And sanguine streams the slippery ground embrue.
First stretching out his arm, in sign of peace,
He cries aloud, to make the combat cease :
' Rutulians, hold ! and, Latin troops, retire !
The fight is mine ; and me the gods require.
'Tis just that I should vindicate alone
The broken truce, or for the breach atone.
This day shall free from war the Ausonian state,
Or finish my misfortunes in my fate.'

Both armies from their bloody work desist,
And, bearing backward, form a spacious list,
The Trojan hero, who received from fame
The welcome sound, and heard the champion's name,
Soon leaves the taken works and mounted walls :

Greedy of war where greater glory calls,
He springs to fight, exulting in his force;
His jointed armour rattles in the course.
Like Eryx, or like Athos, great he shows,
Or father Apennine, when, white with snows,
His head divine obscure in clouds he hides,
And shakes the sounding forests on his sides.

The nations, overawed, surcease the fight;
Immoveable their bodies, fixed their sight;
E'en death stands still; nor from above they throw
Their darts, nor drive their battering-rams below.
In silent order either army stands,
And drop their swords, unknowing, from their hands.
The Ausonian king beholds, with wondering sight,
Two mighty champions matched in single fight,
Born under climes remote, and brought by fate,
With swords to try their titles to the state.

Now, in closed field, each other from afar
They view; and, rushing on, begin the war.
They launch their spears; then hand to hand they meet:
The trembling soil resounds beneath their feet;
Their bucklers clash; thick blows descend from high,
And flakes of fire from their hard helmets fly.
Courage conspires with chance; and both engage
With equal fortune yet, and mutual rage.

As, when two bulls for their fair female fight
In Sila's shades, or on Taburnus' height,
With horns adverse they meet; the keeper flies;
Mute stands the herd; the heifers roll their eyes,
And wait the event—which victor they shall bear,
And who shall be the lord, to rule the lusty year:
With rage of love the jealous rivals burn,
And push for push, and wound for wound, return;
Their dewlaps gored, their sides are laved in blood;
Loud cries and roaring sounds rebellow through the
        wood:
Such was the combat in the listed ground;
So clash their swords, and so their shields resound,
    Jove sets the beam: in either scale he lays
The champion's fate, and each exactly weighs.

On this side, life, and lucky chance, ascends;
Loaded with death, that other scale descends.
Raised on the stretch, young Turnus aims a blow
Full on the helm of his unguarded foe:
Shrill shouts and clamours ring on either side,
As hopes and fears their panting hearts divide.
But all in pieces flies the traitor sword,
And, in the middle stroke, deserts his lord.
Now 'tis but death or flight: disarmed he flies,
When in his hand an unknown hilt he spies.
Fame says that Turnus, when his steeds he joined,
Hurrying to war, disordered in his mind,
Snatched the first weapon which his haste could find.
'Twas not the fated sword his father bore,
But that his charioteer Metiscus wore.
This, while the Trojans fled, the toughness held;
But, vain against the great Vulcanian shield,
The mortal-tempered steel deceived his hand:
The shivered fragments shone amid the sand.

Surprised with fear, he fled along the field,
And now forthright, and now in orbits wheeled:
For here the Trojan troops the list surround,
And there the pass is closed with pools and marshy
  ground.
Æneas hastens, though with heavier pace—
His wound, so newly knit, retards the chase,
And oft his trembling knees their aid refuse—
Yet, pressing foot by foot, his foe pursues.

Thus, when a fearful stag is closed around
With crimson toils, or in a river found,
High on the bank the deep-mouthed hound appears,
Still opening, following still, where'er he steers:
The persecuted creature, to and fro,
Turns here and there, to escape his Umbrian foe:
Steep is the ascent, and, if he gains the land,
The purple death is pitched along the strand:
His eager foe, determined to the chase,
Stretched at his length, gains ground at every pace:
Now to his beamy head he makes his way,
And now he holds, or thinks he holds, his prey;

Just at the pinch, the stag springs out with fear,
He bites the wind, and fills his sounding jaws with air:
The rocks, the lakes, the meadows, ring with cries;
The mortal tumult mounts, and thunders in the skies.
    Thus flies the Daunian prince, and, flying, blames
His tardy troops, and, calling by their names,
Demands his trusty sword.   The Trojan threats
The realm with ruin, and their ancient seats
To lay in ashes, if they dare supply,
With arms or aid, his vanquished enemy:
Thus menacing, he still pursues the course
With vigour, though diminished of his force.
Ten times already, round the listed place,
One chief had fled, and t'other given the chase:
No trivial prize is played; for, on the life
Or death of Turnus, now depends the strife.
    Within the space, an olive tree had stood,
A sacred shade, a venerable wood,
For vows to Faunus paid, the Latins' guardian god.
Here hung the vests, and tablets were engraved,
Of sinking mariners from shipwreck saved.
With heedless hands the Trojans felled the tree,
To make the ground inclosed for combat, free.
Deep in the root, whether by fate, or chance,
Or erring haste, the Trojan drove his lance;
Then stooped, and tugged with force immense, to free
The encumbered spear from the tenacious tree;
That, whom his fainting limbs pursued in vain,
His flying weapon might from far attain.
    Confused with fear, bereft of human aid,
Then Turnus to the gods, and first to Faunus, prayed:
'O Faunus! pity! and thou, mother Earth,
Where I thy foster-son received my birth,
Hold fast the steel! If my religious hand
Your plant has honoured, which your foes profaned,
Propitious hear my pious prayer!' He said,
Nor with successless vows invoked their aid.
The incumbent hero wrenched and pulled and strained:
But still the stubborn earth the steel detained.
Juturna took her time; and, while in vain

He strove, assumed Metiscus' form again,
And, in that imitated shape, restored
To the despairing prince his Daunian sword.
The queen of love—who, with disdain and grief,
Saw the bold nymph afford this prompt relief—
To assert her offspring with a greater deed,
From the tough root the lingering weapon freed.

Once more erect, the rival chiefs advance:
One trusts the sword, and one the pointed lance;
And both resolved alike, to try their fatal chance.

Meantime imperial Jove to Juno spoke,
Who from a shining cloud beheld the shock:
'What new arrest, O queen of heaven! is sent
To stop the Fates now labouring in the event?
What further hopes are left thee to pursue?
Divine Æneas (and thou know'st it too),
Foredoomed, to these celestial seats is due.
What more attempts for Turnus can be made,
That thus thou lingerest in this lonely shade?
Is it becoming of the due respect
And awful honour of a god elect,
A wound unworthy of our state to feel,
Patient of human hands, and earthly steel?
Or seems it just, the sister should restore
A second sword, when one was lost before,
And arm a conquered wretch against his conqueror?
For what, without thy knowledge and avow,
Nay more, thy dictate, durst Juturna do?
At last, in deference to my love, forbear
To lodge within thy soul this anxious care:
Reclined upon my breast, thy grief unload:
Who should relieve the goddess, but the god?
Now all things to their utmost issue tend,
Pushed by the Fates to their appointed end.
While leave was given thee, and a lawful hour
For vengeance, wrath, and unresisted power,
Tossed on the seas thou could'st thy foes distress,
And, driven ashore, with hostile arms oppress;
Deform the royal house; and, from the side
Of the just bridegroom, tear the plighted bride:—

Now cease at my command.'   The thunderer said ;
And, with dejected eyes, this answer Juno made :
' Because your dread decree too well I knew,
From Turnus and from earth unwilling I withdrew.
Else should you not behold me here, alone,
Involved in empty clouds, my friends bemoan,
But, girt with vengeful flames, in open sight,
Engaged against my foes in mortal fight.
'Tis true, Juturna mingled in the strife
By my command, to save her brother's life,
At least to try ; but (by the Stygian lake—
The most religious oath the gods can take)
With this restriction, not to bend the bow,
Or toss the spear, or trembling dart to throw.
And now, resigned to your superior might,
And tired with fruitless toils, I loathe the fight.
This let me beg (and this no fates withstand)
Both for myself and for your father's land,
That, when the nuptial bed shall bind the peace
(Which I, since you ordain, consent to bless),
The laws of either nation be the same ;
But let the Latins still retain their name,
Speak the same language which they spoke before,
Wear the same habits which their grandsires wore.
Call them not Trojans : perish the renown
And name of Troy, with that detested town.
Latium be Latium still ; let Alba reign,
And Rome's immortal majesty remain.'
    Then thus the founder of mankind replies
(Unruffled was his front, serene his eyes) :
' Can Saturn's issue, and heaven's other heir,
Such endless anger in her bosom bear ?
Be mistress, and your full desires obtain ;
But quench the choler you foment in vain.
From ancient blood, the Ausonian people sprung,
Shall keep their name, their habit, and their tongue :
The Trojans to their customs shall be tied :
I will, myself, their common rites provide :
The natives shall command, the foreigners subside.
All shall be Latium ; Troy without a name ;

And her lost sons forget from whence they came.
From blood so mixed, a pious race shall flow,
Equal to gods, excelling all below.
No nation more respect to you shall pay,
Or greater offerings on your altars lay.'
Juno consents, well pleased that her desires
Had found success, and from the cloud retires.
    The peace thus made, the thunderer next prepares
To force the watery goddess from the wars.
Deep in the dismal regions void of light,
Three daughters, at a birth, were born to Night:
These their brown mother, brooding on her care,
Indued with windy wings, to flit in air,
With serpents girt alike, and crowned with hissing hair.
In heaven the Diræ called, and still at hand,
Before the throne of angry Jove they stand,
His ministers of wrath, and ready still
The minds of mortal men with fears to fill,
Whene'er the moody sire, to wreak his hate
On realms or towns deserving of their fate,
Hurls down diseases, death, and deadly care,
And terrifies the guilty world with war.
One sister plague of these, from heaven he sent,
To fright Juturna with a dire portent.
The pest comes whirling down: by far more slow
Springs the swift arrow from the Parthian bow,
Or Cydon yew, when, traversing the skies,
And drenched in poisonous juice, the sure destruction
    flies.
With such a sudden, and unseen a flight,
Shot through the clouds the daughter of the Night.
Soon as the field inclosed she had in view,
And from afar her destined quarry knew—
Contracted, to the boding bird she turns,
Which haunts the ruined piles and hallowed urns,
And beats about the tombs with nightly wings,
Where songs obscene on sepulchres she sings.
Thus lessened in her form, with frightful cries
The Fury round unhappy Turnus flies,
Flaps on his shield, and flutters o'er his eyes.

A lazy chillness crept along his blood ;
Choked was his voice ; his hair with horror stood.
Juturna from afar beheld her fly,
And knew the ill omen, by her screaming cry,
And stridor of her wings.   Amazed with fear,
Her beauteous breast she beat, and rent her flowing
    hair.
' Ah me ! (she cries) in this unequal strife,
What can thy sister more, to save thy life ?
Weak as I am, can I, alas ! contend
In arms with that inexorable fiend ?
Now, now, I quit the field ! forbear to fright
My tender soul, ye baleful birds of night !
The lashing of your wings I know too well,
The sounding flight, and funeral screams of hell !
These are the gifts you bring from haughty Jove,
The worthy recompense of ravished love !
Did he for this, exempt my life from fate ?
O hard conditions of immortal state !
Though born to death, not privileged to die,
But forced to bear imposed eternity !
Take back your envious bribes, and let me go
Companion to my brother's ghost below !
The joys are vanished : nothing now remains
Of life immortal, but immortal pains.
What earth will open her devouring womb,
To rest a weary goddess in the tomb ?'
She drew a length of sighs ; nor more she said,
But in her azure mantle wrapped her head,
Then plunged into her stream, with deep despair,
And her last sobs came bubbling up in air.
    Now stern Æneas waves his weighty spear
Against his foe, and thus upbraids his fear :
' What farther subterfuge can Turnus find ?
What empty hopes are harboured in his mind ?
'Tis not thy swiftness can secure thy flight ;
Not with their feet, but hands, the valiant fight.
Vary thy shape in thousand forms, and dare
What skill and courage can attempt in war :
Wish for the wings of winds, to mount the sky ;

Or hid within the hollow earth to lie!'
The champion shook his head, and made this short
    reply:
'No threats of thine my manly mind can move;
'Tis hostile heaven I dread, and partial Jove.'
He said no more, but, with a sigh, repressed
The mighty sorrow in his swelling breast.
Then, as he rolled his troubled eyes around,
An antique stone he saw, the common bound
Of neighbouring fields, and barrier of the ground—
So vast, that twelve strong men of modern days
The enormous weight from earth could hardly raise.
He heaved it at a lift, and, poised on high,
Ran staggering on against his enemy;
But so disordered, that he scarcely knew
His way, or what unwieldy weight he threw.
His knocking knees are bent beneath the load;
And shivering cold congeals his vital blood.
The stone drops from his arms, and, falling short
For want of vigour, mocks his vain effort.
And as, when heavy sleep has closed the sight,
The sickly fancy labours in the night;
We seem to run; and, destitute of force,
Our sinking limbs forsake us in the course:
In vain we heave for breath; in vain we cry:
The nerves, unbraced, their usual strength deny;
And on the tongue the faltering accents die:
So Turnus fared: whatever means he tried,
All force of arms, and points of art employed,
The Fury flew athwart, and made the endeavour void.
   A thousand various thoughts his soul confound:
He stared about, nor aid nor issue found:
His own men stop the pass, and his own walls sur-
    round.
Once more he pauses, and looks out again,
And seeks the goddess charioteer in vain.
Trembling he views the thundering chief advance,
And brandishing aloft the deadly lance:
Amazed he cowers beneath his conquering foe,
Forgets to ward, and waits the coming blow.

Astonished while he stands, and fixed with fear,
Aimed at his shield he sees the impending spear.
  The hero measured first, with narrow view,
The destined mark ; and, rising as he threw,
With its full swing the fatal weapon flew.
Not with less rage the rattling thunder falls,
Or stones from battering engines break the walls :
Swift as a whirlwind, from an arm so strong,
The lance drove on, and bore the death along.
Nought could his sevenfold shield the prince avail,
Nor aught, beneath his arms, the coat of mail ;
It pierced through all, and with a grisly wound
Transfixed his thigh, and doubled him to ground.
With groans the Latins rend the vaulted sky :
Woods, hills, and valleys, to the voice reply.
  Now low on earth the lofty chief is laid,
With eyes cast upwards, and with arms displayed,
And, recreant, thus to the proud victor prayed :
' I know my death deserved, nor hope to live :
Use what the gods and thy good fortune give.
Yet think, oh think ! if mercy may be shown,
(Thou hadst a father once, and hast a son),
Pity my sire, now sinking to the grave ;
And, for Anchises' sake, old Daunus save !
Or, if thy vowed revenge pursue my death,
Give to my friends my body void of breath !
The Latian chiefs have seen me beg my life :
Thine is the conquest, thine the royal wife :
Against a yielded man, 'tis mean ignoble strife.'
  In deep suspense the Trojan seemed to stand,
And, just prepared to strike, repressed his hand.
He rolled his eyes, and every moment felt
His manly soul with more compassion melt ;
When, casting down a casual glance, he spied
The golden belt that glittered on his side,
The fatal spoil which haughty Turnus tore
From dying Pallas, and in triumph wore.
Then, roused anew to wrath, he loudly cries
(Flames, while he spoke, came flashing from his eyes),
' Traitor ! dost thou, dost thou to grace pretend,

Clad, as thou art, in trophies of my friend?
To his sad soul a grateful offering go!
'Tis Pallas, Pallas gives this deadly blow.'
He raised his arm aloft, and, at the word,
Deep in his bosom drove the shining sword.
The streaming blood distained his arms around;
And the disdainful soul came rushing through the
    wound.

PRINTED IN GREAT BRITAIN
AT THE UNIVERSITY PRESS, OXFORD
BY VIVIAN RIDLER
PRINTER TO THE UNIVERSITY